A History of Child Psychoanalysis

Child analysis has occupied a special place in the history of psychoanalysis because of the challenges it poses to practitioners and the clashes it has provoked among its advocates. Since the early days in Vienna under Sigmund Freud, child psychoanalysts have tried to comprehend and make comprehensible to others the psychosomatic troubles of childhood and to adapt clinical and therapeutic approaches to all the stages of development of the baby, the child, the adolescent and the young adult.

Claudine and Pierre Geissmann trace the history and development of child analysis over the last century and assess the contributions made by pioneers of the discipline, whose efforts to expand its theoretical foundations led to conflict between different schools of thought, most notably to the rift between Anna Freud and Melanie Klein.

Now taught and practised widely in Europe, the USA and South America, child and adolescent psychoanalysis is unique in the insight it gives into the psychological aspects of child development, and in the therapeutic benefits it can bring to both the child and its family.

Claudine Geissmann is a psychoanalyst (IPA) and a lecturer in child psychiatry and Director of the Children's Mental Health Centre at the University of Bordeaux. The late **Pierre Geissmann** was a psychoanalyst (IPA) and Professor of Child Psychiatry at the University of Bordeaux.

THE NEW LIBRARY OF PSYCHOANALYSIS

The New Library of Psychoanalysis was launched in 1987 in association with the Institute of Psycho-Analysis, London. Its purpose is to facilitate a greater and more widespread appreciation of what psychoanalysis is really about and to provide a forum for increasing mutual understanding between psychoanalysts and those working in other disciplines such as history, linguistics, literature, medicine, philosophy, psychology and the social sciences. It is intended that the titles selected for publication in the series should deepen and develop psychoanalytic thinking and technique, contribute to psychoanalysis from outside, or contribute to other disciplines from a psychoanalytical perspective.

The Institute, together with the British Psycho-Analytical Society, runs a low-fee psychoanalytic clinic, organizes lectures and scientific events concerned with psychoanalysis, publishes the *International Journal of Psycho-Analysis* (which now incorporates the *International Review of Psycho-Analysis*), and runs the only training course in the UK in psychoanalysis, leading to membership of the International Psychoanalytical Association – the body which preserves internationally agreed standards of training, of professional entry, and of professional ethics and practice for psychoanalysis as initiated and developed by Sigmund Freud. Distinguished members of the Institute have included Michael Balint, Wilfred Bion, Ronald Fairbairn, Anna Freud, Ernest Jones, Melanie Klein, John Rickman and Donald Winnicott.

Volumes 1–11 in the series have been prepared under the general editorship of David Tuckett, with Ronald Britton and Eglé Laufer as associate editors. Subsequent volumes are under the general editorship of Elizabeth Bott Spillius, with, from Volume 17, Donald Campbell, Michael Parsons, Rosine Jozef Perelberg and David Taylor as associate editors.

ALSO IN THIS SERIES

NEW LIBRARY OF PSYCHOANALYSIS
—— 30 ——

General editor: Elizabeth Bott Spillius

A History of Child Psychoanalysis

CLAUDINE AND PIERRE GEISSMANN

Preface by Anne-Marie Sandler and Hanna Segal

Foreword by Serge Lebovici

Published with the assistance of the Melanie Klein Trust,
the Anna Freud Centre and the French Ministry of Culture

London and New York

First published as *Histoire de la Psychanalyse de l'Enfant*
by Bayard Presse, Paris, in 1992

English language edition first published 1998
by Routledge
11 New Fetter Lane, London EC4P 4EE

Simultaneously published in the USA and Canada
by Routledge
29 West 35th Street, New York, NY 10001

Typeset in Bembo by M Rules
Printed and bound in Great Britain by
MPG Books Ltd, Bodmin, Cornwall

British Library Cataloguing in Publication Data

A catalogue record for this book is available from the British Library

Library of Congress Cataloging in Publication Data

Geissmann–Chambon, Claudine.
[Histoire de la psychanalyse de l'enfant.   English]
A history of child psychoanalysis / Claudine and Pierre Geissmann.
p.   cm.
Includes bibliographical references and index.
1. Child analysis–History.   I. Geissmann, Pierre.   II. Title.
RJ504.2.G4513   1998
618.92′8917′09–dc21
97-12477
CIP

ISBN 0-415-11020-3
ISBN 0-415-11296-6 (pbk)

Contents

Preface

We are very happy to have the opportunity to introduce Pierre and Claudine Geissmann's *History of Child Psychoanalysis* to an English-speaking audience. This remarkable work is of the greatest importance because it is the first detailed study of the development of child psychoanalysis. It is quite surprising that there are so few studies of the way child analysis has developed, as the basic tenet of psychoanalysis is that our adult development has its foundations in the inner life of the child within us. In this excellent volume the authors follow the history of child analysis from its beginnings, starting with the analysis of Little Hans, through to its contemporary developments. The Geissmanns give the background against which these developments have occurred and need to be assessed, and explain in detail and in depth the differences in technique and theory between the pioneers and the different schools which have subsequently developed.

The authors emphasize the rich contributions that the psychoanalysis of children has brought to psychoanalytic theory and practice, in regard to work with adults as well as children. They study the various schools of thought in the child psychoanalytic world, and elicit the unique contribution of each. They discuss what these schools have in common, and in what ways they differ.

The major sponsors of this translation, in addition to the French Ministry of Culture, have been the Melanie Klein Trust and the Anna Freud Centre (formerly the Hampstead Clinic, founded by Anna Freud). This collaboration is in itself a tribute to the authors' scientific objectivity and integrity.

Anne-Marie Sandler and Hanna Segal

Acknowledgements

First and foremost we would like to thank those who opened up the world of child psychoanalysis to us: Serge Lebovici, René Diatkine, James Gammill and Hanna Segal. Their clinical and theoretical experience and the diversity of their respective viewpoints have been very precious indeed.

We would also like to thank those who were kind enough to let us visit them, and to share their experience and reminiscences: Simone Decobert, Yolanda Gampel, Ilse Hellmann, Betty Joseph, Serge Lebovici, Sidonia Mehler, David and Estela Rosenfeld, Anne-Marie Sandler, Hanna Segal, Frances Tustin and Rodolfo Urribarri.

We were much stimulated and helped in our research by the group of child psychoanalysts who meet regularly at Françoise Caille's house, some of whom make up the Editorial Committee of the *Journal de la psychanalyse de l'enfant*. The seminar on the history of child psychoanalysis that we held in Bordeaux was also very useful. Pascale Duhamel, Mireille Fleury, Dominique Dujols and Marcel Boix were particularly helpful in assisting us to collect a large number of documents.

We are indebted to the young child psychiatrists and psychoanalysts and the members of the psychiatric teams who work with us for their questions, their curiosity and their remarks, which led us to get involved in this history in the first place. This history is also theirs in part.

Danièle Guilbert of Bayard Editions was of constant and warm assistance with her careful reading of our text and her criticisms, which were helpful and to the point.

We are very grateful to Dr Hanna Segal, to Mrs Elizabeth B. Spillius, to Professor J. Sandler and to Mrs Anne-Marie Sandler for having made this publication possible and for having efficaciously helped us with the difficult task of translating this book into English. Thanks are owed especially to Mrs E. B. Spillius who has read our manuscript carefully, and patiently revised our English.

We should like to acknowledge the financial help of the Melanie Klein Trust, the Anna Freud Centre and the French Ministry of Culture; their grants allowed us to overcome the difficulties we have encountered in the translation.

Finally, we must say a very big thank you to Claude Dugrava, who carried out the difficult job of the transcription of our manuscript in his usual very competent fashion.

Foreword

SERGE LEBOVICI

We should not delude ourselves about the current success of a number of works on various aspects of psychoanalysis, different periods in its history and the movements which have left their mark. What a large proportion of the reading public is looking for is a whiff of scandal. The work of Claudine and Pierre Geissmann offers something quite different: it is the fruit of a tremendous amount of work, reading and classifying a great number of unpublished works, or works which are rarely consulted or referred to. The authors have no hesitation in telling us about the interpersonal conflicts which illustrated some of the relationships between the pioneers of this relatively new field. But they know full well that a simple reminder of everyday life in a new field of science does not enable one to reconstruct the history of that science, all the more so when its roots need to be laid bare by the methodical work of a true archaeologist.

Throughout this book, Claudine and Pierre Geissmann show that the application of psychoanalysis to children has always been a challenge for psychoanalysts. Witness the clashes which are still going on today in psychoanalytical construction and reconstruction. The prototypical model of mental functioning can be found in the paradigm of infantile neurosis, which, it must be admitted, is no longer a universal model because of the interest currently shown in psychoses and borderline states. Contempory child psychoanalysts have also shown the importance of a second paradigm: child autism.

We will therefore follow the authors as they discreetly enter the 'parents room', and rediscover in the nursery the 'ghosts' of those who are no longer with us, to use the classic metaphor of Selma Fraiberg.

From the onset of the Wednesday sessions held in Freud's apartment in Vienna, the first disciples of this small circle amassed observations which could be classified as protopsychoanalysis of the child. It is difficult to know whether these observations were just accumulated in order to give a basis to

Freud's theories. If this were so, one could compare these psychoanalysts to the surrealists, who recommended relating their dreams to their children. In similar fashion, but reversed, as it were, these psychoanalysts were relating the dreams of their children to their colleagues.

However, it is difficult to know whether these protopsychoanalysts also interpreted these dreams to their children. There is no doubt, however, that Freud and his first disciples, closer or more distant, did undertake the psychoanalysis of at least one of their own children.

In Vienna, and then in Berlin and Budapest, the psychoanalytical world was very small, and analysis of the children of the members of this circle was no secret: this was the case for Anna Freud, Hilda Abraham, Melanie Klein's son, Eric, and perhaps one of Jung's children.

Circumstances brought Anna Freud and Dorothy Burlingham into close contact and they stayed close: Dorothy's two sons were analysed by Anna. She was also able to undertake analysis of one of their friends, who had been abandoned by his mother, and she contributed to his upbringing. She had news of him when, grown up and holding a university position in the United States of America, he wrote to her asking if she would let him have the notes she had made during his treatment and the drawings he had left with her. In his book, *A Child Analysis with Anna Freud,* the adult Peter Heller (1990) relates the history of his childhood in Vienna, his memories of his analysis with Anna Freud and the comments that he thinks are justified on the subject.

Claudine and Pierre Geissmann pose a number of questions which remain valid, about which we shall make some brief comments:

1 Do observations of the child, and the very young child in particular, reveal the nature of the workings of the unconscious?
2 Does child psychoanalysis enable infantile amnesia to be removed more easily and does it permit better reconstruction of the past because of its chronological proximity?
3 Does child psychoanalysis exist or is it just a form of psychotherapy derived from psychoanalysis?

1 The psychoanalytical observation of the child

For many modern psychoanalysts, the child observed is the real child, not the model child of psychoanalysis. However, present-day work on the attachment of the child to its parents and on the early interactions that can be observed would tend to invalidate the Freudian theory of the genesis of the representation of the object: the process of subjectivation starts with the nucleus of the Self and perceptions of maternal care. One then goes from the interpersonal process of interaction to intersubjectivity, which shows that the young infant becomes aware of the existence of thought in its partners. To use a personal formula, I still believe that the child invests in its mother before it perceives her but I also believe that its action – its perceived action – on her contributes to registering her as the 'maternal gender'. For her part, the mother acts by introducing into the care and attention she gives the child her own imaginary and phantasy life. At this point one can speak of phantasy interaction, enriched by the various episodes which take place, the scenarios by which the interaction is organized, and the possibility of their enriched narration afterwards. Thus the psychopathology of development not only conforms to the metapsychological profile of Anna Freud's Hampstead Clinic, it also introduces the inter- and intra-subjective relation enriched by the intergenerational transmission of conflicts, i.e. by the history of the conflicts of the parents with the grandparents of the child. Education and culture enable the filiation and affiliation processes to be combined.

2 Psychoanalytical (re)construction through psychoanalyses of children

In general, treatment of children should enable infantile amnesia to be removed more easily. However, experience shows that reaction formation and traits of character which shape the transference neurosis in the adult are extremely well established in the latency stage, when the child has no wish to confide in anyone. No doubt the therapeutic alliance advocated by Anna Freud and the softening up of the defences that it offers on the one hand, and the processes of the child's play which the Kleinian school assimilates with associations of ideas, enable the interpretative process to be pursued, which is most certainly considerably facilitated by the fact that there are several sessions a week. The fact nevertheless remains that this easing of the system of social censorship, and therefore of some of the strata of the super-ego, does not facilitate work on the derivatives of the unconscious. It is probable that the interpretation of the child psychoanalyst can hardly relate to the latent material, that concerning the preconscious. In adult psychoanalysis, the situation is often quite similar and enables a reconstruction of the causes and effects of the repetitions of the past. But the construction itself arises from fertile periods, those where the mature narcissism of the two protagonists provides a wealth of identifications through generative and metaphorically creating empathy. From this point of view the authors emphasize the contribution made by Melanie Klein and post-Kleinian psychoanalysts: projective identification is a normal stage of development where the capacity of the mother (and of the child psychoanalyst) for reverie 'detoxifies' the devastating effects. In these circumstances, the child psychoanalyst is in a position to contain the identificatory projections and to offer their construction. The child of psychoanalytical theory is thus a child reconstructed through its own development and constructed via the interpretations of its psychoanalyst.

3 Does child psychoanalysis exist?

The preceding considerations would seem to prove that it does, but the difficulty in ensuring perfect constancy and neutrality of the psychoanalytical framework makes a real course of treatment somewhat difficult. Claudine and Pierre Geissmann show the importance of a solid psychoanalytical background for those who wish to become child psychotherapists. However, this is unfortunately not always the case, if only because many future analysts begin their careers working in centres restricted to children.

Claudine and Pierre Geissmann's book is not just a history of child psychoanalysis. It gives an outline of the field as a whole, which, one can see, did not just flower in Vienna, Berlin or London, but has also blossomed in South America and throughout Europe. The authors show in detail the influence of psychoanalysis on the development of child and adolescent psychiatry in France, and describe the work of its forerunners: Eugenie Sokolnicka and Sophie Morgenstern. They mention Françoise Dolto and are kind enough to speak very highly (too highly, some would say) of the influence I and my friend and colleague René Diatkine have had on the field in France. At a time when neuro-biological psychiatry and neuro-psychology claim to exercise a dominant influence on the work of child psychiatry, in particular by their so-called 'objective' assessments, Claudine and Pierre Geissmann's book shows the importance of the psychopathological approach that psychoanalysis alone can offer, both to the child who is sent to the psychiatrist and to his or her family.

This book should be read thoroughly – it validates over a century of clinical work and research. Throughout that time child psychoanalysts have been the pioneers of the development of psychoanalysis; they have tried to understand and make understandable to others the mental and psychosomatic troubles of childhood and adopt a clinical and therapeutic approach to all stages of development: that of the baby, the child, the pre-adolescent, the adolescent and the young adult.

Introduction

What? You have had small children in analysis? Children of less than six years? *Can* that be done? And is it not most risky for the children?

(S. Freud, 1926: 214)

It can be done very well. It is hardly to be believed, what goes on in a child of four or five years old. Children are very active-minded at that age; their early sexual period is also a period of intellectual flowering. I have an impression that with the onset of the latency period they become mentally inhibited as well, stupider. From that time, on, too, many children lose their physical charm. And, as regards the damage done by early analysis, I may inform you that the first child on whom the experiment was ventured, nearly twenty years ago, has since then grown into a healthy and capable young man, who has passed through his puberty irreproachably, in spite of some severe psychical traumas. It may be hoped that things will turn out no worse for the other 'victims' of early analysis. Much that is of interest attaches to these child analyses; it is possible that in the future they will become still more important. From the point of view of theory, their value is beyond question.

(S. Freud, 1926: 215)

As we can see, child psychoanalysis has been practised since the beginning of the twentieth century. It has been very successful therapeutically, and has made an incomparable contribution to psychoanalytical theory both in the wealth of material supplied and in the therapeutic potential that it offers. In our practice of psychoanalysis, we have been able to observe daily the reality of the findings of our predecessors, Sigmund Freud first and foremost. We saw the possibility that we ourselves might be able to contribute something to the theorization of child psychoanalysis in particular and to psychoanalytical theory in general.

Yet at the same time we felt that we were practising an art in which no

1

apparent training was given and which seemed to be considered by adult psychoanalysts as a sort of sub-specialization, practised by women or psychologists. In the press, anything to do with child psychoanalysis tended to be found in the 'agony column'; there was rarely any mention of the unconscious or of child sexuality.

For all these reasons we became interested in the nature of child psychoanalysis and the identity of the child psychoanalyst. Our participation in conferences and working groups outside France, particularly in Britain, rapidly led us to the conclusion that a study of the subject in a single country – ours – would lead to a totally inadequate and partial view of the situation. There were difficulties elsewhere, of course, but they appeared to us to be quite different from our own. We were, for example, greatly impressed by the considerable progress that seemed to have been made in our field in Britain.

While working on the history of the child psychoanalysis movement, we initially found only individual 'histories'; but the real subject of our research was a collective history. Reading the texts in this field was not easy, since few have been translated into French. We therefore undertook the translation of texts from English, Spanish, German, etc. We also wanted to meet the eyewitnesses to this history, and that took us from London to Buenos Aires, and from New York to Vienna.

Our research produced a wealth of documents from which it became apparent we would have to make a selection and decide on a general theme. We decided not to retain too much of the anecdotal material. The reader is drawn to the anecdote because of what it might reveal of forbidden secrets, but is prevented from considering the fundamental problems because their interest is diverted by these same anecdotes. So we turned our interest to the development of the vocation of this or that pioneer of psychoanalysis and to their social and cultural background, and decided to put aside the scandals and personal conflicts unless they were of psychoanalytical interest. Where a conflict of ideas ostensibly arose out of a personal conflict, it seemed more interesting to us to look into the conflict of ideas underlying the personal arguments.

In search of this collective memory, we went to the cradle of child psychoanalysis, to Vienna, where psychoanalysis itself had its infancy. But which Vienna?

Was it the Vienna we visited, where number 19 Berggasse (Freud's consulting rooms) has been turned into a small and rather unimposing museum, the Vienna from which, one needs little reminding, Freud was expelled in 1938?

Was it that of the screen-memory, recast by our culture, a Vienna which was both gay and inhibited, carefree and yet neurotic, the breeding ground in which a more or less depraved sexuality was simmering?

Was it that of Sigmund Freud, whose family had come to live there when he was a little boy, the Vienna that he dreamt of conquering later on, in spite of all the difficulties he could expect?

Was it that of Bruno Bettelheim, the town in which he and his parents had always lived, which had been at the heart of the most powerful empire in the world, the second most important city in Europe (after Paris), the town which went on disintegrating like its rulers, who persisted in self-destruction and committing suicide and whose preoccupation with madness led them to build the most beautiful mental hospital in the world (the Steinhof)? The city where Sigmund Freud invented psychoanalysis but also where Wagner von Jauregg won the Nobel Prize for having discovered the malarial treatment for paralytic dementia or where Sakel had devised the insulin cure for schizophrenia? The city whose art and culture were so prodigious (Herzl, Brahms, Mahler, Kokoschka, Strauss, Schnitzler, Krafft-Ebing, Klimt, Martin Buber, Rainer Maria Rilke, to mention but a few)? (See Bettelheim, 1990 [1986].) The city of Anna Freud's cosseted childhood, where she witnessed the misery of its children at the end of the 1914–18 war, which was to lead her and her socialist and Zionist friends to try to find psychoanalytical means to help them?

Or is it that of Melanie Klein, the city of her happy childhood, where she studied art history and that she had to leave to follow her husband?

While taking into account the cultural foundations on which psycho-analysis was built, it did not seem to us that psychoanalysis was specifically Viennese, as is generally accepted, which is evidence of resistance to admitting the universality of its discoveries. Besides, as we shall see, psychoanalysis in general, and child psychoanalysis in particular, was to become tinged with British imperturbability, American pragmatism or Argentinian enthusiasm, but its foundations would remain the same from one country to another, perhaps because of emigration. In short, the unconscious is not Viennese, even in children.

We are going to try to show how child psychoanalysis has been built up, from its beginnings in Vienna and throughout the world. We shall see that the problems undergone during its development were to become confused with other issues, such as that of the place of women in society (which is, of course . . . to look after children), or that of psychoanalysis being practised by those who were not also qualified medical practitioners and who were also asked to treat children medically (passed off as an 'educational' activity!). More importantly, factors internal to the practice of psychoanalysis, in particular the development of a number of many-sided theories could be observed. We have therefore gone into the history of those who practised child psychoanalysis and have investigated the ideas which enabled it to make progress.

But we have also followed a phantasized course. We will see how, with

3

the geographical spread of ideas and human emigration, psychoanalytical thought was to lead to a lack of understanding between psychoanalysts: Americans were not to know Kleinian concepts; Anna Freud's ideas would not reach South America; American and British thinking would become a dead letter to the French. It was the myth of the tower of Babel all over again:

> And the whole earth was of one language, and of one speech. And it came to pass, as they journeyed from the east, that they found a plain in the land of Shinar; . . . And they said, Go to, let us build us a city and a tower, whose top may reach unto heaven; and let us make us a name, lest we be scattered abroad upon the face of the whole earth. And the LORD came down to see the city and the tower, which the children of men builded. And the LORD said, Behold, the people is one, and they have all one language; and this they begin to do: and now nothing will be restrained from them, which they have imagined to do. Go to, let us go down, and there confound their language, that they may not understand one another's speech. So the LORD scattered them abroad from thence upon the face of all the earth: and they left off to build the city. Therefore is the name of it called Babel.
>
> (Genesis 11, vv. 1–9, King James version; *Bab el akka* means the Gate of God, a play on words with the Hebrew *balal*, meaning 'to mix')

In 1961, Wilfred R. Bion interpreted this myth as being the history of the development of language in a group dominated by the assumption of dependence. The tower is a threat to divine supremacy and carries a messianic hope (pairing group). If this hope is fulfilled the unity of the group is broken. In simpler terms, any group which threatens to appropriate truth for itself runs the risk of being more powerful than the appointed or symbolic leader. The internal laws of the group cause it to break up into splinter groups so that it will not be exposed to truth, which is always unbearable. The schisms or splinter groups are the various languages: people no longer understand each other; they no longer speak the same language.

All psychoanalytical groups are exposed to this evolution, reflecting group resistance to the acquisition of new ideas which seem to go beyond the word of the founding father. This is very true in the case of child psychoanalysis. In 1963 Bion (1963: 64–6) stressed that it is the increase in knowledge as such that is punished, as the representative of the drive (the drive for knowledge = K).

We came across this Babel-like scattering in our peregrinations through various societies and countries and we did indeed get the feeling of a group resistance to knowing what the 'true essence' of a child was.

We therefore did not think it necessary to mention *every* important figure in *every* country. Rather, we chose to write about those individuals who seemed to us to be the most representative in the field we have chosen, that of the history of child psychoanalysis. Others were not retained. We could have mentioned Ferenczi and his little man-rooster, Arpad (1933), or Adler. We could also have mentioned the Dutch or Italian schools of child psychoanalysis, for example. Our choices may be arbitrary, but they have nevertheless enabled us to focus on individuals and countries.

This history has been divided into three parts, covering the chronological element, a geographical element showing how ideas have spread around the world, and an element of phantasy: a phantasized geography. There are therefore three sections: 'The day before yesterday', the origins, in Vienna; 'Yesterday', in Vienna, Berlin and London; 'Today', in London, the United States, Argentina and France. A final short section deals with the outlook for the future: 'And tomorrow?'

PART I

The day before yesterday: beginnings in Vienna (1905–20)

Introduction

This period, the building up of psychoanalysis by Sigmund Freud, would also see the outlines of what was to become child psychoanalysis. Well before 1900, Freud had already worked in paediatric departments. Following the publication of Freud's *Three Essays on the Theory of Sexuality* in 1905, the Psychoanalytical Society of Vienna started to become interested in the sexuality of young children. The Society's Wednesday evening discussions became very heated, all the more so since those present were using examples taken from their own families, mentioning the 'exploits' of their own young children. Carl Jung in Zurich and Karl Abraham in Berlin also took part enthusiastically, and corresponded with Freud on the subject. His correspondence with Jung, through which permeates the unease which would lead to their separation, sometimes takes an amusing turn; for instance, when Freud writes to Jung: 'I hope Agathli [Jung's daughter] is original and hadn't heard the story of Little Hans?' At other times it is moving, such as when Mrs Jung tries to get the dual message across to Freud that it is not easy to be the father of his children, nor that of . . . Jung. 'I wanted to ask . . . if you were sure that your children could not be helped by analysis. One is not to the son of a great man without impunity if one has such difficulty in casting off ordinary fathers . . . wasn't your son's broken leg in the same vein?' (Freud and Jung, 1974).

The publication of the analysis of little Hans in this climate was a significant event, because it confirmed Freud's theoretical views and also because it demonstrated that it was possible to carry out analytic treatment on a young child under certain conditions.

It was difficult at that time to know where this interest in child psychoanalysis would lead. Should the number of observations of the child be multiplied in order to confirm psychoanalytical theory? Should the dream of a psychoanalytical education to ensure the prevention of neuroses be pursued? Sándor Ferenczi's communication at the Salzburg conference in 1908

9

entitled: 'What practical guidance does the Freudian experience provide for the education of the child?' was a step in this direction. Should there be more analytical treatment for children? How should this be carried out?

The group was teeming with ideas. Hermine Hug-Hellmuth was the most persistent in her research and was the first to carry out analytical treatment on children. A teacher by training, she held bold views on child sexuality and education, for which many would never forgive her. Her murder and the particular circumstances surrounding it provided the opportunity for hateful attacks on Freudian theories.

1

Sigmund Freud

In the beginning, my statements about infantile sexuality were founded almost exclusively on the findings of analysis in adults which led back into the past. I had no opportunity of direct observations on children. It was therefore a very great triumph when it became possible years later to confirm almost all my inferences by direct observation and the analysis of very young children – a triumph that lost some of its magnitude as one gradually realized that the nature of the discovery was such that one should really be ashamed of having had to make it. The further one carried these observations on children, the more self-evident the facts became; but more astonishing, too, did it become that one had taken so much trouble to overlook them.

(Freud, 1914a: 18)

Sigmund Freud's discovery and elaboration of psychoanalysis was something which took much longer than is generally recognized.

When, with the help of a bursary, the young Sigmund Freud went to attend Charcot's courses in Paris in 1885, he was 29. He had already done considerable work in the field of neuro-pathology, histology in particular, but, as he himself said: 'I understood nothing about neuroses at that time' (1925a). However, he did become interested to some extent in young children early on and published a number of works on both unilateral and bilateral cerebral paralysis in children (Freud and Rie, 1891; Freud, 1893). In 1886, he spent several weeks in Adolf Baginski's paediatric department in Berlin. He was then appointed head of the new neurological unit at the public Institute of Paediatrics in Vienna run by the paediatrician Kassowitz. 'Freud held this position for many years, working there for several hours three times a week and he made there some valuable contributions to neurology' (Jones, 1953, Vol. I: 233). At the same time he set up in private practice as a 'specialist in nervous disorders'. His patients became less and less 'neurological' and more and more 'nervous'. For the former there was no effective treatment anyway. With the latter he mainly used suggestion and hypnosis, and this led him to the theoretical and clinical field where he was to come into his own. Freud had said: 'from the very first I made use of hypnosis in *another* manner, apart from hypnotic suggestion. I used it for questioning the patient upon the origin of his symptom' (Freud, 1925a: 19).

To develop his technique, Freud had based himself on an observation by his friend Josef Breuer dating back to 1880–2. Hypnosis had enabled Breuer to find in Anna O. links between symptoms of severe hysteria and reminiscences of 'traumatic' experiences going back in particular to a period when she was looking after her sick father. The therapy used abreactions:[1] it was a cathartic treatment. It was while trying for many years to understand this case in the light of experience with other patients that Freud was able to make progress. In particular the question was to elucidate the erotic transference that the patient had made to Breuer and his positive countertransference. Breuer was not able (or unconsciously did not want) to see the phenomenon, in spite of the phantom pregnancy of his patient during the treatment and the jealousy of his wife. He even went as far as saying that Anna O.'s sexual side was surprisingly underdeveloped. To get beyond this stage, Freud had to discover the mechanism of repression, the existence of the unconscious, the role of transference and the major role played by sexuality.

But in 1895 Freud had not yet reached that point. His reflections led him to write *Studies on Hysteria*. He himself said on the subject (Freud, 1925a): 'In the case histories which I contributed to the *Studies* sexual factors played a certain part, but scarcely more attention was paid to them than to other emotional excitations. . . . It would have been difficult to guess from the *Studies on Hysteria* what an importance sexuality has in the aetiology of the neuroses' (p. 22).

The progress from catharsis to psychoanalysis was not easy: it can be dated to the period 1895 to 1900–2. These dates correspond to Freud's self-analysis, which indicates the energy he must have expended, the resistance he must have had to overcome and the inward searching he would have had to perform. Didier Anzieu's excellent book *L'auto-analyse de Freud* (1986) is proof of this.

Having discovered the role of 'trauma' in the genesis of hysteria, Freud was obliged to admit that there was a still earlier trauma to which the present trauma referred. The earlier trauma was a seduction, a sexual transgression, generally paternal in origin. The notion that the trauma itself was of an essentially sexual nature was not easily admitted, and Breuer had fled from this. But the truly agonizing reappraisal was the discovery of the active role played by the child in sexual seduction, and even more so, the discovery of the imaginary role of the adult in the seduction scene. It was at this point that Freud pronounced his celebrated renunciation of his 'neurotica'.

A century later, the active sexual role of the infant is not always acknowledged, not only by opponents of psychoanalysis, which is after all only quite natural, but even by a large number of psychoanalysts themselves, whose theories show that these factors have not been taken into consideration, even if they consciously and officially admit their existence.

Freud resisted as long as he could. His first thesis was that sexual advances by adults led to early stimulation of the child. 'He did not at first believe that such events could arouse immediate sexual excitement in the child. It was only later, nearing puberty that the memory of the incidents in question would have an effect' (Jones, 1953: 353).

In 1895 Freud had written that reminiscences only become traumatic *years after* the events themselves have taken place. In 1896 it was a question of 'slight sexual excitement' in the early infantile period but purely auto-erotic, there being no relation between the excitement and another person. In 1897, after having intuitively discovered erotogenic zones, he made a fundamental discovery: more than simply responding to a perverse act by the parents or to the simple sexual desires of its parents towards it, a child has incestuous desires towards its parents, generally the one of the opposite sex. Ernest Jones describes this research in detail:

> Even then Freud had not really arrived at the conception of infantile sexuality as it was later to be understood. The incest wishes and phantasies were later products, probably between the ages of 8 and 12, which were thrown back on to the screen of early childhood. They did not originate there. The most that he would admit was that young children, even infants of six to seven months old [(!)], had the capacity to register and in some imperfect way to apprehend the meaning of sexual acts between the parents that had been seen or overheard (May 2, 1897). Such experiences would become significant only when the memory of them was re-animated by several phantasies, desires or acts . . .
>
> The first forms of sexual excitation in early childhood that Freud recognized were what are now called pre-genital ones and concerned the two alimentary orifices, mouth and anus. These could still be regarded as auto-erotic. It was much harder to admit that the young child might have genital wishes concerning a parent which could in many respects be comparable with adult ones. And to recognize the full richness of the child's sexual life in terms of active impulses was a still further step that Freud took only later with his usual caution. . . .
>
> Even in *The Interpretation of Dreams* (1900) in which the Oedipus complex is described, one finds what might be called an encapsuled fossil from earlier times in which it is assumed that children are free from sexual

desires; the footnote correcting it was only added in the third edition of the book (1911).

There is therefore no doubt that over a period of some five years Freud regarded children as innocent objects of incestuous desires, and only very slowly – no doubt against considerable inner resistance – came to recognize what ever since has been known as infantile sexuality. As long as possible, he restricted it to a later age, the phantasies being believed to be projected backwards on to the earlier one, and to the end of his life, he chose to regard the first year of infancy as a dark mystery enshrouding dimly apprehensible excitations rather than active impulses and phantasies.

(Jones, *The Life and Work of Sigmund Freud,* Vol. I, 1953: 355–6)

In 1914, Freud stated this discovery of infantile sexuality with the utmost caution. It is true that the uncovering of the infantile libido had already won him some most violent attacks, but Freud's own mental resistance had also to be reckoned with its repression ever active, as is normal:

Enquirers often find more than they bargain for. One was drawn further and further back into the past; one hoped at last to be able to stop at puberty, the period in which the sexual impulses are traditionally supposed to awake. But in vain; the tracks led still further back into childhood and into its earlier years.

(Freud, 1914a: 17)

And, further on, he notes:

If hysterical subjects trace back their symptoms to traumas that are fictitious, then the new fact which emerges is precisely that they create such scenes in *phantasy*, and this psychical reality requires to be taken into account alongside practical reality. This reflection was soon followed by the discovery that these phantasies were intended to cover up the auto-erotic activity of the first years of childhood, to embellish it and raise it to a higher plane. And now, from behind the phantasies, the whole range of a child's sexual life came to light.

(Freud, 1914a: 17–18)

Freud thus made this discovery against his will. In 1925 he noted: 'I was not prepared for this conclusion and my expectations played no part in it, for I had begun my investigation of neurotics quite unsuspectingly' (Freud, 1925a: 24).

One could still protect oneself with the 'medical' aspect of sexuality: its chemistry was as yet unknown, but it governed sexual excitation and meant that neuroses resembled endocrine disorders such as Basedow's disease (hyperthyroidosis) (Freud, 1925a: 25).

14

Because infantile sexuality was a novelty in those days, Freud's discovery was

a contradiction of one of the strongest human prejudices. Childhood was looked upon as innocent and free from the lusts of sex, and the fight with the demon of 'sensuality' was not thought to begin until the troubled age of puberty. Such occasional sexual activities as it had been impossible to overlook in children were put down as signs of degeneracy or premature depravity or as a curious freak of nature. Few of the findings of psychoanalysis have met with such universal contradiction or have aroused such an outburst of indignation as the assertion that the sexual function starts at the beginning of life and reveals its presence by important signs even in childhood. And yet no other finding of analysis can be demonstrated so easily and so completely.

(Freud, 1925a: 33)

But how was this to be demonstrated? As we shall see, between 1902 and 1910 it would be necessary to study *the children themselves* (the effects of that decade are still being felt today).

It was during the meetings of the circle of Freud's first students that this study of children was undertaken. The Wednesday psychoanalytical evenings which, from 1902 onwards, took place in Freud's rooms, were to become the Wednesday Evening Sessions. The Psychoanalytic Society of Vienna, founded in 1908, arose out of these meetings, which then became part of its official activities. Reports of these meetings dating back to 1906 are still available to us (see *Minutes of the Vienna Psychoanalytic Society*, vols I–IV, 1906–18).

The task the members of this rather mixed group set themselves was to endeavour to understand psychoanalysis and to gain ground in this field. They did this with the various means at their disposal, some by analysing patients, others by commenting on philosophical, psychological or literary texts, and yet others by studying themselves. In this last category we might mention Rudolf von Urbantschitsch, who, on 15 January 1908, gave a paper entitled: 'My developmental years until marriage.' The participants discussed in learned fashion whether his onanism was harmful or whether it was just the struggle against the urge to masturbate that was harmful. An analysis of the speaker was then undertaken. Freud analysed his feminine side and his exhibitionism. Hitschmann emphasized that 'it is of great interest to know what has become of a man with such a history (1906–8, p. 283); Isidore Sadger studied his perversions and indicated that 'It is a question whether the speaker is really quite as healthy as has been asserted' (p. 284); Max Graf (the father of little Hans) said that 'one would have to assume that the speaker is severely hysterical'. Freud said that this was not so, since neurosis does not exist when repression is successful. In his response the 'speaker' acknowledged his 'psychic sadism', but disputed that he was a homosexual or a pervert (p. 285).

We have mentioned this discussion to show that in this sort of atmosphere, talking about one's own children would not be found shocking in any way.

One sentence from the *Three Essays on the Theory of Sexuality* clearly indicates the tasks assigned to the Wednesday researchers:

> A formula begins to take shape which lays it down that the sexuality of neurotics has remained in, or been brought back to, an infantile state. Thus our interest turns to the sexual life of children, and we will now proceed to trace the play of influences which govern the evolution of infantile sexuality till its outcome in perversion, neurosis or normal sexual life.
>
> (S. Freud, *Three Essays on the Theory of Sexuality*, 1905: 172)

These tasks are mentioned again in the article on little Hans: 'With this end in view I have for many years been urging my pupils and my friends to collect observations of the sexual life of children – the existence of which has as a rule been cleverly overlooked or deliberately denied' (S. Freud, *Analysis of a Phobia in a Five-Year Old Boy,* 1909: 6). The parents of little Hans, Max Graf and his wife, 'had agreed that in bringing up their first child they would use no more coercion than might be absolutely necessary for maintaining good behaviour'. These remarks echo those of Freud in 1905 (*Three Essays on the Theory of Sexuality*): 'A thorough study of the sexual manifestations of childhood would probably reveal the essential characters of the sexual instinct and would show us the course of its development and the way it is put together from various sources' (1905: 173).

Often forgotten is the fact that right at the beginning of the article on little Hans (the first ten pages) there is an observation of a normal child; these were observations made of Herbert Graf between 3 and 5 years of age, from 1906–8. In his observations, Freud noted elements demonstrating the castration complex, the significance of infantile curiosity, sibling rivalry and, in particular, a polymorphously perverse disposition. The phobia of 'being afraid of being bitten by a horse in the street' crops up at this point, which permits the actual analysis to take place.

As we can see in this example, Freud distinguishes quite distinctly between psychoanalytical *observation* and psychoanalytical *treatment* very early on in the history of psychoanalysis. The observations mentioned above led to Freud's 1907 paper entitled: 'The sexual enlightenment of children'. In the original edition, the child was still called Herbert: anonymity was not complete. This paper is part of a discussion, commonplace for that period, about the interest of such information, the time chosen for divulging it, the way to do it, and so forth.

16

It was therefore after two years of observation – and an upbringing 'with no more coercion than might be absolutely necessary – that the child became phobic. The parents were very worried: 'I am sending you a little more about Hans – but this time I am sorry to say material for a case history' (Freud, 1909: 22).

Initially, the occurrence of this infantile neurosis must have been very distressful in a circle which was working on the aetiology of neuroses. Besides, was this not an indication of the eventual harmfulness of an upbringing without coercion and with sexual information? We know that these ideas of Freud's were very much criticized at the time. Finally, had the parents not committed some errors in their upbringing? Through the observation from the age of 3, we know that the mother had threatened to have the 'widdler' of Herbert–Hans cut off by Dr A if he continued to masturbate, that his parents sometimes (often?) let him sleep in their bed, that the mother had called his penis a 'filthy thing'. These occasional accounts imply an atmosphere which would make the child feel guilty: the parents too, for that matter. Guilty because of the fear, that modern child psychoanalysts know well, of having not brought up their child correctly and of having been the cause of the child's neurosis. Add to that the fact, which we owe to Jean Bergeret's penetrating study (1987), that other histories are hidden behind this analysis: the systematic scotomization of the role played by the mother seems to indicate the existence of an intentional omission on Freud's part, for he knew this particular mother well (he had analysed her) and was obliged to suppress highly significant details so as not to embarrass the three protagonists.

Whatever the case may be, the child temporarily became a 'pathological case' and the treatment decided on was psychoanalysis. Freud appears to have been very happy with this outcome, which would enable him to study a neurosis *in statu nascendi*, the father being the most suitable person to carry out the analysis, with Freud as supervisor.

We cannot and do not wish to present the psychoanalysis of Hans in this present work, where our intention is to limit ourselves to a historical viewpoint (*vertex*). Those readers who are already acquainted with the case will be bored by the repetition, and those who are not acquainted with it or only slightly will perhaps be prompted to read or reread it.

Yet, this case of child psychoanalysis in history is deserving of more than a passing mention. For one thing it was the first time it had ever been done, and if the credit goes to Freud for inspiring the method, devising the theory, supervising the case, and writing it up, he was not the analyst. This was in fact Max Graf, who undertook this first case. He was not a doctor, he did not have any experience, he was not of the female sex (see below) and, in any case, he was the father of the child. We have often observed in our own supervisory seminars the miraculous treatment carried out by young and inexperienced doctors. These first cases often benefit from inspired intuition, perhaps because the resistance to insight,[2] which starts to develop at the beginning of their psychoanalysis, has not yet blinded them. One has then to wait for these psychoanalysts successfully to finish their own personal psychoanalysis before seeing their 'therapeutic gift' and their insight reappear.

This was probably the only psychoanalysis that Max Graf ever undertook. It was very distressing for him and Freud's support was essential. When Freud wrote: 'It was only because the authority of a father and of a physician were united in a single person, and because in him both affectionate care and scientific interest were combined, that it was possible in this one instance to apply the method to a use which it would not otherwise have lent itself. [*Ungeeignet*]' (Freud, 1909: 5). This was undoubtedly true at the time, because no child psychoanalyst existed at this time, and in fact only the father could have done it. However, one is bound to add that without Freud it would never have happened.

Today's reader might question the psychoanalytical nature of this treatment, which is vastly different from the 'technical' conditions under which psychoanalyses are now conducted. First, it would be reasonable to take Freud's own opinion into account: he published the case under the title '*analysis* of a phobia in a five-year-old boy'. The benevolent neutrality on the part of the father was no doubt lacking, but his paternal bias was nevertheless tempered by his concern to let the child express himself and it was underpinned by Freud, who had to sustain a double transference: that of the father and that of Hans himself, who knew Freud not just through his father, but directly. Freud had offered him a rocking-horse(!) for his third birthday.

This analysis was carried out with at least as much rigour as all the others practised in 1908. The child recounts his dreams, confides his theories and sexual practices, evokes his anxieties and his symptoms; what the father does not understand, the child explains. For instance, when Hans says that he does not touch his 'widdler' any more and his father takes him to task for nevertheless still wanting to, Hans lectures him, saying: '*Wanting's* not *doing*, and doing's not wanting.' In the same way, Hans says he wishes his sister Anna were dead, and his father says that a nice little boy should not wish such things. Hans retorts that he has the right to *think* it. His father does not immediately understand, and says that that is not nice. Hans explains: 'If he thinks it, it *is* good all the same, because you can write it to the professor', referring his analyst father back to his supervisor! At this point, Freud writes a footnote: 'Well done, little Hans! I could wish for no better understanding of psychoanalysis from any grown-up.' The father elicits associations from his patient: 'Tell me, quickly, what you are thinking about . . . and what else.' The interpretations are made, in classic fashion, in the transference: 'the big giraffe is me', etc. At one point, the supervi-sor–professor takes part in the analysis directly: the father and son consult him. Freud allows himself to venture an interpretation, which would be the turning point: 'I then disclosed to him that he was afraid of his father pre-cisely because he was so fond of his mother.' The symptoms started to improve rapidly from that point and the little boy showed proof of a truly rare 'clarity of mind' says Freud (today we would say that he had gained in insight).

In May 1908, after five months of daily analysis, the child was considered cured, the symptoms having disappeared. The child gave up this game of question and answer with his father and started asking himself questions about the exact nature of his relationship with his father ('I belong to you too.'). The father wrote up the remaining unanalysed material, to which Freud responded: 'our young investigator has merely come somewhat early upon the discovery that all knowledge is patchwork'. The father added that 'the boy would have gone out for walks soon enough if he had been given a sound thrashing' (which he had not). That was a case of double transfer-ence well disposed of!

The treatment in this particular case therefore consisted of an analyst lis-tening in a benevolent fashion to what a child of 5 was saying while remaining as neutral as possible, and supervised by Freud. Listening to the daily events, dreams and memories enabled the analyst to elicit associations of ideas which in turn enabled the child to bring back forgotten memories and thus to reconstruct his primal phantasies. The analysis of the transfer-ence (through Freud) and the interpretations made in that transference enabled the child gradually to gain a better understanding of his inner world, to the point that he no longer needed to repress it, that he no longer needed his symptoms.

This case can therefore truly be considered to be an analysis, even in the sense that we understand the word today: it was indeed the first case of child psychoanalysis. In passing, we would just like to mention the 'deferred action' concept, which for a large number of French psychoanalysts means that psychoanalysis for children must be ruled out. Referring to the phrase spoken by little Hans: 'My widdler will get bigger as I get bigger; it's fixed in, of course', Freud observed that this was a *deferred* effect (the emphasis is Freud's) of the maternal threat of castration expressed fifteen months previ-ously. At the time, the threat was not carried out; but the effect of the analysis was to give it some sense, bringing the fear of castration to the fore and causing the child to make this defiant statement. Contrary to what one often reads, this deferred effect can happen well before puberty.

In his annotations, Freud announced that he would demonstrate, in a very systematic fashion, that this case supported the theory of infantile sexuality he had expressed in 1905 (*Three Essays on the Theory of Sexuality*), what it contributed to the understanding of phobias, and, finally, what it contributed to the understanding of the mental life of the child and to its upbringing from a psychoanalytical viewpoint.

The point here is neither to comment on nor even to give a summary of this major theoretical text. However, we would like to emphasize the point to which the founder of psychoanalysis came to rely on the psychoanalysis of a child, clearly stated as such, to raise and solve a large number of theoretical problems concerning not just children but psychoanalysis in general. Moreover, he was often to refer to this case in a number of later works.

To the malicious critics of the time who described a child with such polymorphous perversity as 'degenerate', to those who, on the contrary, deplored that such a courageous child should thus be perverted by psychoanalysis, to those who accused Freud and Max Graf of putting ideas into Hans' head, to those who, on the contrary, denied any value to infantile discourse, Freud responded calmly with a scientific and humanistic disquisition, which, in our opinion, is one of his finest texts. The normality of infantile neurosis is mentioned, as is the fact that 'no sharp line can be drawn between "neurotic" and "normal" people – whether children or adults'.

The biological factor is not forgotten: 'Predisposition and the eventualities of life must combine before the threshold of this summation is overstepped.'

Problems of upbringing are mentioned; first, those within the scope of child psychoanalysis: Freud believed that the 'pedagogical experiment' (meaning sexual education) could have gone further in this case. But on the general problem of education, he had already adopted the sceptical position which he was to maintain throughout:

> the information gained by psychoanalysis . . . can claim with justice that it deserves to be regarded by educators as an invaluable guide in their conduct towards children. What practical conclusions may follow from this, and how far experience may justify the application of those conclusions within our present social system, are matters which I leave to the examination and decision of others.
>
> (Freud, 1909: 146–7)

When, at the end of this study, Freud expresses the idea that this particular case had not 'strictly speaking taught [him] anything new', we do not think that he was criticizing any psychoanalysis of children that might take place in the future, but rather was reaffirming the similarity of the process of infantile neurosis in both adults and children. Indeed, in the same sentence he indicates that these facts that he already knew were perceptible in adults 'less distinctly and more indirectly'. Moreover, in 1910 he rectifies as follows (footnote added to the *Three Essays on the Theory of Sexuality*, 1905: 193–4):

When the account which I have given above of infantile sexuality was first published in 1905, it was founded for the most part on the results of psychoanalytic research upon adults. At that time it was impossible to make full use of direct observation on children: only isolated hints and some valuable pieces of confirmation came from that source. Since then it has become possible to gain direct insight into infantile psychosexuality by the analysis of some cases of neurotic illness during the early years of childhood. It is gratifying to be able to report that direct observation has fully confirmed the conclusions arrived at by psychoanalysis – which is incidentally good evidence of the trustworthiness of that method of research. In addition to this, the 'Analysis of a Phobia in a Five-Year-Old Boy' (1909) has taught us much that is new for which we have not been prepared by psychoanalysis: for instance, the fact that sexual symbolism – the representation of what is sexual by non-sexual objects and relations – extends back into the first years of possession of the power of speech. I was further made aware of a defect in the account I have given in the text, which, in the interests of lucidity, describes the conceptual distinction between the two phases of *auto-erotism* and *object-love*³ as though it were also a separation in time. But the analyses that I have just mentioned, as well as the findings of Bell . . . show that children between the ages of three and five are capable of very clear object-choice, accompanied by strong affects.

The epilogue to the story of little Hans is well known. In 1922 Hans–Herbert was 19 and went to see Freud. He said to the great man: 'I am little Hans.' He was well and, in particular, he had weathered his adolescence well, as he had difficulties resulting from the divorce of his parents. It was satisfying to be able to oppose this result to the indignant critics of 1909, when 'a most evil future had been foretold for the poor little boy, because he had been "robbed of his innocence" at such a tender age and had been made the victim of a psychoanalysis' (p. 148). See also the chapter on Hermine Hug-Hellmuth.)

Jean Bergeret (1984, 1987) shows us Herbert Graf once again in 1970 (at the age of 67!) greeting Anna Freud at a conference in Geneva with the same words. 'I am little Hans.' The aim of Bergeret's book was to delve further into the things which had remained unvoiced in the analysis in 1909, and in particular to give more prominence to the problem of the 'basic violence' of this case. We also find interesting this author's suggestion that this case was in fact a continuation of Freud's own self-analysis and that in 'Hans', he had found more than just an echo of his own childhood, which up to that point he had tended to scotomize. Equally fascinating reading is Hans–Herbert Graf's (1972) autobiography *Memoirs of an Invisible Man*. This man, son of a writer and music critic, whose godfather was Gustav Mahler, had a very rich professional career, first as an opera singer and then as a producer. He was director of the Metropolitan Opera of New York from 1936 to 1950 and worked on all the great stages of the musical world. He does not seem to have been at all unhappy in his personal life either. He died in 1973.

Let us go back to the Psychoanalytical Society of Vienna in 1909 (see *Minutes of the Vienna Psychoanalytic Society*, vol. II, 1908–10). At its meeting on 12 May, Freud stated: 'We simply do not understand children and only since Hans do we know what a child thinks' (p. 230). Perhaps what he meant to say was: we know that a child *does* think. Reitler blames the parents, which was quite common at that time and not really a modern idea at all: 'Undeniably, mistakes were made in his education, and these were indeed responsible for his neurosis' (p. 232). Max Graf was present at the meeting and defends himself: Hans had a 'strong sexual predisposition *Anlage*, which awoke a premature need for love; this in turn became too strongly linked with his parents' (p. 235). Freud also comes to his defence: 'not *that* many mistakes were made, and those that did occur did not have *that* much to do with the neurosis' (p. 235). In fact, it was a question of constitution: Hans had 'a strong predisposition to sexuality'.

Many of Freud's students studied their children. It is a pity that we do not have any notes prior to October 1906, but, as early as 7 November 1906, Bass (a general practitioner) indicates that his child was extremely sensitive to light up to the age of 2; the sudden striking of a match would make him sneeze. On 23 January 1907 Federn observed that his child, aged 13, was showing an aversion to certain foods, which were those also disliked by his mother. On 27 March Reitler talks of a little girl of about 8 or 9, who he seems to know quite well. She was enuretic and had an obsessive ritual which consisted of using the chamberpots of her brothers and father and then having to wash herself 'until she bled'.

On 12 May 1909, the session where Hans is mentioned, Bass continues to report: his little boy only talks about 'these things' with his mother. He thinks that a woman need only look into the eyes of a man to conceive a child.

On 17 November 1909, Heller talks about his children: vomiting and spending a long time on the toilet are the symptoms he has observed, along with a compulsive need to bite (his brother) and a 'strange' aversion to kisses.

On 16 March 1910, Friedjung talks about a little boy of 6 and a half. The boy's father (himself?) sleeps with him and perhaps the child has felt his father's penis in erection. Whence a dream: a large black man plunges a rod into his chest. It would also seem that he had witnessed his parents during coitus – after a dream he started to make moaning noises similar to those made by his mother during coitus. However, things were not taken any further because Friedjung did not want to ask the child 'suggestive' questions.

On 25 February 1914, Weiss talks of a little boy just over 1 year old who tries to undo the buttons of his mother's blouse. Tausk mentions a little girl who gets on his back and says, embarrassed when her mother enters, 'That's not the thing to do.' Federn mentions two children for whom the mother's breast takes on a sexual connotation; Friedjung a small boy who always makes ironic remarks about male visitors, but never about women visitors. Sachs mentions a boy of about 7 or 8 who fell in love with his step-mother. On 18 March Federn and Weiss mention their children again. On 20 May Tausk, Friedjung, Weiss and Landauer also mention similar material that they have observed.

What can thus be gleaned from the minutes of the Psychoanalytic Society of Vienna is perhaps only the fossilized remains which have been preserved by the stenographic talents of Otto Rank. It is more than likely that the observation by the first psychoanalysts of their own children gave rise to a much larger mass of documents which have not yet come to light.

Notes

1 Abreaction is an emotional discharge whereby the subject liberates himself from the affect attached to the memory of a traumatic event in such a way that this affect is not able to become (or to remain) pathogenic.
2 Insight consists of the acquisition of knowledge of one's own unconscious. For Hanna Segal it is the central factor of the therapeutic process. As to the analyst, it means his capacity to apply the awareness he has of his own unconscious to the interpretation of the behaviour of his patient (Money-Kyrle, 1956).
3 Emphasis added.

2

Carl Gustav Jung: divergent views

Concurrently with the work being done in Vienna, another group of young doctors, both men and women, had got together in Zurich around Evgen Bleuler and Carl Jung to discuss Freud's ideas, and very quickly began to apply them. The rapidity with which they did this is indicated by a few biographical details. As Christian Delacampagne reports, (in Jaccard, 1982, vol. I: 246), Jung, the son of a Protestant minister, became a medical assistant at the Burghölzli (the Zurich mental hospital) at the age of 25. He was to become the chief physician in 1905, at the age of 30, and in 1906 he discovered Freud's theories. In fact according to William McGuire (Introduction to the *Freud–Jung Correspondence*, 1974: 9–10), Jung had read *The Interpretation of Dreams* in 1900 but had not understood it (a remark made by Jung himself); he then went back to the book in 1903. In fact, most of Jung's publications from 1902 to 1905 contain quotes from Freud.

Bleuler and Jung thought that they might be able to get to the root of the problem of schizophrenia (still called 'dementia praecox' by Jung at that time) using this new theory. Bleuler had conducted an episodic correspondence with Freud from 1904, and Jung corresponded regularly with him from 1906 to 1912. Throughout these few years the Burghölzli seems to have been more attractive than Vienna, for we note the visit of Karl Abraham and also of Max Eitingon, Herman Nunberg, Ernest Jones and Sándor Ferenczi. All these pioneers of psychoanalysis would go to Vienna later on.

While this Swiss group studied the theories of the unconscious and psychoanalytical treatment with enthusiasm, the problems of infantile sexuality seem to have given rise to many more reservations. It is all the more interesting, therefore, to see Jung take an interest from the outset in the treatment of children. On 13 May 1907, Jung wrote to Freud: 'At the moment I am treating a 6-year-old girl for excessive masturbation and lying after alleged seduction by the foster-father. Very complicated! Have you had any

24

experience with such small children?' (Freud and Jung, 1974: 45).

Of course, Jung knew full well that Freud did not have this experience and one can see that this rapidity, this impatience of Jung's to get to the 'applications', could be construed as a forerunner to the rivalry which was to grow and flourish between them. Perhaps it was pressure from Jung that led to Freud's insisting that his students obtain material about children. However, looking further ahead at what Jung was to say about this analysis, one is surprised by its antiquated nature (it is 1907):

> Except for a colourless and affectless, totally ineffectual representation of the trauma in consciousness, I have not succeeded in obtaining any abreaction with affect, either spontaneously or suggested. At present it looks as if the trauma is a fake. Yet where does the child get all these sexual stories from? The hypnosis is good and deep, but with the utmost innocence the child evades all suggestions for enacting the trauma. One thing is important: at the first setting she spontaneously hallucinated a 'sausage which the woman said would get fatter and fatter'. When I asked where she saw the sausage, she quickly said: 'On the Herr Doktor!' All that could possibly be wished of a transposition! But, since then, everything sexual has been completely occluded. No sign of D. pr [dementia praecox]! With respectful regards, yours very sincerely, Jung.
>
> (1974: 45)

He was therefore talking about <u>hypnosis and not analysis</u>, in the sense that Freud understood it in 1907.

Freud gave a lecturing response to this questioning ten days later, on 23 May 1907:

> In your six-year-old girl, you must surely have discovered in the mean time that the attack is a fantasy that has become conscious, something which is regularly disclosed in analysis, and which misled me into assuming the existence of generalized traumas in childhood. The therapeutic task consists in demonstrating the sources from which the child derives its sexual knowledge. As a rule, children provide little information but confirm what we have guessed when we tell them. Questioning of the families is essential. When it is successful, the most delightful result analyses. In regard to Bleuler I should add: the *Three Essays* do give a clear picture of autoerotism. Psychically negative, if you will.
>
> Another reason why the child fails to talk about it is that, as your observation shows, she enters immediately and fully into the transference, as your observation also shows.
>
> (1974: 48)

In fact, in his answer, Freud assumed that they were talking about analysis and not hypnosis. But this was probably the first opinion given by Freud on transference during child analysis: it is not only possible, but full and complete and can give rise to these negative reactions (i.e. silence).

In 1908 we note a significant bone of contention in the correspondence. On 14 April Freud writes: 'Oddly enough, I have been reading in your Amsterdam paper that child hysteria does not enter this context [Jung had written that, "In any case, hysteria in children and the psychotraumatic neuroses form a group apart"] whereas I myself have been toying with the idea of working up my analysis of hysterical phobia in a five-year-old boy for the Congress' (1974: 81).

Jung replies on 18 April: 'Child hysteria must fall outside the formula applicable to adults, for whom puberty plays a large role. A specially modified formula must be established for child hysteria' (1974: 83). The attentive reader will have understood that we have here the nub of a fundamental question. Jung's objection is still evoked today, with a few variants, by a number of (adult) psychoanalysts. In effect, there is still a tendency to refer to the Freudian deferred-action theory, often placing it at the phase of puberty, in order to deny both the problem of the structure of infantile neuroses and the possibility of a cure by psychoanalytical means. Freud responds very quickly and with great precision. The following day, he writes (p. 140): 'Only the sentence on hysteria in children strikes me as being incorrect. The conditions here are the same, probably because *each thrust of growth creates the same conditions as the great thrust of puberty*[1] (each increase in libido, I mean).' One can guess that the lack of attention given to this indication by Freud would long encumber the debate on child psychoanalysis. The rest of this letter, dated 19 April, also needs to be quoted: Freud excuses Jung in a grandiose manner: 'I know that it will take you time to catch up with my experience of the past 15 years'. Four lines further on one reads the better-known declaration taken up by Jones (1955: 488): 'I thoroughly dislike the notion that my opinions are correct, but only in regard to a part of the cases. (Substitute point of view for opinions). That is not possible. It must be one thing or the other'. Here Freud puts the weight of his fanaticism (the word is his) on defending the correctness of his theories, and what we understand here is that he insists not only on the sexual aetiology of hysteria, but also that he refuses to differentiate the infantile psyche from that of the adult.

On 17 November 1909, a year-and-a-half later, Freud takes up this discussion again with the same insistence at the meeting of the Psychoanalytical Society of Vienna. Jones includes this remark in the appendix to volume II of his biography of Freud (1955: 493–4):

The objection that the hysteria of childhood appears to have no 'reminiscences' behind it was brought forward also by Jung. Two points, however, are neglected here: (1) In a child hysteria occurring between six and eight we have no right at all to underestimate the previous history, since the decisive impressions occur in the years between two and four. The shortness of the period elapsing since these reminiscences is compensated by the magnitude of the changes that occur rapidly at this time in life.

The second fact mentioned by Freud is 'organic repression'. By that he means not a "cerebral" function, but a fact of civilization: the vertical position of the human being which represses smell, in particular. In the same way, as the child grows up he or she gets further away from the ground. He adds: 'This [organic] repression makes possible an hysteria in earliest infancy, indeed even in an animal.'

As a follow-up to this remark, Freud demonstrates the archaic origin of neuroses and outlines what would later become the psychoanalytical observation of the infant:

> In the matter of anxiety one has to remember that children begin their experience of it in the act of birth itself. It is also noteworthy that every affect manifests itself originally as an hysterical attack. It is only a reminiscence of an event. The pediatrist should be able to enlighten us about the origin of affects. Most children have a trauma. After it they behave like hysterics. I refer to the weaning from the breast, and this has to be taken into account as a significant psychical trauma to the pleasure of the nutritional impulse. . . . Such children can, for example, come to dislike milk.
>
> The technique of this child study has not such poor prospects as it might seem. One will have to make use of an intelligent nurse (and specially favourable cases, of the mother herself) who will observe the child continuously and report anything of note – rather like the indirect observation of psychotic patients.
>
> The investigation of childhood life will for some time yet, be dominated by the knowledge we gain from adults. But that is not an ideal state of affairs.
>
> (Jones, 1955: 494)

On 19 January 1909, we can see that Jung in turn takes an interest in the observation of infants. He notes that 'baby pains' (convulsions?) are related to the sucking organ and seem to precede the first 'active attempt to mimic': looking at a bright object, opening the mouth, clicking movements of the tongue, etc. This does not seem to interest Freud very much. As we know, we need to wait for Rene Spitz and then Esther Bick to come along and follow up this lead, which had been uncovered but not explored.

However, the same day Jung speaks about his 4-year-old daughter, Agathli. We quote the full observation here, in spite of its length, for its historical interest and so as to be able to understand Freud's reluctance to consider it entirely authentic:

Contributions by my 4-year-old Agathli: the evening before Fränzli's birth I asked her what she would say if the stork brought her a little brother. 'Then I shall kill it', she said quick as lightning with an embarrassed, sly expression, and would not let herself be pinned down to this theme. The baby was born during the night. Early next morning, I carried her to my wife's bedside; she was tense and gazed in alarm at the rather wan-looking mother, without showing any joy; found nothing to say about the situation. The same morning, when Mama was alone, the little one suddenly ran to her, flung her arms around her neck and asked anxiously: 'But, Mama, you don't have to die, do you?' This was the first appropriate affect. Her pleasure over the baby was rather 'put on'. Up till now the problems had always been: Why is Granny so old? What happens to old people anyway? 'They must die and will go to heaven' – 'Then they become children again', the little one added. So someone has to die in order to make a child. After the birth A.[gathli] went to stay for some weeks with her grandmother, where she was fed exclusively on the stork theory. On her return home, she was again rather suspicious and shy with Mama. Lots of questions: 'Shall I become a woman like you?' 'Will I then still talk with you?' 'Do you still love me too, not just Fränzli?' Strong identification with the nurse, weaves fantasises about her, *starts making rhymes and telling herself stories.* Often unexpectedly fractious with Mama, pesters her with questions. For instance, Mama says: 'Come on, we'll go into the garden,' A.[gathli] asks: 'Is that true? You're quite sure it's true? You're not lying? I don't believe it,' etc. Scenes of this kind were repeated a number of times, all the more striking because they were about quite irrelevant things. But once she heard us talking about the earthquake in Messina and all the people that had been killed. She literally hurled herself on to this theme, had to be told the story over and over again; every bit of wood, every stone in the road could have tumbled down in an earthquake. Mama had to assure her hourly that there were certainly no earthquakes in Zurich. I had to assure her too, but she came back again and again to her fears. Recently, my wife hurried into my room looking for some books; A.[gathli] wasn't leaving her a moment's peace, my wife had to show her all the pictures of earthquakes and volcanoes. A.[gathli] would pore over the geological pictures of volcanoes for hours on end. Finally, on my advice, my wife enlightened A.[gathli], who showed not the least surprise on hearing the solution. (Children grow in the mother like flowers on plants.) Next day I was in bed with influenza. A.[gathli] came in with a shy, rather startled look on her face, wouldn't approach the bed, but asked: 'Have you a plant in your tummy too?' Ran off merry and carefree when this possibility was ruled out. Next day a fantasy: 'My brother [a fantasy hero] is also in Italy, and has a house made of glass and cloth and it doesn't fall down.' During the last two days, no trace of fear. She merely asks our female guests whether they have a child or whether they had been in Messina, though with no sign of anxiety. The three-year-old Grethli ridicules the stork theory, saying that the stork brought not only her little brother, but the nurse as well.

What an enchantment such a child is! Only recently A.[gathli] praised the beauty of her little brother to her grandmother. 'And look what a pretty little boy's bottom he has' [in Switzerdeutsch: *Buobefüdili*].

(Freud and Jung, 1974: 199–200)

On 25 January Freud replies: 'But surely you recognize the main features of little Hans' story. Mightn't everything in it be typical?' In his following letters Jung insists on giving more details. Freud insists, with, as we have seen, some humour: 'I hope Agathli is original and hadn't heard the story of little Hans?' (9 March).

Jung denies this, indicating on 11 March: 'My Agathli's achievements are original: she has never heard of Little Hans. We simply listen and interfere as little as possible.' He gives a few more details: the difference from the analysis of Hans is that Jung, as he himself states, does not seem to interpret, at least not at the time. However, in the letter dated 10–13 July 1909, we learn that this observation has become an 'analysis'. 'I am about to finish the analysis of Agathli.' In spite of the 'end' of this 'analysis', he continues to tell Freud of his discoveries in his abundant correspondence. Freud seems in general to have made only cautious responses, but it is possible that Jung might have considered this exchange as supervision. In 1910, Jung speaks of it as if it were an analysis, and even a case to be published: 'my child analysis' (6 April). It does in fact appear (under the name of Anna) in 'Conflicts of the infantile mind' (Jahrbuch, 1910, vol. II: 1) and then in the form of a booklet.

Freud had mixed feelings about this publication, whether because of his rivalry(?) with Jung or for more fundamental reasons, and tried to explain his position to Jung, again in humorous fashion:

I have reread with pleasure the charming story of the children (see Worcester, Anna and Sophie), but regretted that the scientist did not entirely overcome the father; it is a delicate relief when it might have been a vigorous statue, and because of its subtlety the lesson will be lost on most readers. In the children's fear that their father intends to drown them, one glimpses the symbolism of water-dreams (disguised childbirth). The analogies with Little Hans are developed only here and there; you forget that the reader is by definition a simpleton and deserves to have his nose rubbed in these things. Your reviews and abstracts show a freedom and humour that I would like to see in the *Zentralblatt*.

(letter of 18 August 1910)

Jung replies on 31 August:

I knew of course that I could not quite disown the father when writing about my Agathli, but I do not think this personal note will worry the initiates. The analogies with Little Hans should have been developed if only it had been possible to keep these explanations short. I had the feeling that I would have had to say very many things I wanted to avoid. The thicker a work is, the less it is read. Finally, one must after all leave something to the reader's imagination. I wonder very much what the critics will make of this feminine counterpart to Little Hans ('Poor little boy, poor little girl'[2]).

(1974: 350)

Jung does not only relate his observations of Agathli. In another text he mentions little 'Freddy', who seems to have been Manfred Bleuler. Eugen Bleuler does not seem to have appreciated the publication of this material (see letter from Freud to Jung dated 26 April 1910; 1974: 312). Jung even took an interest in Martin, one of Freud's sons, but does not go as far as publishing the material concerning him (letters dated 18 January and 17 February 1911; 1974: 384 and 394, respectively). In the abundant correspondence of 1911 one also finds Jung's attempts to have Freud modify one of the passages of *The Interpretation of Dreams*. Jung appears to want to have the psychoanalysis of children taken more seriously and takes objection to the passage where Freud excepts children's dreams from the general rule. Jung says this should be reconsidered, and cites as an example one of his daughter Grethchen's dreams (Grethe was born in 1906, Agathli in 1904):

My daughter Grethchen gave me excellent proof of the importance a child's dream can have. She dreamt of her 'little friend Hans who had pulled his felt bonnet completely down over his head (so that his head was hidden) and she had to swallow it.' Another time she had dreamt of a wolf 'who was sitting in the tunnel.' She is now five. Her knowledge of the prepuce and glans is quite remarkable.

At that same period his wife, Emma Jung, intervenes in the discussion. Freud had spent three days in Küsnacht with the Jung family before going with the Jungs to the Weimar congress (21–2 September 1911). The conversation must have been quite lively. Very early on Emma realizes intuitively that relations between the two men will eventually deteriorate. 'Your dear wife, well known to me as a solver of riddles', writes Freud on 1 September. The 'dear wife' then writes to Freud behind her husband's back on 30 October (p. 452): 'I have been tormented by the idea that your relation with my husband is not altogether as it should be. . . . I don't know whether I am deceiving myself when I think that you are somehow not quite in agreement with "Transformations of Libido".' She complains of Freud's resignation at seeing his own children possibly living their lives against him, and fears that this resignation might extend to his spiritual sons. She adds, with a touch of self-criticism: 'Do not count me among the women who, you once told me, always spoil your friendships' (1974: 452). In his letter to Carl Jung dated 2 November Freud tries, more or less skilfully, to satisfy Emma by showing that he is interested in children, in his own children: 'My son Ernst is well. My daughter Sophie is better but nothing has been decided yet. The rest of them are fine. I hope to hear the same of you and your little barnyard. Very cordially . . .'.

We do not have Emma's reply to Freud, but a very moving, second letter was written by her on 6 November 1911 in which she tries to point out to Freud his paternalism. 'Do not think of Carl with a father's feeling: "He will grow, but I must dwindle," but rather as one human being thinks of another, who, like you, has his own law to fulfil. Don't be angry with me'.

In this letter she mingles the fatherly feelings of Freud towards Jung and those towards his own children. The result is an ambiguous but quite revealing discourse:

> I wanted to ask . . . if you are sure that your children would not be helped by analysis. One certainly cannot be the child of a great man with impunity, considering the trouble one has in getting away from ordinary fathers . . . Didn't the fracture of your son's leg fit in with this picture? . . . When I asked you about it you said you didn't have time to analyse your children's dreams because you had to earn money so that they could go on dreaming. Do you think this attitude is right?
>
> (1974: 456–7)

The emphasis that Jung places on the analysis of children, which we have mentioned at some length, and the correlation with the analysis of his own children both probably went to deepen Freud's reticence about child analysis in general. His sarcastic reply, as reported by Emma Jung, is a good example. Although very intuitive by nature, she does not seem to have picked up the irony in Freud's remarks; at all events, she takes him literally. Jung talked a lot about child analysis. In a letter dated 17 October 1911 (p. 450), he mentions a number of other observations

> which have forced me to conclude that the so-called 'early memories of childhood' are not individual memories at all, but phylogenetic ones. I mean of course the *very early memories* like birth, sucking the thumb, etc. There are things whose only explanation is *intra-uterine*: much of the

water symbolism, then the enwrappings and encoilings which seem to be accompanied by strange skin sensations (umbilical cord and amnion). Just now my Agathli is having dreams like this; they are closely related to certain Negro birth-myths, where these envelopments in slimy stuff also occur. I think that we shall find that infinitely more things than we now suppose are phylogenetic memories.

Freud does not respond to these suggestions, which sow the seeds of the 'cosmic' developments that Jung will try to bring to psychoanalysis later on. Yet these views were to be taken up in part by Ferenczi ('Thalassa: A theory of genitality', 1933), who was to have the ear of the master more readily.

Other elements were to dissuade Freud from following Jung's suggestions. As we have seen, his analysis of Agathli was suspect in Freud's eyes and in the 1907 case, the technique used owed more to hypnosis than to psychoanalysis. In addition, Jung did not undertake the analyses of children himself, delegating them to women trained specially for that purpose. In his report to the 1st International Congress of Paedology in 1911 (*Congress Report*, Brussels, 1912, vol. II: 332–43) Jung wrote:

> Such analyses are better carried out by women. I have already trained a number of ladies in psychoanalysis, mainly with the object of treating children. It seems that, for women, this is destined to become a worthwhile, new profession. I leave my analyses of children to one of my women assistants and, after much experience, I have arrived at the conclusion that women, because of their natural psychological intuition, are by far more apt than men at this sort of work.

Among the women trained by Jung to undertake child analysis we should mention 'Sister' Moltzer. Maria Moltzer (1874–1944) was the daughter of the owner of the Dutch manufacturing company Bols. She was a nurse and underwent training in analysis with Jung. She was analysing an 11-year old girl whose case Jung had used for the paper entitled 'On psychoanalysis in children' given at the Brussels conference mentioned above. This was a case of a school phobia. In his paper Jung omitted to mention little Hans. He indicated, and it is instructive to find the source of an idea still commonly held today, that a child under 8 is not capable of being interested in the train of its thoughts and that an 'indirect method' is therefore necessary. This method is the observation of psychological events which he had already presented in his paper entitled 'On the conflict of infantile mind'. However, older children could benefit from analysis 'almost' as much as adults; but such analyses were a 'laborious task' for the practitioner because the children had too much respect for him (Graf-Nold, 1988: 162).

Jung had trailed along a whole retinue of women to the congress of Weimar (1911). In addition to his wife Emma, and 'Sister' Moltzer, the delegation included Beatrice Hinckle-Eastwick, Sabina Spielrein, Antonia Wolff, Martha Böddinghaus and Mira Gincburg. Concerning the last named, Jung had written to Freud on 5 August 1909 (p. 243):

I have a pupil, a Polish Jewess, Frl. Dr Gincburg, who is really clever and has a very nice way with her in analysing children. She assisted me most efficiently at the outpatients' clinic all through the summer term. Now she is looking for work of the same kind. I remembered that you often find yourself in the position of having to recommend a suitable person for children. Might something be arranged with Frl. G.[incburg]? I'm afraid I know of nothing for her. She wouldn't be too demanding.

Mira Gincburg (1887–1949) was to marry Emil Oberholzer, who had undergone an analysis with Freud in 1912. She and Oskar Pfister were to found the Swiss Psychoanalytical Association. The couple emigrated to the United States in 1938 and became members of the New York Society. Emil Oberholzer was a specialist in Rorschach, and Mira Oberholzer was designated 'one of the very first child analysts' by William McGuire (1974), editor of the Freud–Jung correspondence.

Irrespective of the value one gives to the child analysis practised by Jung and 'Sister' Moltzer, the paper Jung gave in Brussels caused quite a commotion. According to Jung (letter of 29 August 1991), the chairman was furious, calling him an odious person. People got up and left the room, 'One Danish doctor flew into a rage with me; I didn't deign to answer him and that made him more furious than ever, for the rabble likes to be answered in kind'. All this makes one think that on this occasion Jung must have in fact spoken from an analytical point of view, with the reactions that that would have aroused in 1911. However, it does seem, and we will come back to this in Chapter 4, on Hermine Hug-Hellmuth, in particular, that the concept of child analysis caused more violent reactions than that of analysis for adults, in particular amongst educationalists.

However, as we know, the understanding between Freud and Jung was to dwindle rapidly. In 1911 Jung had already opened hostilities by wanting to widen the concept of libido. By 1912 their relationship was losing its amicability. In 1913, they finally broke off. The work of Jung and his disciples from that date forth cannot therefore be assigned to psychoanalysis.

Notes

1 Emphasis added.
2 An allusion to a critical remark by Mendel.

3

Karl Abraham: the 'father' of Melanie Klein

A third focal point for psychoanalysis was Berlin, prior to World War I, where Karl Abraham was also taking an interest in the observation and analysis of children. He had worked at the Burghölzli with Jung for a number of years and knew Jung's daughter, Agathli, and was also conversant with the discussions taking place in Vienna and had heard of little Hans. It was therefore not surprising that he should undertake a close observation of his only daughter, Hilda. 'On two occasions I have had to give her a glycerine enema. Since then she has told me every day that she doesn't want another injection, but she says this without real affect and, on most occasions, even with a rather arch smile. She does not show any other anal-erotic tendencies[!]', he writes to Freud on 7 April 1909 (Freud and Abraham, 1965: 77). Hilda was then 2 years and 4 months. Two months earlier, Abraham had questioned Freud about the history of a little 6-year-old girl who engaged in reciprocal masturbation with her brother by touching genitals with the feet.

As to Hilda, we know from her biography (1974) of her father that this observation was just the beginning of a more complete study that Abraham was to undertake on his daughter. To our knowledge, it is the first document in which the person actually concerned recounts an analytical history: being analysed by one's own father. The fact that Hilda Abraham was a training psychoanalyst (British Psycho-Analytical Society) perhaps explains this particular case.

This undertaking 'could give rise to some apprehension' says Anna Freud in the Preface; but she was talking about undertaking the biography of her own father, not the circumstance in which a father had analysed his daughter. She does not allude to this at all; which is understandable, given her almost complete silence on the subject of her own analysis with her father.

So it would appear that this observation of the child started very early on. The 1909 note quoted above does not seem to be part of Hilda's memories, nor is it known to the editor of Karl Abraham's biography, Dinora Pines. This work situates the beginnings of observation in 1910; Abraham wrote an article about it entitled 'Some illustrations of the emotional relationship of little girls towards their parents'. However, he did not publish it until 1917, and even then he changed the first names. He also reported some of his daughter's words in the 'Children's Corner' of the *Zentralblatt*. Hilda Abraham (p.100) remembers that when she was 4 or 5 years old her father spent some time with her after lunch.

> I remember that he took me in his arms, then carried me or led me to his consulting rooms, a room which I only entered on those occasions. He would sit me on the carpet and I would play with the chess pieces or some of the draughts and he would sit in a chair and doze off; I would keep quiet until he woke up and came to play on the floor with me . . .

Her analysis started when she was 6 and a half, and lasted two months, November and December in 1913. The symptom which had alarmed Karl Abraham was a very pronounced tendency to daydream, which was very disrupting both at school, where she was not learning anything, and at home. In this context Hilda remembers that one day she was doing her homework, sitting beside her mother, when she was suddenly brought out of her daydreaming 'by my mother's fist banging on the table which made both me and my books jump'. She had confessed to masturbating and one day had even been caught in the act.

The analysis consisted of walks with her father (lasting an hour?), probably on a daily basis. This was the object of a report, which remained strictly confidential until Mrs Abraham gave it to her daughter one day. Hilda in turn gave it to her second analyst, Hilde Maas, who gave it to Dinora Pines, who inserted it into Karl Abraham's biography, published in 1974. Hilda had died in 1971.

Reading this account by Karl Abraham, one can see how carefully he carried out a detailed analysis of all the material offered by his daughter while respecting the child's personality. At the outset he explains to her why he is doing the analysis 'in my capacity of doctor'. He thus gets her to recount her terrifying phantasies: wicked monkeys, a flame which suddenly shoots up from the floor, and a third theme, which is at first repressed. Abraham proceeds while reassuring the child and setting her mind at rest as to the unreal nature of these dreams (there are no monkeys, there is no flame). Thus reassured, the child remembers a third theme: giants. This enables the father–analyst, while continuing to reassure her (there are no giants) to suggest that, sometimes, some children are afraid of dogs when in reality they are afraid of people. The child understands immediately (this was the first session), but refuses the session the following day. 'Resistance', Abraham notes. The therapy continues in the form of daily walks. Children are

devoured; there are robbers. With the latter, the child is sufficiently ambivalent for the analyst to detect a transference, interpreted immediately ('The
wicked man was none other than myself'). She then starts to ask for more
sessions: 'Your patients come to see you often, don't they?'

At the end of December, the analysis comes to an end owing to a tonsil-
lectomy, but there is one further session. By this time the phantasies are 'half
pleasant, half terrifying'. She thinks about them much less often.

In her memoirs, Hilda recounts that her father did not mention her anxieties about castration, although they were quite evident. Perhaps because
she was a girl.

Abraham's private patients included some children, but it would seem that
he didn't think that this should make any difference to his work with adults.
In 1913, he published a paper entitled 'The effect on the psyche of a 9-year-
old child of the observation of sexual relations between its parents'. The
paper describes a little girl subject to bouts of acute anxiety, in whom he was
able to bring to light this 'observation' and the traumatic effects that followed. In 1916 his daughter recounts that he was treating a boy of about 12
who was not making progress at school (1974: 168). It is improbable that
these two cases were isolated.

It can be said that the psychoanalysts of the time, like Abraham, saw no
theoretical or practical objection to treating children by analysis. It was
only later that obstacles arose.

However, the analysis of children is a difficult art. Abraham nevertheless
encouraged his pupils and analysands to practise it. This was the case with
Melanie Klein, whom he encouraged to continue with the analysis of her
son when she hesitated, faced with the anxiety symptoms he presented. On
7 October 1923, Abraham wrote to Freud (Freud and Abraham, 1965:
339):

> In the last few months, Mrs Klein has skilfully conducted the psycho-
> analysis of a three-year-old with good therapeutic results. This child
> presented a true picture of the basic depression [*Urmelancholie*] which I
> postulated in close combination with oral erotism. The case offers amaz-
> ing insight into the infantile instinctual life.

With this general view of the period from 1895 to the 1914–18 war, we can
see that, just as psychoanalysis itself was being built up, the beginnings of
what was to become child psychoanalysis were also being outlined.

At this stage, however, it was still not known whether child psychoanalysis would be in the form of psychoanalytical treatment of infantile
neuroses, naturalistic observation of children, and their sexuality in particular, or pedagogical applications, among which two main preoccupations
already stand out clearly: sexual education and psychoanalytical education.

'Psychoanalytical education' is a temptation which appears very early

on: would it not be possible to prevent neuroses by an appropriate education? In Zurich Oskar Pfister thought so as early as 1908–9. However, there
was no question of liberating sexuality – rather the contrary – but rather of
substituting conscious suppression for unconscious repression: 'The essential
object of psychoanalytical education is to conquer sexual images already present but repressed which prevent normal development and often cause
disorders of the mind' (Pfister, 1913). Unconscious, evil forces had to be
mastered by the moral faculties of the mind.

In a discussion which took place at a meeting of the Psychoanalytic
Society of Vienna (see *Minutes*, vol. II, 1908–10) on 4 May 1910, Tausk
asked: 'For where is it to lead, if one tells children things, in analysis, that
contradict the present outlook of civilization?' (p. 514). He thought that
children should be given a *Weltanschauung*. Freud replied that prevention
would be more effective if children were not submitted to so much pressure,
which in turn leads to repression.

The most heated discussions took place in Vienna and were about sexual
education. The initial discoveries about infantile sexuality lead the first psychoanalysts to propose early and complete education-information for
children. However, there were reservations and much opposition. For example, at the meeting which took place on 18 December 1907, Hitschmann
explained that ever since it had become known that sexual trauma was not
as important as originally thought, owing to the discovery of phantasy, the
necessity for sexual information had been less evident; it could be introduced at 8 to 10 years. Isidore Sadger thought that, in any case, the parents,
being ignorant themselves, would not be capable of giving their children a
sexual education. Abraham, invited to this meeting, was sceptical: trauma
could not be prevented by education; at school this information was not of
any great use, it was the mother's love and tenderness that the child required.
Freud remained prudent: might sexual education not prove to be a sort of
preventive vaccination against trauma? Probably not, but it could counterbalance its effects. An interesting note: Freud said that sexual education
should not be undertaken in a neutral and detached fashion: 'The child
should feel a certain amount of sexual excitement, such as is appropriate to
the subject, and this should not be feared.' The gravity of neurosis would
thus be limited, but not avoided: it was not a panacea.

At the Congress of Salzburg in 1908, Ferenczi, from Budapest, entitled
his report: 'What practical indications does the Freudian experience offer for
the education of children?' (Ferenczi, 1908).

Another meeting was given over entirely to this theme, on 12 May 1909.
The public then had a problem. There was even a competition to find the
best solution to the problem of sexual education, which gave rise to an
anthology of suggestions. On this subject Heller stated that 'the results of this
event exceeded our worst fears'. Among the solutions offered, apart from

the traditional stork, was the 'botanical' one. Freud considered that these partial solutions were indeed quite unsatisfactory and that, after all, sexual education should be a task for the school, but that children should not be subjected to a sudden 'shower' of information. 'Sexual education should above all make them understand that these are loving acts, that in doing this the parents show how much they love each other. As to sexual intercourse, children should be enlightened on the subject at school, in biology lessons.'

The problem of child psychoanalysis proper was to be taken up by Freud more seriously in 1914, when he wrote *From the History of an Infantile Neurosis* (the Wolf Man). However, this work was not published until 1918, which often leads people to believe that it was written much later. Freud indicates that in this particular case he is only interested in the neurosis of the child that this patient had once been. He compares (Freud, 1918: 8–9) the analysis undertaken 'on the neurotic child itself' and that undertaken on the adult in whom the disorder of childhood comes out by means of recollection. 'It may be maintained', he writes, 'that analysis of children's neuroses can claim to possess a specially high theoretical interest (1918: 9).' It is work that is 'particularly difficult', but the later layers, which can be noted in the adult, are absent, thus enabling the neurosis to be recognized more easily.

It should be remembered that it was in this work that Freud mentioned the spectacular example where a dream which took place at the age of 4 'brought into deferred operation his observation of intercourse at the age of one and a half' (p. 109). The possibility that a very young child can witness and register significant events, shown here with great perceptiveness by Freud (see also pp. 119–21), appears to us to be the theoretical foundation of any discourse on child analysis. Furthermore, the possibility of a deferred action at the age of 4 indicates that, at least from that age onwards, psychoanalysis of children is possible.

Freud's interest in the observation of children is unfailing and he demonstrates this outstandingly in the game with the reel, where he uses a game he has seen played by his grandson as a basis for his theory. This game with the reel, which we hesitate to quote since it has been mentioned so often – almost always misinterpreted and out of context – is important, we believe, because it constitutes a rare testimony to the attention Freud gave to children and because of the discovery it led to. Related in *Beyond the Pleasure Principle* (1920), the repetition of an act implying unpleasure associated with clinical symptoms of traumatic neuroses in fact enabled the first formulation of the death instinct. This strange link between a child's game and the death instinct, formulated in 1920, no doubt made a great impression on Melanie Klein.

Later, Freud comes back to this branch of psychoanalysis: in 1933 he writes in *New Introductory Lectures on Psycho-Analysis* (34th lecture):

But there is one topic . . . which is exceedingly important and so rich in hopes for the future, perhaps the most important of all the activities of analysis. What I am thinking of is the application of psychoanalysis to education . . . my daughter, Anna Freud, has made this study her life-work . . .

(pp. 146–7)

This text makes a distinction between psychoanalytical education and child analysis:

> We had no misgivings over applying analytical treatment to [neurotic] children. . . . It turned out that a child is a very favourable subject for analytic therapy: the results are thorough and lasting. . . . The inevitable deviations of analyses of children from those of adults are diminished by the circumstance that some of our [adult] patients have retained so many infantile character-traits that the analyst . . . cannot avoid making use with them of certain of the techniques of child analysis.
>
> (p. 148)

Twenty-five years after the meetings of the Psychological Society of Vienna, Freud's basic tenets of child analysis had not been repudiated. We shall now follow the progress this practice and theory was to make with his pupils.

4

Hermine Hug-Hellmuth: pioneer and most obstinate of Freud's disciples

The life and work of the pioneer of child psychoanalysis, Hermine Hug-Hellmuth, have passed unnoticed for more than half a century. Mentioned in passing by Helene Deutsch and Anna Freud, commented on a little less succinctly by Melanie Klein, it was not until 1974, fifty years after her death, that Colette Chiland translated the text on her techniques into French and wrote an article about her (see Hug-Hellmuth, 1921, and Chiland, 1975).

In 1988, the author ran a research group on this subject and the result was two theses, written by Marcel Boix (1990) and Dominique Dujols (1990) at the end of their psychiatric studies. In that same year, in Zurich, Angela Graf-Nold's book was published in German, a 374-page work dedicated entirely to Hermine Hug-Hellmuth and to the history of the beginnings of child psychoanalysis. Apparently Jungian in inspiration, the work is concise and well researched. The author asserts that Mrs Hug-Hellmuth was chosen by Freud to represent him in the field of child psychoanalysis because of her great – perhaps too great – fidelity, her 'absolute orthodoxy'. She is presented as being incapable of deviating one iota from the Freudian line, and therefore as more or less manipulated by those supporting the 'orthodox' line. The work is extremely well documented, even if the author's argument did not convince us.

In 1991 a book by George MacLean and Ulrich Rappen on the life and work of Hermine Hug-Hellmuth was published in English. These authors insist on the rich personality of Hug-Hellmuth and aim to rehabilitate her in the psychoanalytical world. They reproach Graf-Nold for a lack of any significant archive material and for only using autobiographical allusions published by Hug-Hellmuth herself in her works.[1] We should also mention an article by Wolfgang Huber in 1980, Loïse Barbey-Thurnauer's article in the *Journal de la psychanalyse de l'enfant* in 1989, and finally, a short, four-page, chapter in Silvia Ines Fendrick's work *Fiction des origines* (1989).

This discretion could be connected to Hug-Hellmuth's will, in which, only a few days before her death, she expressed the wish that 'no account of her life and her work should appear, not even in psychoanalytical journals'. As late as 1980, Anna Freud reminded MacLean and Rappen of this dying wish, indicating that they should respect it. These authors point out that they chose to ignore this reminder. Besides, one could question the melancholic nature of this will, written by a woman who had always had a strong depressive tendency.

In fact, this silence is probably due to factors of an entirely different nature. Neither her will, nor the outcry caused by the publication of *A Young Girl's Diary* (1919), nor even her death explain it sufficiently. We believe it is more logical to attribute the oblivion into which this pioneer of psychoanalysis has fallen to the resistance shown in general to child psychoanalysis.

HER LIFE

Hermine Wilhelmine Ludovika Hug, Edle (Lady) von Hugenstein, was born in Vienna on 31 August 1871 into an old Catholic family of noble and military origins. Her father, Hugo Hug, Ritter von Hugenstein, had been born in Prague on 6 November 1830. A captain in the Imperial army, wounded at the Battle of Königgratz in 1866, he finished his career as a lieutenant-colonel at the War Ministry. On 17 January 1864 an illegitimate daughter, Antonia Farmer, was born to him, the same Antonia Farmer who later called herself Antonia Hug and who was the mother of 'Rolf'. She was the daughter of a Miss Farmer, of humble origins. Because of his background, and as was the custom in the Imperial and Royal Army, the military court forbade Hugo to marry the mother and to acknowledge the child, Antonia. In 1869, he married Ludovika Achelpohl. These details are the fruit of the research done by MacLean and Rappen. As we shall see further on, the debate about the *A Young Girl's Diary* has given rise to all sorts of criticism and speculation. These very precise details are in total contradiction to the suppositions put forward until 1991, i.e. that Antonia was only two years older than Hermine, and that they were born of the same mother, whose name was Leiner. Yet the suppositions were convenient and made the friendship between the two girls mentioned in the *Diary* easy to understand, and the fact that their 'author's' name was Greta Lainer. Convenient, but probably untrue.

Ludovika took her husband's illegitimate daughter in and made a home for her. MacLean and Rappen say that the year 1869 was given as her date of birth by her father as a way of passing her off more easily as the couple's legitimate daughter.

The birth of Hermine in 1871 was surrounded by deaths: the death at 2 weeks of a first daughter in 1870; the death of her paternal grandmother in 1872; the death at 1 month of another daughter in 1874. All this occurred in the midst of family difficulties of one sort or another, mostly financial. One can imagine the problems encountered by the child Hermine, caught among an illegitimate sister, all these deaths, and parents obviously much too preoccupied to provide her with a satisfactory 'container'.[2]

The climate deteriorated further when the mother caught tuberculosis in 1875; when Hermine was 4. The illness was serious and Ludovika died in 1883. Between the ages of 4 and 12 Hermine had therefore lived with her half-sister Antonia, her sick mother, an aunt who had come to help the family out, and her father.

Ludovika, who was a cultivated woman, musical and linguistically gifted, seems to have been the person who undertook Hermine's primary education, since she did not go to school until she was 11. It was this secondary education that led her to become a school mistress. Both she and her half-sister were teachers for a number of years.

In 1897, at the age of 26, Hermine enrolled at the University of Vienna, probably as a student who attended lectures but was not obliged to sit exams. This would appear to be the first year in which women were admitted to university. A year later her father died, and she decided that she wanted to be more than just a school mistress. She prepared to sit a sort of university entrance exam and went as far as working in Prague for several years with this in mind. (Prague was part of Austria at that time.) In 1904, at the age of 33, she went back to the University of Vienna, but this time as a full student. In that same year Antonia finished her university studies and obtained a Doctorate of Philosophy with a thesis entitled: 'Contribution to the history of the text *Fragments* by Novalis.' In 1909, Hermine presented a thesis centred on the subject of physics, but in the Faculty of Philosophy. It would seem that she was captivated by the personality of Marie Curie and by the feminist symbol she represented: but in those days, although women could enrol at the University of Vienna, they could only do so in philosophy or medicine. Her essay – sixteen pages written in a hand typical of a school mistress – was entitled: 'Research into the physical and chemical properties of radioactive deposits on positive and negative poles.' In fact, this doctorate of philosophy did not take her into the domain of scientific research in physics and chemistry, but into a more commonplace field, to a higher teaching diploma: she was now able to teach in a secondary school. However, her taste for research would take her into a new scientific field: psychoanalysis. But at this point two major events took place, one which would foreshadow her death and one which would govern her life.

The first of these events was the developments taking place in the life of her half-sister Antonia. When she had finished her studies in 1904, she

founded a rural educational centre for adolescents of both sexes with boarding facilities in a place called Mürzzuschlag. This centre was run in the spirit
of the reforms in teaching methods which were then in vogue. She founded
the establishment with the principal of the school she had been working at,
Rudolf Rossi von Lichtenfels, and his wife, who was to be the bursar. In
fact, Antonia was Rudolf's mistress, by whom she had a son in 1906 who
was given the name of Rudolf Otto *Helmut* Hug: it was he who would
become the notorious 'Rolf'. The educational centre did not do well and
von Lichtenfels went elsewhere, after having another affair, this time with
the family's nanny. Antonia took her son to Vienna, where she lived in a
succession of apartments.

Hermine was quite alarmed by the dramatic turn of events in her half-
sister's life. To begin with, Hermine was a very shy young woman, prudish,
with no friends. Antonia's conduct shocked her and, although in theory she
was in favour of a certain form of feminism, she could not in all good conscience condone the situation. Further, she clearly perceived in Antonia a
sort of repetition of her father's life story, since Antonia had also been his
illegitimate daughter. All the lies in relation to society and the secrets surrounding the birth of the children must have preoccupied her considerably.

The other event that was to govern the rest of her life was her encounter
with Isidore Sadger: this psychoanalyst, a member of Freud's inner circle,
was to become her family doctor in 1907. Given all the difficulties just mentioned, it is no surprise to learn that she very quickly began analysis with
him, which was to last about three years. At the same time her intellectual
interests also turned to things psychoanalytical, the works of Freud in particular, to such an extent that she soon decided to make it her profession.
Between 1910 and 1912, she abandoned teaching little by little and ended
up by retiring entirely. She was then 40 and had been teaching for twenty
years.

After her analysis, Hermine remained very attached to Sadger, her only
friend until her death. We may presume that, in a fatherly way, he gave her
guidance in her plans for becoming a psychoanalyst. As he would say himself later on (in 1925, at the trial): 'Since she was not a doctor I helped her
with her work, to protect her from making any *faux pas* [in French in the
original].' Here is probably one of the earliest examples of collaboration
between medical and non-medical people to enable them to practise psychoanalysis. Ilse Hellman (I. 4) has told us that this practice still existed in
Britain in 1991.

From the outset, Hermine was a very modern psychoanalyst. She had
undergone quite a long analysis for that era, focusing on her symptoms and
her difficulties of the moment, related to her problems as a child. A number
of deciding factors led to her becoming a child psychoanalyst: identification
with her analyst, of course, but also the combination of a searching mind,

43

the discoveries she had made about herself, and the observations she had made of 'Rolf,' aged 4 in 1910.

As we shall see, Hermine did not become a member of the Psychoanalytical Society of Vienna until 1913. We must therefore suppose that between 1910 and 1913 she became conversant (through Sadger?) with the subjects that were being debated, and the group problematics, for the subjects she worked on throughout these three years were strangely similar to those which interested the early psychoanalysts, Freud himself in particular.

A typical example, for instance, was the meeting of 15 December 1909, where, in response to Tausk, who argued that a sexual education did not cause any inhibition in the emotional life of the child, Freud indicated that he had 'wherever possible avoided drawing conclusions – even less given directions – on education from our current knowledge. Which is why [he would] not contest that there was a legitimate problem and why he would be pleased to receive a paper for *Sammlung* setting out the impressions that a teacher might have on psychoanalysis.' Hermine got the message.

In addition, the events which had perturbed the Psychoanalytical Society of Vienna, in particular the conflict with Adler, made the strengthening of the 'Freud' group useful. The debate surrounding the election of Margarete Hilferding in April 1910 was probably symptomatic of Adler's tactics. Increasing the number of his followers inside this little group appeared to him to be the means of ensuring a majority for himself and thus, he probably thought, of imposing his views on psychoanalysis. It was no mere chance that it happened to be Isidore Sadger, always an orthodox follower of Freud, who fought against the admission of Hilferding. He used feeble arguments for the purpose, bordering on the perverse, stating that a woman could not be admitted to the ranks of psychoanalysts: it was in fact the first time that such a state of affairs had occurred. Freud himself intervened, saying that a refusal on those grounds would be a gross inconsistency in a psychoanalytical society. The following year, in October 1911, Margarete Hilferding left the Psychoanalytical Society of Vienna along with Adler and presided over the Adlerian individual psychology movement. She had been the first woman to be admitted to the Vienna society; later she died, in 1942, in Theresienstadt concentration camp.

The second woman was Sabina Spielrein, one of Jung's pupils, elected in 1911, but she too was only present for a year. She left Vienna for Switzerland in 1912, and was Jean Piaget's analyst. In 1923, she returned to Russia and became one of the first members of the Russian Psychoanalytical Society. She was murdered in 1941 by the Germans in the synagogue in Rostov.

Following the successive departures of Margarete Hilferding and Sabina Spielrein, Hermine, as the feminist, was destined to become a member.

We can thus see in outline how Hermine Hug von Hugenstein's vocation as a child psychoanalyst is consistent with her taste for research, the inner necessity of continuing her self-analysis, the very disrupted climate of her early years with, no doubt, a profound desire for reparation, with her (unstructured) commitment to the movement for the emancipation of women of the day. It is also consistent with the wishes of her former analyst and with the internal necessities of the Freudian movement within the Psychoanalytical Society of Vienna. The fact that Freud was anxious that his disciples should go deeper into the field of child psychopathology through direct observation was, as seen in the preceding chapter, another source of inspiration for her vocation.

Although it is evident that the birth of her nephew was a serious concern for Hermine, we do not believe, as some do, that Rolf was the origin of her vocation and the only subject of her professional research; on the other hand, Rolf was of course a privileged source of observation, as he was the only child in her small circle. But they did not live under the same roof, or only occasionally; we have seen that the two half-sisters did not get on, for many reasons, and, to make matters worse, Antonia's political convictions tended toward the antisemitic German nationalists, totally opposed to Hermine's ideals.

Her activity within the Psychoanalytical Society of Vienna was remarkable; she attended every meeting. On 29 October 1913 she presented a paper on the work of Stanley Hall. The paper does not appear to have been published. It was undoubtedly no mere chance that during that particular meeting Freud happened to remark that 'play enables a child to live out its drives; by playing with dolls it satisfies its various sexual tendencies'. On 11 February 1914 the speaker is 'Hug' [*sic*] once again, but there are no minutes of the meeting: the subject was 'children's games'.

Freud held the work of Hug-Hellmuth in high regard. He recommended that her theories be applied, even in his own family. In a letter to Karl Abraham dated 22 September 1914, he wrote (Freud and Abraham, 1965: 197):

> My grandson is a charming little fellow who manages to laugh so engagingly whenever one pays attention to him; he is a decent, civilised being, which is doubly valuable in these times of unleashed brutality. Strict upbringing by an intelligent mother enlightened by Hug-Hellmuth has done him a great deal of good.

Lou Andreas-Salomé also held Hug-Hellmuth in high regard, saying, albeit with some ambivalence that she was impressed by the depth of her scholarship.

External events were soon to leave their mark on the work of the psychoanalysts. The portents of World War I, its declaration, its length, the absence and death of so many young people, and the changes it was to bring to the Austro-Hungarian empire would all influence psychoanalytical thinking.

In addition, for Hermine the period was marked by important personal problems: her half-sister became ill in February 1913, moved several times, came back to Vienna for a short time with 'Rolf'; it is possible that they lived with her for several weeks. Antonia had tuberculosis; she went back to Bolzano (Bozen), probably for the climate, and died on 2 February 1915.

As we have already indicated and contrary to what is said by a number of authors, Hermine was not at all attached to Rolf and was not particularly keen on seeing him. Moreover, Antonia did not want to leave him with her, and in her will she names a Dr Schlesinger as his guardian. The child, who was 9 at the time, was first of all entrusted to the von Horvath family, friends of Antonia, then to another family, the Pesendorfers. In 1917, when he was 11, Rolf went back to live with his aunt for a few weeks. His guardian then died. This period of Rolf's life is somewhat obscure. Tausk was then chosen as his guardian, probably at the suggestion of Hug-Hellmuth and Sadger.

The child began to become known to a number of psychoanalysts, and there are indications which suggest that Siegfried Bernfeld tried to undertake psychotherapeutic treatment with him. Tausk himself had enough of his own problems, and after he committed suicide in 1919, Sadger became Rolf's guardian. When he was older he was placed in a number of re-education centres. The 'delinquent' nature of his personality was noted by his three guardians, but none of the therapeutic or re-educational measures was successful. Hug-Hellmuth, we must reiterate, did not have much to do with him, probably finding him beyond the reach of any therapeutic assistance. She did not like him, had always refused to have anything to do with his education and had not treated him. It was probably for these very reasons that he in turn detested her. However, there is no justification at all for saying that she failed either with his education or with his treatment, or that her relationship with him was too close. In 1924, Rolf was 18 and Hermine Hug-Hellmuth 53. Rolf killed her without premeditation: he broke into her house, she awoke and he wanted to 'silence her'. The murder caused quite a stir, but we will come back to this later on. All the records of the trial that we have been able to consult show that the murder was committed out of panic. Nevertheless, the media and the public reacted as if it were a murder which had been ruthlessly planned and executed. Facts were distorted; this dramatic news item had put psychoanalysis on trial: it was psychoanalysis that was held responsible.

Stern, about whom more later, and whose reactions will then become more comprehensible, gave his opinion shortly after the trial was over, on 20 March 1925, in a front-page article in the newspaper 'Das

Unterhaltungsblatt', published by the *Vossisches Zeitung* (one of Graf-Nold's documents in her 1988 book):

> Over and above the people concerned, this crime takes on a different significance. It shows just how dangerous psychoanalysis can be when it purports to be more than just a scientific theory or a therapeutic treatment, when it tries to interfere with culture, education or children. At the same time this murder is a demonstration of the argument that we, the critics of psychoanalysis, have constantly put forward – unfortunately in vain: the early manifestations of sexual behaviour alleged by psychoanalysis are in fact a psychological disorder and have nothing to do with ordinary child psychology. What Dr Hug-Hellmuth calls 'Child Psychology' is in fact mostly about a 'nephew' psychology.

Hug-Hellmuth's observations of her nephew are then taken up again to show that Rolf's sadistic tendencies and early manifestations of sexual behaviour are evidence that he was not a normal child but a born criminal. It should be pointed out here that Hug-Hellmuth had made similar observations concerning the Stern children, but the Sterns did not conclude for all that that their children were born criminals! Furthermore, ten years earlier it had been William Stern who had called little Hans a 'monster'.

Opportunistically, Alfred Adler gave a lecture on the subject at the *Volksheim* (The People's House) in Vienna on the night of the trial. His talk was published next day in the *Wiener Arbeiterzeitung* (Adler, 1925), with the glaring headlines: 'Incorrigible Child or Incorrigible Theory? Some Remarks about the Hug Case'.

Adler protested at the idea that Rolf was a 'born' murderer, as had been stated in court. Isidore Sadger had said that in any case by the age of 5 nothing more could be done for him, but Adler argued that nothing was more destructive than denying hope to a child by saying: 'You will finish up in prison.' To predict misfortune is tantamount to inducing it. Adler's discourse was aimed at the opinion generally accepted by psychoanalysts that the early years are a determining factor in the life of a child. For Adler, the destiny of the individual depended largely on social factors. In this article he advocates the founding of 'Educational institutes for children-deprived cases'. Such an institution would prevent children from becoming criminals. In choosing to give the 'Hug case' (ambiguous, since one doesn't know if the 'case' concerns the nephew or the aunt) maximum publicity, in order to settle old scores with Freudian theories of psychoanalysis, Adler showed his opportunism and his 'political' sense.

Of course, we might be in agreement with his discussion on the subject of the pessimistic view, still sometimes met in certain psychoanalytical circles, which would transform the saying, 'It's the first five years which are important' into 'After 5 it's too late.' But we might then go on to say that the purpose of psychoanalytical treatment is precisely to treat that which has undergone poor development: it does not follow that institutionalizing 'deprived cases' is a necessity. The institutes that Adler dreamt of have since seen the light of day, and have not had the results he expected.

Rudolf von Urbantschitsch also published an article in the women's page of the *Neue Freie Presse* on 29 May 1925 (Graf-Nold, 1988). Very close to Freud, von Urbantschitsch chose to treat the subject by speaking highly of Hug-Hellmuth's last two books and refrained from unwarranted remarks about her private life. Given Freud's aversion to these intrusions, it is possible that, directly or indirectly, he was the instigator of the article. 'The two works combine a great wealth of knowledge and observations on which a modern practice of child education can be built . . . But beyond her knowledge, the author shows kindhearted qualities which underline each and every line of her books and which embellish and warm each world.' He argues that any educational effort that Hug-Hellmuth might have made was doomed to fail in the case of this fatherless child, spoilt by his mother, tossed to and fro by life. By the time she could have done something, the child was too old; it was effectively too late.

Graf-Nold, who, as we have seen, seems to represent the Jungian viewpoint, has some very harsh words to say about this stand, which, she thinks, reflects the 'political' concerns of the IPA (International Psychoanalytical Association); she is amazed that neither Friedjung, who knew her well, nor even Freud himself took a stand. We believe that von Urbantschitsch did that for them, taking care, as was Freud's wish, to remain within the bounds of discretion and respect for Hug-Hellmuth's private life.

Nevertheless, there were two official stands: first, that of Siegfried Bernfeld in the *International Journal of Psycho-Analysis* – a few lines announcing her death and her desire that neither herself nor her work should be discussed; and second, that of Joseph Friedjung, who, at the end of 1924, had written an obituary for the *Zentralblatt für Psychoanalyse und Psychotherapie*, cited by MacLean and Rappen. After having regretted 'strongly the all-too-early loss of this brave psychoanalytic pioneer', he points out 'that she was the first who would confirm through immediate observation Freud's daring theories about the true character of the child' (MacLean and Rappen, 1991: 43). Concerning *A Young Girl's Diary* he says: 'For the psychoanalytic school it was a valuable, human document. For her enemies, it was the subject of malicious assault and nasty suspicions' (p. 44). He concluded by saying: 'She acknowledged in a moving manner the deplorable opposition to the growing importance of psychoanalytic insights for education. Our scientific movement has much to thank her for. Her work will be a valuable source of psychoanalytic literature for the future' (p. 44).

In 1945, we find a few remarks by Willie Hoffer, a young psychoanalyst when Hermine Hug-Hellmuth was carrying out her final work and someone we will meet again in Chapter 5, on Anna Freud.

Her primary aim was to harmonize psychoanalytic aims with those of the family, school and society. Hug-Hellmuth's first step was to practice child analysis in the child's home or in a children's ward. . . . She spent most of her time finding out secrets that the child had intentionally withheld from educators – and thus she opened the door to the child's fantasy life. As she did so, the child tended more and more to act out his conflicts, to the great bewilderment of his parents. This of course often endangered the continuation of treatment. However, where it did continue, improvement often followed . . . her attempts were mainly characterized by the treat-ment of children of latency and prepuberty and were aimed at a better adaptation of these children to the environment by alleviating superego demands and by encouraging sublimation of instinctual drives.

(cited in MacLean and Rappen, 1991: 281)

For the reader who is curious to know more, we should perhaps mention the nephew, Rolf: he was deemed to be sound of mind although thoroughly perverse, and condemned to twelve years' imprisonment for manslaughter and robbery with violence, to a 'hartes Lager'[3] every three months, and was required to spend every 8 September, the anniversary of the murder, in a dark cell. When he was released he pestered Helene Deutsch and Siegfried Bernfeld, demanding to undergo analysis(!) and asking for money. He met with refusal and then disappeared into the Austria of 1933, and nobody ever seems to have heard of him again.

HER WORK

The first work that Hermine Hug-Hellmuth did was undoubtedly that on 'colour hearing', since it was essentially autobiographical and, we might say, self-analytical, in the sense that when she had finished her analysis and had obtained sufficient insight, she continued her own self-analysis, in fact right up to the end of her life, as can be seen from her writings and correspon-dence. The first work is the clearest from this point of view (along with *A Young Girl's Diary* perhaps). The phenomenon that she described had per-turbed physiologists for many decades and they had tried to find an 'organic' explanation. One is reminded of the famous poem by Rimbaud ('*A noir, E blanc, I rouge, U vert, O bleu: voyelles Je dirai quelque jour vos naissances latentes . . .*', 1872). G. Fechner had worked on the subject briefly in 1871; as had Eugene Blander, who had the same symptom in 1879; in 1890, the subject was discussed at the first International Congress of Physiological Psychology (colour-hearing). In 1893, Flournoy presented a monograph on 'The Phenomen of Synopsy'. Freud therefore must have known about it when he carried out his experiments with cocaine.

This work can be seen as in close connection with that part of Freud's self-analysis revealed in *The Interpretation of Dreams* (1900). Hermine had wanted to prove that she too was capable of carrying out scientific work using her own self-analysis and applied herself, not to demolishing the physiological explanations but to studying the psychoanalytical dimension of the phenomenon. She did not hesitate to place synaesthesia[4] right back at the outset of a child's mental activity, a child with a conflictual sexual and erotic problem, or eventually an anal–erotic problem, at an age when it does not possess the ability to sublimate. All this must have delighted Freud, who, as early as 1911, was apprised of this conscientious study, in the form of fifty-two handwritten pages, probably beautifully written in copperplate.

Freud wrote to Jung in 1911 asking if this article could be published in the *Jahrbuch* (Freud and Jung, 1974, letters 289 F, J. 292, 239 F). He did not obtain satisfaction. Jung used the pretext of editorial delays. Freud replied on 10 January 1912: 'I will not now be sending you Dr Hellmuth's work; I have sent it to the new journal *Imago*'. Sadger had no doubt mentioned Hermine to Freud, so he would have known all about her by then.

Publications from 1911–13

Her first psychoanalytical work to be published was one entitled 'The Analysis of a Dream of a 5½-Year-Old-Boy', probably because her work on hearing in colour had been subjected to editorial delays. This first paper appeared in the *Zentralblatt für Psychoanalyse und Psychotherapie* (1912a), as did the next two; it was signed 'H. Hellmuth'. Since there is no explanatory documentation, one can only suppose that Hermine wanted to mark her arrival in the psychoanalytical family with a new name. Of course, one must also note that as a literary pseudonym she had chosen one of Rolf's Christian names: Rudolf Otto Helmut Hug. He is also the subject of the article, or at least one of his dreams is. She does not hide this fact: she is 'Aunt Hermine'.

'Aunt Hermine, Aunt Hermine, I so afraid!' said Rolf, 'a big bear wants to eat me. . . . There was also a big picket fence there and lots of pointed arrows on top. The bear wanted to hug me with his front paws. In the middle of the ceiling there was a gigantic black spot, no, a big blot' (MacLean and Rappen, 1991: 52).

Conscientiously, the author analyses the circumstances in which the dream took place, the events of the previous day, the associations with each of the elements of the dream; these associations are a mixture of what Hug-Hellmuth remembers of what the child said, the answers he gave to the questions she asked about these fragments of his dreams and the constructions offered by the author. She picks out nipple–penis material (the arrows), anal material, and connects it all to a desired but inaccessible father image (the child was brought up without a father). At no time does she offer to interpret the dream to the child, which is logical. She is determined to note just how much this dream confirms the Freudian theories of the dream as a hallucinatory fulfilment of a desire.

Her next two articles also appeared in 1912 in the same journal (1912b, c) and were on the subject of the psychoanalytical analysis of cases of lapsus: this time they were about other children, adults and two autobiographical experiences.

Her fourth article, again in 1912, appeared in *Imago* (1912d), and was about the child and its representation of death; it was later translated into English by Anton Kris and appeared in the *Psychoanalytic Quarterly* in 1965. In this paper her nephew is only very briefly mentioned (three and a half lines). The other examples were drawn from non-psychoanalytical observations of children, which she reinterprets, and from observations made by Jung. She reminds the reader of what Freud thinks of the death wish in children and how he showed that children do not consider death in the same way as adults (see *Interpretation of Dreams*, Freud, 1900; see also the minutes of the meeting of the Psychological Society of Vienna on 5 October 1910). She demonstrates the intensity of these death wishes and the childish belief in the reversibility of death. As MacLean and Rappen note, the work which has been published since on the subject does not have much more to add.

Her fifth article, still in 1912, 'On colour hearing: an attempt to clarify the phenomenon on the basis of the psychoanalytical method' (1912e), was the first work she had undertaken, which had been the object of such shillyshallying by Jung. Freud had said about it (289 F, 28 December 1911; Freud and Jung, 1974: 235–6): 'I have received a splendid, really illuminating paper about colour audition from an intelligent lady Ph.D. [*eine kluge Frau*]. It solves the riddle with the help of our psychoanalysis.'

It was at this point that she founded a column called 'About the true nature of the infantile psyche' in the journal *Imago*; she wrote editorials of sorts, had articles on child psychoanalysis published in it, and published her own articles and reading notes. She continued to write the column until 1921.

Publications in 1913

In 1913 Hug-Hellmuth published no fewer than ten articles, three in *Imago*, others in various psychoanalytical journals. For the most part they are psychoanalytical studies of children, the others being about the psychology of women. She studied the problem of the earliest memories of the child, and wrote: 'Here two contrasts are mixed together – the mystery that creates life, and death that finishes life. A terrified child's soul trembles between them' (cited in MacLean and Rappen, 1991: 79). In 'The Nature of the Child's Soul' (1913a) she states: 'Everyone realizes that the child's intellectual and affective development begin immediately in the first few weeks of life' (cited in MacLean and Rappen, 1991: 89). She places masturbation in the first months of existence and underlines the sexual and erotic nature of a child's first games (playing with dolls), and the sucking of the thumb. From this she draws conclusions for education and for the general comprehension of the human being. Some ideas can be considered to be pessimistic and are no doubt drawn from her personal experience: 'A deficit in love during childhood cannot be compensated for by later attachment. The loneliness of the child's soul resembles a fruit that a worm has destroyed from inside, leaving its surface looking immaculate' (cited in MacLean and Rappen, 1991: 90).

One of her works in 1913 was more important: the 170-page monograph entitled: *The Mental Life of the Child: A Psychoanalytical Study* (1913b). This was the fifteenth treatise edited by Freud (*Schriften zur angewandten Seelenkunde*) and published by Deuticke. Rapidly translated into English, by James Putnam and Mabel Stevens, it was published in 1913 in English. There was a second German edition in 1921.

The work was an illustration of Freud's ideas on infantile sexuality using many clinical cases. For the sake of objectivity she takes her examples mostly from the observations of children, their own in particular, made by psychologists who were not psychoanalysts. According to Graf-Nold, who counted them, Hug-Hellmuth cites stories of her nephew eighty times, but she cites the children of the psychologists William and Clara Stern fifteen times (they had written two books on their own children in 1907 and 1909), and she also cites little 'Bubi', the son of Gertrude and the zoologist Ernst Scupin, fifty times (their own observation of him had been published by them in the form of a journal from 1900–10). In addition to the already well-known topics of the Oedipus complex, the castration complex, the problems of masturbation and guilt, a number of less well-known notions become apparent: the 'muscular sense' of children under the age of 12 months which, she says, should be linked to the movements of the foetus inside the body of the mother. Cutaneous and muscular erotism are the primitive forms of sexual sensations. So is the pleasure of scratching oneself, she says. Certain pleasures of smelling, in particular that of a thumb which has been sucked all night, are of a directly sexual nature. This quest for smells might also be linked to memories of intra-uterine smells, but in any case certainly to ecstatic experiences of sucking the mother's breast: on this point, she recalls the importance of smell in human love life. She also deals with infant masturbation, its dreams and its coprophilia.

Hug-Hellmuth strongly stresses the role of play in the life of the child.

She describes how drives and repressions are linked to its emotional and intellectual progress. This mental evolution will occur along a certain number of 'development lines', which are the sensory functions, the intellect, will, language, feelings, imagination and character. Anna Freud was to take this notion, give it a more stable foundation and develop it considerably; but the person who originated it was forgotten.

In Elizabeth Young-Bruehl's book (*Anna Freud, A Biography*, 1988) one reads (p. 72) that in 1915 Anna Freud had translated an article by James Putnam, who had 'translated into English Hug-Hellmuth's work on "Play Therapy"'. She also says that

> Hug-Hellmuth had updated her pre-War work on play therapy with an extended paper at the 1920 Hague Congress, which Anna Freud had heard. She also reported to the Vienna Society on her play sessions with children, usually in their homes; but it was left to Melanie Klein and Anna Freud to turn this play technique into a properly psychoanalytic method.
>
> (Young-Bruehl, 1988: 160)

However, as we have just seen, this 'article' was a 170-page book, and is not about 'therapy through play' but, amongst other things, the *observation* of play and the theoretical conclusions that can be drawn (the English translation of which did not appear until 1919). The term '*play therapy*' is rather scornful, even disparaging, and amounts to saying that this was nothing to do with psychoanalysis.

In 1920, as we shall see, Hug-Hellmuth developed a theory of child psychoanalysis in which play is mentioned as one of the methods of analysis; but she never mentioned 'play therapy'.

The response

The 1913 work in which Freudian concepts on infantile sexuality were strongly illustrated was widely read and caused immediate reactions.[5] The *Wiener Medizinischen Wochenschrift* complains that 'mothers will be disgusted with the observation of their happy and innocent children' (1914: 842). 'It is a question of neologism in the psychiatric sense of the term, when one claims as sexual the impulses of the human body, especially those that have to do with food and [its] evacuation', one reads in the *Jahrbuch für Psychiatrie und Neurologie* (1913: 461). For Stanley Hall, writing in the *American Journal of Psychology* (1914: 461), 'the author's point of view is too narrow'.

William and Clara Stern, through the use of the observations that they had published on their own children, felt that they in particular stood accused; it was the last straw. William Stern protested openly at the annual meeting of the German Psychiatric Society (1913). We shall quote at length from extracts from this text, since it shows just how violent the reaction was.

The case of little Hans has prompted Freud's pupils to go even further. . . . Psychoanalysis should restrict itself to developing the positive contributions it has made to psychology such as the ideas of repression, abreaction, displacement of affects, the role of unconscious drives, and not let itself be invaded by the obnoxious weeds on which it will choke. Psychoanalysis will drop even lower than phrenology or chiromancy. . . . The theory of infantile sexuality is built on analogies with adult behaviour. The enormous distance between the analyst and the 'analysand' in the case of the application of psychoanalysis to children is particularly dangerous and exposed to analogies, the source of many errors. . . . For a child, the sudden awareness of unconscious motivations can only have a negative effect . . . it will result in taking away their innocence [*Entharmlosung*], it is snatching away their naivety. In a healthy child, what is unconscious should remain so [*das was unbewusst, auch das, was unbewusst sein soll*]. He who with his coarse hands attacks this process, is also attacking the development of the psyche. . . . Why not analyse an embryo? There too, Hug-Hellmuth stops at nothing: you can't even laugh at such nonsense. How we should pity these young creatures on whom the parents, teachers or doctors are experimenting in the name of 'education.' What irreparable damage will be done when the educator introduces a psycho-sexual hypertrophy into the psyche of the young child by force?

Had not Freud already looked after little Hans with a 'total lack of regard for his education' and, in addition, the connection between Hans' analytical treatment and the disappearance of his phobia was more than tenuous. Besides, if the interpretations of Freud were exact, little Hans would have been 'the most remarkable psychic monster ever seen, a five-year-old sexual monomaniac'. The Sterns feared an epidemic of child psychoanalysis through 'psycho-sexually infected teachers'. The existence of a 'Psychoanalytical Teachers' Union' in Zurich was extremely distressing. And was it truly in the interests of education to take Alfred Adler on to the editorial board of a teachers' journal, even if he had distanced himself somewhat from the sexual monomania of Freud?

The Sterns therefore decided to publish an official protest, in particular in the *Zeitschrift für Angewandte Psychologie* (1913–14: 380, cited by Graf-Nold, 1988) and in the *Zeitschrift für Jungenderziehung* (1914: 299, cited by Graf-Nold, 1988). This protest was signed by thirty-one important people, mostly teachers, five university professors and the doctor in charge of the Breslau municipal lunatic asylum.

Danger: The Encroachment of Child Psychoanalysis

The signatories hereto, members of the children's study group of the Union for School Reform, believe it is their duty to inform the friends of Childhood and the teaching profession of the dangers arising from the recent trials concerning the application of the psychoanalytical method to children and adolescents.

Without taking a stand concerning the scientific significance of the basic ideas of psychoanalysis, nor on the therapeutic application of the method to adults, the signatories declare:
1. The assertion that the psychoanalytic method shows that research on childhood to date is erroneous and that psychoanalysis has become the only possible scientific psychology applicable to childhood, is unjustified.
2. The spread of the psychoanalytical method with a view to its application in the practice of normal education is reprehensible [*verwerflich*]. Undergoing psychoanalysis can lead to the durable psychic infection of the victim with its premature sexual sensations and representations and can thus provoke 'loss of innocence' [*Entharmlosung*]: this is a great danger for our young people. The eventual educational-successes of their method as alleged by psychoanalysts can in no way justify the devastating damage done to a developing soul.

(Stern, 1913–14)

One petition invariably leads to another, and there followed a 'protest [*Verwahrung*] against the erroneous condemnation of child psychoanalysis' shortly afterwards, organized by Pastor Oskar Pfister in Zurich (cited by Graf-Nold, 1988), which was signed by twenty-three Swiss teachers, psychologists and doctors. Edouard Claparede, Theodore Flournoy, Oskar Pfister and Eugenie Sokolnicka were among the most well-known of the signatories. This was a 'moderate' declaration in which the signatories first of all state that they agree with the fact that psychoanalysis is just a method and no different from any other and reject its application to normal children, 'for all that it might lead to loss of innocence'. But for children with disorders it was an incomparable method for specially trained educators to heal them and give them back their 'innocence' [*Verharmlosung*]; but one should be warned against 'child psychoanalysis carried out by dilettantes'. Teaching was very much interested in the development of a scientific 'pedanalysis', there was more to psychoanalysis than just sexuality. Finally, from a scientific point of view, 'pedanalysis' would bring to light those interpretations which comply with the norm.

Pastor Pfister had at that time just published a 400-page volume, *The Psychoanalytic Method* (Pfister, 1913), prefaced by Freud. Jung had not been forgotten, however, and had contributed a paper on 'Psychic disorders in children'.

Pfister was looking for a middle road between Jung and Freud, and reproached the latter for mixing up eroticism with sexuality. He himself favoured an asexual libido, as did Jung. He felt that Stern's protest was in part directed at him, since he was actively in favour of using the 'method' in the instruction and education of children. Some three months later he published 'Zur Ehrenrettung der Psychoanalyse' (Pfister, 1914: 305–12), in which he repeats that: 'Freud's sexual theory is neither the basis nor an evident consequence of psychoanalysis. . . . This sexual theory is rejected by a large number of "pedanalysts." It was a theory which was historically necessary and which represented an immense progress; but I do not find it accurate.'

These positions on theory led Pfister to be very severe with Hermine Hug-Hellmuth:

> Her works . . . are taken as an example of the pretentious and ridiculous nature of psychoanalysis. Many 'pedanalysts' of my acquaintance deplore this publication in many respects, and take exception to . . . her affirmations, while recognizing the interest of her observations of children. And in any case, psychoanalysis does not consist of [the ideas of] a single individual only.

Hug-Hellmuth's publication appeared just prior to the 4th International Congress in Munich on 7 and 8 September 1913, at which the split between Freud and Jung was consummated. This was also no doubt the moment when Freud wrote *On the History of the Psycho-analytic Movement* (1914) in which he indicated (p. 18):

> In the beginning, my statements about infantile sexuality were founded almost exclusively on the findings of analysis in adults which led back into the past. I had no opportunity of direct observations on children. It was therefore a very great triumph when it became possible years later to confirm almost all my inferences by direct observation and the analysis of very young children . . .

Further on (p. 38) he says:

> The revolutionary discoveries of psycho-analysis in regard to the mental life of children – the part played in it by sexual impulses (von Hug-Hellmuth [1913]), and the fate of those components of sexuality which become unserviceable in the function of reproduction – were bound early to direct attention to education and to stimulate an attempt to bring analytic points of view into the foreground in that field of work. Recognition is due to Dr Pfister for having, with sincere enthusiasm, initiated the application of psychoanalysis in this direction and brought it to the notice of ministers of religion and those concerned with education.

Hug-Hellmuth fought valiantly in support of Freud's ideas, and opened the way for psychoanalysis of the child based on the recognition of the theory of infantile sexuality. Even if her publications were judged to be too orthodox and clumsy, she had indeed won her election to membership of the Psychoanalytical Society of Vienna, becoming a member on 8 October 1913.

To that point her work had referred only to analyses undertaken as a result of observations of children. Knowing her modest, consciencious, almost scholastic nature, one can imagine that she was waiting for her recognition as a psychoanalyst by her peers before taking patients into her consulting rooms or, as we shall see, going into their homes. She did treat a number of adults, mainly women, but her principle activity was to be the psycho-analysis of children. This activity was to supply the material for her future publications.

Publications of 1914 *Education & Treatment should go hand in hand*

As early as 1914, Hug-Hellmuth had published a paper entitled 'Child psychoanalysis and pedagogics' (1946) about the psychoanalysis of children, which thus shows that she had already begun her activities in this field. We therefore believe that the first child psychoanalyst to have worked systemat- ically in the field must have started working in 1913. This, of course, would have given her a considerable anteriority in relation to her successors. Anna Freud was 18 at that time and Melanie Klein had only become acquainted with Freud's *Interpretation of Dreams* in 1910, and undergone psychoanalysis in 1914.

In the above-mentioned article, Hug-Hellmuth suggests that child psy- choanalysis should consist of both the education and the treatment of the child at the same time. This is not psychoanalysis applied to education but, on the contrary, the educational nature that psychoanalysis should assume. She relies on love (in transference?) in both its positive and its negative aspects, and insists on the non-cognitive elements: 'The mental processes of *SEL* . the child are more influenced by feelings than by intellect.' Finally, she thinks that part of the job of (child) psychoanalysis is also to give a certain kind of education to the parents.

That same year, Hug-Hellmuth (1914a) also published 'Children's Letters'; these are fascinating documents which she used, as was her wont, to defend Freudian ideas.

Publications from 1914–24

From 1914–24 Hug-Hellmuth published thirty-three works, mostly in the field of child psychoanalysis. There are also a number works about the family, understanding women in psychoanalytical terms, the neuroses of war. We shall stick to those concerned with the history of child psychoanalysis and to the three major works: *A Young Girl's Diary* (1919), 'On the technique of child analysis' (1921) and *New Ways to the Understanding of Youth* (1924).

A young girl's diary

Although the famous *A Young Girl's Diary* was not published until 1919, it was obviously written in 1914 or 1915, since Freud's Preface consists of a letter to Hug-Hellmuth dated 27 April 1915. As to the title, a preferable translation would have been 'Diary of a young adolescent girl' or 'Diary of a halfgrown young girl' (*Tagebuch eines halbwüchsigen Mädchens*). It was probably not published earlier owing to the war; and a publisher was also needed. The work was thus one of the first in a series planned by Freud under the banner of 'International Psychoanalytical Publications'; this means of publication, subsidized by a 'grateful patient' and organized by Sándor Ferenczi, Otto Rank and Ernest Jones, would enable psychoanalysts to be independent of the publishers (Graf-Nold, 1988).

In fact, the work was sponsored entirely by Freud and the IPA. If proof were needed, Freud's very flattering Preface is evidence enough:

Letter to Dr Hermine von Hug-Hellmuth

The diary is a little gem. I really believe it has never before been possible to obtain such a clear and truthful view of the mental impulses that characterize the development of a girl in our social and cultural stratum during the years before puberty. We are shown how her feelings grow up out of a childish egoism till they reach social maturity; we learn what form is first assumed by her relations with her parents and with her brothers and sisters and how they gradually gain in seriousness and inward feeling; how friendships are made and broken; how her affection feels its way towards her first objects; and, above all, how the secret sexual life begins to dawn on her indistinctly and then takes complete possession of the child's mind; how, in the consciousness of her secret knowledge, she at first suffers hurt, but little by little overcomes it. All of this is so charmingly, so naturally, and so gravely expressed in these artless notes that they cannot fail to arouse the greatest interest in educators and psychologists. . . . It is your duty, I think, to publish the diary. My readers will be grateful to you for it.

(Freud, 1919c [1915]: 341)

The 'Diary' relates the sentiments, sensations and feelings of a young adolescent girl from 11 to 14 years of age; it describes the sexual awakening of the adolescent, but also the emotional and to some extent the 'social' awakening, all swathed in the romanticism so typical of the time and of its author. For us it is a delicious piece of literature. Perhaps it would be written differently today, as Neyraut points out in his Preface to the 1974 edition, but we are not so sure. This charming young lady also had the additional merit of confirming the Freudian theories of infantile sexuality.

There is no doubt in our minds that Hug-Hellmuth wrote this work of fiction with the object of propagating the theories she had upheld for years in an acceptable form of packaging. It also enabled her to continue her self-analysis, since it is relatively easy to follow Hermine's own life in the stories of 'Rita'.

The response

We might think it strange today that she did not wish to sign her work. However, those were the days before romantic fiction was fashionable and the book caused quite a stir. It was quite remarkable to see a young girl describing her sexuality so precisely and in such detail chorused Monty Jacobs, Kurt Schneider, August Aichhorn, Peter Panter, Barbara Low, Lou Andreas-Salomé and Stephan Zweig. Cyril Burt, of the Psycho-Analytical Society of London, also admired her, but thought it necessary to demonstrate that it could not have been written by a young girl. We firmly believe that the other authors of reading notes or commentaries had understood this, but had closed their eyes to the fact.

Helene Deutsch would say later on (1973): 'People were insisting that the diary was a figment of her imagination, to which I replied that if that were so, Dr Hug-Hellmuth was not only an excellent psychologist but also a very talented writer.'

For the opponents of psychoanalysis, evidence of the fictitious nature of the work also enabled them to throw doubt on the contents. Charlotte Bühler was a Professor of Child Psychology in Dresden, and later in Vienna. In Vienna she represented a current absolutely opposed to psychoanalysis, to the point that the word itself and the name of Freud were never pronounced in her presence. She herself was interested in the diaries of children and, in the Preface to one of her own works, expressed the opinion that 'this work tallies remarkably with the ideas of Freud, but very badly, in [her] opinion, with the development of a normal young girl.' Her pupils Joseph Krug and Hedwig Fuchs continued to make every effort to demonstrate that this diary could not have been written by a child, even well after Hug-Hellmuth's death.

A futile demonstration, as we have seen. However, reserved as always, modest and timid, Hermine Hug-Hellmuth did not dare to reveal the truth: she had the first edition published without her name appearing, even as editor. No one in Vienna was taken in; here she really was *the* child psychoanalyst. This novel was a material manifestation of all her previous writings, in particular the publication of the children's letters. She only dared to reveal herself as editor in the third German edition (1923) but always fiercely denied that she was the author. She even pretended to attest, in the face of all evidence, to the authenticity of the manuscript, which, unfortunately had been destroyed; she said she had known the author well, but that she had unfortunately just died, at barely 20 years of age. Besides, 'how could one doubt the authenticity of a diary prefaced by Freud himself?'

Her defence was so weak that her friends did not insist. However, this controversy did not prevent her book from selling 10,000 copies, having three German editions, two in English (the 1921 London edition was banned), and three in French (1928, 1975 and 1988). Today, it is one of the most quoted works in child psychoanalysis.

On the technique of child psychoanalysis

The second work that we shall mention is the report that Hug-Hellmuth presented at the International Congress in The Hague in September 1920: 'On the technique of child analysis'. Colette Chiland translated this article into French (see Hug-Hellmuth, 1921) and followed it with some very pertinent considerations on 'Child psychoanalysis, in 1920 and in 1974' (1975). She supposes that the paper was not really read at the conference, but we have not found any evidence to support this supposition. On the contrary, it would seem that Hug-Hellmuth did agree to present a paper, among such famous names as Freud, Karl Groddeck and Karl Abraham.

There were also some very interested listeners in the audience; in addition to Anna Freud and Melanie Klein, who had been invited, Oskar Pfister and Eugenie Sokolnicka should be mentioned, both presenting papers. A few months before (1920) Sokolnicka had published an analysis of a child with an obsessional neurosis (see I. 3). Melanie Klein had also read her article on the psychotherapy of a child (*her* child) at a meeting of the Psychoanalytical Society of Budapest in 1919.

The beginning of this article is a veritable manifesto of child psychoanalysis, in Hug-Hellmuth's sense of the word. We would like to quote *in extenso* from it:

The goal of both child and adult analysis is the same: to recover mental health, to re-establish a balance of the psyche disturbed by impressions both known and unknown to us.

The task of the doctor [the analyst] is over once recovery has taken place, whatever road the patient takes from the point of view of the ethical judgement of his behaviour in relation to the outside world; it is sufficient that that human being is once again able to work and live life to the full, and that he no longer threatens to succumb to the aggressions and deceptions that life might hold. Therapeutic and educational analysis [*Heilerziehung*] should not just be satisfied with releasing the young human being from his suffering, it should also give him moral, esthetic and social values. Its object is not the mature human being, the being who, having learned to take life in his stride, is able to assume his acts, but the child, the young person who, because he is still developing, needs, under the educational guidance of the analyst, to gain enough strength to become a person conscious of his goals and armed with will. The analyst, teacher and therapist, should never forget that, above all else, *child analysis is a constant analysis of character and education.*

This is not about remedial teaching, or educational recommendations which take psychoanalytical theory into account, but rather psychoanalysis which takes educational requirements into account. The criticisms of the Swiss teachers in 1913 had been heard: Hug-Hellmuth was being very prudent. But one can also see more than just prudence: whether it was simply a 'strategic retreat' before the violence of the assaults of the critics, or that she had changed her point of view, she really does seem to think that the analyst should retain an 'educational' perspective in his work.

Is this not an echo, perhaps distorted(?), of Freud's remark in 1910 (*Five Lectures on Psycho-analysis*, 1910 (1909): 48): 'You can if you like regard psycho-analytic treatment as no more than a prolongation of education for the purpose of overcoming the residues of childhood.' Here, of course, Freud is talking about adult psychoanalysis.

Colette Chiland remarks that in his later work *Analysis Terminable and Interminable* (1937), Freud indicates that the analyst is sometimes the model (*Vorbid*) and sometimes the teacher (*Lehrer*), still in relation to adult psychoanalysis.

This question of the relationship between education and psychoanalysis was to permeate all subsequent discussions on child psychoanalysis and foster a lack of understanding, both on the part of teachers who were not psychoanalysts (who reacted very early on, as we have seen) and on the part of 'adult' psychoanalysts. As far as Hug-Hellmuth was concerned, the relationship seems to have been obvious, and this can be seen clearly if her various works are compared. Elsewhere (in particular, and in detail, in *New Ways to the Understanding of Youth* (1924), which is mentioned further on), she develops the advantages of personal psychoanalytical knowledge, or theoretical psychoanalytical knowledge for teachers, whose task is then to educate in an enlightened and understanding manner. It is indeed psycho-analysis proper that we are talking about, even if in the definition she spells out its nature of *Heilerziehung* (educative and therapeutic analysis).

Provided, however, that the child is older than 7 or 8. At an earlier age it is advisable to follow the instructions given by Freud in 'Little Hans'. Education should be based on a knowledge of psychoanalysis. Also, 'as Freud said', 'the fact that infant care, both physical and mental, is mainly done by women, means that we must train kind, intelligent women [*kluge, gütige Frauen*] for the job of psychoanalytical education'. She is echoing, with no apparent criticism, an opinion put forward by Jung. (see Chapter 1).

On the contrary, for children over 7 years of age, Hug-Hellmuth advo-cates treatment similar to that for the adult, with a number of technical modifications, for which she gives the three following reasons:

1 The child is brought in by its parents.
2 The adult is suffering from past events, the child from present events (this is not at all obvious to us, since we believe that the child *too* has a past).
3 The child does not have sufficient narcissistic interest at this stage to force him to change. Hug-Hellmuth indicates here that the same applies to a number of adult women patients, which, *ipso facto* considerably weakens her argument.

In addition, when the child is only about 7 or 8, one must be content with partial success only, so as to not intimidate it 'by a brutal breach of his thoughts and feelings . . . thereby disturbing him further, rather than setting him free'. Here, the response to the attacks of 1913–14 is quite evident; but it is difficult to know whether this is a climbdown, or an ironic remark which is not meant seriously.

With children between 14 and 18, analysis is often undertaken as for an adult, except perhaps insofar as the couch is concerned: the lying position can give rise to situations which are too distressing at this age to enable any consistant analytical work to be carried out. Hug-Hellmuth remarks, 'I have not been able to observe that the success of analysis was endangered in any say just because of sitting face to face' (Chiland, French translation, p. 198). Here, contrary to the opinion put forward by Graf-Nold, Hug-Hellmuth takes a position on theory which is different from that of Freud; we shall find other examples elsewhere. We also know that in at least two cases, that of a 17-year-old girl with obsessions, and that of a 6-year-old girl suffering from a disabling phobia, Hug-Hellmuth did use the couch (MacLean and Rappen, 1991). Of course, this was also the case with her adult patients.

As to children in the latency period, in this article she pays particular attention to describing the *setting*. First of all, one can avoid insisting on the analytic goal that is being pursued. Some patients 'know in advance or learn fast' what it is all about; with others, those who are too young, or who do not suffer, or who are 'mentally defective', one can undertake treatment without forcibly drumming explanations into them that they would not understand. 'Experience and tact should be the sole guide.'

The initial interview is carried out with the parents. But the child must not be relegated to an adjoining room, since that would be humiliating and distressing and lead to needless additional resistance. As with the initial interview, the analysis should be carried out at the patient's home. The object is to avoid needless resistance, since the child is not motivated in the same way the adult is by the payment of fees, and might behave capriciously and not turn up to a session. In addition, even at that time parents had great difficulty in sending the child to the analyst (Chiland, French translation, p. 207). In such a context, the desire expressed by the child to visit the home of the analyst should be understood as a manifestation of positive transference, to which one should not respond with an acting out, since it might prove fleeting. However, we do know (through Anny Katan, mentioned by MacLean and Rappen, 1991: 31) that Hug-Hellmuth also had children coming to her surgery.

The first session is very important, as it enables the analyst to decide on the strategy to be followed, which will be different for each child. With children who refuse any dialogue whatsoever, Hug-Hellmuth advises facilitating transference by using a number of strategems (telling it about the misdemeanours of another child, for example), and thus conceives what was later to become Anna Freud's 'therapeutic alliance'. With younger children (7–8 years old) it might be useful to play; this would enable dialogue to begin, and enable the analyst to become more familiar with the symptoms and the character of the child; sometimes play might be used throughout the treatment. But sometimes play is also a 'symbolic action', equivalent to verbal communication in adults: it is the 'wordless admission'. Here she is formulating the role of play in child analysis, such as it was to be developed by Melanie Klein. The use of play teaches her that, in children, 'mental processes generally take place in strata quite different [from that of the adult]'. 'With children, many impressions, although they do not reach the threshold of consciousness, still leave clear traces in the mind.'

> [With adults], analysis does not render conscious memory traces of the primal scene (Freud, *A Child is Being Beaten*, 1919) whereas [with children] the process of the fusion of new impressions [with memory traces] takes place perhaps in the preconscious, and it remains for later experiences, higher stages of development, to bring them into consciousness.

We repeat that she was not the inventor of 'play therapy' as has been said, but she did invent the use of play – such as the dream or free association – in child analysis. As we have seen, there is even the outline of a reflection foreshadowing Kleinian theories on symbolism.

Another problem concerning the setting is time: there has to be a compromise between the school obligations put forward by the parents, and the 'regulation' six sessions of adult analysis. 'I have always found that a reduction in the number of sessions to three or four a week in no way endangers the success of the analysis, *if it is continued for long enough*.'[6] Here, too, Hug-Hellmuth is respectfully distancing herself from the Freudian rules. On the other hand, she does hold to 'strictly respecting the length of the sessions'. For her that means a session is made up of so many minutes (50, 55 or 60 minutes, depending on the patient), and under no circumstances should the duration be reduced, or increased, even if one is very curious as to what might be said after the 60 minutes are up.

This is part of what Hug-Hellmuth calls the 'child's requirements' of the analyst and which tend to be so easily forgotten in many 'psychoanalytical psychotherapies' today. Another 'requirement of the child' is for the listener to be kind and full of understanding, to have an affectionate concern for 'trifles', constant vigilance, to forget nothing, and not to mix up things that were said in the initial sessions.

Of course, the analytic *process* will operate with the aid of transference, which is often a 'rising tide'. A 'strong positive transference' poses no problems for Hug-Hellmuth, unlike Anna Freud. Of course, to speak of transference 'requires . . . considerable prudence in the formulation because basically, in spite of everything, the child is not prepared to exchange his parents for a stranger, even if he has every reason to do so.' But Hug-Hellmuth has none of the reservations that Anna Freud was to show later on. 'Parental authority and early educational influences still continue to play a part', she says, but instead of drawing the Anna Freudian conclusion that transference is difficult to induce, she writes that 'for him, the analyst also embodies the imago of the father or the mother far more than for the mature patient'. This transference is also ambivalent, and a negative transference is rapidly perceptible, generally in the form of a fear of betrayal, mistrust, anxiety and jealousy with regard to the conversations between the analyst and the parents. Interpretations are tackled under the name of 'explanations': the negative transference is explained as 'saying nothing out of defiance', and the positive transference 'in the sense of being ashamed of belittling oneself or of belittling one's parents by a remark made in front of the analyst . . . or of the expression which is soon used, "Now I have told you everything"' (French translation, p. 204). She also believes that a negative transference is generally more easily admitted by the child) than a positive transference. One can but think that at this point Melanie Klein, who was present in the audience, must have been listening very carefully.

(We should remember that she had been 'invited' to this Congress in The Hague, as had Anna Freud.)

Analysis of the resistance, especially where sexual problems are concerned, requires great tact and judgement. 'The main thing in child analysis is the analyst's *intuition* concerning the sick mind of his patient.' This definitely has a very modern ring to it. Moreover, one should not expect an immediate and favourable response of the child to the interpretation. In fact, this would be somewhat suspect: this is what 'well trained children who say "yes" to everything, but who think "no" and act accordingly' do. It is in a much later session that a child will say something which shows that he or she has taken on board the explanation given. But this acceptance remains unconscious and unformulated, unlike in the adult; with the child it is often a change in behaviour which proves to the analyst 'that the pains one has gone to have not been in vain'. 'Intuition and patience are the foundations which must be laid right from the first contact with the young patient, so that trust is housed between solid foundations and a solid roof', Hug-Hellmuth concludes (French translation, p. 207). Here it is not of Anna Freud or Melanie Klein that one is reminded, but of W. R. Bion: in modern terms one would be talking of a firm container and insight.

This paper also tackles the question of the relationship with the parents, on which the author dwells at length. The difficulties with parents in those days are astonishingly similar to those we meet with today. One must be patient with them, never forgo contact. 'I hold analysis of one's own child to be an impossibility', says Hug-Hellmuth. Here, too, she takes an opposing view to that of Freud with 'little Hans' and to that of Jung of course. It is difficult to know whether she knew that Melanie Klein was analysing her own son and that Anna Freud had been analysed by her father; but we can suppose that each of the two listeners must have reacted to this.

It is striking to note that she 'defends' parents; there are nearly always blunders in any education, and it is difficult to avoid either excessive severity or excessive affection. If the parents had undergone analysis before the child, 'in all likelihood, fewer children would need to be analysed'. However, she does not say that parents should be analysed *after* the child has presented the symptoms, as one sometimes hears today (see Mannoni, 1970).

The paper also touches on the problem of the 'placing' of the child. A temporary removal from the family *sometimes* has favourable results but, on the whole, psychoanalytical treatment in an institution is problematic because the child finds it difficult not to talk about his analysis to those around him, which means a break in confidentiality and, in addition, he may become the butt of jokes on the part of his classmates concerning the sessions. Even today these problems have not been overcome. Hug-Hellmuth dreamt of 'psychoanalytical centres for young people' (*Psychoanalytischen*

Jugendheimen). What form the treatment in such centres would take, she cannot tell:

> I do believe that the most important requirement should be exceptional tact, a lot of experience in education and considerable talent to successfully overcome the great difficulties in psychoanalytical treatment which are certain to arise due to the promiscuity of school life. The jealousy of the analysands with regard to the others, comparisons, which are not always favourable to the analyst into whose hands the patient has been put, the impossibility of preventing the children from talking about their analysis amongst themselves, are all things which should not be underestimated. However, I nevertheless believe that such centres for young people would go some way to resolving or to lessening the problem of controlling the difficult child, an area where many parents and schools have met with failure.
>
> (p. 197, French translation)

Graf-Nold (1988) wonders how such well-known people as August Aichhorn, Siegfried Bernfeld, Anna Freud or Oskar Pfister might have reacted to these remarks in view of the fact that they had recently set up their own youth centres. Colette Chiland (1975), with her knowledge of modern institutions, dreamt instead of the analysis 'that we are lucky enough to be able to carry out in our surgeries, a bit like the rest and recreation due to the soldier after battle'.

To sum up, this early paper contains the well-structured basis of what was to become child psychoanalysis: framework, process, negative and positive transference, interpretation, resistances, the problem of parents. In the same way that the first message the child communicates to the analyst contains the nucleus of his or her neurosis, this first scientific communication contains, perhaps in syncretic form, the core of psychoanalytic work with children. The various tendencies that we shall encounter later on will develop along the lines already laid down, only giving more emphasis to this or that aspect.

A clear differentiation has been introduced: the psychoanalytic treatment of children, although it may play an educational role, is different from education, even though psychoanalysis may have shed some light on it. Anna Freud contributed to the development of these notions, as we shall see.

Lectures

Hermine Hug-Hellmuth was also involved in the teaching and dissemination of the ideas of psychoanalysis. In 1916 she gave nine lectures at the Union for Feminine Culture. In 1920 she was invited to the Berlin Institute of Psychoanalysis; she even inaugurated the lectures for future psychoanalysts. She had hesitated to go to Berlin, but Freud insisted, and in a letter from Karl Abraham to Sigmund Freud dated 10 June 1920 (Freud and Abraham, 1965) one reads that Hermine Hug-Hellmuth would give 'a lecture at the start of the August–September term, her travel expenses will be paid and she can stay with Karen Horney and her husband. Anything that the lecture might yield would thus be all profit for her. The polyclinic is putting its premises at her disposal'. This only goes to underline in how much esteem she was held by Freud and Abraham. Her lecture was entitled: 'Psychoanalytical knowledge of the child'.

According to Wolfgang Huber (1980), she also gave lectures on the subject of 'Psychoanalysis and Education' at the Urania centre for continuing education in Vienna, probably in 1921. In 1922–3 she undertook a series of lectures on 'The psychology of the child', and a seminar on pedagogical questions.

In 1922 the Psychoanalytical Society of Vienna organized outpatient consultations. She was also appointed Director of the Educational Committee set up in 1923. According to MacLean and Rappen (1991), Anna Freud succeeded her in this position some years later. The consultations of the Educational Committee were for children aged from 2½ to 15. Hug-Hellmuth hoped that advice given in this form would find favour with the Administration and be integrated into Social Welfare.

New ways to the understanding of youth

The lectures that Hermine Hug-Hellmuth gave to a much wider public (parents, teachers, educators, school doctors, kindergarten and social workers) complemented her activities as a consultant. (It would seem that later on Anna Freud was to take up the idea of 'Lectures for Educators', see later.) Twelve of these lectures were published together in 1924 in a book entitled *New Ways to the Understanding of Youth*. Hug-Hellmuth died just before the book was published, but it seems nevertheless to have been very successful. Moreover, her death was announced in the *Illustrierte Kronenzeitung* with the headline 'Murder of the *writer* Hug-Hellmut' and in *Neue Freie Presse* as 'Mysterious Death of Woman *Writer.*'

In 1925, Karen Horney commented: 'The book makes known what analysis has discovered about the child's development and the difficulties which this encounters and indicates the possible line of attack for the educational worker. . . . The book has great value, not only for educators interested in analysis but for analysts themselves' (cited in MacLean and Rappen, 1991: 36). A letter from Alix Strachey to her husband (11 February 1925) is far less pleasant in tone: the book evidences a mess of sentimentality covering the old intention of dominating at least one human being – one's own child: I really believe a book like hers might do more harm than good. It gives parents and teachers a new leverage. Now they know that all children masturbate and have phantasies, and so on they'll be much sharper in detecting them and in general interfering (all for the best) with their private lives. Thank god Melanie is absolutely firm on this subject. She absolutely insists on keeping parental and educative influence apart from analysis and in reducing the former to its minimum, because the most she thinks it can do is to keep the child from actually poisoning itself on mushrooms, and to keep it reasonably clean, and teach it its lessons.

(Strachey and Strachey, 1986: 200–1)

MacLean and Rappen (1991) have given a summarized translation of Hug-Hellmuth's *New Ways to the Understanding of Youth*[7]; we were able to have access to the translation of the first lecture through J. Finck.

A glance at the titles of the lectures is instructive: (1) Ways and Goals of Child Rearing; Basics of Freudian Theory; Basics of Psychoanalytic Terminology. (2) Early Disappointments; The Child's Emotional Attitude toward the Environment. (3) About the Unconscious. (4) The Sexual Drive. (5) The Child's Sexual Curiosity; About Sexual Education. (6) Educational Difficulties in the Family and in School. (7) The Child's Anxiety. (8) Fantasies of Children and Adolescents. (9) Children's Play. (10) Children's Dreams. (11) Mental Health. (12) Psychoanalytic Educational Counseling (see MacLean and Rappen, 1991: 154).

'*Adults also too easily forget their own childhood*' she says in Lecture 1, with its specific interests, wishes and follies. 'Their critical view of the child's spontaneity leads to tragic mistakes. They apply their *own standards*. These are the reasons why adults don't fully understand. They lack the most important knowledge of the unconscious'[8] (MacLean and Rappen, 1991: 155). 'Adults therefore overestimate or underestimate the child's mind. . . . They therefore cannot plumb the depths of the child's mind, from whence originate the emotions which determine the light and the shade in the life of the individual and of whole peoples'.

Hug-Hellmuth sets out for her readers the first Freudian topic with the talent of a great educationalist and does not hesitate to use some of the cases she herself has dealt with, from the 12-year-old girl who was afraid of needles to the 14-year-old girl who was subject to fits of compulsive laughter.

She ends the lecture with these words: 'Knowledge of psychoanalysis is essential for the Judge who carries out a job with great responsibility, for the teacher and the educator into whose care the young person is entrusted to guide him so that he blossoms successfully.'

We have noted an interesting remark in Lecture 9 concerning children's play. Whereas in her preceding works she considered the use of play during analysis more as a strategy destined to replace free associations, here she mentions the Hungarian psychoanalyst Sigmund Pfeiffer (1919): 'Analysing a number of infantile games he [Pfeiffer] proves the similarity between them and other products of the unconscious like fantasies and dreams . . . and lapses. . . . Suppression, displacement, condensation, symbolization, identification, and rationalization all contribute to the eventual form of the play' (cited in MacLean and Rappen, 1991: 192–3). And she goes on to give examples.

This is one of the discoveries that was rightly attributed to Melanie Klein and that, moreover, is still not unanimously accepted by psychoanalysts today. However, if the account of her theory concerning play in child analysis was given at the Salzburg conference in 1924, and developed in the articles dated 1926 and 1927, then Hermine Hug-Hellmuth could, of course, have had no knowledge of them. The premises of the theory, and more precisely the question of the analogy between play and the products of the unconscious mind, however, were tackled by Melanie Klein as early as July 1919 in a lecture given to the Hungarian Psychoanalytical Society, entitled 'The development of a child', published in 1921. Did Hug-Hellmuth not know about Melanie Klein's work or did she scotomize it? Perhaps Sigmund Pfeiffer was the first to mention it: his paper 'The manifestation of the infantile erotic drive in play: the position of psychoanalysis in relation to the principle theories concerning play' was dated 1919. It has to be said that Melanie Klein does not mention Pfeiffer either; in Anna Freud's biography (Young-Bruehl, 1988) he is mentioned in one line: he 'wrote one of the foundational works on play therapy' (p. 160). It really does not matter very much; the concept had been created. Hermine Hug-Hellmuth had adopted it, quoting its author.

The drama surrounding the death of Hug-Hellmuth could not but arouse the psychoanalytical world: they publicly expressed their gratitude to this pioneer, then she was almost forgotten. Anna Freud mentions her very little except to say that she was her only predecessor, but only by a short time. In fact, Hermine Hug-Hellmuth preceded her by a good ten years. Melanie Klein is a little more prolix, acknowledging her talent but criticizing her theoretical positions in her usual energetic fashion, so that the tribute she pays to her remains ambiguous.

Did they really know her? What one can reconstruct of the personality of Hermine Hug-Hellmuth suggests that when Anna Freud appeared in psychoanalytical circles Hermine felt immediately threatened by a rival who was all the more formidable since she embodied legitimacy itself: not only was she the daughter of her idol, but her merit became obvious almost immediately. Hermine never spoke of her, but she moved aside little by little as Anna took her place. What she represented for Anna is no doubt more complex: she would most certainly not have been attracted to such a 'motherly' image. In a letter to Angela Graf-Nold dated 4 December 1979, Anna Freud wrote:

> All that I can say is that she was the first person in Vienna to undertake analysis of children, and that I knew this when I myself became a member of the Psychoanalytical Society of Vienna. Naturally, I often saw Hermine Hug-Hellmuth at the meetings of the Society, but I did not have any [*so gut wie keinen*] personal contact, so to speak; I did not seek to be taught by her; at the time it seemed preferable for me to go my own way.'

As to Melanie Klein, her biographer, Phyllis Grosskurth (1986), recounts that she met Hug-Hellmuth at the conference in The Hague, that she tried to have a discussion with her, but was met with standoffishness. It is easy to imagine the warm and enthusiastic Melanie Klein trying to speak to the timid Hermine Hug, and quickly giving up. In her unpublished autobiography (1959b), Melanie Klein states:

> Dr Hug-Hellmuth was doing child analysis at this time in Vienna, but in a very restricted way. She completely avoided interpretations, though she used some play material and drawings, and I could never get an impression of what she was actually doing, nor was she analysing children under six or seven years. I do not think it too conceited to say that I introduced into Berlin the beginnings of child analysis.
>
> (cited in Grosskurth, 1986: 93)

Of course, Hug-Hellmuth did not interpret things in the same way as Melanie Klein, but if the latter had taken the pains to read her works she would have understood that interpretation was part of Hug-Hellmuth's analytical technique, the technique she had set out in The Hague. MacLean and Rappen (1991) observe that, in the climate of the period 1920–30, Melanie Klein criticized in the work of Hug-Hellmuth that part which was later taken up (at least to start with) by Anna Freud: no analysis of children under 7, the establishing of a therapeutic alliance, the educational role of the analyst. In the same way, Anna Freud did not like in Hug-Hellmuth that which she criticized Melanie Klein for doing: interpretation of negative transference, a clear separation between the educational and the analytical, the use of play.

It was the destiny of Hermine Hug-Hellmuth, who gave to psychoanalysts the basics of child psychoanalysis, first of all to be imitated without being acknowledged, then decried and finally forgotten.

Perhaps Hermine Hug-Hellmuth was just a simple woman, shy and reserved, sensitive and, towards the end of her life, somewhat depressed; perhaps she had almost no friends and perhaps she was restrained in her social dealings; perhaps she did not construct a grand theory, as Melanie Klein and

Anna Freud were to do later on, for example; perhaps she had exchanged somewhat rapidly her belief in Catholicism and the love of her nobleman of a father for a devout and unbounded belief in Freud and her analyst; perhaps she felt unduly guilty about not having been able to help her nephew; perhaps she did have all these faults and others besides, but she was a human being, an intelligent, cultivated, sensitive and loyal woman who put all her talent and her obstinacy into the cause of psychoanalysis, a gallant foot soldier in the Freudian troops, never hesitating to stand up and be counted no matter what blows she might receive. Her work, buried for sixty years, is being unearthed at last: and that work was the invention of child psychoanalysis.

Notes

1 We had already written this book in November 1991 when a selection of texts by Hermine Hug-Hellmuth was published in French by Dominique Soubrenie (1991). Prefaced J. Le Rider, a number of these papers had never been translated into French previously. Contrary to the opinion of the prefacer, we do not believe that the work of Soubrenie means that historians of Freudian texts will have to 'considerably revise' their views. Indeed, the accent in the book is placed on the 'wretched bad fairy', and on the 'devastating effects on family ties' caused by the first cases of child psychoanalysis. These arguments reverberate like an echo of the earliest criticisms against the psychoanalysis of children as formulated by Pierre Janet, the Sterns or André Gide, for example. There has always been, in our opinion, and as history shows, two diametrically opposing points of view on the same material, depending on one's opinion as to whether the self-know-ledge brought about by psychoanalysis is of interest or not. In addition, it is to be regretted that J. Le Rider did not have access to the most recent sources of infor-mation, i.e. the work of MacLean and Rappen (1991), or the theses of Dujols (1990) and Boix (1990) (University of Bordeaux), both of which offer new ele-ments and put the facts in a different light.
2 'Container' in the sense given by Wilfred Bion; the quality of a maternal object able to 'contain' a baby's anxieties.
3 A strict labour camp.
4 Phenomenon to which the person in question is subjected, consisting of an abnormal relationship between the sensations perceived by different sensory sys-tems.
5 The details of these reactions can be found in Angela Graf-Nold's (1988) remark-able documentation.
6 Our emphasis.
7 In Dominique Soubrenie's book (1991) the translation of lectures 9 and 12 appears.
8 All our emphases.

PART II

Yesterday: two schools, three cities – Vienna, Berlin and London (1920–45)

Introduction

During this period (1920–45), Anna Freud, in Vienna, following in the footsteps of her father, and Melanie Klein, in Berlin, following in the footsteps of Karl Abraham, then in London after his death, were each to found their own school of child psychoanalysis.

Their research took them into different fields. With great enthusiasm, Anna Freud worked on the application of psychoanalysis to the child, in the field of education and observation. She was certainly interested in the psychoanalytical treatment of children, but remained reluctant about the existence of child psychoanalysis *per se* because of the technical and theoretical problems, which, at the time, she thought insuperable.

Melanie Klein, on the other hand, envisaged carrying out psychoanalytical treatment of children from the outset. She developed and perfected her methodology – analysis through play – and, little by little, as she made her clinical discoveries, began to question the foundation of some of Freud's theories.

Psychoanalysts of the period tended to side with one or other of the two, for they rapidly constituted opposing schools of thought. They were to meet up again in London in 1938 after the Freud family had emigrated from Vienna, and the result was one of the most dramatic confrontations in the history of the psychoanalytic movement: the 'Controversial Discussions'. The Kleinian school was accused of diverging so much from Freudian theories that at one point it was proposed that they be excluded from the Freudian analytical movement. They were obliged to justify their position and demonstrate that they were in fact faithful to Freudian thinking, which they did in a series of theoretical treatises (see King and Steiner, 1991).

The presentation of these articles and their discussion by representatives of both schools within the British Psychoanalytical Society took place in war-torn London between 1941 and 1944. During one of the working sessions the sirens sounded the alarm but the discussion was so heated that no one was inclined to leave the meeting and take shelter. At the next meeting a proposal was put to the vote: in future, if there was an air-raid alert, the meeting would be disbanded.

Vienna, Berlin and London were the scenes of intense activities centred on child psychoanalysis. We shall try to give an account of this creative climate by highlighting some of the personalities of the Viennese school around Anna Freud, and some of those of the English school around Melanie Klein.

France managed to remain remarkably aloof from the enthusiasm of the movement during this same period. However, two Polish immigrant psychoanalysts tried to introduce psychoanalysis to Paris. First, Eugenie Sokolnicka, analysed by Sigmund Freud and Sándor Ferenczi, who tried to introduce psychoanalysis to the literary world of the NRF *Nouvelle revue française*, but without much success. Then came Sophie Morgenstern, analysed by Eugenie Sokolnicka, who worked as a child psychoanalyst alongside Professor Georges Heuyer in the child neuro-psychiatric unit at La Salpêtrière hospital in Paris.

None the less, they remained isolated cases and were soon forgotten. We decided to take an interest in them, and in their work, to bring them out of the oblivion into which they had fallen, and also try to understand why they have disappeared so completely from our collective memory.

The reader interested in the introduction of child psychoanalysis to the United States will have to wait until Part III: we decided not to treat the pre-1940 period in America separately, because the hiatus due to the rise of the Nazis and the 1939–45 war was not felt in the same way there as it was in Europe.

5

Anna Freud, the daughter:
psychoanalytical education and observation

In the spring of 1966 Anna Freud was invited to give a lecture at the first meeting of the American Association for Child Psychoanalysis in Topeka, Kansas. The theme she chose was: 'A brief history of child psychoanalysis'. 'It is logical', she said, 'that when psychoanalysts pursue a new venture they start by looking at their own history. They thus grasp the importance of past experience in present actions and in what they expect from the future.' In this lecture she indicated what she thought child psychoanalysis was. She described her work at the Hampstead Clinic in London, where 'students are trained in psychoanalysis which is a method of treatment, a means of investigation, a theory which calls for critical examination and expansion, a body of knowledge which can be applied to a good many needs of the community. . . . The choice of the aspect or aspects of psychoanalysis [he or she will study] throughout his or her future career is up to the individual' ('A short history of child psychoanalysis', in *The Writings of Anna Freud*, 1965–80, vol. 7: 48–58).

The ideas and work of Anna Freud are not very well known in France. Her global vision of the psychoanalyst, i.e. someone who, having studied a new science, can throw new light on human behaviour and is not put off by the interpersonal side of psychoanalytical treatment, won her only incomprehension and criticism. Her conception of child psychoanalysis was of course intimately bound up with her personality (she even made a study of herself, as her father had done before her), and with the personal, professional and social choices she had made on reaching adulthood. As her biographer Elisabeth Young-Bruehl (1988) recounts, Anna Freud was almost certainly much influenced at that time by what her father had said in 1918 in *Lines of Advance in Psycho-Analytic Therapy* (Freud, 1919a [1918]). Talking about the future, Freud imagined that one day

it is possible to foresee that at some time or other the conscience of society will awake and remind it that the poor man should have just as much right to assistance for his mind as he now has to the life-saving help offered by surgery; and that the neuroses threaten public health no less than tuberculosis, and can be left a little as the latter to the impotent care of individual members of the community . . . institutions or out-patient clinics will be started, to which analytically-trained physicians will be appointed, so that men who would otherwise give way to drink, women, who have nearly succumbed under their burden of privations, children for whom there is no choice but between running wild or neurosis, may be made capable, by analysis, of resistance and of efficient work. Such treatments will be free . . .

(p. 167)

To understand the work of Anna Freud one has to look at the various elements that she takes into account and the way that she links them together. Linking the psychoanalytical treatment of the child to psychoanalytical psychology, and to the possible contribution of psychoanalysis to the child's adaptation to life, she presented her conception of child psychoanalysis at the conclusion of her lecture thus: 'I would like to think that this new Association [the American Association for Child Psychoanalysis], on the occasion of its first convention, is committing itself to a similar wide outlook on the subject and thereby will shape the future of child analysis in the United States' ('A short history of child analysis', 1966, in *The Writings of Anna Freud*, 1966–80, vol. 7: 58).

In 1920, 'the temptation to apply the new analytical knowledge to the upbringing of children was almost irresistible', wrote Anna Freud in 1965 in her book *Normality and Pathology in Childhood* (p. 4). She linked this temptation to the discoveries made in the therapeutic analyses of adult neurotics, which had brought to light 'the detrimental influence [on the child] of many parental and environmental attitudes'. 'It seemed a feasible task', as Sigmund Freud had advocated earlier, to alter 'the conditions of upbringing and to devise thereby what was called a "psychoanalytic upbringing" serving the prevention of neurosis'. This psychoanalytic upbringing was soon to lead to reflections on psychoanalytic teaching, which was in itself the origin of the setting up of the psychoanalytic observation of the child. The material collected by the new child experts was to contribute to 'the systematic building up of a psychoanalytic child psychology, and the integration of the two kinds of data, direct [observation of the child] and [that] reconstructed [from adult sources], became a rewarding task' (p. 9). These instruments were put to work in the search for more knowledge about the development of the young infant and its disorders. The study of the problems of the child's adaptation to its environment was also advocated.

The public persona of Anna Freud was somewhat different from her private self, according to the people who knew her. Ilse Hellmann, who speaks very warmly of her, (I. 4) says that her public persona was somewhat reserved and distant, and that she replied to questions in short sentences. She was attentive to others, could be very warm with her students, but rarely spoke of herself. Her approach was austere and she did not seek to be attractive. She was said to be very shy. The private person was, by contrast, cheerful and happy, and often very entertaining when among friends, most of whom she knew from Vienna. She loved to sew and had made a lot of the clothes for the children at the Hampstead Nurseries, for example. At the weekend, in her country home, she loved to ride. Having chosen the path of discretion, she refused several offers to write her autobiography. It is true that on many occasions she had been very hurt by what was said about herself, her family and her father.

In her book *From War Babies to Grandmothers*, Ilse Hellman (1990) describes Anna Freud both in her work as an educationalist and in her daily life with the children in the Nurseries. 'On her daily visits she noted some of the difficulties the children presented; she listened to them, she watched them, she discussed them with all the people concerned with them, and gradually the problems became clearer, as they unfolded. She had a great gift in her ability to make sense of what seemed at first incomprehensible' (p. 15). Of her work as an educationalist, Hellman added:

The outstanding impression, and one that remains with me, was her capacity to register every detail of what was reported to her and form a clear picture of the patient . . . she always asked the relevant questions needed to complete the picture, and she would always point out to us those features of which we needed to take greater note or be more aware. This is a gift I have met in very few analysts. It was as if she had known the patient in person.

(p. 15)

HER CHILDHOOD

Anna Freud was born in Vienna in December 1895, the sixth and youngest of the Freud children. There had been six births in eight years. Anna would later say that if contraception had existed, she probably would not have been born, for her parents were not ready, mentally, physically or financially, for yet another child. This was also the year in which Sigmund Freud reached a vital stage in his self-analysis, which was to lead to his work on the interpretation of dreams.

Anna was not breast fed and, along with her closest brother and sister, was very quickly entrusted to the care of a young nursemaid, Josefine. She therefore had three mother images present daily around her: her mother,

Martha, her aunt Minna (when she was a year old), and Josefine, from the earliest days after her birth. She became very attached to Josefine in particular, who stayed with her until the end of her first year at school. Anna got the impression that she was 'special' for her, that she was Josefine's favourite. In this maternal substitute one can perhaps see the origins of her interest in what she was to call the 'psychological mother' figure. It is probably the analysis of this deep bond with Josefine and the memory of a traumatic experience that happened with her in a park (Josefine having disappeared, Anna went off in search of her and got lost) that led to the following remarks in her article entitled 'About losing and being lost' (1967 [1953]): 'It is only when parental feelings are ineffective or too ambivalent, or when aggression is more effective than their love, or when the mother's emotions are temporarily engaged elsewhere, that children not only feel lost but, in fact, get lost' (in *Writings*, vol. 4: 311–12).

In general, on reading the various biographies written about her, one notes the lack of emotion shared between Anna and her mother during Anna's childhood. Sophie, the second of the Freud daughters, seems to have been the mother's favourite. Mathilde, the eldest, appears to have been her father's favourite until she got married. Anna seems to have had difficulty finding her place; she knew what it was to be the youngest, which meant 'the experience of being left out by the big ones, of being only a bore to them, and of feeling bored and left alone' (Young-Bruehl, 1988: 37) Her father seems to have become very important to her early on. A childhood memory disclosed by Anna, at the age of 20, to her friend Lou Andreas-Salomé, confirms the feeling she seems to have felt of being able to penetrate a magical, mysterious and beautiful world with him: Listening to Anna talk about her father. . . .

> When they went collecting mushrooms he always told them to go into the wood quietly and he still does this; there must be no chattering and they must roll up the bags they have brought under their arms, so that the mushrooms shall not notice; when their father found one he would cover it quickly with his hat, as though it were a butterfly. The little children – and now his grandchildren – used to believe what he said while the bigger ones smiled at his credulity. . . . The children were paid in pennies for the mushrooms they had found while the best mushroom of all (it was always Ernst who found it) got a florin. It was the quality and not the quantity of mushrooms that mattered.
> (Quote from the journal of Lou Andreas-Salomé in Young-Bruehl, 1988: 36; also quoted by Peters, 1979: 72)

Anna became an intrepid little girl with a taste for adventure, and liked to follow her big brothers when they went swimming or boating. But at home she was the model of what a good little girl should be, always smartly dressed, charming and tidy. She learned to knit and became mad about knitting. She was soon vying with her sister Sophie, who she thought was more beautiful and clever than she was. Anna tried to compensate for what she saw as her inferiority by being more intelligent, more mischievous and, a little later on, a better student at school. The rivalry between the two girls was to surface again when Sophie got married. At that time Anna was a teenager and it is quite possible that her father's decision that she should not be present at the wedding, although of course to do with her ill health, which often took her away from Vienna, was primarily due to the fact they did not get on and bickered constantly, making everyday life for the Freud family very difficult. It would appear that Anna suffered greatly because of this difficult relationship with her sister, and one wonders whether it was not something akin to this rivalry which appeared years later when she met Melanie Klein.

Anna started school when she was 6, very quickly became bored and complained all the time, but she did get good grades. For some reason she harboured the feeling that her lisp had partly spoilt her school life. She also detested the teaching methods, especially learning by rote. Writing and reading would be her remedies against boredom. What she liked in particular, recounts her biographer Elisabeth Young-Bruehl, were stories which were real. What she wanted most, she writes, 'was not' to 'escape into unreality, but' to be 'as grown up as her siblings', to be 'accepted and appreciated in her real family' (Young-Bruehl, 1988: 50). We can find confirmation of this need to be anchored to reality in the introduction to her lecture on 'The Ideal Psychoanalytical Institute', given in Chicago in 1966 at the request of her friend Hans Kohut.

> At an age before independent reading, when children are read to or told stories my interest was restricted to those which 'might be true'. This did not mean that they had to be true stories in the ordinary sense of the word, but they were supposed not to contain elements which precluded their happening in reality . . . To my own surprise, I have not changed very much in this respect: the Ideal Psychoanalytic Institute also claims my interest only in so far as it is capable of becoming true.
>
> ('The ideal psychoanalytic institute: a utopia',
> 1966, in *Writings*, vol. 7: 73–4)

She also wanted to compete with her father in the field of languages. At school she learnt English and French. She became interested in Italian when on holiday there. However, she did neither Latin nor Greek, since she would be going to a 'Lyceum' and not to a 'Gymnasium'. Contrary to a number of his close friends, who by sending their daughters to a 'Gymnasium' would enable them to later go on to become doctors, for example, Sigmund Freud did not want his daughters to go to university; their future, he thought, was in marriage. Towards the age of 13 or 14 Anna started to take an interest in her father's foreign visitors. He even let her sit, silent, in a corner, on the library ladder and thus be present at the Wednesday evening meetings of the Vienna Psychoanalytical Society.

In 1908, just before her father went to the United States, Anna had to be operated on for appendicitis. The operation was successful, unlike that of her sister Mathilde. However, over the next few years she was to lose weight and tended to walk with a stoop.

Early in 1912, at 17½ years old, Anna obtained her final-year diploma at the Lyceum. She began to wonder about her future: she was to have gone to Italy with her aunt Minna for a few months, but then Sophie announced she was getting married and Minna had to stay in Vienna. So, Anna went off alone to the boarding house in Merano, where Mathilde had also been. At that time Freud seems to have been worried about Anna's health: he wanted to see her in better physical shape and also tried to avoid any mental stress, which is why he advised her not to return to Vienna for her sister's wedding. As a reward, he went to see her at Easter and they went off to visit Venice together. For Anna, it was the realization of one of her dreams, to travel alone with her father. In fact, at that time she complained of troubles which she did not fully understand. She did not really feel ill but went through periods of profound fatigue, feeling 'stupid and exhausted' after bouts of daydreaming, consisting of weaving beautiful but complicated stories filled with many characters, in order, says her biographer, to fight her tendency to masturbate (Young-Bruehl, 1988: 59). We shall come back to these troubles, for ten years later Anna was to write one of her first articles, entitled 'Beating Fantasies and Daydreams' in which she describes the conflicts and phantasies connected with masturbation.

Sophie's wedding was to lead to great changes in the Freud household, since Anna then became the only daughter at home. The departure of his daughters to get married and of his sons to continue their studies was a difficult period for Freud. The years of 1912–13 were also darkened by the dissent of some of his disciples. He had just written *Totem and Taboo* (1912), the central theme of which was sons waiting for or desiring the demise of their father. In a letter to Sándor Ferenczi in July 1913, Freud wrote: 'in order to live for a few weeks, analysis-free, in Marienbad, my next company will be my little daughter, who is now developing so gratifyingly (you have surely long ago guessed this subjective condition of the "choice of the caskets")' (Freud and Ferenczi, 1993: 499; 9 July 1913). In the essay alluded to here ('The theme of the three caskets', 1913, S.E. 12: 289–301), Freud had studied 'a man's choice between three women'. At the time he was 56 and Anna 18. He still had an intense desire to please and to be loved, he did not want to give up the love of women, felt lonely, and was frightened at the idea that Anna too might leave him. He was depressed, knowing how vain it was to try to win back the love of the woman, the love that the child first received from its mother. He dreamt of finishing his life with her, while all the time realising what he was asking her to do. Did Anna feel her father's trouble when she wrote to him, worried, from her grandmother's in 1914: 'How am I to make do for six children all by myself next year?' (Freud and Andreas-Salomé, 1972: 32, 30 July 1915; see also Young-Bruehl, 1988: 62–3).

For ten years, until his first cancer operation, Freud worried about Anna's possible departure from home. She was as necessary to him as smoking (Freud and Andreas-Salomé, 1972: 113, 13 March 1922; Young-Bruehl, 1988: 117). In 1919, after the death of Sophie, he offered her the ring given to members of the Committee in recognition of her devotion to his cause, to psychoanalysis. Both their professional and personal relationships became closer. Together they weathered the grief of this death, together they took care of the two young children Ernst and Heinerle, aged 6 years and 13 months respectively.

Several young men showed interest in Anna, but each time she rejected them, either on the advice of her father, or because she thought they were really only interested in her father. She was reluctant to think of herself as the object of someone's love. At one point, in 1923, at the end of her first analysis with her father she thought she might go to live in Berlin and wrote as much to Max Eitingon (Young-Bruehl, 1988: 118). However, her father's illness put paid to this idea and she remained with him.

HER PROFESSIONAL COMMITMENT

In June 1914, at the age of 18, Anna passed the exam which would enable her to become a school teacher the following year. She remained in this position for five years, until 1920, thus spending the war years in Vienna, at the family home. The previous year, in Merano, she had begun to read her father's works and from 1915 began to do translations of psychoanalytical articles, concurrently with her teaching work. In 1917 she became ill with tuberculosis, owing mostly to hunger, cold and overwork, and had to stop working. Her health was one of the reasons given for her resignation from the teaching profession in 1920. In fact, in the autumn of 1918 she had decided to undergo an analysis with her father, the first stage of which lasted until the spring of 1922, at the rate of six one-hour sessions a week.

After the war, in the period 1918–20, Anna made a number of acquaintances and moved in circles which were to have a great influence on her personal life. Her two brothers, Martin and Ernst, were members of the Jewish Zionist movement in Vienna and Berlin. This enabled her to meet Siegfried Bernfeld, a militant socialist and Zionist. At that point he was in the process of founding an institute, the Baumgarten Institute, for war orphans and Jewish children who had been abandoned. At the end of the war Anna had done some work for the American Joint Distribution Committee on a voluntary basis. This Jewish–American committee collected funds to help Jewish children who were war victims, orphans or homeless, and Anna would place them in institutions or in families. The Baumgarten Institute was to be financed by the Joint Distribution Committee, and Bernfeld and another analyst who was to become famous, Willi Hoffer, were to devise the educational system to be used in the institute. Before long Bernfeld, Hoffer and Anna had formed a working group to reflect on education and child psychology. A fourth, older, member, who already had considerable experience of working with children and adolescents, was to join the group not long after its formation: August Aichhorn. Already well known, Aichhorn had for a number of years been the director of a municipal institution for delinquent adolescents on the outskirts of Vienna and had just been admitted as a member of the Vienna Psychoanalytical Society. Anna had already had experience of working with deprived children as a school teacher. With Aichhorn she was to use this experience; he regularly took her with him on his visits to institutions and services dealing with delinquent children. Aichhorn was also writing a book at that time, entitled *Wayward Youth* to be published in 1925 and prefaced by Freud. As the drafting of the book progressed it was discussed in the working group. We will come back to this important aspect of her vocation when we discuss Anna Freud and the institutions she founded.

Anna became a member of the Vienna Psychoanalytical Society in 1922, at the end of the first stage of her analysis with Freud. Through her father, who had invited her to stay, she had been in touch with Lou Andreas-Salomé for some months. Their correspondence, which lasted for a number of years, shows how Anna had found a constructive maternal and feminine image in Andreas-Salomé. She found support, understanding and warmth in this relationship. In 1923, when Anna thought she should perhaps put some distance between herself and her father and move to Berlin, his illness became such that she had to give up the idea entirely and, on the contrary, led to a strengthening of their desire to stay together. Anna therefore set up practice in Vienna and began to take on a few patients. At the same time, with the help of Paul Schilder, she was able to accompany the morning rounds in Professor Wagner-Jauregg's Department of Psychiatry at the University Hospital of Vienna. Here, she met Heinz Hartmann. Forty years later, in her 'Curriculum Vitae of a Lay Analyst' given in a speech of thanks at Jefferson Medical College, where she had just received an honorary Doctorate, she was to say:

> Familiarity with the symptomotology of psychiatry was offered to me
> thanks to the permission to attend the rounds in the psychiatric teaching
> hospital of Vienna, then under Professor Wagner-Jauregg. This was an

exciting time in the particular department where I was a guest with Paul Schilder as first and Heinz Hartmann as second clinical assistant. The ward rounds, especially when led by Schilder, were highly instructive and what they taught was never forgotten by me. We all listened spellbound to the revelations made by the patients, their dreams, delusions, fantastic systems, which the analytically knowledgeable among us fitted into a scheme.

('Doctoral Award Address', in *Writings*, vol. 5: 512)

It was at this point that she decided to accept her father's proposal to take up her analysis with him again.

One of the difficulties of Anna's work as a child analyst, of which she was conscious, was her need to have a much closer relationship with her patients than was professionally required. She mentioned this to Max Eitingon (Young-Bruehl, 1988: 132), for she found it difficult to talk to her father about it. Among the first patients she analysed were children, those of Dorothy Burlingham. (We shall come back to this point when we talk about the positive transference that Anna Freud wanted to set up in child analysis.) At that point she had just met Dorothy, with whom she was to establish a warm and complex relationship. Over the years Dorothy was to become her life companion, sharing her children with her. Anna was to become a second mother to the Burlingham children, just as, to a certain extent, her aunt Minna had been to Anna and her siblings. It is difficult to give an opinion on the nature of the relationship between the two women, since even the opinions of the biographers are divided. We shall content ourselves with the remarks made to us by those who were close to Anna Freud and whom we have met personally. For them (I. 3 and I. 4) the relationship between the two women was not homosexual, but the fact of having been a mother to Dorothy's children was of great importance to Anna, who, through them, had her own family. It was also at this time that she met Eva Rosenfeld another positive maternal figure, about whom we will say more when we discuss the various institutions of children which Anna Freud was to found.

Anna Freud and psychoanalytical institutions

Anna Freud became a member of the Vienna Psychoanalytical Society in the spring of 1922, at the age of 27. At that time adult analysis could not be practised in Austria unless one was also a medical practitioner, so she officially became a child analyst. She presented a largely autobiographical paper, drafted with the help of Lou Andreas-Salomé, on the fantasies of some beaten children and day dreams entitled: 'Beating Fantasies and

Daydreams'. She attended the 1920 conference in The Hague, the first international conference after the war, as an invited guest. But it was as a member of the International Association that she attended the Berlin conference in 1922. Having already translated a number of psychoanalytical works from English, she then threw herself into publishing, devoting her time to two projects in particular: the German edition of her father's *Gesammelte Schriften*, finished in 1924 and the English translation of the same work, *Collected Writings* (see Young-Bruehl, 1988: 147), for which she acted as consultant to the Stracheys, who were doing the translation. In 1924, Anna took Otto Rank's place on the Committee and received the ring from her father. This was most certainly a very important moment for Anna: she was no longer a subordinate, having replaced the youngest of the six spiritual sons of her father.

In 1923, she was appointed secretary of the International Teaching Committee, which had been set up by Max Eitingon and whose object was to streamline the requirements for the training of psychoanalysts. This organization never got off the ground because the members of the American Association refused to accept students who were not medical practitioners.

When the Vienna Psychoanalytical Institute was founded in 1925, she became its secretary. It was a training institute, modelled on that of Berlin and its director was Helene Deutsch, with Siegfried Bernfeld as second-in-command. Even before the Institute was founded, Anna and a few other young psychoanalysts, including Heinz Hartmann and Wilhem Reich, had formed a study group. Soon she was also running a seminar on child analysis. Her friend, August Aichhorn, had devoted himself to the analysis of delinquents and criminals, as had Siegfried Bernfeld and Willi Hoffer. Together they were to continue their reflections in an informal study group on psychoanalysis as applied to teaching called the 'Kinderseminar'. This Kinderseminar was later to become a group dealing with child psychoanalysis in general. These various experiences were soon to give rise to some valuable theoretical work, which has remained a cornerstone in the field: August Aichhorn's work on adolescents (which we shall come back to), Siegfried Bernfeld's lectures on teaching given to the members of the Institute and to educators in Vienna, Anna's own lectures for educators and, of course, her various works on the techniques of child psychoanalysis in the years 1925, 1926 and 1927, on which we will go into further detail later. Rene Spitz, Helene Deutsch, Marianne and Ernst Kris were all to take part in and benefit from these seminars.

In 1927, at the age of 32, Anna became general secretary of the International Psychoanalytical Association. She was to be elected and re-elected Vice President of this organization several times and finally became Honorary President in 1973.

The problem of the training of psychoanalysts was of concern to Anna

Freud throughout her lifetime. She was in dispute with the International Psychoanalytical Association (IPA) on several occasions over the question of the recognition of child psychoanalysis and lay analysis, but never quite broke off relations. As we shall see later, she even went as far as creating her own training course for child psychoanalysts at the Hampstead Clinic, since she was not able to get child psychoanalysis on to the IPA curriculum. The training dispensed at Hampstead was finally recognised by the British Psycho-Analytical Society in 1970, and candidates of the Society were then able to train at the Hampstead Clinic.

In a lecture given in 1968 at the New York Psychoanalytical Institute ('Difficulties in the path of psychoanalysis', 1969 [1968], in *Writings*, vol. 7: 124–56) she again emphasized the necessity for strict training for analysts: 'The task of the analyst is not to create, i.e. to invent, but to observe, explore, understand and explain.' In the 1966 lecture at the Chicago Institute on the 'ideal institute' she had already broached the subject, as we have seen ('The ideal psychoanalytic institute: a utopia', 1966, in *Writings*, vol. 7: 73–93).

The selection of analysts seemed to her to be a formidable task; she was in favour of lay analysis, as was her father. She stressed the need to respect originality, using the pioneers as an example, saying 'the greatest contributions to analytical theory and technique and clinical analysis were made by people with very different professional backgrounds and *in spite of* all sorts of personal characteristics, individual qualities and idiosyncrasies, or perhaps, *because of them*' (ibid.) Her ideal institute would accept only full-time candidates, and would enable them to work in the fields of both adult and child analysis, because, she added,

> Since we now possess a technique of child analysis which is not merely a derivative of adult technique, but equivalent to it, it is no longer necessary to relegate child analysis to the end of training after the candidate has familiarized himself with the classical technique . . . [candidates] will be trained in both and may specialize in either in the future.
>
> (in *Writings*, vol. 7: 82–3)

Teaching was essential, whether the theory or the history of the discipline, but above all, future analysts should 'go into this new field actively and explore it with an adventurous and pioneering spirit' (ibid.).

For Anna, observing, exploring, understanding and explaining meant that the candidate should, in study groups, learn how and when to carry out the diagnostic assessment, so as to be able to reflect on whether child analysis was appropriate or not in the light of an understanding of the child's development. The analyst must also have undertaken direct observation of young children, so as to 'be able to complete the theory he has been taught about earlier development with direct observation of these processes of development at the time that they occur' ('The ideal psychoanalytic institute: a utopia', pp. 73–93, 1966, in *Writings*, vol. 7).

She also thought that future analysts should be taught to apply the understanding of analysis to related fields. This could be done in two different ways: one would be to modify classic techniques with new objectives in mind, psychotherapy for instance. The other would be to use one's theoretical knowledge and the experience acquired to deal with problems of upbringing, education, prevention, and so forth. 'It is a serious, though frequent, mistake to confuse these two methods of application by introducing analytical techniques into schools instead of analytical understanding' (ibid.).

Anna Freud fought all her life within the IPA for the recognition and training of child psychoanalysts, and for full-time training; but she was very much in the minority in this. She was, however, faithful to the teachings of Freud both in her ideas about lay analysis and in her conception of child analysis.

Anna Freud, psychoanalytical education, psychoanalytical teaching and psychoanalytical institutions

In the first chapter of *Normality and Pathology in Childhood*, published in 1966, Anna Freud wrote: ' it did not take more than one or two decades . . . before a number of analytic authors ventured beyond the boundaries of fact finding and began to apply the new knowledge to the upbringing of children. *The temptation to do so was almost irresistible*' (p. 4).[1] In his article in *La Psychiatrie de l'enfant* (1984b: 17), Serge Lebovici stresses the fact that 'in the first part of her professional career [Anna Freud] was a psychoanalyst and educator who did not separate the two activities and the theoretical foundations on which they are both based'. There are at least four possible origins for this orientation, which we must again stress was not that of her father.

Anna started out as a primary-school teacher, working at a municipal primary school in Vienna for five years. In her training year she had done a course at a municipal centre for deprived children, and became interested in teaching methods.

The end of the war found her and her brothers influenced by the socialist and Zionist movements. As we have seen, she worked for the American Joint Distribution Committee on a voluntary basis. She closely followed the setting up of the Baumgarten Institute by Siegfried Bernfeld and Willi Hoffer. She also attended the lectures given by Bernfeld to the Vienna Psychoanalytical Society from 1920 onwards. With Bernfeld and Hoffer she set up a psychoanalytical study group, the 'Kinderseminar', which met at the Berggasse. August Aichhorn was soon to join them. He introduced Anna to the welfare services in Vienna: 'He drags me [on Fridays] to all the most

remote regions of the city and shows me institutions and welfare arrangements and we meet the people involved in them. And that is really very
interesting, a special and very impressive world' (Young-Bruehl, 1988:
100–1). With Willi Hoffer they set up a course of psychoanalysis as applied
to teaching, open to both the Institute's candidates and to the educators,
teachers and social-welfare officers working for the municipality. They contributed to a magazine called *Zeitschrift für Psychoanalystische Pedagogie*, the
management of which was soon taken over by Willi Hoffer. This magazine
was to play an important role in the development of child analysis until its
closure in 1938.

In 1965, Anna was able to write: 'The alumni of the Vienna Course for
Educators can still be found in responsible positions in the children's field all
over the world, and quite especially in the United States' ('A short history
of child analysis', 1966, in *Writings*, vol. 7: 51). Peter Blos and Erik Erikson
are two such examples (see vol. 3: 2).

Quite rapidly, Anna herself went on to give lectures to the future educators, and these were later published in a book entitled *Psychoanalysis for
Teachers and Parents* (1930). We shall come back to these later on.

A third motivation, perhaps more complex in origin, had to do with her
relationship with her father; in particular, her desire to help him defend his
theories on psychoanalysis. As we have seen in the chapter on Hermine
Hug-Hellmuth, psychoanalysis was being attacked for attempting to intervene in the observation and education of children. Anna and her friends
thought they should go about things differently.

A fourth motivation stems undoubtedly from the interest Anna and her
friends had in teaching, directly linked to 'the therapeutic analyses of adult
neurotics which left no doubt as to the detrimental influence of many
parental and environmental attitudes and actions' (1965: 4). The idea that
parents could do damage to their children either by giving them too much
love or by depriving them of love is a constant in all Anna Freud's works
written in the period 1920–30, as it is in those of August Aichhorn. This
finding went together with the generous idea that 'by enlightening parents
and altering the conditions of upbringing [one could] devise thereby what
was called hopefully a "psychoanalytic education" serving the prevention of
neurosis' (1965: 4).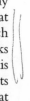

> The body of psychoanalytical knowledge grew gradually, one small find-
> ing being added to the next. As new discoveries of pathogenic agents
> were made in clinical work or arrived at by the changes and innovations
> in theoretical thinking, they were lifted out, translated into warnings and
> precepts for parents and educators, and became part and parcel of psy-
> choanalytic upbringing.
>
> (p. 5)

Here, one can see the outline of a great current in child psychoanalysis, which remains strong even today to a greater or lesser extent. In 1965, Anna Freud had to admit that: 'in spite of many partial advances, psychoanalytic education did not succeed in becoming the preventive measure that it set out to be . . . There is . . . no wholesale "prevention" of neurosis'. However, she also knew that: 'There are of course instances where an "analytic upbringing" helps the child toward finding adequate solutions which safe-guard mental health; but there are also many others where inner disharmony cannot be prevented and becomes the starting point for one or the other kind of pathological development' (p. 8). We shall come back to this again, when discussing the initial works of Anna Freud the psychoanalyst and her notion of the 'bad parent'.

This generous ambition began to take shape in the form of various insti-tutions. First the Baumgarten Institute, founded by Siegfried Bernfeld and Willi Hoffer after the 1914–18 war, and the Oberhollabrünn Institute, founded in 1918 by the city of Vienna and run by August Aichhorn. In 1920, it was transferred to St Andrä in Lower Austria, where it remained, still under the direction of Aichhorn, until 1922. There was also the first school set up by Anna in 1925, run by her friend Eva Rosenfeld (Young-Bruehl, 1988: 135–6). Dorothy Burlingham's children attended this school, as did Eva Rosenfeld's son and a number of other children of friends. The idea was to give disturbed children an appropriate learning environment. We should also mention the Jackson Nursery, founded together with Dorothy Burlingham in 1937 in Vienna for deprived children under 3. Unfortunately, for obvious historical reasons, this experiment only lasted a year, but it was a forerunner to the Hampstead Nurseries, set up in London in 1940.

Anna Freud's lectures were mainly designed for the educators of the wel-fare centres run by the municipality of Vienna, which were the most recent educational innovation by the socialist municipal council. The object of these centres was to take care, outside of school hours, of children who were in physical or moral danger if they remained in the family home, as a pre-ventive measure to stem the rising tide of abandoned children. In the first three lectures she emphasized the need to win the favour of the parents of these children, since it depended on them whether the children would attend the centre regularly or not. She stressed that a child's education began the day it was born, before going on to talk about the instinctual drives of the child and the latency period. In her fourth lecture Anna Freud went into the relationship between psychoanalysis and teaching. For her, the most important question for the educator was to know which methods of education are the most appropriate and which should be avoided at all costs, so as not to jeopardize the entire development of the child. She believed that a psychoanalytical pedagogy, based on psychoanalytical data, should consist of indicating, for each age, the appropriate dose of satisfaction permitted and the limitations imposed on drive. Psychoanalysis provides three fundamental elements enabling the construction of this analytically informed education. First, it is able to criticize teaching methods as they exist at present. Second, through its tenets, it widens the educator's knowledge about humankind and it makes the understanding of the complex relationship which exists between the child and the adult educator even more important. Third, as a method of treatment, it can try to repair the damage done to the child during the educational process.

Starting from the hypothesis (ibid., p. 54) that education has a very important influence on children in certain areas, she wonders what would happen 'if the adults in the child's environment were careful not to affect him in any way'. She was very interested in the experiments of the Russian analyst Vera Schmidt, who had founded a home in Moscow in 1921 for thirty children aged 1–5 years. Schmidt nicknamed the institute the 'children's home-lab'. It was almost a department of scientific experiments. This small group of children was looked after by specially trained women educators, whose job was to observe the drives and emotional demonstrations of the children while remaining quite calm. When the experiment had to be called off, for reasons to do with the Stalinist era, Anna lamented: 'The question of knowing what merit one should attribute to the earliest upbringing will now remain unanswered until such time as another experiment of this sort can be carried out under more favourable conditions' (p. 55). In these remarks one can see the evidence of a new line of enquiry, one which would lead her to the psychoanalytical observation of infants (Hampstead Nurseries).

August Aichhorn's book *Wayward Youth* was published in 1925. It caused quite a stir throughout Europe, and remains topical even today, not so much for the terminology used, which seems somewhat old fashioned now, but because of the ideas it expresses. The work profoundly influenced several generations of psychoanalysts working in institutions and with adolescents. In his preface, Sigmund Freud stressed the importance of this work:

> None of the applications of psycho-analysis has excited so much interest and aroused so many hopes, and none, consequently, has attracted so many capable workers, as its use in the theory and practice of education. It is easy to understand why; for children have become the main subject of psycho-analytic research and have thus replaced in importance the neurotics on whom its studies began . . .
>
> (Freud, 1925d: 273)

Recognizing that he may have played a modest part in this particular application of psychoanalysis, Freud was not, however, one to play down the social value of the work done by his friends the educators: 'From the experience and the success of August Aichhorn', Freud would draw 'two lessons': first, the educator must be trained in analysis, otherwise the object of his efforts, namely the child, will remain an enigma: simply teaching the educator about psychoanalysis is not sufficient. In addition, he stressed 'that the work of education is something *sui generis*: it is not to be confused with psychoanalytic influence and cannot be replaced by it' (p. 274).

In his book Aichhorn recounted his experience over a number of years as a teacher in charge of an institution for problem adolescents. He had considerable clinical experience. With the help of the psychiatrists working with him he first of all tried to define the population of children and adolescents needing institutionalized re-education. His work was based on a wealth of descriptions of clinical cases. 'Psychoanalysis is a tool which can assist us', he said, 'just as psychology is a tool' (1973: [1925]: 33). 'From what they [the children] tell us and from other elements in their behaviour, we can draw conclusions which we then fit into the way re-education is carried out.' He stressed the importance, when examining the children, of distinguishing between the manifestation or the symptom of deficiency and the deficiency itself, and of establishing a link between them in the same way as there is a link between the symptom of a disorder and the disorder itself.

If running away from home or stealing are only symptoms of the state of neglect, Aichhorn wrote, 'the manifestations are only of interest insofar as they serve diagnostic purposes; what needs to be treated is the deficiency' (p. 43). Wondering about the 'predisposition to mal-adaptation', he acknowledged that there might be a hereditary tendency here, but for him (and in this he was revolutionary for his time) adaptation also depended on the emotional relationship the child had with its initial entourage. This is what psychoanalysis had uncovered.

> The study of the causes of defective adaptation is not concerned with looking for what made the latent mal-adaptation appear, but with establishing what caused it. The cure for mal-adaptation can therefore not consist of removing the manifestation of mal-adaptation, while leaving the latent mal-adaptation to subsist (for example by treating the symptom, or using coercive measures); you have to go back to the constituant factors of the mal-adaptation in order to also remove the latent mal-adaptation.

And he adds (p. 45): 'Re-education will be all the more effective the less it lingers on the manifestations in its attempt to reduce the latent deficiency. That supposes a modification of the structure of the ego.'

The population of children and adolescents described by August Aichhorn presented defective adaptations that today we would describe as serious behavioural disorders, character neuroses, psychopathy, neurotic disorders and borderline cases. In his institute for re-education Aichhorn was to study the mental structure of each child very carefully. Once the diagnosis had been made, he made up groups of children and adolescents which were as consistent as possible for the educators who were to look after them. In this he acknowledged having been influenced by the work of Sigmund Freud in his *Group Psychology and the Analysis of the Ego* (1921).

For Aichhorn there must be transference as a lever for education or re-education to be effective. Doing his utmost to be precise, he tries to individualize this concept in teaching by differentiating it from the transference in analytical treatment as described by Freud.

> From the point of view of re-education, when we talk of transference, we mean the emotional relationship which is established between the child and the educator, without, for all that, insisting that it is exactly the same thing as that which occurs in psychoanalysis. In the same way, 'counter transference' means the emotional attitude of the educator to the child. It is evident that the relationship of a young person to his/her educator will be based on relationships previously experienced in relation to other people.

For Aichhorn, the educator must, if he wants to be effective, 'above all else', bring the child to the point of positive transference. 'He must methodically try to obtain the child's affection knowing full well that as long as he does not have it, no educational action will be possible' (1973 [1925]: 114). It is interesting to note here the similarity between the views of Aichhorn, talking about the re-education of children and adolescents in difficulty, and those of Anna Freud, talking about the necessity of a therapeutic alliance based on positive transference by the child if it is to undergo analytical treatment (A. Freud, 1926). For both, in 1926, negative transference induced a state in which neither re-education nor analysis was possible.

Everything would therefore be done in this institute for re-education, to encourage a positive transference from the outset, from the arrival of the child. The educators, Aichhorn writes, should show their *joie de vivre* and their tolerance to the aggressions of the children and adolescents. 'The less the institution looks like a restraining institution and the more it looks like a normal environment the easier it will be for the child to develop favourably' (1973 [1925]: 139). The frustrations inflicted on the children should be as light as possible. It is therefore 'an imperative educational condition', he writes (p. 141), that 'the meals in our institution should be the same for everybody, children and staff alike, made in the same kitchen, on the same stove, and served on the same plates'. (We know from experience in the institutions with which we ourselves are involved how easy it is for many little difficulties, many little oppositions, to stand in the way of achieving this ambition.)

Aichhorn also champions the idea of assigning a mixed couple of educators to each group of children.

The role of the female educator in a group of boys should not just be limited to that of the good housewife concerned with order, cleanliness of the house, the linen and the children themselves, she should use her position to favourably influence, in an educational sense, the personal relationships she has with the children.

He also thinks it is important that the staff be attached to the head of the institution, as he is the leader and 'the attitude of the educator to the leader automatically creates parallel attitudes in the relationships of the children to the educator'.

Aichhorn believed that the role of the biological parents in the formation of the child's disorders was crucial. In some cases 'the lack of love of the parents for their children was also felt objectively by us. In other cases it was only felt by the child.' In the first instance, he was talking about children who had undergone brutal rejection on the part of adults; in the second 'it was a lack of love between the parents who concentrated their emotions on the child. The child could easily feel that he was not loved for himself and reacted with antisocial behaviour' (1973 [1925]: 151). In the work of Aichhorn we can see the idea of inadequate, incompetent and even bad parents voicing itself for the first time. We shall return to this notion, for at that time neither Anna Freud nor August Aichhorn were able to differentiate between the real image of the parents and the parental imago internalized by the child.

In the final chapters of his book, Aichhorn stressed the pathogenic influence of an inadequate development of the ego and the superego in cases of inadequate adaptation. He considered that the foundation of social development lay in a 'primary adaptation to reality'. This adaptation is linked to the normal growth of the various functions of the ego, which can be impeded by both internal and external factors. An absence of primary adaptation leads to an impossibility in adapting to the cultural values of the community in which the child is called upon to grow up. Having failed to establish emotional ties with his love objects, he is then not able to construct the identifications which should have become the centre of a strong and effective superego. According to Aichhorn, owing of course to this lack of superego, the child no longer has any barriers against the instinctual forces which are in him and his ego is no longer able to tell him how to behave according to the rules of society. In this, too, Aichhorn was close to the theories of Anna Freud and, of course, therefore in complete disagreement with the initial theories put forward by Melanie Klein.

From this first work onwards, the concept of 'psychoanalytical education' made great strides, in spite of Anna Freud's remarks in 1965, when she questioned the idea which had not become the preventive weapon it ought to have been. There can be no prevention of neurosis, she wrote:

The very division of the personality into an id, ego and superego presents us with the picture of a psychic structure in which each part has its specific derivation, its specific aims and allegiances, and its specific mode of functioning. By definition, the various psychic agencies are at cross-purposes with each other, and this gives rise to inner discords and clashes which reach consciousness as mental conflicts.

(1965: 8)

This great advance was primarily used later, in the service of prevention in the United States. There was an ultimate extension in Françoise Dolto's 'Maisons vertes'. But in institutions for re-education the idea gradually disappeared, to be replaced by that of specific psychotherapeutic treatment in educational institutions.

Anna Freud and the psychoanalytical observation of the child: her contribution to the theories of Hartmann

Anna Freud was to make observation of the child one of the pillars of the psychoanalytical system she constructed: it was a question of completing the understanding given by psychoanalytical treatment. She was present every day in the institutions for young children that she founded. Ilse Hellman noted her remarkable qualities as an observer of young children, to which it should be added that she also listened daily and with great attention to the staff who were looking after them (I. 4).

Over the years the psychoanalytical observations of children were gradually to form a framework covering the various areas of the psyche. The knowledge thus acquired was methodically recorded in the Index of the Hampstead Clinic.[2] This contributed also in the creation of what was to become a psychoanalytical psychology of the child. To determine the interest Anna Freud took in this task one need only read her works, beginning with those of 1926, 1927, 1928, and continuing right through to the update in 1972–3 of her 1936 work *The Ego and the Mechanisms of Defence*, carried out with the assistance of Professor Sandler and the team at the Hampstead Clinic (J. Sandler with Anna Freud, 1985).

According to Anna Freud, it was in 1905, following the publication of Sigmund Freud's *Three Essays on the Theory of Sexuality*, that the first generation of analysts began to observe and record the behaviour of their own children, with regard to infantile sexuality, the Oedipus complex and castration anxiety. They were soon joined by a number of child specialists, who had themselves been analysed and were at liberty to observe the reactions of children on numerous occasions outside the analytical setting. Then, given populations of children with behavioural disorders were observed: for example, delinquents. Next, it was certain phases of the child's development: for instance, the initial relationship with the mother. After that it was specific difficulties (feeding, thumb sucking, separation anxiety, etc.). Wars, she wrote, enabled the study of traumatic situations: children surviving the concentration camps, being placed in orphanages, or having to be adopted (1951).

It was necessary to build up systematically 'a psychoanalytic child psychology', using 'the integration of the two kinds of data, direct and reconstructed. . . . While reconstruction of childhood events from the analyses of adults kept its place, reconstructions from the analyses of older children and findings from analysis of the youngest were added to it' (1965: 9).

She stressed that direct observation of the child by psychoanalysts was done with some reluctance. First, in the initial stages of psychoanalytical research, direct observation was considered to be quite negative. For the pioneers, their 'duty' was to emphasize the differences between observable behaviour and hidden impulses, rather than the similarities between them. Therefore, it was necessary to establish the fact that beyond obvious behaviour could lie unconscious motivations. Finally, the analytical technique itself needed to be perfected and the next generation of analysts, who had a tendency to confuse the content of the unconscious with its overt derivatives, had to be won over. This uncompromising attitude was, however, modified little by little. It was recognized that, in the treatment of the adult, what the analyst explored was not the unconscious mind itself but its derivatives. Interest was shown in slips of the tongue, faulty and symptomatic actions which revealed preconscious and unconscious impulses, dream symbols and typical dreams. However, it was important not to fall into the trap of 'wild' analysis.

Attention then turned to defence mechanisms as material for observation.

> The manifest appearance of children and adults became even more transparent for the analyst when attention was extended from the content and the derivatives of the unconscious mind, i.e. from the impulses, fantasies, images, etc., to the methods employed by the ego to keep them warded off from consciousness. Although these mechanisms are automatic and not conscious in themselves, the results achieved by them are manifest and easily accessible to the observer's view.
>
> (1965: 15–16)

Thus, with repression, if it is successful, 'nothing becomes visible on the surface' (p. 16) and, as Anna Freud emphasizes, one is surprised at the apparent absence of greed and aggression in a child. Other mechanisms, on the other hand, offer more tangible results to the observer. These are the reaction formations: overconcern, shame, disgust, pity, which can only be acquired by the child at the price of internal struggles against exhibitionism, messing, cruelty. The observer should also take an interest in sublimations and projections. In this Anna Freud was influenced by her father's work, *Inhibitions, Symptoms and Anxiety* (1926b). Moreover, it was due to this detailed observation that she was able to show evidence of, and describe, an additional defence mechanism: identification with the aggressor.

Over time, child behaviour was studied. '*Orderliness, time sense, cleanliness, unagressiveness* are unmistakable pointers to bygone conflicts with anal strivings' she writes (1965: 18). '*Exaggerated manliness* and *noisy aggression* are overcompensations which betray underlying castration fears' (p. 19).

A child's attitudes and activities became material for observation; children's play activities and games a source of information: for instance, watching the way a small boy played with his train might show his interest in parental intercourse, or in the inside of the body. What a child ate and how and what it wore or did not wear were all clues. 'Since each item is tied genetically to the specific drive derivative which has given rise to it, they permit conclusions to be drawn from the child's behaviour to some of the concerns and conflicts which play a central role in his hidden mind' (p. 21). Here, of course, Anna underlines the possible trap for the analyst which consists of falling into symbolic interpretation, the consequence of which would only be to increase the patient's anxiety and heighten the resistance. It would be a mistake to confuse observation (e.g. food preference) with analytic work (I. 3).

Then, after the defence mechanisms of the ego, the ego itself became the subject of observation. The psychology of the ego was included in psychoanalytical work. 'So far as ego and superego are conscious structures, direct, i.e., surface, observation becomes an appropriate tool of exploration, in addition to and in cooperation with exploration of the depth' (p. 22). The various ego functions were then studied: the child's ego control over the motor functions, the development of speech, memory, the synthetic function. If the discovery of the primary and secondary processes was due to analytical work, for Anna Freud, 'the difference between the two processes can be seen at a glance . . . in extra-analytic observation of infants in the second year of life or of preadolescents and adolescents' (p. 23).

In certain areas direct observation even became Anna Freud's method of choice for understanding the mind, in contrast to analytical exploration, for analysis had its limitations. She was thinking of the preverbal period and of all the disorders where transference is not possible. However, she immediately added a moderating element to this concerning very young children in particular. If, for instance, the various forms of separation anxiety were observed for the first time in crèches, 'vital facts such as the sequence of libido development and the infantile complexes, in spite of their manifest derivatives, remained unnoticed by direct observers until they were reconstructed from analytic work' (p. 24).

Finally, there are areas where direct 'observation, longitudinal study and child analysis work in combination'. A study of this sort, an observation of the behaviour of a very young child (16 months) (Hampstead Nurseries) and his analysis in later childhood (9–12 years) (Hampstead Clinic) is reported by Ilse Hellman and Ivy Bennett in Hellman's *From War Babies to Grandmothers* (1990: 31–54).

After some initial work in 1924–5, Anna again tried, in 1937–8, to carry out this type of psychoanalytical observation of very young children at the Jackson Nursery, which she opened in Vienna. It was a day nursery for children from deprived families under the age of 3 and they came with or without their mothers. The work was interrupted by the dramatic events which were to take her to London. She took it up again at the Hampstead Nurseries from 1940–5. 'The organization of the institution was ideal for the purpose of observation.' She was able to select both the children and the practical arrangements concerning them. Contact was maintained with the children on a 24-hour basis. Circumstances were such that some of them entered the nursery at 10 days and stayed there until the end of the war. Some of the children remained in close contact with their mothers.

'It was thus possible to observe the stages of libidinal and aggressive development, the process and the effects of weaning and the education of the sphincters, the acquision of language and the various functions of the ego with their individual variation' Anna Freud writes ('A short history of child analysis' in *Writings*). Equally important were a number of factors which could lead to distortions: for instance, the absence of the father, the absence of family life, the impossibility for the child to observe the parent's sexuality as he normally would, and so forth. The observers were requested to imitate the attitude of the analyst during sessions by letting the attention float freely and following it wherever it led. The contents of the observation cards were discussed in study groups. 'The participants knew that they were doing more than just collecting data: they compared the behaviour of the children with analytic theories about the hidden tendencies of the mind.'

After the closure of the Hampstead Nurseries at the end of the war the work of Anna Freud continued at the Hampstead Clinic. The Hampstead Index was developed, and the concept of developmental lines, so well described in *Normality and Pathology in Childhood*, was elaborated. On the theoretical level we can see how much Anna Freud's commitment to the psychoanalytical observation of the child was to be important in her work on the ego and its defence mechanisms. We shall come back to this work in the next chapter.

We can now try to understand the part played by Anna Freud in Heinz Hartmann's elaboration of ego psychology. Anna Freud and Hartmann were admitted to the Vienna Psychoanalytic Society at about the same time ('A short history of child analysis', 1966, in *Writings*, vol. 7). 'In analysis he was like a brother, not much older than I was: to be more precise, a halfbrother, since to a certain extent we shared the same father. We also entered the field of ego psychology almost at the same time, in 1930.' Anna adds that she entered the field in a rather conventional manner, by studying the defence mechanisms of the ego against impulses, whereas Hartmann, in a more radical fashion, was interested in a new angle, the autonomy of the ego. The first debate on the subject in which they both took part took place in 1936 at the Vienna Society over the first two chapters of Anna Freud's book: *The Ego and the Mechanisms of Defence* (1936). This is probably the most criticized part of Anna Freud's work, at least in France. Some consider that the part given over to the study of synthetic and adaptative functions of the ego in this work is excessive.

> Whereas other psychoanalysts stress the responsibility of the ego and the superego for turning us into neurotics, Hartmann and I have reinforced this aspect of analytical theory which shows in convincing fashion the immense effort carried out by the ego and the superego to preserve our health.
>
> ('A short history of child analysis', in *Writings*, vol. 7)

In a lecture entitled: 'Heinz Hartmann: a tribute' (1965 [1964]), given at the New York Medical Academy on 4 November 1964 for Heinz Hartmann's 70th birthday, Anna Freud underlined a number of similarities between her theories, as she had been able to formulate them from the data gained at the Hampstead Child Therapy Clinic, and the fundamental concepts of Hartmann's theory of ego psychology.

'For instance,' she says,

> I commonly use in our practice at the Hampstead Clinic, in particular in what we call the 'diagnostic profile' which serves to assess the development of the child, especially its psychology, the study of the development of the 'aconflictual' and autonomous ego as described by Hartmann, the study of the defensive organization of the ego and the vicissitudes of instinct development.

She stresses the interest of Hartmann's work, which looked at the maturing and developmental aspect of the growth of the ego. She even found particularly enriching Hartmann's concern to verify 'whether the autonomous functions of the ego are disturbed by the defensive functions'.

Anna Freud also finds of fundamental interest Hartmann's idea of 'the preponderance of certain functions of the ego in relation to other functions', and therefore his interest in the functions which undergo early or late development with regard to drives and also how its other functions develop. It was by taking Hartmann's concept into consideration that she devised the idea of developmental lines, which are therefore 'the result of the interaction of maturation, adaptation and structuration'.

She goes on to reiterate that she supports Hartmann in his refusal to take into account only the material supplied by the patient during analysis and when he emphasizes the value of direct observation. In the face of the critics she even maintains that Hartmann's theories are in line with the historical development of psychoanalysis. She is referring to the Sigmund Freud of 1900–1, who at that time had become interested in faulty and symptomatic actions, daydreams and children's dreams.

As a child psychoanalyst, she also concurs with his concept of infantile neurosis, especially when he says that the term is often used incorrectly. She believes, like Hartmann, that it is a misnomer to use the term 'infantile neurosis' to describe troubles specific to childhood, which are simply non-organic upsets of vital bodily functions and are limited to a single function, She approves too of Hartmann's work on the relationship between psychoanalysis and moral values. Like him, she accepts the idea of a double force 'exerting pressure on the personality and the constituent parts of the ego, helping the individual to acquire a moral sense when the tendency of the id is to work in the opposite direction' ('A short history of child analysis', in *Writings*, vol. 7).

However, these remarks of Anna Freud should be put into perspective: they were made at a conference whose object was to extol Heinz Hartmann. In fact, it would appear that she agreed with him a lot less than these remarks might lead us to believe, to the extent that at the end she reminds the audience: 'I hope to have convinced him now, even at this late stage, that far from being a silent critic, I am a vigorous supporter of his work.' Some of those close to Anna Freud (I. 3) told us during interviews that there were times when she thought that this work was in a sense a distortion of psychoanalysis. Because of her long and deep affection for Hartmann, this is something that could only have been said in private. It is true that she tended to be more interested in variations of the normal than in severe disorders. It is also true that she was interested in deviations from the norm, the maturing of the ego and problems of adaptation. However, her main interest, as she wrote often and at length, was to study the conflicts between the various agencies of the mind and inside the mind. It also seemed to her that direct observation tended to corroborate a number of discoveries made through reconstructions which had taken place during analytic treatment.

Anna Freud and analytic treatment of the child

As we have seen, it was in 1923, after the first phase of analysis with her father, that Anna Freud started to undertake analytical treatment of children. As a lay analyst, she was not able to undertake analytical treatment of adults in Austria (she only did this later on). Among her first little patients were the

Burlingham children, Bob and Maby. It is interesting to note the difficulties she met with during the treatment of children, for they are not without importance to her theories. In fact, in a letter to Max Eitingon, Anna states them clearly, as her biographer, Elisabeth Young-Bruehl, points out: 'I think sometimes that I want not only to make them healthy but also, at the same time, to have them, or at least something of them, for myself' (1988: 133). She believes these affects to be 'stupid', being well outside the framework of any professional commitment of the analyst insofar as treatment is concerned, and that they would, in the long run, also be damaging to the work done with the child.

Concurrently she organized seminars on the subject of child psychoanalysis at the Vienna Training Institute from 1925 onwards. In a letter to Max Eitingon mentioned by Young-Bruehl (1988), Sigmund Freud speaks of the lectures given by his daughter:

> The most enjoyable event right now is Anna's course on child analytic technique. I suppose that she communicates with you about it. But it is really the general opinion that she knows how to hold the attention of her audience. She tells me the content of each lesson on the evening before, and I am especially gratified that she does not, like a student, simply apply what she has learned elsewhere; she is unconstrained as she deals with the subject, she judges for herself and knows how to assert the particularities of this kind of analysis. Compared to the opinions of Klein, hers are conservative, one might even say reactionary, but it looks as if she is right.
>
> (p. 163)

Melanie Klein had indeed made her appearance in the field of child psychoanalysis. At the Salzburg Conference in 1924, she had given a paper on the technique of 'early analysis'. This conference happened at a particularly difficult moment, since it took place as Otto Rank was leaving the Vienna Society. Melanie Klein might have echoed some of Rank's ideas, especially that of original anxiety, but her differences of opinion with him far outweighed the similarities.

Anna Freud was not to reply until 1927 at the Innsbruck Conference, and her reply was based on the lectures she had given in 1926 at the Vienna Training Institute (A. Freud, 1927). Put together in book form under the title *Introduction to the Technique of Child Analysis*, these papers were the official opening salvos in the war of opinion with Melanie Klein. The object of the papers was to reply to Melanie Klein's assertions, but there was also a didactic content in that she was also imparting this new science to the students at the Vienna Institute and drawing the outlines of what was later to be called the Vienna School, as opposed to the Berlin School, which then became the English School, headed by Melanie Klein. Although quite well received by the members of the Vienna institution, this work of Anna Freud's was to be the object of very severe criticism, by Ernest Jones in particular, who even refused to let it be published in England, where it was only finally to make its appearance after the war.

The debate fired by Anna Freud's book was to become entangled with another, also very intense one: that surrounding lay analysis. Jones was also involved in this conflict, for he represented a compromise between the position of the American School, which required analysts to also be qualified medical practitioners, and that of Sigmund Freud, who said that psychoanalysis should also be practised by those who were not medically trained. It is of interest to note this point, for the fortunes of child analysis, as we shall see, were often linked to those of lay analysis. More often than not, those who became interested in child analysis were women who were not medically trained. The question revolved around children, women and the non-medically trained: all the ingredients required to turn child analysis into a by-product of adult analysis. Of course, there were also some who took pleasure in claiming that Freud was on the side of the lay analysts because his daughter was one. But things were not quite that simple: it was one of Freud's fundamental beliefs that one did not necessarily have to be a doctor to be an analyst. It is also evident that for both Sigmund Freud and his daughter to remove lay analysts, teachers and psychologists from psychoanalysis was to cut themselves off from a wide public interested in analysis and which in Vienna was seen as being very important, i.e. teachers at all levels and those in charge of the various administrative departments responsible for child welfare.

Introduction to the Technique of Child Analysis appeared in German in 1927 and was in book form the material contained in a series of lectures given to the Vienna Psychoanalytical Institute in 1926 (A. Freud, 1926). These were to be published in 1946 in the form of *The Psycho-Analytical Treatment of Children* (1926–45). It is interesting to study this work carefully, the first written formulation of her ideas, not for the purpose of criticizing it, which has been done often enough, but in order to try to understand more fully her line of thought and how it evolved. Moreover, the work is very moving in that it is a fine description of the early emotions that every young child analyst encounters when in contact with his or her first patients. It was to Anna Freud's merit that from 1927 onwards, both in her personal work and in her work with her colleagues, she was able to adapt her ideas and did so right into the 1970s, when she agreed to elaborate and expand on the principal themes with Joseph Sandler and in the seminars given at the Hampstead Clinic.

The first of the four lectures was entitled 'An introductory phase in the analysis of children'. In passing, and for the record, one cannot help but notice that Melanie Klein is mentioned in the second sentence and that Anna Freud shows her disagreement with Klein from the outset, and disagrees with the statement that Klein made to the effect that 'an analysis is of the greatest benefit also to the development of a normal child'. However, the greater part of the lecture was devoted to what Anna Freud called 'the phase of preparation for analysis, of breaking [the child] in'. It is a question, she says of 'rendering the small patient analysable as one would an adult, i.e. making it aware of its disorder, inspiring it with confidence in both analysis and analyst, changing the external recourse to analysis into an inner determination'. Using examples, she shows how 'the conditions necessary for the commencement of a true analysis: the feeling of suffering, confidence and acceptance of the treatment' could or could not be aroused in her small patients. The means she uses to 'establish a bond strong enough to be able to sustain the analysis to come' seem to us today to be somewhat inadequate, but having said that, they do square with everything that spontaneously goes through the mind of the young psychotherapist when he/she starts out. The child's affection must be gained and it must be shielded from influences which might be harmful to the analytic work.

The second lecture was entitled 'The methods of children's analysis'. She first goes back over the preparatory phase which opens the way for analysis and where, for example, she shows herself to be 'the little girl's ally and criticizes her parents with her'. She then goes on to discuss what techniques are possible in the analysis of the child by comparing them with those used for adults. She shows first of all how to use material from the child's dreams and day dreams and how to analyse its drawings. For her these are means of communication. However, she stresses the fact that this material cannot be used as with the analysis of an adult, for the child 'refuses to associate'. It is this lack of association, she says, that led analysts such as Hermine Hug-Hellmuth, or Melanie Klein, to look for another technique in compensation, which they believed they had found with the analysis of a child's play activities.

The third lecture was entitled 'The role of transference in the analysis of children'. From the outset Anna Freud questions Melanie Klein's play technique. She thinks it is of 'great value if one is talking about observation of the child', and finds it excellent with children who have not yet reached the level of speech. However, she energetically refutes 'the use Melanie Klein would like to put it to' in the psychoanalytical treatment of the child. It does not seem 'reasonable' to her to assimilate the activities of a child at play with the associations of the adult. Furthermore, she refutes Melanie Klein's position when Klein 'strives to find behind each of them [the child's gestures while playing] the symbolic value they might have'. Anna Freud emphasizes that a child lacks the notion of purpose. 'With an adult we do not consider ourselves justified in ascribing a symbolic significance to every one of his acts or ideas, but only to those which arise under the influence of the analytical situation which he has accepted' (p. 30). Here Anna Freud mentions transference – which alone can give a symbolic significance to acts, which without it would remain unimportant – and we touch upon one of the deepest divergences between the techniques of Anna Freud and Melanie Klein.

Anna Freud maintains that the child does not go through a real transference neurosis. It has to be said that the arguments she puts forward are not very convincing, since they are essentially bound up with the positive transference, which she believes must be introduced into the relationship with the child for treatment to take place. However, she also gives two other theoretical reasons which would justify the impossibility of a transference neurosis. She thinks that the child is not ready 'to produce a new edition of his love relationships' ('Introduction to psychoanalysis', *Writings*, vol. 1: 44). Indeed, she says, the first objects of the child's affection, its parents, still exist for it as 'real love objects'. The second argument she gives is that, contrary to adult analysis, where the analyst can remain a shadow for his patient, the child analyst must be 'anything but a shadow'. So, she adds logically, such a clearly defined personality can only be a bad object for transference.

Anna Freud concluded the lecture by stressing the number of practical difficulties met with in child analysis. We have, she says, 'to establish a permanent means of obtaining information about the child'. In the absence of cooperation on the part of the child's parents, she believes that the child might even have to be removed from the family environment and placed in an institution in order to undergo analysis. She then outlines a description of this type of institution, run by an analyst, where the analyst could become the object of transference. However, she finishes her lecture by acknowledging a contradiction, since the disadvantages of removing the child from the family surroundings immediately become evident. She can imagine just how difficult the child's return to the family home, 'where it has become a stranger', will be, living with people from whom the child has had to be 'separated with difficulty and not without violence'.

The fourth paper was called 'The Analysis of Children and their Upbringing'. Surprising in more ways than one, this paper shows clearly how Anna Freud was feeling her way along when setting up her analytical technique, a caution in part due to the place and role she gives to the superego of the child. She was to demonstrate that the child analyst had two difficult and effectively contradictory tasks to carry out: 'he has to analyse and educate, that is to say in the same breath he must allow and forbid, loosen and bind again'. This necessity for the analyst is related to the weakness of the child's superego, which means that the analyst 'must succeed in putting himself in the place of the child's Ego ideal for the duration of the analysis'. This is explained by the fact that she thought, at that time, that the child's superego had not yet become 'the impersonal representative of the obligations undertaken at the behest of the outside world'. For her, at that point, the child was still very much linked to its real parents.

Anna Freud found herself facing a dilemma which she did not know how to resolve. For the treatment to be carried out properly, the child had to be detached from the parents, but, if the analyst detaches the child from the parents there is a risk of the child's finding the analyst, lacking the superego that the analyst represents, with liberated instincts and therefore of being unable to adapt to society. A second contradiction appeared: if, in order to avoid the liberation of the instincts the analyst becomes, as she proposes, the educator of the child at the same time, what happens to the analysis? She therefore concludes, wisely, or with resignation, that analysis should be reserved for the children of analysts only, or at the most for those moving in analytical circles, i.e. for those with a background where one would hope that the parents would undertake the educational task from an analytical point of view. She concluded this not very optimistic lecture by stressing the positive side of child analysis. She saw three particular points: (1) the possibility of changing the character of a child under analysis much more rapidly than that of an adult; (2) the possibility of influencing the superego; and finally (3) the possibility of facilitating the child's adaptation to its surroundings.

A fifth paper was given a little later on, at the time of the 10th International Psychoanalytical Conference in Innsbruck, in 1927, and was included in the French translation of *The Psychoanalytical Treatment of Children*. Its title was: 'The Theory of Children's Analysis'. Three papers on child analysis were presented at this conference, which shows the interest of the psychoanalysts of the day in child analysis. One of the papers was given by Melanie Klein. Anna Freud stressed that this growth in interest in child analysis on the part of analysts was due to the three services it had rendered to date. First it had confirmed the ideas gleaned from adult analysis: next, by direct observation of the child, it had completed these ideas, as 'Mrs Klein' had demonstrated, she added; and finally, it had opened the road to a field of application, i.e. teaching. She then emphasized what she believed to be the two essential aspects of the work with children. First, she goes back to the idea that the child analyst should be both educator and analyst and justifies her theoretical position with clinical examples. In the second part of her paper she stressed what she believed to be 'the most important difference in the principle of child analysis compared to adult analysis', and that difference concerns the superego. Insofar as she considers that, contrary to adult analysis, the superego of the child has not yet reached an autonomous state, the action of the analyst on the superego had to be two-pronged; analytic and educational. In the last part of the paper she goes back to the necessity for the analyst to have a pedagogical attitude, which should render him or her capable of probing and of criticizing the educational influences to which the child is submitted, or even, when necessary 'to take their task away for the whole duration of the analysis from the educators and assume it himself'. Not only does she stress the need for the analyst to grasp the child's internal state, but she also thinks he or she must be able to 'determine exactly the external state in which the child finds itself'.

The interest of these lectures is, of course, essentially historical, for Anna Freud's point of view changed considerably over the years. We will come back to this point. However, the lectures did have a considerable influence on the development of child analysis throughout the world. They also provided a focus for those who treated child analysis disparagingly, and for those who were hostile to Anna Freud herself in particular.

In these papers Anna Freud based her theories about the superego of the child on clinical cases − actual treatments for children. It should be remarked, however, that with her friends Siegfried Bernfeld, Willi Hoffer and August Aichhorn, she had already adopted this theoretical point of view in the framework of their definition of psychoanalytical education. This theory was in fact based on the idea that a child was malleable, had a superego which was not yet formed, was very dependent on its real-life parents. Furthermore, its mental changes could be put down to a change in its external surroundings.

Anna Freud wrote *The Ego and the Mechanisms of Defence* in 1936. This work was much less controversial than her earlier writings and gave her an international audience and base. 'It was necessary to write *The Ego and the Mechanisms of Defence* in order to explain the fundamental thesis that historic development became both the structure, and the model for functioning, at the point when the ego was able to reach a homeostatic balance between external requirements, those of the id and external reality, and those of the superego', wrote Serge Lebovici (1984b: 22). Anna Freud positions her book with reference to the following two works of Sigmund Freud, *Group Psychology and the Analysis of the Ego* (1921) and *Beyond the Pleasure Principle* (1920), which marked a change in direction. 'The odium of analytic unorthodoxy no longer attached to the study of the ego and research was definitely focussed on the ego-institutions.' Anna Freud therefore placed her work in the perspective of a continuation of that of her father (1936: 4).

Using Sigmund Freud's *Inhibitions, Symptoms and Anxiety* (1926b) as a base, she set out to describe one by one the various defence mechanisms as the ego uses them to defend itself both against assaults from excitation of the instincts and from external excitation. She brings to light a new defence mechanism of the ego: identification with the aggressor. For her, this was one of the strongest defence mechanisms against external objects which generate anxiety. It was the discovery of this defence mechanism which led some to say that she was essentially interested in the adaptation of the ego to the outside world. To sum up her work with this statement would be profoundly unjust, however, for she was essentially interested in the way in which 'the ego adapts its defence mechanisms to the dangers which threaten it both from within and from without'. It is in the point of secondary repression, the point when infantile neurosis is created, that she was interested.

Anna Freud's theories were to evolve over the years, as we shall see when we look at the controversies with Melanie Klein in the period 1940–5 and the work which makes up the final part of her book *The Psychoanalytical Treatment of Children*, finally published in 1946. We shall also look at her final work, evidence of her later activities at the Hampstead Clinic, published by Joseph Sandler with Anna Freud in 1985: *The Analysis of Defense.*

But in the years which followed her first papers, Anna Freud had already abandoned the preparational phase of child analysis, with the setting up of a positive transference, under the influence of Berta Bornstein, a Berlin analyst who had come to live in Vienna and who began to develop what was called the 'analysis of defence'.

She also went back on her insistence that the child's analyst should also be its teacher. She also finally abandoned the idea that it was only possible to carry out child analysis in the latency period and came round to the idea of analysis at a very early age. However, she always stressed the importance of verbalization, insofar as this was 'known to be the indispensable prerequisite for secondary process thinking' (1965: 32).

As we shall also see, she never abandoned the idea that 'what is called transference neurosis with children' does not correspond totally to what can be observed with adults. She also continued to believe that the forming of the superego remained linked to the resolution of the Oedipus complex. Finally, she never used the concept of the death instinct. For a long time she developed the idea of secondary aggressivity, a reaction to frustration; in this sense she inspired Hartmann's theory of aggressivity. It should also be noted that she never used or integrated into her theories the concept of the internal object, or at least not formulated as such.

In conclusion, we would stress Anna Freud's wide concept of the field of child analysis, a vast science, serving which one finds what she called the body of 'childhood specialists'.[3] Psychoanalytic treatment is but one of the aspects of this field. She was interested in the child from birth until it left adolescence. It is therefore not correct to say that she was not interested in or did not treat very young children because of her own poor relationship with her mother. She was interested in young children, but thought that, on a theoretical level, it was not possible to analyse them before verbalization and secondary processes had been achieved. In general, one can say that she was interested in all ages, and in variations from the norm rather than in very severe disorders. It would seem that this was more out of disinterest in these severe disorders, than an outright rejection of them (I. 3).

Today, a number of English analysts, who knew both Anna Freud and Melanie Klein well, say jokingly that, if Anna Freud preferred children to psychoanalysis, Melanie Klein preferred psychoanalysis to children. Beyond this type of remark, two essential differences do appear in the concepts of Anna Freud and Melanie Klein, which we shall go into in detail in the next chapter. They differed profoundly both in their concepts and in their theories of the development of the young child. In addition, and from the outset, their conceptions of the field of child analysis differed profoundly.

Notes

1 Our emphasis.
2 See chapter 11.
3 This was how she liked to describe the psychotherapist–psychoanalysts trained at the Hampstead Clinic (I. 3).

6

Melanie Klein: early object relationships

Melanie Reizes was born in 1882 in Vienna, where she spent her childhood and adolescent years. She left the city in March 1903, when she married Arthur Klein. At no time during this period did she meet Sigmund Freud, or even hear about him or his work.

Melanie Reizes' family was Jewish: her mother was from a cultivated, liberal, Jewish background, her father from a family of orthodox Jews. Both families had produced Rabbis.

Melanie's father was a doctor and was 50 when she was born. His family had wanted him to become a Rabbi, but he had succeeded in getting himself released and had managed to sit and pass the equivalent of a baccalaureate (university entrance exam) and then go on to become a medical student and to qualify as a doctor, without the assistance of his family. His first marriage was a traditional one, but he and his first wife later separated. He married Melanie's mother, Libussa Deutsch, when he was over 40. She was much younger, at 25, and very beautiful. At that time a medical practitioner did not necessarily earn very much money, and this was Moritz Reizes' case. His wife was obliged to open a shop for exotic plants and animals in order to make ends meet.

When Melanie was 6 years old, a providential windfall improved the family's situation considerably. They moved into a larger apartment and her father bought a dentist's surgery to complement his medical practice. Hanna Segal (I. 1) recounts that Melanie remembered vividly this change in living quarters and the material well-being that went with it.

Melanie was the youngest of a family of four. At the time of her birth her eldest sister, Emily, was 6, her brother, Emmanuel, 5 and her second sister, Sidonie, 4. She was not really desired and was not breast fed, as the others were. In spite of this, she had a happy, harmonious childhood, in a close-knit family.

She greatly admired her father, was very impressed by his great culture and learning, his intellectual capacities and his gift for languages (he had taught himself about ten European languages). He was always ready to answer her many questions, but their relationship was not really close; his favourite was her older sister, Emily, writes Hanna Segal (1979). Above all, during Melanie's adolescence he suffered from serious mental deterioration, which got steadily worse until his death, when she was 20.

Little Melanie adored her mother. This is evident from fragments of her autobiography: "'My relation to my mother has been one of the great standbys of my life. I loved her deeply, admired her beauty, her intellect, her deep wish for knowledge, no doubt with some of the envy which exists in every daughter'" (in Grosskurth, 1986: 69). In reading this declaration made by Melanie Klein towards the end of her life, is one to believe, as Didier Anzieu (1982) suggests, that she was inclined to idealize her because death was not far off, feeling the necessity for good internal objects? Was it not also perhaps that after the self-analysis that accompanied the writing of *Envy and Gratitude* (1957) she had rediscovered a relationship with her mother that was rid of these destructive factors of envy?

In fact, they actually lived apart for only a very short time, since Melanie lived with her mother until she left to get married at the beginning of 1903, and again from 1907 until 1914, the year of her mother's death at Melanie's home in Budapest.

Klein's biographer, Phyllis Grosskurth, wonders about the maternal qualities of Libussa Reizes at length in her book. This energetic mother, who, in the last years of the father's life, had been able to provide for her family by working, and thus prevent it from being split up, had also energetically intervened in her daughter's married life when she had felt her to be in difficulty. For all that, was she a possessive mother, as Phyllis Grosskurth seems to think, wishing to recreate a home by taking her daughter's place in the eyes of her son-in-law? And did Melanie submit too easily to her?

Melanie replies in part in her autobiography: "'I threw myself as much as I could into motherhood and interest in my child. I knew all the time that I was not happy, but saw no way out'" (in Grosskurth, 1986: 42). We shall return to this unhappy period in Melanie Klein's life when we talk about her children.

Melanie's upbringing was liberal and permissive, religion playing only a very minor part, and Melanie herself was not at all religious. With the exception of one incident when she was 9 or 10 years old, in which, because she was very attached to her French governess, she became interested in Catholicism, Melanie was a life-long atheist. However, she did like some of the Jewish customs and felt great solidarity with the Jews. She had witnessed the persecutions in the intolerant Vienna of her childhood, and she was to meet them again in Budapest, when Béla Kun's government was overthrown and she was obliged to flee with her husband. In her autobiography she had this to say:

> In my attitude of sympathy with Israel also enters a feeling which, though it may have originated in the state of persecution of the Jews, extends to all minorities and to all people persecuted by stronger forces. Who knows! This might have given me strength always to be a minority about my scientific work . . .

> (Grosskurth, 1986: 84)

While Melanie's early childhood was very happy, it was on entering the latency period that she encountered death for the first time, with the death of her sister Sidonie, aged 9, when she herself was 5 years old. The little girl, suffering from tuberculosis and spending regular periods in hospital, had spent the last few months of her life in bed at home. This was when she taught Melanie to read and write; wanting to pass on her knowledge to her.

Death was to strike Melanie's siblings a second time: her elder brother Emmanuel died after a long and debilitating illness just as she was about to get married. He had had rheumatic fever as an adolescent, with heart complications and, knowing he would not live long, had given up the idea of doing medicine. They had become attached early in Melanie's adolescence through the poems she wrote, which her brother admired. He became very confident about his sister's talent and hoped that she would succeed where he had failed. 'He wished fate would give her as many happy years as the days it was going to deprive him of', writes Hanna Segal (1979). Melanie most certainly felt she was the trustee of her brother's and sister's desire to live, which she would have to try to achieve if she was to respect their memories and be worthy of their affection.

Curiously, however, on reaching adolescence, Melanie gave up the idea of studying medicine, which she had so much wanted to do. Up until then she had been a very bright student: her father had helped her work at her Greek and Latin so that she could go to university. She regretted this decision all her life. She had often thought, according to Hanna Segal (I. 1), that if she had been a qualified doctor the attacks against her would have been less violent. It was indeed one of the arguments used against her by Ernest Glover at the time of the 'Controversies' to deny any credibility to her work with psychotics. One might well ask why she gave up the idea of doing medicine: the apparent reason is her marriage. She frequented her brother's circle of friends and at 17 became engaged to one of them – a particularly bright engineering student called Arthur Klein. By linking her destiny to his she felt that she had to give up the idea of studying medicine because they would be required to live in small towns, far from universities. However, there were probably deeper, more unconscious motives. Her brother, whose illness was getting worse and who knew he did not have long to live, gave up his medical studies and began to live an unhappy and chaotic life. It is more than likely that, influenced by this situation, she did not feel she could allow herself to undertake what her brother had decided to abandon. She did, however, enrol at the faculty and did a two-year course in art history.

In 1902, Melanie was 20. Her father died in April of that year, and in December her brother died of a heart attack. She had not seen him for some time; ill and depressed, he had been travelling abroad.

In March 1903, at the age of 21, and not long after these deaths, Melanie got married and left Vienna. For several years she was to live in small towns, first of all in Slovakia, with her in-laws (with whom she got on very well), and then in Silesia. Very early on she realized that her marriage would not be a happy one. She had two children: Melitta, in 1904, and Hans, in 1907. She tried to take refuge in 'maternal love', as she wrote, but very soon she was to go through periods of depression accompanied by various somatic complaints. More and more frequently she had to leave her children in order to rest or undergo a cure of some sort or other. It was then that her mother took over from her. In a letter dated February 1908 her mother wrote to her from Krappitz (Hans was 1 year old at the time): 'It was no surprise that I went down like that, when I had to witness your intense suffering and could not help you" (Grosskurth, 1986: 49).

Melanie Klein was certainly not able to look after her two children in their early childhood as much as she would have liked. For them she was the depressed mother, often absent. Being conscious of the situation, she came to feel quite guilty about it.

Klein's biographers are divided as to the origin of this state. Several theories have been put forward: some put these disorders down to a naturally depressive tendency, following the two successive deaths in the family, others stress the matrimonial disharmony, and yet others say that it was because she was shut away in small provincial towns, far from Vienna, the capital, and the vibrant cultural life she had known.

In 1910, her husband found a job in Budapest and the family moved there: this was a turning point in Melanie Klein's life. She was treated for a nervous disorder and her state of health improved. But, most importantly, she began to read one of Sigmund Freud's books, one much talked about at the time: *The Interpretation of Dreams* (1900). Hanna Segal writes that thus 'began her life-long interest in psychoanalysis' (1979: 31).

The year 1914 was marked by the birth of her third son, Erich, and the death of her mother. It was also the year she met Sándor Ferenczi and underwent psychoanalysis with him. It is probable that it was personal reasons (to improve her health) that drove her to undertake this treatment, at a time when she was feeling particularly vulnerable and depressed after her mother's death. The analysis was to last until 1919, with interruptions due to the war and to the mobilization of Ferenczi. In the preface to the first edition of *The Psycho-Analysis of Children* (1932: 10) she expresses it thus:

> Ferenczi was the first to make me acquainted with Psycho-Analysis. He also made me understand its real essence and meaning. His strong and direct feeling for the unconscious and for symbolism, and the remarkable *rapport* he had with the minds of children, have had a lasting influence on my understanding of the psychology of the small child. He also drew my attention to my capacity for Child Analysis, in whose advancement he took a great personal interest, and encouraged me to devote myself to this field of psycho-analytic therapy, then still very little explored.

According to Hanna Segal (1979), Melanie Klein was to reproach Ferenczi later on for not having analysed the negative transference in her treatment; she also disagreed with him about his invention of 'active techniques'. It is interesting to note the influence of Ferenczi, who showed her what not to do during therapy. However, he most certainly also helped her to resolve many of her personal problems, which enabled her in particular to envisage separation from her husband.

Klein was introduced to Sigmund Freud in 1917 at a conference of the Austrian and Hungarian psychoanalytical societies. She read her first paper, entitled 'The development of a child', in 1919 at a meeting of the Hungarian Psychoanalytical Society, and it was published in 1921. The quality of her paper was recognized and enabled her to become a member of the Budapest Psychoanalytical Society. We shall come back to this, since the child mentioned in the article was her son Erich.

In 1919, the fall of Béla Kun was followed by repression and a wave of antisemitism, which finally drove the Klein family from Budapest. Arthur went to Sweden and Melanie and the children to her in-laws. She continued, meanwhile, with Erich's treatment.

In 1920, at the conference in The Hague, where Hermine Hug-Hellmuth was also present, Klein met Karl Abraham. She was so impressed by him that in 1921 she decided to set up practice in Berlin as a child and adult psychoanalyst, becoming a member of the Berlin Psychoanalytical Society in 1923. Her husband was to rejoin her there and they had a house built, but in 1924, after two more years together, they finally decided to separate for good. On the professional level, the years between 1921 and 1925 were years of intense work and a large number of publications. In 1924, she persuaded Karl Abraham to let her undergo analysis with him. This was no easy matter, for as a rule he did not take as patients colleagues living in Berlin. Hanna Segal tells us that this analysis lasted nine months; others say fifteen. It came to an end with the abrupt death of Abraham in December 1925. This time the analysis seems to have been for professional reasons, although Hanna Segal states that Melanie Klein had not been satisfied with her analysis with Ferenczi. James Gammill told Didier Anzieu that she took it up again because of the 'need to deepen the understanding of oneself in order to understand one's patients better'. These remarks were apparently based on something Melanie Klein is supposed to have said to Gammill in confidence.[1] This analysis had a profound effect on her; it led her to a true understanding of the analytical process. Abraham encouraged her to continue her studies on child analysis. In the 1932 preface to *The Psycho-Analysis of Children*, Melanie Klein wrote: 'At the First Conference of German psychoanalysts at Würtzburg in 1924, in connection with a paper I had read upon an obsessional neurosis in a child, he said, in words that I shall never forget: "The future of psychoanalysis lies in play technique."' She harboured a deep sense of gratitude and an unfailing admiration for Abraham for the rest of her life and his death was another cruel blow. Here, too, as with the death of her sister, even more so than with that of her brother, she was determined to continue his work. She always quoted him as her authority, believing that her work was a development of his, writes Segal (1979). She thereafter proceeded with her self-analysis on a regular basis. We can see an example of this in her 1940 work entitled: 'Mourning and its relation to manic-depressive states', in which she worked on the dreams she had in connection with the death of her son Hans.

The years 1924–5 were the period of the marriage of her daughter Melitta, a young doctor, to Walter Schmideberg, an older psychoanalyst and friend of Sigmund Freud and Max Eitingon. It was also the beginning of a very important love affair for Melanie, about which she talked very little, but which seems to have lasted on and off well into the period in London.

However, the death of Karl Abraham had a considerable effect on her standing within the Berlin Psychoanalytical Society, since Abraham had supported her. According to Hanna Segal, life became very difficult for her, since many of the members of the society supported the work that Anna Freud was doing. It was therefore with pleasure that she accepted the invitation of Ernest Jones, Alix Strachey (who had been to Berlin to undergo analysis with Karl Abraham) and Joan Rivière to give a series of lectures in London in 1925. The visit went so well that in 1926 she decided to move there permanently, and became a member of the British Society in 1927 at the age of 45. She took her son Erich to England with her in 1926, Melitta joining them in 1928. Her eldest son, Hans, who had followed in his father's footsteps and become an engineer, decided to remain on the Continent with his father. Klein was to remain in Britain until her death at the age of 78 in 1960. 'She never regretted the decision to move', states Hanna Segal (1979). From that time on, it would seem that she never suffered from any serious bouts of depression again (I. 1). Her work was to become her life from that time on.

Melanie Klein received a good grounding in psychoanalysis: several years of analysis at the rate of five sessions a week with two exceptional analysts. Was this sufficient to create Melanie Klein, the analyst? In his two articles 'Comment devient-on Melanie Klein' (1982) and 'Jeunesse de Melanie Klein' (1985), Didier Anzieu discusses her creative genius. For him (1982),

> creation of any breadth only happens at the waning of a crisis. For Melanie Klein the crisis was that of mid-life, the time when one enters maturity. . . . Two great cities, two great men, gave this youngest daughter, who had been dominated for so long by her siblings, this cultured exile with her insatiable ambition to be admired, her chance: Sándor Ferenczi in Budapest when she was 35, Karl Abraham in Berlin when she was 42.

For all that, should we adopt Didier Anzieu's remark: 'One does not *become* Melanie Klein: no sooner had she begun her work than she *was* Melanie Klein'?

In her autobiography (1959b), Melanie Klein stresses that she had a gift for observation – from the age of 8 or 9 she would observe children younger than she was: this unconscious habit was to continue, in particular, in her relationships with her own children and into her work on her own personal analysis. In addition, she says that she was very disappointed in the results of education early on and was rapidly convinced 'of the existence of something much deeper, the unconscious, which needed to be sorted out in order to change whatever it was that represented the difficulty for the child' (p. 33). By the time her son Erich (Fritz) arrived on the scene she firmly believed that change in a child's behaviour would not be brought about by education alone – even if it did follow psychoanalytical precepts – but by having the child undergo sessions of analysis.

We think this remark is very significant in that it shows clearly that Melanie Klein had little interest in 'psychoanalytical education', one of the roots of her conflict with Anna Freud, and also her certitude about the work that needed to be done in exploring the unconscious. She herself, going back over her life and her work in her autobiography, was unable to answer the question often asked of her about the reasons for her practice and theories.

> After all, I was inexperienced, I did not even know that I had a gift and had to find my way intuitively. I have often been asked about how I managed to bring to a successful conclusion the analyses of the children that I did, about the most unorthodox fashion in which I carried them out, often contrary to the rules established for adult analysis. . . . I am still unable to say how it was that I felt that I had to reach their anxiety and why I proceeded as I did. But I knew by experience that I was right, and

up to a certain point, the beginning of my play technique began with my first case.

Hanna Segal (1979) says that Melanie Klein 'described herself as primarily a very passionate person'. Her personality indeed appears to have been fascinating and complex, and it is difficult to put together her many and sometimes contradictory facets, as we know them, through what has been written about her and the remarks made to us by people who knew her well.

Ilse Hellman (I. 4) for example, who from 1940 was one of Anna Freud's close collaborators, had the opportunity of knowing Melanie Klein in her private life, because Melanie was interested in art and liked to discuss it with Ilse's husband, an art historian. Ilse Hellman describes her as a pleasant person, if perhaps overdramatic, lively and vivacious. On a professional level, however, she sees her quite differently. Her relationship with Anna Freud remained an enigma to her: 'How could these two women have remained a few seats from each other, side by side, in the front rows at the meetings of the British Society, without ever saying a word to each other for years?' For her, Melanie Klein frightened other people, yet she also describes her as being very beguiling: during conferences, for instance, great numbers of students tended to gather around her, and Ilse Hellman remembers being one of them.

Everyone agrees that in middle age she was still a very beautiful woman, charming, with great charisma. Her hats are mentioned, always different and always chosen with great care and taste for each conference, where they always managed to create quite a stir.

Hanna Segal (I. 1) mentions her warmth, her extraordinary vitality, her interest in people, which meant that she knew how to listen and that she was always there when her friends were in need. Anne-Marie Sandler, however, (I. 3) speaks rather of someone ambiguous, formidable, caustic in discussions, who could be frightening. The literature shows that she was the object of much love, but also of much hate, and that she had implacable enemies.

One explanation for these contradictions might be that, like Sigmund Freud, she remained faithful to her ideas, to the work she had done and had to do, and when there was a divergence over her work with her friends or her colleagues, she chose her work, even if it meant breaking off with friends and colleagues. Hanna Segal writes that 'She said once that compromise was necessary and useful in political matters within a psychoanalytical society as well as in the world; but there would be no compromise in scientific matters' (1979). The most stinging and most hateful attacks made against her were and are those concerning her relationship with her children. It would appear that once again there was confusion between reality and phantasy. How could a woman, capable of carrying in her head and giving life in her books to such monstrous babies, with such sadistic impulses towards the mother's body, produce in real life children who would not suffer from having such a mother?

Thus the death of Hans in 1924, in a mountain-climbing accident, was construed by some to be suicide. At a 'Melanie Klein Day' held in Paris in 1982, his brother Erich felt the necessity to mention this accident again, thus no doubt hoping that the truth would finally be acknowledged and the rumours laid to rest.

Melanie's quarrel with Melitta was, of course, widely used as ammunition with which to attack her. When she was still quite young, Melanie would take Melitta to psychoanalytical conferences with her; it was at one of these that she was to meet her future husband. It is of interest to note that in the 1932 Preface to the first edition of *The Psycho-Analysis of Children*, Melanie Klein says (p. 12): 'let me very heartily thank my daughter, Dr Melitta Schmideberg, for the devoted and valuable help which she has given me in the preparation of this book'. The quarrel was to occur three years later, while Melitta was undergoing analysis with Edward Glover. The latter, who until then had always endorsed Melanie Klein's views, dissented with her over her article: 'A contribution to the psychogenesis of manic-depressive states' (1935). Melitta was to side with her analyst and to show the same acrimony towards her mother. It is difficult – impossible? – to understand the reasons for such undying hate, which led Melitta to break off all contact with her mother, to the extent that she did not even attend her funeral. Talking about this period which she knew well, Ilse Hellman (I. 4) declared that she had been deeply upset by this quarrel. She said that Melanie Klein never responded to her daughter's attacks. When Ilse Hellman met Melitta at a seminar at the time she still remembers Melitta exclaiming: 'No, but have you read what she's writ-ten? How could she!' Melitta apparently felt persecuted by her mother's work. Should one conclude for all that, as some have done, that Melanie Klein treated her children more like an analyst than a mother? Should one think, as Hanna Segal does (I. 1), that the roots of this quarrel actually went back to Melitta's childhood and the poor relationship mother and daughter might have had because Melanie, depressive or absent, was not able to look after her daughter in a satisfactory fashion? Or was it one of the effects of the transference in the analysis she was undergoing at the time with Glover?

The work that Melanie did with her son Erich in the years between 1919 and 1922 also led to more attacks and more unkind remarks. It is true that in her paper 'The Development of a Child' (1921), Erich becomes Fritz. Should one necessarily conclude, therefore, that she wanted to hide the fact that she had undertaken the treatment of her son? That, at the risk of caus-ing damage to him, she had profited from her son's case to establish her career as an analyst? This would seem to be a case of misplaced criticism if one places it back in the historical context of the time. It is more likely that she changed the child's name in order to protect him, as did other analysts at the time, such as Jung and Abraham, to mention but two of the most famous, when they published papers about their own children (see also her letter to Ferenczi, in Grosskurth, 1986: 91).

A reminder of the facts might perhaps be useful. Erich was born in 1914, a few months after the death of Melanie's mother. She was feeling so alone, depressed and vulnerable that she had asked to undergo analysis with Sándor Ferenczi. In 1919, when she undertook her 'treatment' of him, Erich was about 4 or 5 years old. She was still in Budapest, but her husband was about to leave for Sweden; she knew she would find herself alone and isolated at the home of her parents–in–law in Slovakia. She was obliged to stop her analysis with Ferenczi; she was worried about Erich because of his various inhibitions. She believed in the therapeutic value of analytical treatment, since she had experienced the effects herself. She knew that in undertaking this work she was not unique, nor the first. All the analysts of the period, from 1905 onward, felt concerned about the development of their children and all, or nearly all, had proved their abilities as analysts by analysing their own children; we need only remember Karl Abraham going for walks or playing with his daughter Hilda. It is not at all certain that one should only read into her action, as Didier Anzieu stresses (1985: 28) 'a phenomenon of the displacement of an over–intense and non–liquidated positive transference, an identification with a lost analyst whose function had become introjected into a split part of her ego'.

It should be added that she continued this work in Berlin. Karl Abraham was to help her contain her anxiety in the face of some of the child's reactions, in what today would be called 'supervision'.

In her relationship with her children, Melanie Klein was neither better nor worse than other mothers. It is the study of her work which will enable us to understand her.

HER WORK 1920–40

Melanie Klein's work was considered quite shocking by many psychoanalysts, and to a certain extent still is. In order to understand her better, and before looking at her development and her relationships with those she acknowledged as her two masters, Sigmund Freud and Karl Abraham, we should take a look at what it is that might be considered shocking.

The object of scandal

From the outset Melanie Klein was aware of the negative reception that her work met with. Hanna Segal (1979) reports that Melanie Klein told her that 'when she first produced child material in the Berlin Society there was indignation, not only at her views about children's aggression but also at her talking to children about sexuality in such a direct manner. And this was more than ten years after the publication of Little Hans'. Further on, we will see just how heated the battle for the expulsion of Melanie Klein from the British Psycho-Analytical Society was, because apparently there was more to it than just an additional theoretical contribution or somewhat special clinical practices. In a lecture given in Mexico City in 1981, Jean Laplanche said:

> Nowadays, rather unfortunately in a way, people are no longer trying to burn Melanie Klein [at the stake]. She is simply neglected, left isolated. Sometimes her dogma is adhered to, a bit like following a recipe. Those who isolate and neglect Melanie Klein are those same people who believe in the tenets of a narrow rationalism, those who long ago forgot the interpretative lesson of Sigmund Freud; a lesson, the words of which still reverberate: *In a way Melanie Klein must be right.*
>
> (1981: 561)

The work of Melanie Klein was the result of a combination of personal and historical circumstances. Personal, because at that time as a lay analyst, and not a qualified medical practitioner, she could not practise adult psychoanalysis, just as Anna Freud could not; if she wanted to be an analyst, she would have to be a child analyst. We know, however, that very early on in her career, and already in Berlin, she was analysing adults. Personal, too, because she had two successive analysts; Sándor Ferenczi and Karl Abraham, who not only each had great hopes for child analysis, but also recognized her gift for child analysis and helped her to pursue this field. We should remember what she wrote in 'The Psychoanalytic Play Technique' (1955a: 4):

> I was at times perturbed by the intensity of the fresh anxieties which were being brought into the open. On one such occasion I sought advice from Dr Karl Abraham. He replied that since my interpretations up to then had often produced relief and the analysis was obviously progressing, he saw no ground for changing the method of approach. I felt encouraged by his support. . . . The conviction gained in this analysis [we are talking about Fritz] strongly influenced the whole course of my analytic work.

Historical circumstances, too, because although Melanie Klein first approached child psychoanalysis armed with the theories and techniques of Sigmund Freud, her point of view was to change. Hanna Segal (1979) stresses that, 'Whereas Freud deduced the psychology of the child from the psychoanalysis of adults – with the single exception of Little Hans – she studied infantile conflicts and structure directly in the child'. We should emphasize that, by analysing the child, it was the '*infant*' in it, which was already there, that she expected to see come out in transference. In this we can see how the creative genius of Melanie Klein led her to where Sigmund Freud had never gone, beyond infantile amnesia, which protects each of us, into the domain of the *infant*. Some saw in this a transgression in relation to Freud's works, and he never forgave her for this.

Should we, then, follow Jean-Bertrand Pontalis, when he wrote (1977: 128): 'She took it for granted that in going back further in time she would go deeper, and that at some point she would eventually reach a primal unconscious. Furthermore, by trying to analyse very young children, she would be able to participate in the "birth" of the unconscious and, as one might say, mother it.' In a footnote Pontalis explains that this illusion, or this hope, is plainly expressed from the outset of Melanie Klein's career. He quotes, for instance, from her *Contributions to Psycho-Analysis* (1948a): 'It is profitable and necessary to carry out analysis very early on in order to establish a relationship with the child's unconscious.' Primal unconscious, taking part in the birth of the unconscious, the mothering of the unconscious, all these terms seem to us to be totally foreign to Kleinian thought. Nothing in what she says, in the quote he gives, suggests anything like what he would have us believe, unless one only sees a chronological or genetic dimension to her theories.

So, did Melanie Klein's work do nothing more than move backward in time the processes already described by Sigmund Freud? It is true that she said that when she undertook the analysis of a child aged 2 or 3 years old its unconscious was in essence already constituted. It is therefore not *in statu nascendi*. But her work, and this is in essence where we disagree with Pontalis, cannot be reduced to just this particular dimension. What Melanie Klein states throughout her work is the existence in the young child of an internal world capable of unfolding in the transference that takes place in the treatment of a child by analysis. She also states that this internal world is based on the process of introjection, that it has nothing to do with the process of memorization, which is situated in a chronological continuity. Finally and above all, she says that this internal world is that of the primitive imagos, which must be differentiated from the images of reality, modified as they have been by the process of introjection. Melanie Klein states very strongly that, in the child as in the adult, transference during treatment enables the redeployment of an internal world totally different from the outside world to which the adult has had to adapt, and to a certain extent the young child too. In this, her work is a direct continuation of Freudian thinking. As Jean Laplanche (1983) emphasizes: 'The requirements of Freud and Klein come together, each giving greater depth to the other. This requirement is the recognition of the world of the unconscious, which is something quite different from the forgotten representation of our childhood.'

However, we need to go further still. The internal world, as Melanie Klein describes it, is full of monsters and demons, and this too was a revolutionary idea. The sexuality that she presents – pregenital and not entirely preoedipal, since she describes an early Oedipus complex – is strongly tinged with sadism. Taking up the Freudian structural model, Melanie Klein presents the work of the death instinct. She describes an infant whose first movement is not a gesture of pure love towards its object but a sadistic movement linked to the deflection of the death instinct. 'It is the projection which deflects libido and aggression on to the mother's breast' ('The origins of transference', 1952a). The internal world of the infant that she describes has nothing in common with what the infant shows in its visible behaviour. She takes care to state this in her article 'On observing the behaviour of young infants' (1952c). Here she is touching on something which is a taboo of the human species: the innocence of the infant soul. In one of our meetings with Ilse Hellman, we were struck by her difficulty in being able to accept the concept of envy as described by Melanie Klein. She is certainly Anna Freudian through her training, but her difficulty went beyond that, since she always said she was open to the various psychoanalytical schools of thought:

> I was never able to admit this aspect of Melanie Klein's theories. I took care of a considerable number of babies, especially at the Hampstead Nurseries, and I saw on the face of a twin what could have been the representation of an affect of jealousy, but I never saw anything which resembled envy, at least in babies in the first few months. (I. 4)

Melanie Klein questioned the Freudian theory of primary narcissism. She denied it, and tried to justify herself, as we shall see. In this, she was certainly influenced by the work of a group of analysts in Budapest to which she belonged, along with Alice Balint, Kata Levy and Elizabeth Revesz, and which started to do research in fields connected with the work of Sándor Ferenczi.

> The theory of primary narcissism was brushed aside and these researchers postulated object relationships, a primary link, and a mother–child relationship right from the outset of life. Based on that, Imre Hermann began his work which would lead to the theory of filial instinct and to the concept of clinging.
>
> (Moreau-Ricaud, 1990: 434)

The last revolution that Melanie Klein brought about, although chronologically the first, was the creation of a technique appropriate to child analysis, analysis through play. It was this technique which would enable her to study infantile structures and conflicts directly in the child itself. By doing this, she ignored a certain number of arguments which opposed the application of the principles of adult analysis to the child. This was the origin of her conflict with Anna Freud, for whom the technique of child analysis could only consist in the application of adult analysis. Melanie Klein fundamentally disagreed with and was therefore a rival to Anna Freud, who declared that her own research was a continuation of the work of her father.

Analysis using play activities

'[My] work with both children and adults, and my contributions to psycho-analytic theory as a whole, derive ultimately from the play technique evolved with young children', says Melanie Klein in 1955 in her paper 'The psychoanalytic play technique: its history and significance' (1955a: 123).

It is true that in psychoanalysis theory and technique are very closely linked. By creating analysis using play activities, Melanie Klein was willing to remain faithful to the fundamental rules governing the setting and the basic technique of analysis as it had been elaborated by Sigmund Freud from its beginnings in hypnosis.

Historically, as we have seen, the idea of playing with young children was nothing new in analytical circles in Vienna and Berlin in 1919. Hermine Hug-Hellmuth and Sigmund Pfeifer had already written papers about it, which both the young Melanie Klein and Anna Freud might have heard or might have read. However, no other analyst had ever claimed that play itself was the technique that made it possible to analyse a child. For Klein's opponents, play was *merely the means of applying* adult analysis to children.

There were several obstacles that Melanie Klein needed to overcome in order to succeed. If her principles and technique had been fully established by 1923 as Hanna Segal (1979) reports, she nevertheless fought much longer to get them accepted, and some analysts still refuse, rare though it is today, to accept them.

For her opponents, child analysis was not possible for a number of reasons. These were mentioned in the chapter on Anna Freud, but let us give a brief reminder of them:

- first of all, the very young child is not conscious of his or her disorder or even that he or she needs help, and it is therefore impossible to count on the child's assistance during treatment, contrary to the adult;
- a very young child cannot lie down and let her- or himself go and make free associations;
- a young child remains very attached to his or her parents and thus cannot effect a transference on to the analyst.

- a young child is fragile: it is dangerous to give free range to its drives, at a time when the superego has not developed (the superego only develops after the elaboration of the Oedipus complex).

According to Hanna Segal:

Klein's stroke of genius lay in noticing that the child's natural mode of expressing himself was play, and that play could therefore be used as a means of communication with the child. Play for the child is not 'just play'. It is also work. It is not only a way of exploring and mastering the external world but also, through expressing and working through phantasies, a means of exploring and mastering anxieties. In his play the child dramatizes his phantasies, and in doing so elaborates and works through his conflicts.

(Segal, 1979)

In other words, for Melanie Klein, a child's unrestrained play activities could be compared to what the dream represented for Sigmund Freud, the 'royal road' to the unconscious and to phantasies. Play fills the same function as free association for the adult. She was interested in inhibition in play from a clinical point of view. This symptom in a child seemed to her to be very important, revealing an inhibition in the phantasy life of the child. As with resistance to free association in adults, she believed that interpretation alone could liberate inhibition in play by relieving the underlying anxiety.

In *The Psycho-Analysis of Children* (1932), Klein stresses the fact that, in a symbolic way, children express their phantasies wishes and actual experiences through play. Her technique was to analyse play activity exactly as one would analyse the dreams and free associations of the adult by interpreting the child's phantasies, conflicts and defences. She points out the danger of just picking out the meaning of each separate symbol: all possible transpositions and other mechanisms appropriate to the working out of the dream must be taken into consideration; and it is important to not lose sight of the connection between each factor and reality.

In a letter sent in 1952 to Françoise and Jean Baptiste Boulanger, who were at that time translating *The Psycho-Analysis of Children* into French, she again stressed the relationship between the symbolism of play and the Freudian interpretation of dreams (Grosskurth, 1986: 391):

It is of importance to me to show that there is an analogy between dream elements (Freud) and play elements, that is to say, certain parts of the dream which are considered and certain parts of the play which are considered. In the same way as by analysing the association to dream elements the latent content is revealed, so by analysing the details of the child's play which are equal to associations the latent content of the play elements is revealed . . .

In addition, Melanie Klein defends the theory, and this is linked to her clinical observations, that if the child is effectively not conscious of his or her disorder, in the way that the adult is, he or she is, however, grateful to the adult analyst for resolving their anxiety and is ready to receive assistance.

Her clinical experience led her to believe, contrary to Anna Freud, that this feeling of meeting someone who could resolve his or her anxiety meant that the child would experience an immediate and very strong transference on to the analyst. However, and here too she tramples Anna Freud's ideas underfoot, to do this, one should not hesitate to interpret also a negative transference. The most well-known example is no doubt that of Rita, aged 2 years and 9 months, whom Melanie Klein analysed at the child's home and who was so anxious that she would not stay in her room alone with Melanie. Melanie followed her out into the garden and her interpretation (that Rita was afraid of what Melanie might do to her, and this was related to her nocturnal terrors) enabled the child to go back up to her room and to play with Melanie there. In her article: 'The origins of transference' (1952a: 54) Melanie Klein states: 'Because the life and death instincts, and therefore love and hatred, are at bottom in the closest interaction, negative and positive transference are basically inter-linked'.

Going even further, Melanie Klein intended to demonstrate on a theoretical level why the child can experience a transference on to the analyst. It is not, she writes, the existence of the child's real parents and the dependence of the child on them that prevent transference, since it is not those parents that one meets in the treatment of the child. One is only dealing with the internal phantasized parental figures, the parental imagos here, she asserts. This is the clinical finding that she made during the treatment of children, by carefully examining the child's inner world and the nature of the internal figures as they are transferred on to the analyst.

She furthermore maintains, thus respecting the analytical situation defined by Sigmund Freud, that 'a true analytical situation can only be arrived at by analytical means' ('Symposium on child analysis', 1927). She therefore insists that educational methods have no place here, and that they can only disturb the analytical process. She rebuts Anna Freud's suggestion that liberating a child's impulses in the absence of a developed superego might be dangerous: using clinical examples, she shows the existence of an early superego in children. She describes it as being particularly cruel, to the point that often the ego of the child cannot do battle with it. In attenuating the severity of the superego through his interpretations, the analyst reinforces the strength of the ego, thus ensuring a better development of the child.

The revolutionary aspect of Melanie Klein's theories of analysis through play led her progressively to draw up a specific framework for child analysis from 1919 to 1923. These are known to the majority of analysts and psychotherapists, but we shall nevertheless give a quick outline. The timetable for the sessions are rigidly fixed: 50 minutes, five times a week. The room is specially adapted for children. It only has plain, robust furniture, the wall and floor are washable. Each child should have their own toy box, adapted to the treatment. The toys, small in size, should be chosen with great care. There are little houses, human toys of two different sizes and representing each sex, farm animals and wild animals. She added modelling clay, paper, crayons, string and scissors. The room should have a sink, since water plays an important role at certain points. Play should not be guided by the nature of the toys and no toy should have any special significance, so there should be no telephone or games with rules. The toys should not be wearing specific uniforms or clothing. The choice of small objects was the result of one of Melanie's intuitions: Hanna Segal (1979) recalls that Winnicott greeted this choice as being 'the most significant advance' in this field. On reflection and with experience, one actually sees that it is because of their small size that children project their phantasy world on these toys so easily and so freely, by adopting them immediately.

Her early writings

In the period 1919–40 Melanie Klein wrote numerous papers and two books. Rather than summarize each of these articles or books we thought it more interesting to try to draw out the main ideas from this initial stage of her discoveries and theories. There are, however, a number of essential papers which must first of all be looked at individually.

Hanna Segal (1979) reminds us that 'Freud discovered the repressed child in the adult. Investigating children, Melanie Klein discovered what was already repressed in the child – namely the infant.'

The first article Melanie Klein ever wrote, 'The development of a child', was written partly in 1919 and partly in 1921. The first part, consisting of a paper read at the Hungarian Psychoanalytical Society, enabled her to become a member of that Society, for her work was found to be remarkable and innovative. The second part, in fact the continuation of the treatment of the same child (Fritz), consisted of a paper ('Analysis of young children') read at the Berlin Psychoanalytical Society in 1921, where she had just moved. The two were published as 'The development of a child' in 1921.

This first piece of work gave rise to a lot of comment. First of all because 'Fritz' was in fact her third child, Erich, but also because it was used by her critics to prove that what she was doing was not psychoanalysis. This is not, of course, difficult to do with a first piece of work, when the author is not very sure of her- or himself. This work was done when Erich was between the ages of 5 and 7 years old: he had a play inhibition as well as an inhibition in speaking and in listening; Klein analysed him at home, with his own toys. The goal that she had set herself, and this is much clearer in the second part, was to bring up to the conscious level, as with adult analysis, the unconscious conflicts of the child by using the same rules of interpretation of material and giving special attention to the positive and negative transference. It was for this analysis that she sought the support of Karl Abraham; he encouraged her to continue along the path she had chosen, with the technique she was using.

The article in 1927 was 'Symposium on child analysis', which received much attention. It was read to the British Psychoanalytical Society, and was a reply to Anna Freud's book *An Introduction to the Technique of Child Analysis* published in Vienna in 1927. The strength of the riposte is evident, both in its lively tone and in its uncompromising attitude on the essential features. On reading this article and in view of the evident considerable difference of opinion between the two women, one can see that conflict was inevitable. It would come in the form of the 'Controversies', fifteen years later.

In 1930 the article 'The importance of symbol-formation in the development of the ego' (1930a) appeared, in which Melanie Klein presented the case of Dick, a deeply psychotic (probably autistic) child, she had analysed. From a historical point of view, it should be noted that this article appeared well before Kanner's description of autism in 1943. 'I found from Dick's analysis that the reason for the unusual inhibition in his development was the failure of those earliest steps', writes Melanie Klein. This article was important because it opened the way for the analysis of psychotics, who, until then, had been considered to be irremediable because they were incapable of communicating in symbolic terms. It also gave an important boost to the study of children's disorders.

An article of fundamental importance appeared in 1935 entitled 'A contribution to the psychogenesis of manic-depressive states' (*Writings*, vol. 1: 262–89). It introduced a key element of Melanie Klein's theoretical contribution, the depressive position, and was read, in shortened form, at the 13th International Psycho-Analytical Congress in Lucerne. 'I have emphasized in this paper that, in my view, the infantile depressive position is the central position in the child's development', she writes:

> Failure to work successfully through this position may lead to predominance of one or another of the flight mechanisms referred to and thus to a severe psychosis or a neurosis.
>
> The normal development of the child and its capacity for love would seem to rest largely on how the ego works through this nodal position. . . .
>
> (1937: 289)

It was not until eleven years later, in 1946, that she was to define the paranoid-schizoid position. We should also note that if destructive and sadistic impulses are mentioned at the very beginning of her work, the Freudian distinction between the life and death instincts did not appear in her work until 1932 (in *The Psycho-Analysis of Children*) and was, of course, at the heart of her 1935 article.

Her book *The Psychoanalysis of Children* (1932), dedicated to Karl Abraham, consisted of two parts: the first was made up of the lectures that she gave at the British Psycho-Analytical Society in 1925, and here she mainly talks about the technique of analysis at different ages in childhood. In the second part, more theoretical and written later on, she propounds her hypotheses about the early stages of oedipal conflict and the formation of the superego; she studies the repercussions of the first anxieties on the sexual development of both sexes. We shall come back to this by looking at the main ideas in this first stage of her theorization.

During this first stage, Melanie Klein constructed in much detail, and always from analytical clinical observation, the inner world of the very young infant. She stresses the importance of the oral phase, more specially the second part of that phase, the oral sadistic phase and its influence on later development. She uncovers the psychotic anxieties which lie beneath infantile neurosis and situates the appearance of this phenomenon at about 6 months.

At the beginning of her analytical work, Melanie Klein was very sensitive to the intensity of the conscious and unconscious anxieties presented by the children she treated. She wondered about their origin, and was very sensitive to the aggressiveness that they showed, and felt that for them it was a means of defence. We shall rapidly pass over the play activities of Erna, for example, who made 'eye salads', wished to bite off Klein's nose, and make fringes in it, or played at having two people being roasted by a third, who then proceeded to eat them. For Melanie Klein, there was in this game a symbolic representation of sadistic and cannibalistic attacks by the child on the parents and on herself through transference. Little by little she hypothesized that young children are dominated by the unconscious relationship that they have established with partial objects of the oral stage, which have already been repressed.

Sigmund Freud and Karl Abraham had already both mentioned part-object relationships, but Melanie Klein was to make this one of the pillars of her theory. The introjection of a good and a bad breast are the basis for the construction of the child's inner world. To avoid theoretical misunderstandings, it is necessary to grasp the difference between the definition that Klein gave of the object from that given by Sigmund Freud. For Freud, the object is the object of the drive. For Klein, it is more complex than that: the object is the object of the drive, as Freud says, but it is also the object of the young infant, i.e. a more concrete object, with psychological qualities, and a personality; besides, whether it is a part- or total object, objects can be perceived by the child as being loving, hateful or greedy. This is explained by their origin, since Klein proposes that their construction is the fruit both of the perception that the young infant has of the personality of its mother, and of its own projections of feelings on this object-mother. These internal objects are not a replica of external objects: they are transformed by the process of introjection itself. The young infant thus incorporates objects such as the mother's breast, the father's penis, the combined parental figure. This phantasy of 'combined parents' requires some explanation.

Klein does indeed distinguish between different phantasies of the child. The very first desires and anxieties are related to the mother's body and the father's penis as part-objects. The phantasy of 'combined parents' appears when the father is distinguished from the mother and the reunion of the father and the mother is linked to sexual intercourse, which produces only one figure. Freud had already noted that the child always felt that the primal scene, its perception or its phantasy, was a sadistic scene. Klein stresses this aspect of things and was to show that here the figure hated by the child becomes hateful.

Klein shows that the child can identify with its objects, or feel in *touch* with them. Later on Bion was to build his theories on these very links. Klein's first discoveries concerned the Oedipus complex and in particular its pregenital forms. This was what she called the early Oedipus complex. She was first to contend that the Oedipus complex began in the second half of the oral stage, at the height of the sadistic-oral phase and was linked to the trauma of weaning. Because of this she saw it, initially, as essentially marked by a predominance of hate, which is showed by the extreme attacks made on the mother's body and the phantasies linked to the mother's body and to the parental couple. A little later, in 1934, she was to modify her theory, with the discovery of the depressive position. The beginning of the Oedipus complex was still situated at the same period, but was even more linked to a conflict where both hate and love occurred.

Depending on the phase of libidinal development reached, the child phantasizes the parents, exchanging various libidinal gratifications: nutrition or sucking at the oral stage; exchange of urine or excrements or anal penetration at the anal stage. It was by analysing these situations that Klein came to understand better the relationship of the child to the mother's body and to her breast.

> In the child's phantasy the mother's body is full of riches – milk, food, valuable magic feces, babies, and the father's penis, which (in this oral stage of his development) the infant imagines as incorporated by his mother during intercourse. His mother's body stirs in the child powerful desires to explore it and possess himself of its riches.
>
> (Segal, 1979)

At the same time, Melanie Klein was interested in the superego. Here, too, her theories were to differ from those of Sigmund Freud. For her, the superego was not the heir of the Oedipus complex; it did not occur at its decline, as Freud says, but, on the contrary, is part of the Oedipus complex itself, an integral part and is already present in the primitive Oedipus through the mechanism of introjection of the good and bad breast. She connects the severity of the superego essentially to the child's sadistic impulses. For Klein, the child's superego is more marked by the child's instincts than by its real parents. In this she is also in disagreement with Anna Freud. Klein went on to describe a number of mechanisms out of which the superego originated; first, she thought of a phenomenon something like the law of retaliation, then of an imprint of the impulse in the superego; finally, from 1933 onward, using the mechanism of projection, she was able to explain the creation of an internal forbidding, punitive, object, by the projection by the child of its aggressive impulses onto its internal object.

During the course of the analytical treatment that she practised, Klein was to bring to light the principal defence mechanisms that the ego of the young infant uses to fight against the psychotic anxieties which persecute him or her. In 1933, in 'The early development of conscience in the child', she asserts that persecutory anxiety is the result of the projection of destructive drives. She thus discovers the importance of the mechanisms of splitting (in the ego and in the object), of introjection and of projection. Little by little, she works out a new definition of infantile neurosis. In this she appears to contradict Sigmund Freud. For Freud, infantile neurosis was engendered by the Oedipus complex, unfolded as its resolution declines and is linked to the fear of castration. On the contrary, for Melanie Klein infantile neurosis occurs very early on as a defensive structure against underlying situations of psychotic anxiety. So for her, the going to bed ceremony was part of Rita's infantile neurosis and its aim was to master her underlying psychotic anxieties. The difference between the two theories is considerable. It is not just a chronological difference but a real change in point of view. For Sigmund Freud, the fixation of the libido (or a part of it at a given stage), is the *cause* of what will later on become a pathological process, by means of a regression to these fixation points (deferred action). For Melanie Klein, the fixing of the libido at a given stage is already an *effect* of the pathological process itself; if there is an effect, there must have already been a pre-existing conflict, which is the drive conflict itself. At any stage of development, if aggressiveness and anxiety are excessive, there is a fixation of the libido in order to overcome the anxiety: the deferred action arrives early.

Another important difference between the theories of Sigmund Freud and those of Melanie Klein, and as early on as 1932, was that concerning the development of sexuality in both boys and girls.

A brief reminder of Freud's theories might be useful here. For Freud, both boys and girls have a long period of preoedipal attachment to the mother first of all. At the time of the phallic phase, the little girl discovers that she does not have a penis and attributes responsibility to her mother for this. Hate for and rejection of the first love object follow, and the little girl becomes attached to her father, since she recognizes that he is the possessor of the penis that she covets so much. She asks him for babies as a compensation. In other words, it is the discovery of her castration complex that enables her to tackle her Oedipus complex. Then, after a long phase of sexual latency, she discovers her vagina at puberty. As to the little boy, he remains faithful to his first love object, the mother, tackles his Oedipus complex, and it is when he meets the paternal rival and the fear of castration that he, temporarily, gives up his mother. For the little boy, the Oedipus complex wanes because of his castration complex.

Melanie Klein's theories, on the other hand, imply a long attachment of infants of both sexes to the mother, an oedipal attachment, of course, but also pregenital. The father appears on the scene early on, becoming an object of desire and a rival for both sexes right from the sadistic-oral period. Klein says that the little girl is aware of her vagina very early on. She maintains that, as soon as the little girl turns away from the maternal breast and becomes interested in her mother's body – containing the penis – she goes into a phase of Oedipus conflict, which becomes more and more genital as the father becomes more individualized in relation to the mother. She does not undergo the sexual latency phase. Klein shows a sexuality in the little girl which is 'not a castrated version of male sexuality, but as existing in its own right' writes Hanna Segal (1979). With the little girl, the envy of the penis at the genital stage only appears as a resurgence of oedipal jealousy. With the little boy, the envy of the penis, in order to have the mother, and the fear of castration are of course present and will reach their height at the genital period but, Melanie Klein writes, anxieties already exist before this: the fear of being emptied, the fear of seeing the inside of one's body destroyed, and it is these anxieties which are at the root of the fear of castration.

With Fritz–Erich, Melanie Klein was to take an interest early on in the problem of inhibition. She rapidly concluded that all school activities were underpinned by unconscious phantasies which are to do with a curiosity about the inside of the mother's body, the desire to penetrate it, to attack, even to possess it. One only need read or reread her analyses of Fritz, who was the first and also Erna, John and his crabs, and in particular Dick, the little autistic child. Up until 1934 she used the expression 'epistemophilic *impulse*' to describe the child's desire for knowledge, since this desire appeared to be so fundamental. She defined the unconscious phantasy as being the instinctual representative, then discovered that this phantasy is expressed in a symbolic way in the child's play activities. From then on she enriched her concept of the symbolism which she had defined in 1930 in her article 'The importance of symbol formation in the development of the ego'.

Along with the clinical material, the analysis of Dick, the autistic child, shows the progress of Melanie Klein's thought. Dick had no symbolic activity when she first met him, he was only interested in door handles, which he liked to open and close, and in stations. Little by little he began to play. The phantasies that he staged corresponded to sadistic attacks against the mother's body, which were immediately accompanied by a state of extreme anxiety. Melanie Klein concluded that this huge anxiety of Dick's, too great for him to bear, led him to withdraw all interest in the maternal body and in any other object which might symbolize it in external objects. 'Dick cut himself off from reality and brought his phantasy life to a standstill by taking refuge in the phantasies of the dark, empty, vague mother's body' (1930: 227).

Her 1935 article 'A Contribution to the Psychogenesis of Manic-Depressive States', in which she introduced the concept of the depressive position, was really the beginning of the Kleinian school. This work was to bring her even more enemies who were neither in Vienna nor in Berlin, but in London itself. It was this article which led to the resounding departure from the fold of Ernest Glover.

This article was essential to her theoretical contribution. Until then she had described anxiety phantasies and defences in minute detail; from now on she was to become interested in the child's ego, linking its possible consistency to the working through of the depressive position. From the age of 6 months, she wrote, the child can perceive the mother as a total person. This change marks the beginning of the depressive position, a privileged moment, when the child begins to live his relationship with its other from a different perspective. The infant can now give her his total love and identify himself with her. Introjected, she can protect the child from the internal and external persecutory objects. However, she is not sheltered from attacks, the child's own or those of the outside world. Feelings of loss of object, sadness, nostalgia and also guilt for having attacked her are the affects connected with this position. The main task of the infant's ego, by working through this depressive position is, according to Melanie Klein, to establish in the interior (the ego) a good and sure internal object. This is the necessary condition of future stability. For Melanie Klein, working through the depressive position is therefore a constitutive period, separating the domain of the psychotic from that of the neurotic.

Klein then goes on to describe the defence mechanisms, called manic, which try to cancel out the mental pain linked to the loss of the object. They are denial of reality and omnipotence. But above all she introduces the mechanism of reparation and stresses its fundamental role in the development of the mind. This was to be the main theme of the 1940 article,

'Mourning and its Relation to Manic-Depressive States'. Here we can see the appearance of the creative aspects of the depressive position. Klein describes how, at the height of the depressive position, the ego can mobilize its resources and its love to restore the damaged object.

This article was essential to the work of Melanie Klein because it marked a new turning point. Destructiveness is no longer alone on the scene, the death instinct is organized into a dialogue with the life instinct so that the depressive position appears, as a threat and pain to the ego, linked to the loss of the object; but it is also at the same time a creative movement of reparation, of restoration of the object and its object.

In his paper '*Faut-il brûler Mélanie Klein*' ('Should Melanie Klein be burned?'), Jean Laplanche (1981) stresses these couples, these pairs of opposites which are milestones in the Kleinian system: introjection–projection, good–bad, total–partial, paranoid–depressive. The Kleinian system becomes simplistic and reductive, if one of the poles renders the other negative. We would agree with Laplanche that we need to 'work' them together. On the part–total pair, he writes 'the part is not the part of the whole, it is on another level entirely', in the same way that good and bad are not two opposite, mutually exclusive poles; what is important is the way in which they dialogue with each other, combining and tacking with each other. With the depressive position, Melanie Klein clearly introduced a dialectic rich in potential. We shall see further on how she was to recast her theoretical concepts yet again.

Note

1 'Melanie Klein aujourd'hui.'

7

Eugenie Sokolnicka: psychoanalysis is introduced to France[1]

Her youth: her analyses with Freud and then with Ferenczi

Eugenie Kutner was born on 14 June 1884 in Warsaw into a cultivated Jewish family. Her father was a banker and her mother a militant Polish nationalist.

The Jewish population in Poland at this time was large and, although it suffered from the prevailing antisemitism, it actively took part in the nationalist and democratic struggles of the Poles, since Poland had been carved up between the powerful neighbours Russia, Prussia and the Austro-Hungarian Empire.

Eugenie grew up in an environment where the process of assimilation was in full swing and thus identified herself more with the sufferings of a country reduced to slavery than with her own Jewish background. Several members of her family had taken part in the various Polish uprisings against the occupying powers. Her paternal grandfather had served in the Polish army in 1830; her father's brother had been deported to Siberia after the 1863 uprising. Her mother played such an important role in the movement leading to the 1863 uprising that she was honoured with a state funeral by the Polish government when Poland was finally reunified in 1918 (Pichon, 1934).

As with all children from a wealthy background, Eugenie's education was mainly carried out at home. She was given a French governess, who taught her French. Later on she did the equivalent of secondary-school studies and passed her baccalaureate. In her autobiography, Helene Deutsch mentions the difficulty she herself had had at the same time, in the same city, of persuading her family that she had the right to go to university.

Before she was 20, Eugenie was in France, studying science and biology at the Sorbonne in Paris (Pichon, 1934). She also attended the lectures of Pierre Janet at the Collège de France. Psychologist, pupil of Theodore

Ribot, a doctor in psychiatry and pupil of Jean Martin Charcot, Pierre Janet was the leading exponent of psychology in France. Believing that it was he who had in fact first discovered the existence of the unconscious, he was very bitter about the Freudian discoveries and had no hesitation in attacking Sigmund Freud himself.

Having obtained her degree in science, Eugenie returned to Poland where she married, becoming Eugenie Sokolnicka. It would appear that she then taught for a number of years, and this is borne out by a compendium of science for schools (1916) bearing her name that we came across in the Franco-Polish Library in Paris.

Between 1911 and 1921 Eugenie was to travel a great deal: Zurich, Vienna, Munich, Warsaw and Budapest. One might deduce that she led a very unstable life, but in fact these were the years of her training, in psychiatry first, and then in psychoanalysis, and this was central Europe, torn by war and all its consequences.

In 1911 Eugenie started her training in psychiatry in Zurich. She was to meet Carl Jung here and may have been one of his pupils, although she is not mentioned in any of his writings. In 1913 when Jung's break with Freud occurred, she chose the Freudian camp and went to Vienna to ask to be analysed by Freud. He welcomed her, as he did another former friend and pupil of Jung's, Sabina Spielrein.

Eugenie's analysis was to last less than a year. One can suppose that it took place according to the rules that Freud had just defined in his 1913 article: 'On beginning the treatment': 'I work with my patients every day, except on Sundays and public holidays – that is, as a rule, six days a week. For slight cases or the continuation of a treatment which is already well advanced, three days a week will be enough' (1913b: 127).

This was the period when Eugenie separated from her husband. From April 1914 onwards she was invited to the Wednesday evening sessions of the Vienna Psychoanalytical Society. On the advice of Freud she moved to Munich, a town where there were no psychoanalysts in 1914. However, when war broke out she moved back to Poland. She only remained there a short time and then fled to Zurich before the German and Bolshevik threat. In 1916, she was back in Zurich again and became a member of the Zurich Psychoanalytical Society. On 8 November 1916 she was elected a member of the Vienna Psychoanalytical Society. It was also at this meeting that Hermine Hug-Hellmuth gave a paper entitled 'About the fate of three lesbians'. After this date Eugenie did not attend the meetings of the Vienna Society again until November 1919, when she was to meet Anna Freud, who had recently been invited to attend the meetings.

In January 1918, she was back in Poland and thought of founding a psychoanalytical society in Warsaw. In a letter to Sándor Ferenczi dated 19 January 1918, Sigmund Freud wrote: 'The Sokolnicka woman seems to be in the process of founding a psychoanalytical society in Warsaw.'[2] In fact, she was not able to. It was also at this period, in the spring of 1919 in Warsaw, that Eugenie undertook a six-week analysis of a young boy with an obsessional neurosis. We shall come back to this in due course.

However, Eugenie did not remain in Warsaw. At the beginning of 1920 she went to Budapest to see Ferenczi: she wanted to undergo another analysis with him. This was to last about a year, until her departure for France, where she was to join her brother.

We know something of this analysis through the correspondence between Freud and Ferenczi, who were often to discuss this mutual patient. Judith Dupont has been obliging enough to give us access to this correspondence, which she is translating with a view to publication. In accordance with her wishes, we shall not quote the correspondence verbatim; however, we can mention the essential points. We would suggest that the reader who is interested refer to this huge piece of work, which is to be published in France shortly.

10 February 1920: Ferenczi informed Freud that Eugenie Sokolnicka had been undergoing analysis with him for six weeks and asked him not to mention this to anyone. (The secret was well kept. Ferenczi is often mentioned as being one of Sokolnicka's mentors. However, to date and to our knowledge, no one has ever mentioned this second analysis.)

20 May 1920: The Hungarian psychoanalyst again mentions the presence of Eugenie Sokolnicka in their psychoanalytical group. The meetings of the Psychoanalytical Society of Budapest take place in German, out of respect for her, he writes. In this letter he notes that Sokolnicka has given him a short, but very nice, report of an observation, a copy of which he is enclosing with his letter. We have every reason to believe that this observation is that of the little boy from Minsk suffering from an obsessional neurosis. It was published that same year in the *Internationale Zeitschrift für Psychoanalyse* (Sokolnicka, 1920).

4 June 1920: Freud invites Ferenczi to send him 'more personal details' in his letters. He starting urging this after hearing about Eugenie Sokolnicka's analysis. Ferenczi replies to Freud that same day with a long description of Eugenie's case. He gives Freud copious details and finally asks for his opinion. Eugenie has obviously become a 'controlled' case and even the object of a number of theories. Ferenczi was interested in her frail psychological state. It is obvious that she was not an easy patient: she seems to have suffered from a number of personality disorders. She also seems to bear a grudge against Freud for having adjourned her analysis before it was finished because of her diminishing resources, owing to the initial stages of procedure in her divorce. She often quarrelled with the other ladies in the boarding house where she was staying in Budapest. She is very unpleasant with Ferenczi, who she willingly describes as incompetent, constantly making comparisons with Freud. Ferenczi makes a suggestion as to the diagnosis and, exceptionally, to avoid any possibility of distorting his judgement, we shall quote him in full:

> It was quite striking (and this is what is most interesting from a scientific viewpoint) that my next supposition (personality disorders being like the symptoms of paranoia because they belong to the ego) was confirmed by the fact that an analysis of her character showed up traits of (mild) paranoia. She often dreamt of spies and was frequently worried about what others thought of her. Her fits of erotomania and her virility also fit in well with this partial diagnosis. . . . She feels superior to others, without exception, and in spite of her real talent, I can see in this a marked idea of 'grandeur'.

Ferenczi also stressed the very real depressive tendencies of his patient. Her threats of suicide worried him and forced him not to abandon her. But he also vaunted her capacity as an analyst to Freud; he believed her to be particularly gifted on a technical level.

15 August 1920: Ferenczi interrupts his holidays, because Sokolnicka seems to be taking the momentary interruption of the treatment very badly.

6 January 1921: Ferenczi tells Freud of Sokolnicka's intention to move to Paris, where she will stay with her brother. To date, most historians have thought that Sokolnicka was Freud's emissary in Paris. The only one to have had doubts was Victor Smirnoff (1979). Ferenczi was pleased with the analytic work done by Sokolnicka, which had softened her personality somewhat. She continued her practical training, working in the department of Dr Hollos, who at that time was in charge of the largest lunatic asylum in Budapest, 'The Yellow House' (Gero-Brabant, 1986). She was noted there for her inspired interpretations. Further on in the letter, Ferenczi notes that Sokolnicka still feels insulted by Freud and Otto Rank. (It would appear that she had been in love with Rank but that this was unrequited.) Ferenczi insists that Freud should give her recommendations to his publishers in Paris and to Jankelevitch, his translator.

16 January 1921: Freud replied to Ferenczi, saying that he would give her recommendations (to Payot and Jankelevitch) but only after she had settled in. (Perhaps he feared yet another change of address?) Freud was to help her, but remained very reserved with regard to Sokolnicka: 'Incidentally', he wrote, 'he [Rank] and I do not like her, whereas you most certainly must have "un *faible*" [sic] for that awful woman.'

A few years later, as we shall see, he would change his opinion somewhat.

7 February 1921: Ferenczi protests. He has no particular liking for this patient, but he appreciates her unusual talent as a psychoanalyst.

11 February 1921: Ferenczi confirms Sokolnicka's imminent departure for Paris. He mentions her case once again, saying: 'She does not suffer from a typical neurosis but from a morbid irritability.' She can be furious both with others and with herself. Ferenczi puts the source of her character disorders down to an anger with her father for having presented her with a little sister. Ferenczi asks Freud to see her and treat her kindly so that she can discuss with him her plans for moving to the 'West' (the term is Ferenczi's).

March 1921: Ferenczi is still just as attentive to the behaviour of his patient and asks Freud how she behaved with him. Finally, he emphasizes with modesty that she is still not yet cured.

We thought it important to relate this correspondence, since it enables us to state firmly that Sokolnicka did not come to France at the request of Freud, but of her own accord. In addition, it enables us better to grasp and understand the nature of the difficulties Eugenie Sokolnicka was to meet in her efforts to have psychoanalysis introduced more widely in France.

Eugenie Sokolnicka in France

With Freud's recommendation to his publishers, Eugenie Sokolnicka was welcomed by the circle of the Nouvelle Revue Française (NRF). The group, consisting of André Gide, Jean Rivière, Roger Martin du Gard, Gaston Gallimard and Jean Schlumberger, met at her home each week. They called themselves the 'Club of the Repressed'.

Edouard Pichon (1934) recounts the arrival of Sokolnicka in Paris thus:

For us, French psychoanalysts . . . the arrival of Sokolnicka in Paris in 1921 was a memorable occasion. Freudian thinking was only known at that point through a number of purely theoretical critical studies which did not really enable one to judge its effectiveness. With the arrival of Eugenie Sokolnicka we have a psychologist who has drawn her knowledge of psychoanalysis from the best wells and who is technically able to apply the method to real cases with effect. . . . Her connections drew her naturally towards the NRF literary group in particular. The importance that psychoanalytic ideas began to have in this renowned coterie through her presence was to have a powerful influence on the upper social circles of the city as a whole. And we can testify that because of the multiplying effect of being in vogue, conversations about psychoanalytical theories were the thing of the moment and the only thing that mattered during the winter of 1921–1922; most of the time these theories were mentioned in tones of blissful admiration, alternatively it was in tones of equally superficial mockery, and just as excessive. This vogue might have momentarily irritated some who would have liked to study the question with a little scientific calm. Madame Sokolnicka was criticized for having created this vogue, but one must remember that she contacted those that she was able to; that the literary circles she moved in were far from being negligable, and as soon as she could, she started to contact the medical profession.

During the winter of 1922–3, she gave some lectures at the Ecole des Hautes Etudes Sociales and it was here that Paul Bourget introduced her to Georges Heuyer, a hospital doctor who was at that time Professor Dupre's assistant at the Sainte Anne psychiatric hospital, and it was Heuyer who gained her admittance to this quintessential citadel of French psychiatry.

When we spoke to Henri Faure, he told us an interesting anecdote (given to him by Georges Heuyer) about this crucial moment when she came up against the Parisian psychiatric world for the first time:

When he had reached a venerable age, Professor Georges Heuyer recounted to me several times at his home some of the many vicissitudes of his long career. Amongst other things he liked to reminisce about that strange person, Mrs Eugenie Sokolnicka. Of Polish origin, she had arrived in France in 1921 and had contacted Georges Heuyer in 1922 through Paul Bourget. A lay psychoanalyst, pupil of Jung but analysed by Freud, she wished to be given introductions to the psychiatric hospitals in Paris and to introduce them to psychoanalysis. At that time Georges Heuyer was temporarily holding the post of professor of mental health at Sainte Anne psychiatric hospital and he opened up his department to her. For three months she took part in the weekly meetings with the various psychiatrists where cases were studied and patients were presented. (One of the psychiatrists, René Laforgue, was to be analysed by her later on.) But Georges Dumas tended to ask Mrs Sokolnicka a lot of embarrassing questions. After three months, she asserted that she was not being taken seriously and never went back to Sainte Anne. She set up in private practice.

Although the historians of psychoanalysis have maintained until now that Eugenie Sokolnicka was sent packing from Sainte Anne, in the light of these remarks by Georges Heuyer and from what we ourselves know of her, it seems clear to us that she did in fact leave this stronghold of French psychiatry of her own volition. However, Eugenie did not fail entirely in this highly reticent medical world, since she became René Laforgue's analyst (he was Professor Claude's assistant) and also that of Edouard Pichon, paediatrician, friend of Laforgue and son-in-law of Pierre Janet.

Henceforth, Eugenie Sokolnicka's route would mingle with that of the history of the psychoanalytical movement in France which had really just began.

It is clear that for this analyst, who was not a qualified medical practitioner, who had little or no backing from the Master and who was not recognized by the big guns at Sainte Anne, it would be difficult to impose herself as the founder of a movement. It was the analysand, the pupil, Laforgue, who grasped the torch that his analyst had, voluntarily or involuntarily, surrendered to him.

René Laforgue wrote to Freud, inviting him to Paris to give a series of lectures at the Collège de France (just after Einstein) and asking him to use his influence with Professor Claude to give support to Eugenie – Claude wanted her barred from all clinical work because she was not a medical practitioner. In a short reply, Freud put forward a number of reservations. He was certainly pleased to be contacted by Laforgue 'about whom he had already heard so much' (in 1923, as far as we know, only Eugenie Sokolnicka was in a position to have mentioned Laforgue to Freud, perhaps as part of a 'controlled' analysis). But from the outset Freud put him 'on guard' concerning the subject of the article he and Edouard Pichon had just written, saying: 'One can gain some support by concessions to public opinion or to prevailing prejudices.' Already ill, Freud was obliged to turn the invitation to Paris down, at the same time deeply regretting that he would not be able to come and give some support to Sokolnicka's position. In fact, Freud did back Eugenie right from this first contact made by Laforgue. He was surprised at Laforgue's disagreements with her and said so. He therefore wrote to Laforgue: 'We would have liked to learn that you were on good terms with Madame Sokolnicka for we have known her for a long time and cannot see her as anything but our legitimate representative.'

It is this sentence which has prompted most historians of the psychoanalytical movement to say that she was Freud's emissary in Paris. In fact, it would appear that from the start (1923–4) Freud preferred to use both of them to try to establish psychoanalysis in France. Eugenie Sokolnicka embodied *Laienanalyse* and a certain orthodoxy, but was not well tolerated by the medical establishment and obviously had no widespread 'political' standing in the psychoanalytical world. René Laforgue was suspected of making concessions from the start. His opinions on theory appear to be weak, but he had the ear of the big names of French psychiatry and was a good organizer who rapidly obtained a reputation for himself. Freud appears to have been trying to stage a rather surprising *pas de deux* between Sokolnicka and Laforgue.

But neither Sokolnicka nor Laforgue were really to gain the Master's confidence. Freud was not to find the person he felt he could really rely on until 1926, in the shape of Princess George of Greece, and from the moment that this 'Bonaparte in skirts' (as Roudinesco described her) started to attend to things in France, the name of Sokolnicka disappeared from the correspondence between Freud and Laforgue.

In August 1926, 'the first conference of French language psychoanalysts took place in Geneva. René Laforgue presented a paper entitled: Schizophenia and schizonoia. And on November 4th 1926 Her Royal Highness, Princess George of Greece, Eugenie Sokolnicka, Professor Hesnard, and Doctors Allendy, Borel, René Laforgue, Lowenstein, Georges Parcheminey and Edouard Pichon founded the Paris Psychoanalytical Society (SPP.)'

Odier and de Saussure, two Swiss analysts joined them soon afterwards. And on 20 December Henri Codet was elected as a full member of the 'Society of the Twelve Founders', which was now complete.

Eugenie Sokolnicka was Deputy Chairman of the society (from the end of 1926 until 1928, and René Laforgue Chairman. It would appear that she mainly played the role of technician and teacher (Pichon, 1934), but to chart her progress through the young French psychoanalytical movement is not an easy task. It should be remembered that her teaching was essentially oral in nature and that her knowledge was most certainly passed on during her analytical treatments.

Pichon (1934) states:

So, although Eugenie Sokolnicka held no medical diplomas, she was the only person one could go to to learn about psychoanalysis if one believed, as I did, that there was something there which should not be ignored. I am not one to forget how much I owe her. The long hours of her time she was kind enough to give me in those days, the friendship she continued to show me afterwards: I was able to profit so much from her and I would be an ungrateful wretch indeed not to recognize it.

Eugenie Sokolnicka, who had already practised analysis on children, must have taught this young paediatrician most of what she knew. Later on, at the height of his career, he was to publish a study manual: *The Psychic Development of the Child and Adolescent* (1936).

Whereas Pichon's only object was to build a teaching system using Freudian theories, Sophie Morgenstern, another of Sokolnicka's analysands, was actually making a theoretical and clinical contribution to the field of child psychoanalysis. We do not know exactly when Sokolnicka and Morgenstern (who was also Jewish and Polish and for whom the future was, unfortunately, to provide other points in common) met around the analyst's couch, but it is most likely that this was prior to 1924, for this was the year she arrived in France and shortly afterwards was present at the foundation of the new Department of Infantile Neuro-Psychiatry with Professor Heuyer.

Françoise Dolto, to whom we talked, said she had learned a lot from Sophie Morgenstern. She also told us she had never heard of Eugenie Sokolnicka and seemed to be under the impression that Morgenstern's analyst was Freud himself.

Hanna Segal met Sokolnicka, who was a friend of her parents, when she was living in Geneva. She was about 15 years old at the time. She remembered the wilful seductiveness of this woman, who seemed no longer very young, her quest for adventures with men, her somewhat hectic love life, a state of confusion. At that period the publisher Gallimard was pursuing Eugenie. She also remembered going for a walk with Eugenie, just the two of them, and the present Eugenie gave her: it was a hand-written letter by Freud himself. Hanna was ecstatic because at that time she was a fervent autograph collector.

From about 1932–3 Sokolnicka slowly disappeared from the French psychoanalytical circle that she had worked so hard to promote since its inception. She had not taken part in any international psychoanalytical conferences for some time and no longer gave papers at the most important meetings in France. Her articles in the *Revue française de psychanalyse* became rarer. Her last paper published in this journal (23 May 1932) mentions 'a case of rapid cure' in which she attributes the success of the treatment to the peculiar mental structure of her patient, rather than to her own talent. One can perhaps see in this not the mark of humility but rather the beginning of the depressive spiral and its accompanying self-depreciation.

Her clientele was diminishing. She did not even seem to do any training analysis and her financial resources were considerably diminished.

Whether by chance or historical fatality, Eugenie Sokolnicka's existential crisis took place against the sombre backdrop of the looming world economic crisis: the economic slump that was to bring scarcity, unemployment and rising antisemitism, which in turn prepared the way for the Nazi era.

At the same time, French psychoanalysts 'continue to get worked up about the long-awaited creation of an institute of psychoanalysis which finally happened in January 10th 1934' (de Mijolla, 1982). Marie Bonaparte was appointed Director of the Institute, at 137 Boulevard Saint-Germain, where the teaching of psychoanalysis was begun. A careful selection was made of the teachers to ensure the right 'political' balance. It fell to Eugenie Sokolnicka to deal with 'psychoanalysis of character disorders' on the Wednesdays of 2 and 23 May 1934. It is difficult to know today whether these lectures were actually given, since all the files for 1934 have disappeared from the Institute. (This information was provided by Alain de Mijolla.)

On Saturday 19 May 1934, practically on the anniversary of the death of Sándor Ferenczi, who in earlier times had given her much support, Eugenie Kutner-Sokolnicka committed suicide by turning on the gas in her apartment. Sophie Morgenstern was to take up the torch of child psychoanalysis in Paris.

Analysis of obsessional neurosis in a child: André Gide's Boris

In 1920, Eugenie Sokolnicka published an article in the *Internationale Zeitschrift für Psychoanalyse* entitled: 'The Analysis of a Case of Infantile Obsessional Neurosis'. It aroused wide interest and was translated into

English and published in the *International Journal of Psycho-Analysis* in 1922 and then in Russia in 1924. The article was not published in France until 1968, when it was translated by Dr Gourevitch and published in the *Revue de neuropsychiatrie et d'hygiène mentale de l'enfance*.

In this article Sokolnicka was pioneering new ground, since it was one of the first analyses of children to be published. It came several years after those of Hermine Hug-Hellmuth and was well before the first of Anna Freud's works, but was contemporaneous with the first of Melanie Klein's articles (1921).

The analytical treatment of a 10-and-a-half-year-old boy

In April 1919 a doctor had sent a thin, sickly young boy from Minsk to Eugenie Sokolnicka to be analysed. He was suffering from a phobia of being touched, which meant that his mother was forced to feed and dress him herself. To treat this case, and with the family's cooperation, Sokolnicka applied the usual rules of psychoanalysis which specify the setting. The child was to go to her home, regularly (most likely every day). The treatment lasted for six weeks and was crowned with success in that the symptoms and rituals of the obsession disappeared.

Her observations abound in clinical details. The touch phobia was accompanied by extremely restrictive rituals in which the mother, reduced to a state of slavery, had an active part. If the ritual was broken, the child went into a fit and its state of consciousness was lowered. Sokolnicka refused to accept the diagnosis of these fits by a neurologist as being epileptic and saw in them a manifestation of hysteria. She stressed the significance of the state of relational inhibition and described in minute detail some defence mechanisms of an obsessional nature: undoing and denial.

Analytic treatment depends on transference, which she described as being the pivotal point of the analysis.

> It must be said that at the beginning I had only one thing in mind, to overcome the difficult character of this boy, such an extraordinarily closed mind, and his intellectual inhibition, and contact had to be established one way or another. So my tactic was partly analytic and partly educational, the latter inspired, it is true, by an analytic point of view.

There is a certain analogy here with Melanie Klein's handling of the Fritz–Erich case (which also took place in 1919), especially in the initial stages of the latter's treatment. We should remember, too, that both Klein and Sokolnicka had been pupils of, and analysed by, Sándor Ferenczi. However, Sokolnicka did not use play with this 10-and-a-half year old: he was much older than Fritz–Erich had been (4–5 years old).

So, Sokolnicka used the positive link which had been created – which she called transference – to establish a dialogue with the child and to induce him to change. Daniel Widlöcher (1968) was to stress the fact that in this particular case there is no 'transference neurosis'. It is difficult to adopt a definite position on this point because of lack of sufficient material, but his position is one which echoes that of Anna Freud. Sokolnicka was interested in and worked on the dreams of her young patient using the free associations that he made. The interpretations were classic, to do with the Oedipus complex and castration anxiety. Very quickly, she stumbled on to what he called 'his big secret'. Sokolnicka intervened a lot during the treatment of this particular patient, interventions which she called 'pedagogical', even though the term might not seem quite appropriate today. The analyst in her felt it necessary to introduce sexuality into the treatment, and to undertake the child's sex education. Here we would agree with the comment made on the subject by Widlöcher (1968) when he said:

> This attitude might appear to be pedagogical and normative. However, its significance is somewhat different. By this means, the child's resistance to such material is revealed and examined, the patient then feeling consciously authorized to speak about such matters. The result obtained proves this: the child first of all expresses its guilt and is then able to talk about the 'secret', the sexual implication of which is not revealed until afterwards.

At another point Sokolnicka intervenes quite actively indeed, and says:

> One day, I myself voluntarily provoked him into a state of this kind: when he got to the point of throwing himself on his mother, I seized him firmly by both hands and sat him down in a chair. 'Mummy, Mummy,' he shouted like someone possessed and, without letting go of his hand, I repeated: 'You are unconscious and you are screaming for Mummy! So, how do you know that it isn't Mummy sitting here with you?'

When Ferenczi presented this paper on 'The Consequences of the "Active Technique" in Psychoanalysis' at the conference in The Hague (September 1920) he used this intervention by Sokolnicka as an illustration (1920: 210):

> Sokolnicka recently reported an hysterical act in a child suffering from an obsessional neurosis, which was similarly influenced by activity. She also suggested the very valuable idea that one should try to get at the symptoms that are in the service of the secondary 'gain of illness' by pedagogic means.

Sokolnicka's attitude corresponded perfectly to the definition that Ferenczi gave of his active therapy which, he said, was made up of two stages which should enable the activation and control of erotic tendencies, even if they were sublimated. The first phase was made up of orders whose object was to transform the repressed impulses into an evident satisfaction and to turn them into fully conscious formations. The second was made up of the prohibitions applied to these formations.

What we are probably looking at here is an interaction between Sokolnicka and Ferenczi in the feverish research activities of the 1920s. In this work Sokolnicka does not escape from the specific difficulties of child analysis and the path that she takes is neither that of Anna Freud nor that of Melanie Klein. This was her only publication on child psychoanalysis.

Although this case of psychoanalytic treatment was only to be published in France in 1968, it did leave a trace in French literature well before that, penned by André Gide in his well-known novel *Les Faux-monnayeurs*.

Gide had discovered Freud in 1921 in the *Revue de Genève* (Ronvaux, 1986). Fired with enthusiasm, he wrote to his famous penfriend, Dorothy Bussy, sister of James Strachey (translator of Freud), who at that time was living in Vienna. He even envisaged asking Freud, through Strachey, to preface his work *Corydon* (which Jacques Lacan was later to call the 'Gidean' theory of the libido), and to publish Freud's works in the NRF. Gide explained to Dorothy that *Corydon* could be presented to the French public as being 'translated from the German', i.e. as if it came from abroad, from a different theatrical world, from an unknown author (Roudinesco). Ernest Jones does mention that a note was received, but Gide's letter has unfortunately disappeared and Freud's is not available to the public.

Gide became so interested in psychoanalysis that in the winter of 1922 he began analysis with Sokolnicka, but was so quickly discouraged that he gave it up after only six sessions, perhaps in order to give more thought to the embryo of the novel he had been working on since 1919: *Les Faux-monnayeurs*. Gide's biographer, Jean Delay, can help us to position this novel in the work of Gide. In 1956 he wrote:

For the second time in his life Gide was proposing to put all of himself into one of his books. What he had tried at the age of 20 in *Les cahiers d'André Walter*, he was to undertake again at the age of 50, but with a mastery which was by then quite different. It was no longer to be almost autobiographical, more or less reproducing the real events of his life, but a symbolic transposition of the essential phases of his psychological make-up personified by fictive doubles. The main character, Edouard, the novelist (Gide's alter ego), analyses all the beings he is presented with. In several of the characters the reader who is familiar with the life and works of Gide can recognize the embodiment of his tendencies or conflicts. The main characters are, to use his own expression, carved out of his own flesh and blood, the function of the secondary characters being to set off the main characters.

Gide brings his analyst into the world of the counterfeiters (and this is why it is interesting for us) under the barely disguised but Hellenized name of Sophroniska. He gives her a particularly difficult task to carry out, the treatment of little Boris Lapérouse. Jean Delay immediately grasped that little Boris had a number of things in common with the child in Gide's earlier works *Si le grain ne meurt* and *Journal*, however, he did not seem to be aware of the work Eugenie Sokolnicka had done on the child from Minsk, which was evidently the source of Gide's inspiration.

There are many similitudes between the portrait Gide draws of Boris and the clinical elements which support the theories of Sokolnicka concerning the child from Minsk. Boris expresses himself with the same ambivalence. He suffered from the same taboo of touch. He too had a secret, the magic words of which are written on a parchment: gas – telephone – one hundred thousand roubles (the same words which Sokolnicka reports were in the dreams of her patient). Likewise, he is told this secret by another boy (Baptistin-Monia) who initiates him in the forbidden pleasures. He too practices masturbation. Threats of castration are bandied about; whereas Boris actually loses his father, the child from Minsk only talks about a threat to his father's survival. The nervous disorder then appears.

This is not as simple as it looks. Gide would not be a writer if he had not shuffled details and likenesses around, for instance, by giving the young hero much of his own childhood. Like Boris, the child Gide suffered from a 'sullen and solitary' childhood; shy and clumsy, feeling unloved, he feared the other children at school. His clandestine practices were soon to get him expelled. His parents took him to see Dr Brouardel, who threatened to castrate him surgically. When his father disappeared, his mother became over-possessive. Little by little, nervous disorders began to appear. In *Si le grain ne meurt* Gide recalls in humorous fashion the numerous advantages he was to benefit from, in particular, a chronic absenteeism from school, which he clearly does not seem to have suffered from. As Boris did with Bronja, Gide was to meet both love and relief from his suffering in the 'angelic' form of his young cousin, Madeleine.

It is possible that Gide had heard about the case of the boy from Minsk from Sokolnicka herself during the course of one of the meetings of the 'Club of the Repressed' – there is not much chance that he would have read about it in any of the specialist German or English psychoanalytical magazines. Gide must certainly have asked himself at the time what the consequences would have been for his own life if he had undergone analysis as a child. The description he gives of Boris' treatment and its effects is without doubt an unambiguous answer to this question. From the dialogue between Boris and Sophroniska one can get an idea of what the writer knew of psychoanalysis in the 1920s but there are also undertones indicating the writer's resistance both to Freudian theories and to his psychoanalyst.

Let us have a look at some of the clues Gide gives us about the 'woman doctor'. She is merely a prop for her Viennese theories, as understood by the author, but a few elements of her personality appear between the lines. She has few doubts and is totally absorbed with her subject, which seems to give her both therapeutic satisfaction and triumphant excitement. Doctor 'Sophroniska' explains her method clearly: she lets her young patient talk and tries to gain his confidence. She does not suggest things to him. She attributes Boris' nervous disorders and anxieties to the 'big, shameful, secret'. She sees in the 'anxious' neurosis of her patient a purely psychological reaction to the moral repression of his instincts, which leads to a feeling of guilt.

Edouard is quite sceptical about this new form of treatment. He continually reproaches the doctor for being too inquisitive and for using her method to dismantle the most intimate workings of one's being, violating even the most secret corners of a person's soul. He put it like this:

> Sophroniska spoke to me again about Boris whom, she believes, she has confessed entirely. The poor child no longer has in him the smallest copse, the smallest clump in which to hide from the eyes of the doctor. He has been found out. Sophroniska spreads out for all to see, dismantled, the most intimate workings of his mind like a clockmaker spreads out the pieces of the clock he is cleaning. If after all that the boy does not ring on time, then I'll be damned.

Wilfred R. Bion (1961) echoes this when he says: it is necessary 'to accept the idea that a clock is more than just the sum of the wheels inside it'.

Edouard believes that only the love of Bronja can save the child. When Bronja dies of tuberculosis at the end of the novel, Boris surrenders to the will of his cruel companions and kills himself playing Russian roulette.

So, although Gide was a discerning and attentive listener at Sokolnicka's talks, he had obviously only retained that which did not upset his vision of mankind too much. In spite of Gide's interest in psychoanalysis, and in the person who embodied psychoanalysis for him, he was far from being one of its defenders. Later on, when he had become even more sceptical about the success of psychoanalysis, Gide is reported to have said to Delay that he was delighted that this treatment had not existed when he had been a child. Interference of this sort might have made him other than what he was and he believed that an artist should rid himself of his complexes by himself and through his work, which is a catharsis.

Gide's opinion, which was no doubt a reflection of that of the literary circles of the day, is strangely reminiscent of that of William and Clara Stern (see Chapter 4). Psychoanalysis, because of the knowledge it gives us about ourselves, about the children we once were, and which we still are, is harmful, indeed dangerous, to the men and women we have become.

Notes

1 This chapter is based on the work carried out by Dr Pascale Duhamel for her thesis in psychiatry at the University of Bordeaux II, dated 12 October 1988 and entitled 'Eugenie Sokolnicka, 1884–1934. Entre l'oubli et le tragique' ('Between oblivion and tragedy').
2 Extract of a letter from Sigmund Freud to Sándor Ferenczi, from unpublished correspondence supplied by Judith Dupont.

8

Sophie Morgenstern: the application of child psychoanalysis in France[1]

Sophie Kabatschnik was born into a Jewish family in Grodno, Poland on 1 April 1875. In 1906, at the age of 31, she began her medical studies at the Faculty of Medicine of Zurich University where Professor Eugen Bleuler was teaching. Her thesis on the subject of 'Mineral Elements of the Thyroid Glands' was written, under the direction of Professor Eichhorst, in 1912. She must have got married while still carrying out her studies, for on the cover of her thesis she wrote her name as 'Sophia Morgenstern – Warsaw'. She then left Switzerland for Russia in order to obtain her State Diploma in Medicine so as to be able to practise in Poland (Parcheminey, 1947). But she was back in Zurich again in 1915 where she worked on a voluntary basis at the Burghölzli Clinic, the director of which was Eugen Bleuler. She held the positions of fourth assistant doctor in 1915, third assistant doctor in 1916 and second assistant doctor in 1918; she was appointed first assistant doctor on 1 May 1920. The records of the clinic do not mention the date of her departure, but they do indicate that another first assistant doctor was appointed on 1 April 1923.[2]

In her first year at the Burghölzli, she met and befriended Eugen Minkowski, also an assistant doctor and whose career resembled her own. A Polish Jew, he had studied medicine and philosophy at Zurich University, gone back to Russia to sit his exams again and had moved to France in 1915. He and his wife were to become close friends of Sophie Morgenstern, although they did not share her views on psychoanalysis.

Eugen Bleuler's son, Professor Manfred Bleuler, aged 85 in 1987, remembered Sophie Morgenstern as being 'a vivacious woman, interested in all sorts of things, charming and intelligent'. In a letter sent to Mrs Berna, Chairperson of the Swiss Psychoanalytical Society in 1987, he wrote: 'She was one of the doctors at the Burghölzli who was very highly regarded by my father; she took part in the discussions which were often about Sigmund Freud's views and his correspondence with my father, Eugen Bleuler.'[3] He was unfortunately not able to find any letters or documents concerning her. In addition, there is no trace in the minutes of the meetings of the Swiss Psychoanalytical Society of the period of the presence of Sophie Morgenstern at any of them.

According to George Parcheminey (1947), she came to France in 1924. We have no details concerning the reasons for this move to France. It is true that the path had been opened by her friends Eugen Minkowski and his wife, and by Eugenie Sokolnicka. It is more than probable that she met the latter in Switzerland. Perhaps she even thought she would join this woman with whom she had much in common. We know that Sophie Morgenstern underwent analysis with Eugenie Sokolnicka, but there is no evidence of a definite date. It could have been soon after her arrival in France, but it could also have been started in Switzerland. In 1925, when Georges Heuyer founded the infantile neuro-psychiatric unit at La Salpêtrière, Sophie Morgenstern became his assistant, carrying out work in the laboratory and at the psychoanalysis outpatients' clinic on a voluntary basis. She held the position for fifteen years, until her death.

We know very little about her private life. Her death certificate shows that she was married to Abraham Morgenstern, and that she was his widow, but there are no dates. She had a daughter by Abraham, Laure, whom we shall mention further on.

During the fifteen years of her professional experience in France, from 1925–40, Sophie Morgenstern seems to have been particularly active. She was, first of all, a colleague who was much appreciated by Georges Heuyer.[4] It was Georges Heuyer who wrote the preface to her book *Child Psychoanalysis* (1937a). He praises the service she rendered in the analytical study of child emotional disorders:

> Using the methods of psychoanalysis, she has thrown light on states which to us were obscure and explains psychological problems which seem so complicated and insoluble. Also, a number of these highly emotional, obsessive, troubled and anxious children are treated in an unfettered manner with patience, discretion and with an authority which belies the most gentle charm. Mrs Morgenstern has reformed characters which seemed difficult, reassured troubled children, brought comfort and recovery to children who had unconsciously suffered from the emotional aftershock of abnormal family situations. For eleven years Mrs Morgenstern has helped us on a voluntary basis and we cannot praise her devotion too highly and give enough thanks to the help she has given us and the results she has obtained.
>
> (Fleury, 1988: 5)

Georges Heuyer considered his colleague as having been the first to have used Sigmund Freud's methods with children, and was pleased to acknowledge that she was a pioneer in the use of the special technique of drawing. He said he was convinced of the not inconsiderable contribution of psychoanalysis to child neuro-psychiatry both from the therapeutic point of view and from that of aetiology. Many years later, when he was to distance himself from psychoanalysis, he still retained his regard for this particular colleague. In 1952, in his book *Introduction a la psychiatrie infantile* ('An Introduction to Child Psychiatry'), he mentioned her many times in the chapter on psychoanalysis.

Others, too, have sung her praises. Georges Parcheminey, in the journal *L'Evolution psychiatrique*, emphasized her tact, her indulgence and her clarity when she took part in discussions, and her excessive modesty (1947).

Sophie Morgenstern belonged to the Paris Psychoanalytical Society and became a full member in 1929, and was its Treasurer in 1932 and 1933. She was also a full member of the group 'Evolution Psychiatrique'.

In her fifteen years' work in France, she published fifteen articles and a book. The articles can be found in the *Revue française de psychanalyse*, in the magazines *L'Encéphale, L'Evolution psychiatrique* and the *Gazette medicale de France*. Her book *Psychanalyse infantile (Symbolisme et valeur clinique des créations imaginatives chez l'enfant)* was published by Denoël in 1937. In 1938, two years before her death, she gave a paper at the 15th International Psychoanalytical Congress in Paris entitled 'Le symbolisme et la valeur psychanalytique des dessins infantiles' (see Morgenstern, 1939).

She seems to have been well accepted in her professional circle. Georges Parcheminey (1947: 12–13) comments: 'All her works were characterized by their spirit of observation, their depth of reflexion, their rigour of method and above all by their incomparable degree of scientific integrity.'

Morgenstern taught about infantile neuroses at the Institute of Psychoanalysis of the Paris Psychoanalytical Society from 1934, the year of its founding, until her death in 1940. In that year she was to have given a series of lectures entitled 'The Structure of Neuroses where the Ego is Prevalent', but they were cancelled because of the outbreak of war.

Sophie Morgenstern committed suicide at her home on 16 June 1940, the day after the Germans entered Paris. She had just turned down an offer from Françoise Dolto to go to the south of France, in spite of the fact that all the hospitals in Paris were closed. Her suicide is a mystery and one can only make suppositions about it. It is true that her only daughter, Laure, had died a few years earlier, on the operating table. Her book, published in 1937, was dedicated 'To the memory of my daughter, Laure'. In his obituary, Georges Parcheminey described Laure as being 'an exceptionally gifted person with a promising career in the field of art history and fine arts'. Given her deep love for her daughter, Sophie Morgenstern probably had great difficulty surviving her and initially sought consolation in her work. On top of this, the arrival of the Germans in Paris in 1940 with all the implications this would have had for a Jewish *émigrée*, together with the fact that she would have had to give up all professional and scientific work, was probably the last straw and the reason she took her own life.

HER WORK

Sophie Morgenstern's works show that she had a thorough grounding in the works of Sigmund Freud and, because she spoke German, she could read them in the original German text. She made frequent reference to his work and based her own clinical practice largely on his theories. She believed that children's neuroses were based on the same conflicts as those of adults: they had the same roots, the same structure and served the same purpose as adult neuroses, and were due to disharmony between the instinctual tendencies, the ego and the superego. She adopts Anna Freud's point of view of the superego, as created during the development of the individual. Like Anna Freud, she believed that the child remains very dependent on the person who, at a given point, represents the superego. On the clinical level, she believes that the same manifest neuroses exist in the child and in the adult: anxiety neuroses, phobias, obsessional neuroses. However, she also points out that child neurotic disorders are only transitory in nature; they can occur at the birth of a brother or sister, the trigger being either jealousy or curiosity as to the origin of children. She also stressed the existence of disorders which might be due to feelings of guilt connected with masturbation, with the child fearing harmful consequences. She shows the importance of these neurotic disorders which can impede normal intellectual development, and the risk of a consequent erroneous diagnosis of mental retardation.

Her concept of psychoanalytical treatment for children

In her article, published in 1928, entitled 'Child psychoanalysis', Sophie Morgenstern indicated that she shared Anna Freud's opinion that analysis should only be applied to a child with a neurosis. She believed that one should not anticipate a child's curiosity about sexual questions, but only give a sexual explanation or interpretation of symbolic acts or symptoms as they arose. She thus implicitly criticizes Melanie Klein's position, which was supposed to be that analysis was an indispensable addition to modern education, and therefore judged it necessary for all children as a measure to prevent neurotic disorders. She did not share Klein's idea of the technique to be used in child psychoanalysis either. For Morgenstern, the Kleinian technique was too static, forcing the child to accept unalterable symbols which restrict its imagination. She believed that Melanie Klein, in the way she used her play technique, looked upon all the child's movements as being symbolic acts and interpreted them accordingly. We can see here that Morgenstern clearly positions herself on the side of Anna Freud at a time when the controversy between Anna Freud and Melanie Klein was in full swing. This is undoubtedly one of the first instances of the great mistrust of French psychoanalysts for Kleinian theory and practice.

Morgenstern believed that, in general, it was better to leave the child with its family. Conflicts met during the course of the treatment could therefore be used and this would help the child to understand the origin and the nature of its symptoms. However, she did believe that in certain circumstances separation from the family surroundings would have a beneficial influence on the child's behaviour, even if this was not enough to resolve the psychological conflict. Separation from the parents was only indicated if they created an environment in which therapeutic work became impossible. It is highly likely that she was obliged to resist the French tendency to 'hospitalize' children.

She put a lot of emphasis on the difficulties which can occur at the beginning of the treatment. The conditions in which the initial contact with the child is made are critical, since the child is to be subjected to a treatment, the purpose of which he or she does not understand, imposed by its parents. She believed that often the child did not suffer from his or her behaviour and had learnt to appreciate the advantages of the illness. Like Anna Freud, she thought that the psychoanalyst should use all possible means to create a transference; the child must have confidence in the analyst and it is the feeling that the child has that the analyst understands the child's conflicts that leads to transference. Through this transference the child will express him- or herself more freely, will be able to reveal the most intimate conflicts and will thus enable treatment to progress. Another difficulty in the treatment of children is connected with the particular way in which the child's mind works and the child's behaviour: since magical thought governs the child's world, the analyst has to become familiar with the way in which the child expresses creations of the imagination and understand the symbols that the child uses.

For Morgenstern the purpose of analytical treatment was to improve or to put an end to family conflicts created by the child's neurosis. In children, the unconscious is more easily accessible than in adults, since it does not yet have all the layers it will ultimately acquire. In this too, Morgenstern is close to Anna Freud's concepts. The child's neurosis is an 'actual neurosis'. The layers in the child's mind in which the conflicts are situated can be reached more quickly. The path from the symptom to its origin is less complicated, so, for her, analysis should not last very long and a recovery is more certain than for adults.

She thought that the role of the parents was very important in the case of analytical treatment of the child in many ways. They can intervene by their resistance to the treatment. Faced with this problem, Morgenstern believed that there was little the analyst could do. She gave the example the case of a child of 7 who came to have ideas of suicide, so tormented was he by the question of how babies were born. However, the father forbade the therapist to give any explanations about how babies are born, 'those dirty things'.

The role of the parents is also important because of the lack of maturity of the child's superego, which is not yet autonomous. Insofar as the child's superego is modelled on the moral instructions of the educator, a superego which is too severe would have unfortunate consequences on the child's development. The analyst can sometimes make the parents understand the origin of these moral conflicts and obtain their help in the treatment, but not always. She also believed that advice as to their behaviour towards their child can often be given to parents, that it is not always easy to make them understand the damage they can do with threats concerning masturbation, by the absence of information or false information given about how babies are born. She further believed that in a number of cases of child neurosis, psychoanalysis of the parents would be invaluable.

Morgenstern did not seem to show much interest in psychoses. However, she did believe that analysis in childhood could have a preventive effect against psychosis in adulthood. But the great originality of Sophie Morgenstern was in the techniques she used in child analysis. Wherever possible she advised the use of free association, as for adults. However, she knew this was difficult before the age of 10 or 12, even with a very bright child. Therefore, she tried a number of other techniques: drawing, modelling, play activities. She also tried to analyse the child's dreams.

THE TECHNIQUES SHE USED

Drawings

It was in 1926, in the initial stages of her experience as a child analyst and while working with Georges Heuyer that Sophie Morgenstern was confronted with a particular problem concerning the treatment of a mute child. She used drawings with the child: the analysis enabled a complete recovery of the child in a few months. She related this case in her first article, published in 1927 in the *Revue française de psychanalyse*, and she was to use all or part of it in later articles. It was this same work with drawings that was the starting point of her later research on the symbolic sense of the imaginative creations of the child and which was to be the subject of her book *Psychanalyse infantile* (1937a). The ways in which the child used drawings was a constant object of research throughout her professional life.

Morgenstern believed that neurosis led to exuberance in a child's drawings. The internal conflict inspires artistic creation. Repression makes the imagination more active and leads to a careful search for the subject of the drawing. She seemed to think that the deeper the conflict the richer and more original the artistic work. Drawings also gave the analyst access to unconscious conflicts, and she showed how important symbolism was in most drawings. The apparent content is thus far removed from the actual content. The symbols used are more or less transparent; the more the conflict expressed is repressed, the less transparent are the symbols. She stresses the fact that they are often ingenious, and that they must be understood if the conflicts they express are to be understood. These conflicts are identical to those found in adults.

She takes into account the emotional atmosphere of the drawings, which gives her important information about the depth of the conflict and the seriousness of the neurosis. Anxiety, the most frequent state found, is manifested in different ways: the theme of the drawings, the surfeit and the accumulation of objects on the same page; repetition, whether it be in the repeated representation of the same subject in the same drawing, so much so that it becomes obsessive or hallucinatory, or whether it be in various objects representing the same symbol. She was interested in the expression on the faces of the people represented: eyes can express anxiety but also suspicion or disapproval. She also took into account the excessively large size of objects, because for her size was related to emotional value.

Play

'Play is the perfect means of getting to the root of the enigma of child neurosis.' This was Morgenstern's opinion as expressed in the report she gave at the 5th Conference of French Language Psychoanalysts in 1930 entitled 'Child Psychoanalysis and its Role in Mental Hygiene'. Play often enabled her to make a diagnosis, to read a child's character, to make a prognosis. The whole of the child's emotional life can be observed in its play. The child's choice of play activity and the way it goes about it provide precious information about its unconscious. In play, the child expresses its conflicts, tries to remedy its disappointments, and get its own back on its entourage. It also symbolically carries out its morbid wishes. It can create another world, where it plays roles which satisfy its emotional needs. In using play in treatment, Morgenstern places herself in the same camp as Anna Freud and Mary Chadwick, who use play as a relief for the emotions and only give an interpretation when the child has been sufficiently prepared by the treatment to understand it. She only mentions Melanie Klein in passing, saying that in her opinion Klein interprets each movement to the child and gives an explanation of its symbolic meaning.

Dreams

Morgenstern recognized that the mechanics of dream-building were the same for both child and adult, but believed that the various elements were of a different nature. The censorship is less severe, especially in the very young child; conflicts are expressed more clearly, repression is not as deep, the superego which brings censorship into play is not yet independent. For her, each individual, even when very young, has memories on to which current conflicts are grafted. The whole of the psychic structure may be revealed in the dream: the various stages of sexual development, the nature of the superego.

In general, Morgenstern gave much importance to the creative activities of the child, those which require greater sublimation. Drawings, of course, but also the spontaneous telling of stories that the child itself has made up. The child is thus able to express conflicts: it shows a certain degree of development, the child being able to sublimate the instinctive desires. It seems to her that, through artistic creation, the child is seeking a solution to its problems. Making up stories enables symbolic expressions to be used. These reveal the structure of the personality and emotional conflicts more precisely, perhaps, than play activities and dreams, enabling the ideas of self-importance to be accomplished more fully. These make-believe stories, like the drawings which often stem from the child's daydreaming where imagination plays an essential role, are conscious and voluntary creations. She was also interested in fairy stories and what the child did with them, using material from its own life. Using these materials, Morgenstern worked on the question of guilt, magical thought and the child's idea of death. She was also interested in the child's aggressive tendencies.

Psychoanalytical upbringing

In a lecture given to the Philosophical and Scientific Study Group at the Sorbonne in 1932, Morgenstern said: 'Psychoanalysis, that science of the unconscious and of instinct, is proving to be of ever more precious assistance in education.' She believed the latency period to be of great importance for the development and strengthening of the personality, and put the crucial period in a child's upbringing as between 5 and 11 years, whereas today we would place it in the child's very early years. She considered that knowledge about the development of the instincts and the unconscious could be an important guide to parents, enabling them to help the child channel the instinctual drives into a creative force. Parents had a duty to show more understanding towards the moral conflicts encountered by the child. She believed that a superego which was too severe would lead to deep feelings of guilt and aggressive acts by the child towards itself or toward others. She considered that psychoanalysis enabled one to see manifestations such as 'spitefulness, disobedience, mythomania' in a different light – and it was the duty of the psychoanalyst to point this out to parents. Such manifestations were generally defences against excessive demands made by the family, school authorities or internally by the superego. An oversevere superego could, she believed, even induce a criminal future. She thought that a clear and truthful explanation about where babies come from and masturbation should be part of a child's education. This was the only way to avoid mental disorders.

Domestic tyrants – 'Les bourreaux domestiques' (1934a)

This was a subject which interested Morgenstern's mentor, Georges Heuyer. He believed it to be 'a perverse type of personality whose spitefulness is practised only on members of the family, to the exclusion of all others.' The 'domestic tyrant', i.e. the child who is a pathological tyrant towards his family, belonged to the group of those showing instinctual perversity. In her conceptualization of the domestic tyrant, Morgenstern would try to bring together two theories which on the surface would appear to be poles apart: the innate theory and the psychoanalytical theory. She admitted the possibility of an innate predisposition, but she sought the source of this abnormality in a disturbed development of the libido. She recognized that the isolation of domestic tyrants as a group was apparently in contradiction with the innate and psychoanalytical theories of instinctual perversity, but she justified her position by the clinical observation she had made of children presenting the characteristic symptoms of this disorder over a number of years. The significant feature is the manifestation of aggressiveness and spitefulness but only towards members of the family. Clinical experience had shown her that this abnormality was not related to a disorder of the intellect but to an emotional disorder. The psychoanalytical study of these children enabled her to translate their aggressive acts into a language which could be understood. She thus brought to light the lack of inhibition, the lack of a counterbalance to the instinctual tendencies, and the importance of the role of the Oedipus and castration complexes in this disorder. She believed that psychoanalytical treatment would do put an end to these symptoms connected with family conflicts. However, this was only a proposal, for she said that psychoanalysis had not yet stood the test of time in that particular field.

Sophie Morgenstern was one of the first psychoanalysts to practise child psychoanalysis in France. She worked with Professor Georges Heuyer from 1925–40 at the Department of Child Psychiatry of the University of La Salpêtrière, Paris. Numerous papers, fifteen articles and a book all go to show her intense scientific activity and the recognition of it by her peers since her work was published in several prestigious journals. Her work was a continuation of that of both Sigmund Freud, on the one hand, and Anna Freud, on the other. She held a very important position at the time. One of her pupils was Françoise Marette-Dolto, who acknowledged having following her teachings, in particular concerning children's drawings, but in whose written works Morgenstern is referred to only very rarely. It is difficult to comprehend why she has been forgotten. Was it to do with the upheaval cause by World War II in France? Was it more to do with the changing direction with Georges Heuyer was to take, moving away from child psychoanalysis, even if he continued to speak highly of her, as he did in one of his books published as late as 1952? Is the fact that she has been forgotten due to her tragic death? It is well known that suicide makes the survivors feel guilty, and the circumstances of her own suicide, at the time of the Nazi occupation of Paris, would have exacerbated this guilt.

Others were to take her place but, strangely for psychoanalysts, they were to forget their collective past. She would only be mentioned occasionally, in connection with the drawings of children or a case of psychogenic mutism.

Notes

1 Much of the information in this chapter was provided by the thesis of Dr Mireille Fleury, entitled 'Sophie Morgenstern, éléments de sa vie et de son oeuvre', University de Bordeaux II, 3 May 1988.

2 Information given by Dr Hahn, Assistant Medical Director of the Maison de Santé in the canton of Zurich (formerly Burghölzli), 1987.

3 We would like to thank Mrs Berna, former president of the Swiss Psychoanalytical Society, Dr Daisy de Saugy, archivist of that Society, Dr Hahn of the psychiatric clinic at the University of Zurich, and Dr G. A. Nogler of the University of Zurich, for the research that they were kind enough to do for us.

4 The reader will find information about Georges Heuyer and Sophie Morgenstern in a booklet by J. Losserand published in 1991.

9

The two schools and some
of the main figures

The period between 1920 and 1940 was particularly fruitful, and the group of child psychoanalysts which formed around Anna Freud was very rich in notable personalities. The 'Kinderseminar', the name given by psychoanalysts of Sigmund Freud's generation to the circle she had organized, had rallied little by little: August Aichhorn, Siegfried Bernfeld, Willi Hoffer, Heinz Hartmann, Wilhelm Reich, Jeanne Lampl de Groot, Richard Sterba, René Spitz, Helene Deutsch, Ernst Kris, Marianne Kris-Rie and Anny Rosenberg-Katan. Some were childhood friends, most were Jewish, nearly all were committed to left-wing politics.

This group of analysts was very active. They carried out lectures on education, ran the Vienna Institute of Psychoanalysis, where, in the third year, students were given lectures on the specifics of child analysis, and contributed to and published the journal *Zeitschrif für Psychoanalytische Pädagogik*. The journal was to be discontinued in 1938 and was replaced by the Anglo-American journal *The Psychoanalytic Study of the Child*. They also founded a number of institutions – for re-education (in which Aichhorn, Bernfeld and Hoffer became heavily involved) and kindergartens (in which Dorothy Burlingham, Peter Blos, Erik Homburger Erikson and others became involved) – and took part in consultations organized by the Viennese municipal authorities for children in difficulty.

The spirit of the period was one of pioneering. Private and professional life tended to mingle, all the more so since some of them were undergoing analysis or supervision with the others, and often the families into which they were born were already friends.

Their activity was intense, but the spread of their ideas in the Vienna of the period met with much resistance. We should remember that Ilse Hellman, who at that time was assistant to child psychology Professor

158

Charlotte Bühler, was not authorized by the latter to meet Anna Freud. Moreover, Ilse Hellman says (I. 4) that in the circles in which she originated – the cultivated Viennese upper class – Sigmund Freud's ideas were still very much criticized and scoffed at. She remembered discussions between her parents and Arthur Schnitzler on the subject. Her father's reservations were such that he tried to prevent her from studying psychology, which, however, she finally did with Charlotte Bühler. Anna Freud was later to describe the spirit of that time as revolutionary. Since it is not possible to mention them all in detail here, we present three examples: Anny Katan, Tola Rank and Dorothy Burlingham.

The whole group was to remain friends, in spite of the fact that they were to be scattered geographically, owing to the rise of the Nazis. As soon as the war was over they renewed their links with Anna Freud, whose talent they recognized, and not just because she was the 'heiress'. They tended to meet up at the international congresses and also at Walberswick in the summer, the property in Suffolk belonging to Anna Freud and Dorothy Burlingham.

Anny Katan-Rosenberg (1898–1992)

Anny Katan-Rosenberg was one of Anna Freud's earliest childhood friends, and was three years younger than Anna. Elisabeth Young-Bruehl (1988) recounts how one day when she was 7 Anny splashed Anna and was not even so much as reprimanded by Sigmund Freud. Later on, when Anna was hesitating as to whether to let Anny undergo analysis with her, Anny is said to have let slip: 'You aren't going to let a little splash stand in the way, are you?' (p. 41).

She was the daughter of paediatrician Ludwig Rosenberg. Both he and another paediatrician, Oscar Rie, were friends of Sigmund Freud, with whom, at that time, he played cards every Saturday evening at the Kassowitz Institute. Under the names Otto and Leopold they were to appear in the well-known dream analysed by Freud, 'Irma's Injection'. Oscar Rie also had a daughter called Marianne. Both Anny Rosenberg and Marianne Rie studied medicine and later became psychoanalysts, practising under their married names as Anny Katan and Marianne Kris.

In 1934, Anny Rosenberg was 36. She had undergone analysis with Anna Freud, had been married a first time and had had a child and then divorced. In February 1934, there were riots in Vienna. Anny Rosenberg belonged to a clandestine socialist revolutionary group run by Otto Bauer, which tried to organize a resistance movement. She was a messenger for the group, and helped a number of analysts to escape, among them Margaret Mahler. In 1936, she herself was obliged to emigrate to Holland with her son. Later, she and her second husband, Maurits Katan, were active members of the Dutch Resistance during World War II. They finally moved to Cleveland (Ohio) after the war, where Anny Katan put all her energy into serving the cause of child psychoanalysis.

> After the war, at the instigation and urging of Anna Freud, the Katans came to Cleveland to assist in the restructuring of the Western Reserve University School of Medicine and to establish psychoanalytic training in Cleveland. Shortly after her arrival she began importing graduates of Miss Freud's Child Therapy Course in Hampstead, who formed around her the centre of the child analytic movement in Cleveland. First came 'The Therapeutic Nursery School', now known as the Hanna Perkins School, in 1950, then the Cleveland Child Therapy Course for training non-medical child analysts in 1958, and in 1964 the Child Analytic Clinic where to this day children may receive a full analysis based strictly on need because of the Clinic's sliding fee scale. In 1966 she was a Founding Trustee of the Cleveland Center for Research in Child Development, the umbrella organization that oversees operation of all these various programmes in addition to community outreach services and research projects.
>
> In addition to her work in establishing the child analytic research complex in Cleveland, Dr Katan was perhaps best known for her papers on verbalisation, object removal, stranger distress (as opposed to stranger anxiety), distortions of the phallic phase, and adults who had been raped as children.
>
> (from the obituary by Robert A. Furman, 1993: 834)

She was to remain friends with Anna Freud and in the late 1950s she and her husband bought a country cottage in Walberswick, next to Anna's. She died at her home on 24 December 1992, at the age of 94.

Tola (Beata) Rank (1895–1967)

We mention Tola Beata Mincer here because she was one of the pioneers of child psychoanalysis in Boston, Massachusetts (Roazen, 1990). She also played an important role in the history of the psychoanalytical movement in its early stages.

Otto Rank met this young and very beautiful Polish Jewess when he was in the army and based in Cracow between 1916 and 1918. Just after they were married he took her to Vienna to present her to Sigmund Freud (Roazen [1990] speaks of this as if it were a 'court presentation'). Otto Rank's role in the life of Freud is well known; it was he who was given the responsibility of keeping the minutes of the meetings of the Vienna Psychoanalytical Society. Freud also considered him as his spiritual son for a long time. Although, according to Roazen, Freud made some 'not very flattering' remarks about her in a letter to Karl Abraham in November 1918, she rapidly became a sort of 'daughter-in-law', with access to Freud's inner circle. In a footnote in *Das Unheimliche* ('The uncanny', 1919d) Freud thanks 'Frau Dr Rank' for a remark she made about a question of etymology. Freud had a habit of always acknowledging his sources, but this note indicates that Tola, who had been in Vienna for only a few months, was already taking part in discussions, including scientific discussions. When she gave birth to a daughter, Freud greeted her as if it were his own granddaughter. Tola organized a number of receptions for Freud, since it would appear that Mrs Freud did not appreciate this task very much. She also entertained his intimate friends (Lou Andreas-Salomé, Felix and Helene Deutsch, for example).

Tola rapidly came to play a more active role in the Vienna circle. She contributed to the publication of *Imago* by taking dictation from Freud, as did Anna Freud. In 1920 she was invited to the congress in The Hague, on the same footing as Melanie Klein and Anna Freud (Lieberman, 1985), and she became a member of the Vienna Psychoanalytical Society only a few months after Anna Freud. On 30 May 1923 she gave her maiden paper on the subject of 'The Role of Women in the Evolution of Human Society'.

We can suppose that Tola Rank played an important role in the evolution of the human society of Viennese psychoanalytical circles. The dispute which occurred at this time between Freud and Otto Rank, and which was so distressing for both protagonists and their entourage, arose predominantly because of new theories put forward by Rank about the trauma of birth.

Ernest Jones observed that one of the things Rank believed, contrary to Freud, was the importance of the mother–child relationship at the beginning of life. For our part, we believe that the problem arose because of the importance that Rank gave to the mother. It is more then likely that Tola and Otto Rank worked in close collaboration on this subject, which Rank had first mentioned shortly after his marriage: chapter 7 of his *Don Juan* (1922) was entitled 'The role of the woman', and it is the evolution of human society that is being discussed. He had also written an article in collaboration with Ferenczi entitled 'Prospects in psychoanalysis' (Ferenczi and Rank, 1924), in which Freud would have found additional reasons to be displeased. Two of his favourite disciples were proposing adjustments to psychoanalytical techniques which he could not have found acceptable; in fact, these adjustments were also to do with maternal transference. It was, above all, Karl Abraham who reacted violently to these theoretical and technical proposals; Freud did try to understand these new ideas. Freud explained in his letter (1965: 345–8) to Abraham dated 15 February 1924: 'You should not let yourself be guided by the fact that your work may or may not be to my taste. . . . If every time you had a new idea you insisted on waiting for my approval it would run the risk of becoming very old first'. In spite of his reservations, Freud insisted that the question be left 'open'. He held Otto Rank's ideas to be 'an interesting contribution, the value of which should be recognized by us', but nevertheless added, 'It is not clear to me how prematurely informing a patient that his transference to the physician represents attachment to the mother can lead to a shortening of his analysis.'

It is said that Rank was influenced by Freud's cancer, which had begun to evolve, and that his work was a reflection of his difficulty with the father image. This latter would confirm the fact that, in reaction to the lack of understanding with which his work had met, Rank appears to have suffered a bout of manic-depressive reaction. Jones even wrote that he 'went mad' but this seems to be more of an impassioned description than the truth.

The maternal image that Rank had been talking about since his marriage was very ambivalent. He developed the theme of the primal mother. In *Don Juan* he mentions the wicked old women, the devil's grandmother, the *Rabenmutter* (cruel stepmother), who is often portrayed in children's stories as a witch or a shrew. 'But how did the woman come to be portrayed in such a hostile role?' he wonders at the end of chapter 5. In *The Trauma of Birth* we find 'the wicked primal mother (witch)', who swallows up little children (1968 [1924]: 117), the intrauterine hell (p. 139), the Sphinx, Hecate, the Gorgon and a dozen or so other deadly female demons and primitive divinities (p. 153).

Did Freud hesitate because of this primitive phantasmagoria, when intellectually he glimpsed the progress psychoanalysis could make by opening up in this direction?

The public had rapidly understood this dimension of the quarrel. In a letter to his wife, dated 5 October 1924, James Strachey said that American analysts were saying that 'you should have your father complex analysed by Freud and your mother complex by Rank' (Strachey and Strachey, 1985: 80).

Helene Deutsch seems to confirm the relationship between the work done by Otto Rank and the ideas of his wife when she quotes Tola concerning the reign of the primal mother: she mentions Tola's paper 'Zur Rolle der Frau in der Entwicklung der menschlichen Gesellschaft' (published in *Imago*, 10, 1924) which was published in 1924 (see Deutsch, 1944, vol. I).

Although the same age, Anna Freud did not apparently like Tola, which is perhaps understandable: as 'daughter-in-law' she was a rival; as a woman, she was beautiful and bore her maternal state with an obvious joy – Anna was envious of her. In a letter to Ernest Jones (Roazen, 1990) she dates Otto Rank's 'change in personality' to his marriage. However, she did allow Tola to attend her seminar on child psychoanalysis. In a letter to Max Eitingon dated 14 February 1925 (Young-Bruehl, 1988: 152), Anna writes: 'Frau Rank was present at the last meeting of the Society. Because I had really done her a great injustice in my thoughts, I wanted to make a new attempt to find her pleasant. It did not do any good: I think once and for all that I just can not stand her.' We should add that when Tola Rank was in hospital in Vienna in 1925, Sigmund Freud went to visit her almost every day, during his daily walks.

Tola Rank seems to have been a whimsical sort of person, and somewhat spendthrift. In Vienna she is described as being very elegant, while her husband wore trousers which had been patched. They did not have much money but she lent quite substantial sums to various psychoanalytical publications. She socialized often, but still managed to find time to translate *The Interpretation of Dreams* into Polish, and it was published in that language in 1923. From 1924 onwards her husband travelled frequently between Vienna, Paris and New York. In New York he had a large clientele of analysts pressing at the door of his surgery, which enabled him to make his fortune, or rather would have if Tola, who had moved to Paris in the meantime, had not lived in such a grand style. She lived in Paris for about ten years, frequenting artistic and literary circles with Henry Miller and Anaïs Nin in particular. The latter mentions Tola in her diary, although Nin talks more about Otto Rank, with whom she underwent analysis in Paris (after an initial period with Allendy). They became friends and Otto accepted an invitation to dinner with Anaïs Nin accompanied by his wife. The two women could not stand each other. In 1967 Nin was to write: 'A very disappointing evening. Mrs Rank negative, spent all her time dampening everyone's enthusiasm . . . [she is] cold and curt [with people].' A short time afterwards (1934) Rank brought Nin to New York, where she worked as his assistant–secretary–pupil; she rapidly began taking in patients for analysis herself, but this activity only lasted a year.

Roazen supposes that Tola must have known about the beginnings of psychoanalysis in France, but there is no formal proof of this. However, she did undergo analysis with Mira Gincburg-Oberholzer, perhaps in Switzerland.

When Rank resigned from the Vienna Psychoanalytical Society in 1929, Tola remained faithful to Freud. It would appear that she began her work with children in Paris, but we have no information on the subject.

It seems that it was Helene Deutsch who invited Tola to Boston, where she is presumed to have arrived in 1936. They had met in a public garden in Vienna while taking their respective children for a walk. (Later on the children too were to become friends.) In her autobiography in 1973 Helene Deutsch says that Tola had had great difficulty in establishing her clientele in Boston to begin with because she was not a medical practitioner; friends found her a job, but she surprised everyone by preferring to practice psychoanalysis rather than take up a career as a social worker, which was the job that she had been offered.

Tola and Otto divorced in 1939, but this was simply the endorsement of a split which had occurred much earlier. Rank remarried but was to die in October 1939, just a month after Freud, which is probably more than a coincidence.

According to Roazen, Tola Rank became the most celebrated child analyst in Boston and it was she who trained all the other analysts in this particular field. She chaired the Educational Committee of the Psychoanalytic Institute of Boston and 'everybody adored her'. She wrote a number of articles on the atypical development of children, particularly for the *Psychoanalytic Study of the Child*. With Dr Molly Putnam, she helped found the James Jackson Putnam Children's Center for preschool children. She later gave up supervising the centre to concentrate on training analysis.

Her writings did not have a wide audience and were not considered to be important works. Although several of them remained unpublished, one is mentioned by Helene Deutsch. In her autobiography, Deutsch says that Tola had retained a very neurotic attitude, that 'she suffered from a painful inferiority complex which was totally unjustified'. For Roazen, she had a complex and subtle intelligence, but was more 'sentimental' than 'intellectual' in the academic sense of the word. She remained friends with Helene Deutsch and at the end of her life they lived not far from each other, visiting each other every day. She died in 1967.

Looking back now, says Roazen (1990), Tola Rank seems

a tragic figure, apparently caught up in situations from which there was no escape. According to the diary of Anaïs Nin she was always dressed in black, which corresponds entirely with the memories people have of her at the beginning of her Boston experience; black was elegant but also an indication of a certain depressive tendency. Her success as an analyst in Boston should perhaps be attributed to the extreme sensitivity with which she reacted to the influence of her peer group.

Dorothy Burlingham (1891–1979)

Dorothy Burlingham was born in 1891 in New York, into a well-known American family: her father was the famous glassmaker-decorator Louis Tiffany. While quite young she married Robert Burlingham, a surgeon with manic–depressive disorder. Her father-in-law was a well-known east-coast lawyer and legal expert, and an influential politician. She had four children in rapid succession. Hoping to be able to treat her husband, who had been confined to mental institutions a number of times, she went to see Sándor Ferenczi, and then to Vienna to see Sigmund Freud. She undertook a first analysis with Theodor Reik and then continued with Freud. Fearing that they too would suffer from mental disorders, she entrusted Anna Freud with her children. Anna undertook the analysis of the two older children fairly quickly. It would appear that they were among the first children to be analysed by her.

Dorothy soon became a member of the Vienna Psychoanalytical Society and actively took part in the foundation of the first nursery, where the educators were Peter Blos and Erik Homburger Erikson. She also founded the Jackson Nursery in Vienna with Anna Freud, and later followed the Freud family to London, becoming a member of the British Society in 1938 and a training analyst in 1940.

During the 'Controversies' between Melanie Klein and Anna Freud she actively supported Anna Freud. Together they founded the Hampstead Nurseries and later on the Hampstead Clinic, where Dorothy Burlingham was in charge of research on young blind children and the setting up of the Hampstead Index.

Dorothy published a number of books and articles, often in conjunction with Anna Freud, and analysed many of the analysts belonging to the British Psychoanalytical Society, including Ilse Hellman. She was a very close friend of Anna Freud. In 1988 her grandson, Michael D. Burlingham, published her biography, entitled *The Last Tiffany*, in the United States. Interested readers will find much material about her life and her work in this volume.

MELANIE KLEIN AND THE ENGLISH SCHOOL

The history of the British Psycho-Analytical Society is closely linked to its founder, Ernest Jones. He became a qualified medical practitioner in 1900, first of all becoming interested in neurology and then in psychopathology. He discovered the works of Freud through Wilfred Trotter and tried to put Freud's teachings into practice with a first patient in 1905–6.

In 1907 Jones met Carl Jung, who invited him to Zurich. He was to meet Freud himself at the First International Congress in Salzburg. After living in Canada for a few years (1908–13) he returned to London in 1913 and founded the British Psycho-Analytical Society in 1919. In the following year, he founded the first psychoanalytical journal in English: *The International Journal of Psycho-Analysis*. Four years later he opened the Institute of the British Psycho-Analytical Society. In 1926 he brought Melanie Klein over from Berlin and she was immediately asked to undertake the analysis of his wife and two children.

The members of the British Psycho-Analytical Society were all liberals and humanists by inclination and by training. Some of its members (Alix and James Strachey, Adrian and Karen Steven) also belonged to the Bloomsbury Group.[1] The correspondence of Alix and James Strachey between 1924 and 1925 (Strachey and Strachey, 1985) is very enlightening about the group. Alix was in Berlin at that time undergoing analysis with Karl Abraham and it was here that she met Melanie Klein for the first time. The correspondence highlights the liberal thinking of members of this social class. Joan Rivière, Barbara Low (the only Jewish person amongst them), Susan Isaacs, Sylvia Payne and Dr Edward Glover also made up this first group: they had in common the fact that they had all been analysed in Vienna, Budapest or Berlin. For more than ten years the group evolved in harmony and with great vitality. Melanie Klein and her research influenced them all to a greater or lesser degree: the idea that the Kleinian path could be a deviation never occurred to them.

We shall have a look at three particular members of the group in detail because of the role they played in the history of child psychoanalysis.

Paula Heimann (1899–1982)

Paula Heimann began her career as an analyst in Berlin where she had undergone analysis with Theodor Reik. In 1931 she became an associate member of the Berlin Psychoanalytical Society. The rise of the Nazis in Berlin, and the separation from her husband, Dr Franz Heimann, meant that in 1933 she was able to accept Ernest Jones' proposal to go to England with her daughter, and she became an associate member of the British Psycho-Analytical Society that same year. She underwent analysis again, with Melanie Klein, in 1935. She was always very vague as to how long it lasted but it seems to have gone on until 1953, albeit with a few interruptions. At the insistence of Ernest Jones, she studied medicine and qualified in 1937, and became a full member of the British Society in 1939. At that time she was part of a small group trying to introduce Kleinian concepts to the Viennese, without much success. At the end of 1939, at a joint meeting in London of the British Psycho-Analytical Society and the Paris Psychoanalytical Society, she presented a paper entitled: 'A contribution to the problem of sublimation and its relation to processess of internalization' (published in 1942).

It was during the 'Controversial Discussions' that Heimann was to give full support to Melanie Klein, and actively took part in the scientific and administrative discussions. She presented a first paper entitled: 'Some aspects of the role of introjection and projection in early development', which was discussed during the sixth scientific discussion in October 1943. It would appear that at this time she was undergoing analysis with Melanie Klein, which must have made life difficult, as was her analysis.

She wrote another paper entitled: 'Regression', with Susan Isaacs, which they presented jointly to the group in December 1943 at the second series of scientific discussions. These papers are mentioned below in Chapter 10, 'The Controversies'.

Paula Heimann became a training analyst in 1944. The relationship between Melanie Klein and Paula Heimann seems to have been very complex. From 1935–53 they were very close friends; it would appear that Heimann shared many social activities which were part of Klein's private life, they worked together and one was being analysed by the other. This sort of relationship is difficult to understand in today's context. After their quarrel Heimann made numerous remarks about the inherent danger of mixing an analytic cure with friendship and shared social activities.

Their relationship seems to have begun to deteriorate from 1949 onwards. It was in that year that Heimann gave a paper in Zurich on a subject which Klein disapproved of: countertransference, but the paper was warmly greeted and Heimann thought that Klein had taken umbrage because of this.

Those who knew them well, and held them in high esteem, describe both as intelligent and ambitious people. Heimann, who had been submissive for a long time, chose to become independent, which Klein no doubt did not appreciate. However, it would also appear that Heimann had had the feeling several times that her analyst was stealing her thoughts and using them for her own personal prestige. This is a plausible feeling, fairly common in all analysands, and should be worked on and interpreted by the analyst. Other grounds for discord came to light concerning the British Psycho-Analytical Society. Heimann was in greater favour with the Society than Klein, so much so that at one time she hoped to become its Chairman. She put her failure to do so down to her nuisance of a friend Melanie Klein. It is difficult, however, to say precisely what finally caused them to go their separate ways in 1955. Paula Heimann was to say later on that Klein's paper on envy, presented at the Geneva conference, was the point at which they finally and irrevocably diverged on a theoretical level (Grosskurth, 1986: 414). Their quarrel became official and concrete in 1955 when Klein requested that Heimann resign from the board of the Melanie Klein Trust, and Heimann complied immediately. From that point on, Paula Heimann positioned herself in the group of independent psychoanalysts, and in particular took part in the weekly seminars given by Donald Winnicott.

It would appear that this quarrel was a particularly painful episode in the life of the Kleinian group and they did not say much on the subject. However, it was of course also a great victory for their detractors, who saw in this quarrel yet another instance of Melanie Klein's malign influence. The exclusion of Paula Heimann from the group was used as a weapon against Klein in the battle waged to limit the spread of her ideas, particularly in the United States, but also to some extent in Europe.

Heimann also analysed a number of well-known analysts: Betty Joseph (British, and a member of the Kleinian group) and James Gammill (an American, who trained in London before coming to France (see Chapter 14), to mention but two.

Joan Rivière (1883–1962)

Joan Rivière was part of the intelligentsia of upper-middle class society in Britain from birth, and was one of the sharpest and most brilliant minds among British psychoanalysts of the period. Beneath an apparent detachment, she was to defend the Kleinian 'cause' very passionately indeed. Whereas Susan Isaacs offered Melanie Klein, the *immigrée*, the backing of the academic world, Joan Rivière offered her invaluable assistance in the social field.

Rivière never obtained a university degree of any sort, but she had an excellent background in literature and the fine arts. She had been sent to Germany at the age of 17 to improve her skills in that language, and had married a lawyer, Evelyn Rivière. She began analysis with Ernest Jones in 1915 at the age of 32, and was the first lay analyst in Britain, taking part in the founding of the British Psycho-Analytical Society in 1919. In 1922 she went to Vienna to undergo part of her analysis with Freud himself. She very quickly became involved in the translation of Freud's works with the Stracheys. She was also responsible for translations for the *International Journal of Psycho-Analysis*. Finally, she was a member of the Glossary Committee along with Ernest Jones and Alix and James Strachey, whose work was to translate into English the technical terms used by Freud. As early as 1921 she was also undertaking training activities. She was also one of the analysts of Donald Winnicott and Susan Isaacs, among others.

Joan Rivière and Melanie Klein appear to have met at the 1920 Congress in The Hague, but were only to become friends after the 1924 Congress in Salzburg. At this time they spent the summer holidays together on the Continent and Rivière began to become familiar with Kleinian theory. Later, she was to play an important role in bringing Klein to Britain, and actively supported Klein, not hesitating to incur the wrath of Freud because of it. The correspondence between Ernest Jones and Freud (Freud and Jones, 1993) in the period 1927–30 is quite enlightening: Freud felt betrayed by Rivière, calling her a heretic, and asked Jones to transmit his observations to her. She must have received them, but did not let herself be influenced by them. Rivière had a great admiration for Freud and was very grateful to him, but refused to limit psychoanalysis to the work of Freud alone.

Rivière's natural independence of mind, probably a result of her background and her education, enabled her to confront the world of the

Viennese psychoanalysts with a certain amount of self-assurance when she went there to give her paper 'The genesis of psychical conflict in earliest infancy' in 1936, as part of an exchange scheme between the two societies. This article is remarkable form a scientific point of view: it is a rigorous and objective presentation of Kleinian ideas and their relationship to Freudian theories. It is also a courageous article because, in this particular hostile Viennese world she declares: 'The innovative work of Melanie Klein has led in particular to a very intensive study of these problems by the British Psycho-Analytical Society and, in my opinion, has directly or indirectly influenced the greater part of the work of its members over the last few years' (1936).

She was one of those who tried to facilitate the integration of the Viennese in London in 1938. However, at the time of the 'Controversial Discussions' she vigorously defended the Kleinian position, sometimes replying somewhat brutally to the attacks by Melitta Schmideberg or Barbara Low. But her support was of most value on the scientific level, where she was unbeatable, unlike Ernest Jones. She took part in all the scientific discussions.

Towards 1947, after the publication of Melanie Klein's article 'Notes on some schizoid mechanisms' (1946) she distanced herself somewhat from Klein. She admitted to being uneasy in borderline cases and to dreading being asked to take on psychotic patients; the new aspects of Kleinian theories were alien to her, she no longer felt qualified to belong to the circle of Klein's disciples in the way that the newcomers were, newcomers such as Hanna Segal, Herbert Rosenfeld or Wilfred Bion. However, she actively took part in *Developments in Psycho-Analysis* published in 1952 for Klein's 70th birthday: She wrote the general introduction, which begins with a quote from Freud's *An Autobiographical Study* (1925a: 1): 'I have made many beginnings and thrown out many suggestions . . . Something will come of them in the future.' She made a point of repeating here that Klein's work had been carried out in a field of knowledge which until then had been closed to scientific inquiry (1925a: 36). Whereas 'the general assumption of psychologists (and even some psycho-analysts) has been that the baby *has* no mind and no psychical processes until it begins to express them visibly and audibly in a way adults are accustomed to comprehend', she pays homage to 'the gifted intuitive mothers and women who nurse children' who are not scientists and yet they know 'that a baby does feel and "think" and "know", and react and respond emotionally *i.e.* psychically, to whatever happens to him and is done to him'. In fact, years would go by before 'the scientists' and certain psychoanalysts, educated through the scientific study of mother–child inter-relationships, modified their position concerning Klein's work.

Joan Rivière died in 1962 at the age of 79. She published a great number of papers; we have only mentioned the main ones from a historical view-point. Her influence on the British Psychoanalytical Society was considerable (see *The Inner World and Joan Rivière: Collected Papers 1920–1958*, ed. A. Hughes, 1991).

Susan Isaacs (1885–1948)

Susan Isaacs became a member of the British Society in 1923 after having been elected associate member in 1921. She had three successive analysts: initially, and briefly on the Continent, Otto Rank, then a second phase in London with Fluegel, and then a final phase with Joan Rivière, and this after having met Melanie Klein.

Her training was not medical; she was a teacher. She studied philosophy and then psychology at Manchester University and then at Newnham College, Cambridge. In 1924, she accepted the position of principal at a so-called 'revolutionary' school in Cambridge. It was a nursery school, Malting House School, and it claimed to follow a new educational philosophy:

> The school encouraged . . . children not simply to express themselves randomly but also to 'find out all they can for themselves,' including 'the open expression of sexual interests,' though 'canalized', as Isaacs expressed it, 'by being turned into scientific channels.' The result, she claimed, was a sense of 'pleased concentration' among the children.
>
> (Strachey and Strachey, 1985: 45)

The school seems to have been the object of scandalized rumours. According to James Strachey, it had been nick-named 'the pregenital bordello'. However, children of Cambridge friends of the Stracheys attended it, and Melanie Klein and Jean Piaget (who seems to have been influenced by Isaacs) also visited it before it closed in 1927.

In Britain Susan Isaacs was a pioneer in the study of child development, the first to apply psychoanalytical knowledge to the field. In 1933 she was appointed Head of the new Department of Child Development at the Institute for Education of the University of London. She was still working there at the time of the 'Controversies'.

Ilse Hellman (I. 4), who came to work in London in 1937, remembered having worked with her at that time on letters Isaacs wrote in reply to the readers of the magazine *Nursery World* in which she ran an educational column. Hellman said she had learned a lot from Isaacs.

In 1939 Isaacs gave a paper to the British Society entitled: 'Temper tantrums in early childhood in relation to internal objects'. This was a memorable meeting in many ways: Melanie Klein and a number of her supporters were present but so were Anna Freud, Dorothy Burlingham and

Princess Marie Bonaparte. In the ensuing discussion Isaacs was told that a number of points which she took for granted required further explanation.

Isaacs took an active part in the 'Controversies' giving courageous and intelligent support to Melanie Klein: she presented the text of the first series of scientific discussions 'The nature and function of phantasy'; she also wrote the paper for the second series of scientific discussions on the subject of 'Regression' with Paula Heimann. We shall come back to the text of these papers in the chapter on the 'Controversies'.

However, Isaacs' participation was cut short when her house was bombed in 1944 and she contracted pneumonia. She was to die suddenly in 1948 at a time when she and her Kleinian friends were working on the draft of a document which was to become *Developments in Psychoanalysis*.

Susan Isaacs was one of those who had welcomed Melanie Klein when she came to London to give her lectures in 1925, and when she finally moved to London in 1926. She was fascinated by Klein's theories from the outset and, as we have seen, played an active part in the group's activities. She was a faithful friend without being servile. She insisted on retaining her intellectual independence, as we can see from her correspondence with Klein when she says that although it was with great enthusiasm that she would defend Klein's theories, she wonders what errors she herself and others might have committed that had led to such hostility to those self-same theories. It is no doubt this analysis of her behaviour which enabled her to reply calmly during the 'Discussions', avoiding 'too much pride of possession, too much display,'[2] in a logical, clear and precise manner. She first needed to convince her own colleagues, so much had Klein's work impressed her by 'the very *nature* of her work – the inevitable anxieties it stirs' (Grosskurth, 1986: 327).

Notes

1 Name given to a group of writers, artists and intellectuals who met in the Bloomsbury district of London from 1906, whose members included Virginia and Leonard Woolf, E. M. Forster, John Maynard Keynes and Bertrand Russell.
2 These were her own words in one of her letters to Melanie Klein.

10

'The Controversies' (1941–5): the inevitable confrontation in London

The 'Controversies' have often been mentioned as a mythical period in the history of child psychoanalysis that was better left alone. However, it is now possible to talk openly about them. In 1991, a book called *The Freud–Klein Controversies 1941–1945*, edited by Pearl King and Riccardo Steiner (both members of the British Psycho-Analytical Society) was published. It included the minutes of all the scientific and administrative meetings that took place during the period that was known as the 'Controversies'. We cannot of course give a detailed summary of this voluminous work (958 pages) but we would like to emphasize its considerable historical interest: for the first time we are able to have direct access to the contents of these controversies and we do not have to just make do with a more or less sectarian version by one or other side.

It has often been said that the 'Controversies' were between advocates of Sigmund Freud's theories, grouped around his daughter Anna, and the advocates of Melanie Klein and her theories. In fact, from a scientific viewpoint, the question was to decide whether Melanie Klein's theories followed the lines set out by Freud, or whether her ideas had become incompatible with those of Freud. A reminder of the main tenets of Kleinian theories which were in dispute might be helpful at this point:

- She questioned primal narcissism. Melanie Klein believed that narcissism and auto-eroticism existed but that they were already connected with frustration and with the phantasies about internal and external objects.
- She assumed the existence of an early object relationship, and unconscious phantasies; this was connected with the idea of a rudimentary ego capable of establishing object relationships and of producing mental processes such as introjection and projection.
- She affirmed the existence of pregenital forms of the Oedipus complex, in particular a primitive Oedipus complex, existing parallel to an early

superego, which was not, as Freud suggested, the heir of the Oedipus complex but was a constituent part of the primitive Oedipus.

- She discovered the depressive position and was convinced of the existence of child neurosis (in the sense of Lebovici) in children as young as 6 months old, resulting from the working through of psychotic anxieties.
- She placed great importance on the death instinct, and on the duality between the life instinct and the death instinct;
- She challenged Freud's idea of feminine sexuality, which she said existed in its own right and was not the castrated counterpart of masculine sexuality.

From an administrative point of view the debate was about how the various tendencies in the British Psycho-Analytical Society should be represented and how much influence each should have, in particular with respect to the training of candidates. The discussions were sometimes extremely violent, aggravated by personal animosities, such as that between Edward Glover and Melitta Schmideberg (Klein's daughter), on the one hand, and Melanie Klein, on the other, but more generally by resentments which had been building up for a number of years between the members of the Vienna and London Schools of thought, kept apart initially by their geographical distance. For example, during the debates Anna Freud was heard regretting that the British Society, in the person of its chairman, Ernest Jones, had not judged it necessary to have her earliest work, dated 1927, translated and published in Britain, all the more so because Vienna had always published Melanie Klein's articles.

To try to understand what was at stake during these 'Controversial Discussions', we need to go back to the early 1930s in Britain. Backed by Ernest Jones from the moment of her arrival, Melanie Klein, was able to develop her ideas in a favourable climate. She was listened to and understood; a group of analysts had formed around her, which included Joan Rivière, Susan Isaacs, Donald Winnicott, Nina Searles, Ernest Jones himself and the Stracheys. An initial difference had arisen in the British Society in the period 1934–5, the period of the death of Melanie Klein's son Hans, and of the publication of her work on the depressive position. Her own daughter Melitta and Edward Glover openly became her enemies. In addition, Ernest Jones, who had by then become the chairman of the International Psychoanalytical Association, was becoming worried by the growing differences of opinion between the English school, which was now called the Kleinian school, and the Viennese school of thought. Although in his correspondence with Ernest Jones Sigmund Freud did not attack Melanie Klein openly, he did complain bitterly of Joan Rivière's treachery. She had undergone analysis with him, but was becoming a spokesperson for the Kleinian movement.

It was with a view to reconciling the two groups that in 1934 Sigmund Freud and Ernest Jones decided to hold an exchange of lectures in Vienna and in London: Jones went to Vienna in 1935 to give his paper on 'Early female sexuality' (Jones, 1935) and in return a member of the Viennese school, Waelder, went to London in 1935 to present a paper on 'The problem of the genesis of psychical conflict in earliest infancy' (Waelder, 1937) to the British Society. Joan Rivière then went to Vienna in May 1936 to give her paper on 'The genesis of psychical conflict in earliest infancy' (1936). As we have seen, this latter was a paper defending Kleinian theories, and the notion of reparation in particular. This paper, which was didactic in intent, appears today to be a veritable lecture on the state of Kleinian thought at that time, on the 'innovative work of Melanie Klein'. The questions of oral sadism, introjection and projection, and reparation are dealt with in considerable depth. Rivière did not, apparently, hope to convince, but she insisted:

> Conclusions about impulses and conflicts arising at a date at which the child has almost no means of *direct* expression must be based on the evidence of repetition in the analysis – it is the only source of knowledge of the unconscious mental content existing before consciousness and memory develops fully. I am not expecting therefore immediately to convince you of the validity of our views and our findings, for nothing but analytic experience on the same lines would do so.
>
> (1936: 397).

This idea of the recognition through experience of child analysis was often expressed by Melanie Klein, who regretted that her enemies had not tried to treat a child before expressing their views. (Rivière's paper was published again in 1952 in *Developments in Psychoanalysis* along with the other Kleinian papers discussed during the 'Controversies'.)

However, these exchanges, do not seem to have brought the two points of view any closer together. It was history, in the form of the rise of the Nazis, that was indirectly to precipitate confrontation. A first group of Jewish Viennese analysts had arrived in London as early as 1933 (Paula Heimann and Kate Friedlander among them), but the majority arrived with the Freuds, just before the outbreak of war.

From 1938 a third of the psychoanalysts making up the British Psycho-Analytical Society were continental in origin, mostly from Vienna, but also from Berlin (Hilda Abraham) and Budapest (Michael Balint).

Melanie Klein saw these arrivals as a 'disaster'. 'It will never be the same again', she lamented to Donald Winnicott (Grosskurth, 1986: 241). For their part the *émigrés* were perturbed: they were indirectly reproached with taking patients away from those already established (and would there be enough to go round?), and they were nostalgic for the Viennese group, which seemed to them to have been more friendly and less formal. In 1938 Anna Freud began practising again as a psychoanalyst and ran a private seminar for those wanting to train as child psychoanalysts. In 1939 she turned down a seminar on child analysis at the Institute of Psycho-Analysis because trainee analysts 'who had been analysed or otherwise trained by analysts holding different views would not be likely to benefit from her teaching' (Grosskurth, 1986: 243).

Melanie Klein also admitted that it would have been fruitless to try to blend their teaching. In April 1940 they came face to face in London at a meeting of the Training Committee:

> Miss Freud said (speaking about her work and Mrs Klein's) that her work and that of her collaborators is Freudian analysis, and that Mrs Klein's work is not psycho-analysis but a substitution for it. The reason she gave for this opinion was that Mrs Klein's work differs so greatly in theoretical conclusions and in practice from what they know to be psychoanalysis.
>
> (Grosskurth, 1986: 256)

These remarks were noted by Sylvia Payne and caused a considerable stir in the Kleinian camp, where they were judged to be quite offensive. Some saw in them an Anna Freud sure of herself, heir to and guardian of her father's work. However, these remarks should be put into their historical context. What Anna Freud was defending here, and perhaps first and foremost, was her identity as a 'Viennese' psychoanalyst, the only thing that remained for this group of exiles. The meeting at which Anna Freud had made these remarks took place at the beginning of World War II, at a time when the Viennese found themselves alone in London, at the British Psycho-Analytical Society, because as foreigners they were not authorized to leave the city, whereas the British analysts had either been mobilized or were out of danger in the countryside. Such was the context and climate in which the 'Controversies' began in 1942, when the analysts came back to London.

We will not go into the five Extraordinary Business Meetings which took place between February and July 1942 and concluded with the setting up of the scientific meetings where Melanie Klein and her supporters were invited to defend their works, for, as Edward Glover put it, 'the onus of proof always lay with those advancing new views' (Grosskurth, 1986: 315).

The Kleinians accepted the offer and four papers, by Susan Isaacs, Paula Heimann and Melanie Klein, were put forward for discussion by the group. These discussions were lively, and that over Susan Isaacs' paper lasted a number of months (from January–June 1943). Anna Freud's advocates did not take part in the discussions concerning the last papers.

After having read all the 'Controversies' and a number of commentaries about them, we feel that a few remarks are necessary.

First, one cannot help being struck by the obstinate attitude, indeed mutual suspicion, between the two groups and their evident desire not to be seen to compromise with the other side. It is this desire which enables us to understand why Anna Freud wanted a formal warning ('caveat') to figure at the end of the discussion of the first paper by Susan Isaacs: 'Not answering Mrs Isaacs now does neither mean that we are satisfied with the answers she has given, nor that we now agree with the views she has expressed' (King and Steiner, 1991: 472).

The resolutely combative aspect and the quality of the Kleinian papers is quite evident, as is the way in which the speakers carefully position themselves in line with Freudian theories, supporting their discoveries with reference to Freud's texts. As an example we would quote an excerpt from a letter by Melanie Klein found in the Melanie Klein Trust archives, dated 27 June 1943 and mentioned by her biographer Phyllis Grosskurth, in which she states:

What counts, I think, is to re-establish our position in the Society in respect to the actual value of our work, and that can only be done patiently by giving them at a time no more than they can digest, and also present it in a way which makes this possible for them. . . . I find it necessary, both for the discussions in the Society and with Anna Freud and for our own sake, to refresh our memory on every word Freud has written. This would be a sure foundation from which our discussions can start, and then we might even be able among other things to meet the 'Viennese Freudians' on their own ground.

(Grosskurth, 1986: 313–14)

Conversely, the Anna Freud group seemed immediately to have difficulty in finding arguments, so persuaded was it of the legitimacy of its position, and that it was dealing with a deviation. Certain passages underline this position. For example, Kate Friedlander, in a spontaneous discussion (see seventh discussion of the 'Controversies', King and Steiner, 1991: 585), says: 'The validity of a theory cannot be proved, at least in our science, by its application to therapy. For instance mesmerism and the spring in Lourdes had much better therapeutic results than psychoanalysis. That, however, is no proof for the correctness of the theory behind it.' Another example, is a statement made by Edward Glover, during the same discussion (p. 587, original emphasis): *'But surely this is precisely the matter we are concerned to discuss in the whole of this series, viz. whether these conclusions are valid, or are subjective ideas, in other words, how far Mrs Klein's ideas affect her conclusions and techniques.'*

Consequently, it is not surprising that, as the months and the papers went by, the Anna Freud group took less and less part in the discussions and that finally Glover, initially the main attacker of Kleinian theories, resigned from the British Psycho-Analytical Society, even if other elements, such as his clumsy attack on army psychiatrists and psychoanalysts, had also put him in a difficult position. While on this subject, one might well ask whether Glover's aversion for Melanie Klein was not induced by an element of countertransference which might have escaped him, and which was related to the analysis he was undertaking at the time of her daughter, Melitta Schmideberg, both the analytical situation and the sudden death of Melitta's brother having 'reactivated' in her an early hatred for her mother.

It is also perhaps interesting to note that the discussions often revolved around the works of Sigmund Freud. Each group had 'its Freud', each group purporting to be more Freudian than the other and putting forward, to support its own arguments, one of the aspects of the theories he expressed: the Anna Freud group remaining faithful to his early theories and the Kleinian group putting forward his later works. A typical example is that of the discussions surrounding the death instinct: the Anna Freudians were heard to maintain that the idea of Freud was that it was a purely biological theory in which psychological concepts had no place. The Kleinians retorted that the problem was not to know whether the death instinct was an idea which was acceptable in itself, but rather to envisage the death instinct as Freud had described it when he asserted the duality of the life and death instincts as a basic dialectic in the unconscious, replacing the dialectic opposition of the ego instincts and libido, which became indefensible after the discovery of narcissism. Basing their arguments on various writings of Freud's, such as those in *The Ego and the Id* (1923), *Negation* (1925c) and 'The economic problem of masochism' (1924), the Kleinians maintained that the death instinct was related to mental conflict, the neurosis theory. They maintained that it was at the bottom of the intrapsychic conflict in all his latter works, such as when Freud dealt with masochism or melancholic suicide.

One final remark. The papers given in the 'Controversial Discussions' are of capital importance to Kleinian theories. Not only do they give form to certain basic concepts, but, in addition to the fact that they are rooted in Freudian theory, the Kleinians fully intended to use them to demonstrate the innovative aspects of their ideas.

The object of the first paper 'The nature and function of phantasy'[1] presented by Susan Isaacs, was to clarify the use of the concept of unconscious phantasy. Using Melanie Klein's works, Isaacs looked at phantasy in relation to instincts, the workings of the mind, external reality and to advance mental functions. She considered that unconscious phantasy was the psychic representation of the instincts. 'Every impulse, every feeling, every mode of defence is expressed and experienced in such a specific phantasy, which gives it mental life and shows its specific direction and purpose' (King and Steiner 1991: 278). This is in keeping with the omnipotence characteristic of the infant mind, but also with what Sigmund Freud develops, Isaacs goes on to say, when he describes the existence of a hallucinatory wish-fulfilment, which characterizes the early stages of development. Quoting Freud ('Instincts and their vicissitudes' 1915), she says:

> In so far as it is auto-erotic, the ego has no need of the outside world, but . . . it cannot but for a time perceive instinctual stimuli as painful. Under the sway of the pleasure principle, there now takes place a further development. The objects presenting themselves in so far as they are sources of pleasure, are absorbed by the ego into itself, 'introjected' (according to an expression coined by Ferenczi): while, on the other hand, the ego thrusts forth upon the external world whatever within itself gives rise to pain. (v.infra: the mechanism of projection).
>
> (King and Steiner, 1991: 278–9)

From this Isaacs concludes that

> I am quite aware that Freud, in describing the primary introjection, nowhere calls it an unconscious phantasy. But, as I have already explained, it is to my mind impossible to see how the process of introjection can otherwise be conceived than as operating through phantasy. I therefore hold that we are entitled to claim Freud's concept of primary introjection as a support for our assumption of the activity of the unconscious phantasy in the earliest phase of life.
>
> (p. 279)

She thinks that the earliest phantasies are non-verbal, that they are first of all corporeal, then visual and finally able to be verbalized. Sometimes, however, preverbal phantasies might be expressed later on in a verbal mode. She mentions the example of a small boy observed by Ernest Jones who, seeing his mother breastfeed his younger brother, said while pointing at the other's nipple: 'That's what you bit me with' (p. 313). She describes the earliest phantasies at an oral level, concerning the incorporation and expulsion of objects and parts of the ego. Phantasies are the basis of the initial defence mechanisms of the ego, introjection and projection. 'They are always *experienced* as phantasy' (*Developments in Psychoanalysis*, Klein et al., 1952: 106).

Isaacs gives the example of the mechanism of denial which 'is expressed in the mind of the subject in some such way as: "If I don't admit it [*i.e.* a painful fact] it isn't true". Or: "If I don't admit it, no one else will know that it is true"' (ibid, p. 106). She describes the phantasy in relation to external reality, modelled on it, and in constant interaction with it. Symbolism is the means by which phantasy is linked to the outside world. On finding a symbolic expression of an unconscious phantasy in the outside world, the child understands and can explore this outside world. Hanna Segal says that for

Susan Isaacs 'thinking evolves out of unconscious phantasy through reality-testing' (1979).

For all that, can one believe, as some have argued, that what Sigmund Freud called 'psychical reality' is the equivalent of the unconscious phantasy? It is not quite as simple as it seems, for Freud and Isaacs differ on one important point. For Freud, the phantasy can only be apprehended by its psychical representation. Melanie Klein, on the other hand, sees the phantasy as the ego's response to instincts, the drawing up of defences and object relationships by the ego. For Isaacs, the Kleinian approach to the phantasy is related to the idea that there is enough ego at birth to form rudimentary object relationships and use primitive mental mechanisms such as projection, introjection and splitting (Segal, 1979: 101) Joan Rivière expresses this new and fundamental point of view in the following terms in the general introduction to *Developments in Psychoanalysis*: 'We do not understand the idea of a period of life where there is no synthetic function in activity . . . a synthetic function connected with the development of the ego.'

It is in this remarkably didactic paper that Isaacs gives the definition of the imago, as distinct from the image. It might perhaps be useful to quote it at this point:

> (a) *'imago'* refers to an *unconscious* image; (b) *'imago'* refers (exclusively?) to a person, or part of a person, the earliest objects, whilst *'image'* may be of any object or situation, human or otherwise; (c) *'imago'*[2] includes a reference to the visceral, kinaesthetic and emotional elements in the subject's *relation*[3] to the imaged person, with bodily *links* in unconscious phantasy with the id, the phantasy of incorporation which underlies the process of introjection.
>
> (King and Steiner, 1991: 557)

We should note here how deeply the work of Wilfred R. Bion is rooted in Kleinian thought, much more deeply than some current French psychoanalysts would like to admit. They would like to appropriate Bion's ideas while emptying them of their Kleinian substance, thereby achieving, just as artificially, what others attempted to do fifty years earlier in trying to separate Freudian and Kleinian theories.

The second paper, entitled 'Some aspects of the role of introjection and projection in early development', was written by Paula Heimann (King and Steiner, 1991: 501–30). This paper dealt with the primitive ego and object relations: in it Heimann wanted to show how introjection and projection are instrumental in the formation of the ego and the superego. These two mechanisms are fundamental to Kleinian theories. They exist from birth and remain throughout life. Right from the beginning of life the infant introjects the breast, object of its desire, as much in phantasy as by feeding from it. The infant identifies itself with this introject. This introjection is not just simply a function of the ego, it is part of the ego itself. The term had already been used by Sándor Ferenczi, then by Sigmund Freud, in particular in *The Ego and the Id* (1923), where he says that one can only give up the object of desire by introjecting it and by hoarding it in the ego. What was new about Melanie Klein's contribution here was the importance she gave to the very first introjections of the part-object and of the breast, and then other objects (the parents in particular in the oedipal stage). Heimann then went on to distinguish between introjection and introjective identification, the latter taking place in the ego, and she distinguished it from other introjected objects which make up the superego. While Melanie Klein had initially thought that all introjected objects became constitutive elements of the superego, she later went on to introduce a much greater diversity into their finality when speaking about internal objects. 'They may be experienced as, for instance, feeding, helping, reinforcing sexuality, or, on the contrary, as persecuting and internally attacking the ego' writes Hanna Segal (1979).

Projection also plays an important role from the start of psychical functions. Here again, Paula Heimann considers herself to be in agreement with Freud, particularly with what he wrote in 'Instincts and their vicissitudes' (1915). However, the depth of their disagreement on early object relations should not be underestimated. First, Freud describes an auto-erotic infant (i.e. connecting none of its feelings with an object, the object being the body itself), then a narcissistic infant (taking itself as an object), and finally the infant turns to an object (the mother becomes an erotic object). Heimann acknowledges the existence of auto-erotism and narcissism in the infant, but says that it is linked to object relations using the phantasy and the mechanism of introjection. The infant can thus suck its thumb because it has introjected the breast and can identify its thumb with the breast. 'The important contention of Heimann's paper', writes Hanna Segal (1979), 'is that auto-erotism and narcissism are ways of dealing with frustration and are linked with phantasies about internal and external objects'.

This paper invites three remarks. First, for Melanie Klein, the notion of good and bad should be understood in relation to the ego, which she describes as being initially totally egocentric. The use which is made of this notion by some psychoanalysts, who would like to read into it an abstract idea implying a Manichaean division of the universe, is in fact absent from Kleinian thought. Klein speaks of that which is perceived by the ego as good and bad for it, both inside and outside, which, we repeat, is initially purely egocentric. The second remark arises from the new interpretation Heimann puts on the myth of Narcissus, in a period such as ours when many analysts are so concerned with the 'double'. Heimann stresses that if Narcissus looks at the outside world in the water, he is in fact looking inside himself. 'This element would then describe the unconscious (loved) object phantasy residing inside the subject and that is at the base of the identification of the subject with the object which, in the overt content of the myth, is represented by the faithful reflection of the subject taken by mistake for an object.' At the source of the pain, which leads Narcissus to languish and then to death, Heimann sees a double frustration: 'He suffered not only from his unsatisfied erotic desires, but also from the despair of not being able to relieve the suffering of the beloved object' (footnote of the paper published in *Developments in Psychoanalysis*, 1952: 167). Narcissus did indeed take the reflection of his pain for the pain of the beloved object. Our third remark is to underline the interest of this paper in the understanding of the early superego, as defined by Melanie Klein.

The third paper was presented by both Paula Heimann and Susan Isaacs (1943) and was entitled 'Regression'. This paper is less fundamental to Klein's work, since once she had described the paranoid-schizoid position, after the war, Klein turned away from the notion of regression. The notion of regression is very much present in the work of Freud. He made it the essential mechanism which opened the door to mental disorders, and he linked fixation and regression. The Kleinians differed from Freud's opinion in at least two essential aspects. First, for Melanie Klein the fixation of the libido was not the cause but the effect of the pathological process (Segal, 1979). In addition, Heimann and Isaacs emphasize the much greater inter-relationship between the genital and pregenital stages as seen by Melanie Klein. There is a constant movement to-and-fro here whose primary motor is anxiety. For Melanie Klein, oedipal tendencies already appear on an oral level and the pregenital elements play an important role in genital organization. On a clinical level this implies considering that the appearance of pregenital material is not necessarily a proof of regression. One can perceive the technical implications of this theory in the way treatment is undertaken.

The last paper, entitled 'The emotional life and ego-development of the infant, with special reference to the depressive position', was given by Melanie Klein (1944) herself. It was not published at the time. According to Hanna Segal (1979), in this article she restates the central role of the depressive position and links it more closely to the views of Abraham and Freud by referring to *Civilization and its Discontents*. The paper added two new elements to her theories: her perception of symbolism, modified by the existence of the depressive position, leads her to think that it is 'also concern for the object, love and guilt, which prompts the child partly to displace his interest from the original object and distribute it among symbolic representatives' (1979). In addition, she examined infant feeding disorders in detail, linking them to cannibalistic instincts. She also examined the anxiety and guilt which resulted from them.

This work was not published because, after the war when it was decided to collect her most important papers together into one volume, Melanie Klein had already modified her views and had written several other articles, among them 'Notes on Some Schizoid Mechanisms' in 1946. These articles were included in the 1952 volume entitled *Developments in Psychoanalysis* only translated and published in France in 1966.

The 'Controversies' came to an end in May 1944. In July a new President of the British Psycho-Analytical Society was elected (Dr Sylvia Payne) along with a new Training Committee, in which there were no supporters of Anna Freud. Edward Glover had resigned. However, this situation was not satisfactory to the great majority of psychoanalysts, so in 1945 discussions were initiated with Anna Freud in order to persuade her and her colleagues to come back into training activities at the Institute. The reorganization of the Society in June 1946 made official the existence of three distinct groups within its ranks: the Anna Freud Group, the Melanie Klein Group and another middle-of-the-road, independent group called the Middle Group. For the training of candidates there were to be two courses: Course A was taught by the Kleinian analysts and analysts from the Middle Group, Course B being taught by analysts who were followers of Anna Freud. Both written and unwritten rules defined the representation of the various groups in the management of the Society and in the various training bodies. We shall not go into the administrative details here. However, it might be of interest to mention that in the third year of training the theory of Melanie Klein's work was to be taught to all students and that, following her request, Anna Freud got her training course included in group B.

As Riccardo Steiner (*The Freud–Klein Controversies*, 1991: 907) points out, it was because this gentleman's agreement was carried out to the letter that the British Psycho-Analytical Society did not split up.

In all likelihood the two main protagonists had quite different feelings in 1945. Anna Freud had never had any illusions. She had managed to retain what she always thought was most precious, i.e. the possibility of training students. However, although fatigue and a certain disappointment, coupled with resentment, had led her to contemplate leaving the Society, she did nothing of the sort, probably for several reasons. First, she had doubts about psychoanalytical institutions and this did not encourage her to form a new one. In addition, as Anne-Marie Sandler (I. 3) states, she was deeply grateful to the English for having taken in her father and herself and she did not want to create difficulties in London. Lastly, her status as a lay analyst placed her in a difficult position insofar as recognition was concerned, particularly with American societies, so that, although she was very tempted to go to the United States, she gave up the idea for that very reason. Her position with the British Society was therefore to go for a compromise, but this was accompanied by a great reluctance to take part in any of its structures.

We shall be seeing how she was to move in two different directions, both deepening her research at the Hampstead Clinic (which she founded in 1948) and spreading her ideas in the United States, which became a sort of private 'game reserve' where she benefited from the material and moral support of her friends of the Viennese School who had emigrated there.

According to Hanna Segal, Melanie Klein considered that the overall consequences of the 'Controversies' were on the positive side: she had a group of colleagues and students devoted to her cause, no longer had to justify her theories and could get on with developing her work.

Notes

1 Spelt thus by Isaacs to demonstrate the unconscious nature of the phenomenon.
2 All Isaacs' emphasis.
3 Our emphasis.

PART III

Today: the spread of child psychoanalysis throughout the world from 1945

Introduction

Our object in this section is not to examine the position of child psycho-analysis in every country; rather, we are interested in the spread of the ideas of Melanie Klein and Anna Freud throughout the world, from two view-points. One viewpoint takes into consideration the historical dimension, i.e. the particular moment and the agents who were responsible for the spread of child psychoanalysis in a given country. The other is concerned with the way in which the two schools were able to enter the same territory, become mutually exclusive or coexist freely, in other words, whether the language characteristic of each school was able to be understood and make itself heard.

We have chosen four examples, which are all quite distinct. It was perhaps in Argentina that the opposition between the two schools made itself felt the least. Arminda Aberastury, who introduced child psychoanalysis to Argentina, was initially trained in the Anna Freud school of thought, but later, after she had become acquainted with the work of Melanie Klein, she became a convert to Kleinian theory. It would therefore seem that in her case, and therefore in Argentina as a whole, the influence of the two schools was exerted in a fairly harmonious fashion. Argentinian psychoanalysts were interested in the observation of the child, in the study of the normative and the disturbed, as was Anna Freud, but some of them also did research into serious childhood disorders using input from Kleinian theories.

For a long time the United States remained the private domain of the Anna Freudians. Historically, this is easily understandable in view of the importance the Viennese immigrants were to assume there; it is not so easy to understand from the conceptual point of view, however. Melanie Klein's theories were disdained, ignored even until the late 1970s. When he settled in Los Angeles in 1970, Wilfred R. Bion tried to introduce a number of Kleinian concepts. It would appear that this led to new controversies in the late 1970s.

As with most of Continental Europe, France remained under the influence of Anna Freud's theories. One of her friends, Princess Bonaparte, certainly had an important part to play in this theoretical choice. Kleinian ideas penetrated quite late on, in the early 1970s, and it was difficult to establish a dialogue between the representatives of the two schools.

In Britain, the two schools of thought were forced to put up with each other and from time to time enmities flared up. However, as we shall see, this forced coexistence was to prove extremely fertile for psychoanalysis itself, and with the passing of time, conditions were created in which a dialogue could be instituted, which in no way implied a renunciation of any group identity.

We could have looked at other countries, such as Italy, or The Netherlands where activities in favour of child psychoanalysis were very important. However, they will only be mentioned in passing, for instance, in connection with the fight led by Jeanne Lampl de Groot and her friend Anna Freud concerning the training of child psychoanalysts. Choices had to be made.

11

Britain after 1945

The strides made in child psychoanalysis in Britain in the period after World War II were considerable. It is true that the famous 1946 Barker Report envisaging the creation of one Child Guidance Clinic for every 20,000 inhabitants played a large part in this.[1] This report also proposed a plan for the reorganization of psychiatric hospitals, in conjunction with the National Health Service, enabling the creation of day centres for outpatient treatment and post–cure services. Those in charge of psychiatric institutions then requested the assistance of psychoanalysts, and even went as far as proposing that the latter play a part in the training of psychiatrists. At the same time, an energetic debate was taking place in *The Lancet* concerning the advisability of the continued use of lobotomy and electric shocks as a form of treatment.

A number of the members of the British Psycho-Analytical Society agreed to become involved in this project. However, their participation was limited, owing to their limited number and to the fact that most of them lived in London. Of course, not all of them were interested in child psychoanalysis: some, such as Herbert Rosenfeld and Hanna Segal, chose to concern themselves with psychotics; yet others did not feel at all concerned by this movement towards a more open society.

The influence of the psychoanalysts of the British Society on the treatment of children was concentrated in a few places. We should mention the Tavistock Clinic, where the Institute of Human Relations was set up after the war, and which offered training in child psychotherapy. Many Kleinian psychoanalysts worked there, among them Esther Bick, Martha Harris and Donald Meltzer. We could also mention Anna Freud's Hampstead Clinic, the numerous Child Guidance Clinics such as that at Paddington Green Hospital where Donald Winnicott worked, and the one at the East End Hospital, Kate Friedlander's pilot clinic.

On a theoretical level there were three main currents vying with each

189

other, which, in spite of the inevitable conflicts and rivalry, were the source of a great deal of significant work. The Kleinian school was interested in child psychoanalysis and work with psychotics; Anna Freud and her group concentrated their research on the study of normality in childhood and childhood disturbances. The group of Independents, or Middle Group, had a famous representative in Donald Winnicott. We shall look at how each of these groups evolved in turn.

ANNA FREUD, 1945–82: THE DEVELOPMENT OF
PSYCHOANALYTICAL PSYCHOLOGY

The reorganization of her life

At the end of the war and after the 'Controversies', Anna Freud was tired and depressed. She was to fall seriously ill with pneumonia in the winter of 1945.

A number of the members of her family had perished at the hands of the Nazis: for example, her three aunts (Sigmund Freud's sisters), who had remained in Vienna, had died in concentration camps. The surviving family members were scattered far and wide. Her aunt Minna (who was living with her) had died in London, in 1941.

The outcome of the 'Controversies' had left her bitter and resigned. It is true that the compromise which had been reached within the British Psycho-Analytical Society, and which had led to the creation of the B Course, had meant that she was able to continue training candidates. Although she was on the Training Committee, she nevertheless felt that she was in an isolated minority, facing the Kleinians, from whom she could expect no quarter: 'I know that the Kleinians are hopeless', she wrote to Ernst Kris in 1945 (Young-Bruehl, 1988: 274).

In addition, she had become very critical about psychoanalytical societies, national or international (the International Psychoanalytical Association), for she believed that they were not truly able to promote psychoanalysis in a creative way. There were too many conflicts of interest, personal (because of the various rivalries) or corporate (limiting analysis to medical practitioners only and refusing lay analysts), and ideological.

She felt one very positive aspect, and that was the founding of the Hampstead Nurseries with Dorothy Burlingham and the work that they did there together during the war. Here she felt in tune with herself, working with a population of endangered children, in the community spirit to which she was to remain faithful. With the funds supplied by the American Foster Parents Plan for War Children that Dorothy Burlingham had been able to channel her way, they founded first one, then two and finally three nurseries, and a house in the country for older children. One hundred and twenty very young children (from 0 to 4 years old) finally found places in the London centres. Anna Freud and Dorothy Burlingham defined their goals in 1942 in their book *Young Children in Wartime*: they were to *repair* the physical and mental damage already done to the children by wartime conditions; to *prevent* future disorders connected with the separation from their mothers; to carry out *research* on the psychological conditions essential to child development by studying their reactions to early separation, to the bombing and the destruction; and finally to *teach* those interested the foundations of an education based on a psychological knowledge of the child and, more generally, to look for a model of life in a nursery which could be used in peace-time.

Treatment, prevention, research, and teaching were to be the mainstays of Anna Freud's work in the second part of her life when, after the closure of the Hampstead Nurseries at the end of the war, she founded the Hampstead Clinic. In her book *From War Babies to Grandmothers* (1990), and in the interviews that she granted us, Ilse Hellman spoke of this period with great enthusiasm. She worked at the war nurseries as a superintendent, having been taken on by Anna Freud, who she did not know, because she was a psychologist and had been Charlotte Bühler's assistant in Vienna. The future team around Anna Freud was in the majority made up of Viennese exiles. Hansi Kennedy was one of those who worked in this team (she was only 16 when she started) and then co-directed the Hampstead Clinic (which became the Anna Freud Centre at Anna's death) with Clifford Yorke, as were Liselotte Frankl and Kate Friedlander, who were both to become psychoanalysts like Ilse Hellman. Another was James Robertson, social worker, who went on to become famous in Britain through his work on separation in public hospitals, which, as early as 1950, enabled mothers to be present in the wards when their very young children required hospitalization. The nurseries were open to mothers and fathers alike, day and night, in order to facilitate their encounters with their children. After Hansi Kennedy and Clifford Yorke, George Moran directed the Anna Freud Centre till his death. Anne-Marie Sandler is the present director.

Another important and fundamental idea was to give the children a stable reference in the form of a person, a substitute mother (and if possible a substitute father) and to study the consequences for the child's future development. At that time this was a very innovative idea. The educators and the nurses learned to draw up long-term observations of the children and research was oriented according to these data.

Finally, the staff were all given training: they were taught child psychology, given supervision and some of them also had the possibility of being trained in psychoanalysis, in exchange for their work in the nurseries as it were, since they were paid very little, although bed and board was provided.

On this subject Ilse Hellman recounts how, on the advice of Dr Josefine Stross, the Freuds' family doctor who worked as a paediatrician at the centres, she started to undergo analysis with Dorothy Burlingham. The training dispensed was sufficiently attractive for a large number of students to want to enrol for work in these centres. In spite of the war and the poor financial rewards, there was never any lack of candidates. Moreover, after the war some of the staff wanted training as child therapists. So the Hampstead Child Therapy course was started, but that was after the closure of the War Nurseries.

Of course, at the end of the war the nurseries emptied and a solution was found for the children, within their family circle if that was possible. However, they remained very much attached to their 'substitute mothers', who were careful not to break these ties. Ilse Hellman still has ties with some of them, who do not hesitate to give her a call 'if things are going really badly, or really well' (I. 4). *Infants Without Families*, written in conjunction with Dorothy Burlingham and published in 1944, gave an account of this experience.

We thought it important to recount this experience in some detail because we think it is still applicable today, but also because it is indicative of Anna Freud's unique qualities. With her students and colleagues she was gay, warm, attentive to others and to their difficulties, faithful in her friendships. 'Once she had accepted someone, it was for always', said Anne-Marie Sandler (I. 3), who trained at the Hampstead Clinic before becoming a psychoanalyst with the British Society. But she was more than that; she was a born organizer, which enabled her to found several institutions in succession. One of these had been the Jackson Nursery in Vienna, where she had begun her research on psychoanalytic psychology of the child based on her observations.

In 1946 Anna reorganized her private life, buying a house with Dorothy Burlingham in Walberswick, a small town in Suffolk. Dorothy's children came to stay and so did Anna's Viennese friends, those who had emigrated to the United States in particular: Ernst and Marianne Kris, who were working at Yale University; Anny and Maurits Katan, who lived in Cleveland, Ohio; Hildi and Ralph Greenson, who lived in Los Angeles; Kurt and Ruth Eissler; and, of course, Heinz Hartmann. They and others were to form the circle of Anna's American friends who were to play an essential role in her life over the next thirty years, both financially (through the funds that they helped her to collect – in particular, enabling her to found the Hampstead Clinic and continue her work there) and psychologically (by giving her the moral support she needed for her research and by helping to spread her ideas). Among the private bequests made we should mention that made by Marilyn Monroe; in her will she left a large part of her fortune to her first analyst, Marianne Kris, with the instruction that she should use it to help deprived children. The monies were forwarded to the Hampstead Clinic.

It was Ernst Kris who galvanized Anna into action in 1945, with a memorandum written by and entitled 'MEMORANDUM: Free Associations to the Topic What to Do Next?' Kris was an art historian who had married Marianne Rie, one of Anna's oldest childhood friends. Anna had taken him in analysis in 1938 and the sessions continued each summer at Walberswick for a number of years. He worked at Yale University, where he had founded *The Psychoanalytic Study of the Child* which was to become *the* journal for child psychoanalysis in the United States and would be the main tribune for the researchers at the Hampstead Clinic.

In his memorandum Kris enumerated the current difficulties and made a number of important proposals concerning the future. He believed that it was essential for the group to write the sort of fundamental papers the Kleinians had produced during the 'Controversies', that candidates for training should be selected with great care and trained in 'the Freudian heritage', in what 'we believe to be "true Freudian psychoanalysis"'. (Young–Bruehl, 1988: 271). Training should follow the project of theoretical and clinical formulation, Kris argued, and not be dependent on existing Institutes: 'now psychoanalysis, recognized but very seldom understood, needed to secure its identity' (Young–Bruehl, 1988: 272).

The project appealed to Anna Freud and her friends, Dorothy Burlingham, the Hoffers and Kate Friedlander among others. The latter also believed they should create a clinic for child psychoanalysis, the clinical foundation required for any serious training. The idea took three years to mature, took shape in 1947, and finally came to fruition after a number of different experiments, with the opening of the Hampstead Clinic at number 21 Maresfield Gardens in London in 1951, funded, as we have seen by private donations from America collected by her friends. At the same time Anna Freud travelled throughout Europe and renewed her contacts with the Paris Psychoanalytical Society, of which her friend Princess Marie Bonaparte was a member, the Dutch Society, where her friend Jeanne Lampl de Groot worked, and the Swiss Society. All these societies were to send her candidates to be trained, as would, of course, her American friends; for instance, Ernest Furman from Cleveland was sent to her for training by Anny Katan.

Her work

For some thirty years the theoretical works of Anna Freud were closely linked to her practical, clinical experience and the research she undertook at the Hampstead Clinic. All clinical activity, whether analytical treatment or not, was the object of notes. For a better understanding of her contributions to theory we must look at how the Clinic worked. It was original in that treatment, research and training were truly integrated into all aspects of work; diagnostic assessment and psychoanalytical treatment (five sessions a week) made up the greater part of the clinical work carried out by staff, and trainees under supervision. A small number of children were seen for treatment once or twice a week only; these cases were used to train future child analysts in psychotherapy. In a few cases simultaneous mother–child analyses were carried out by two different analysts. Regular meetings were organized with the mothers of young children in analysis. Less regular meetings were organized for children whose care did not require such a rigid programme or who were older. In a few cases the developmental problems of young children were treated by working with just the mothers.

The Clinic used its preventive and educational services to give advice and support to children and parents alike. Students were also able to familiarize themselves with the system of regular observation which was the cornerstone of the seminar work and which was used to complete lectures on theory and clinical practice. The Well-Baby Clinic, for instance, undertook annually 250 medical and psychological consultations of mothers with their young children. The Mother/Toddler group brought worried and/or isolated mothers together each week and gave them an opportunity to meet other parents in similar circumstances, in the presence of professional staff, while their children played together. The Nursery School was a separate entity and took in children between 2½ and five years old on a daily basis. The Nursery School could call on the diagnostic and treatment services of the Clinic if necessary.

Research was based on carefully recorded material from the cases in analysis, which became the clinic Index. The research groups were many and varied, reflecting the interests of the various staff members and the trainees. These groups were training grounds where clinical problems and their repercussions on theory could be discussed. Some of the research groups already had a long history, with their roots in the research undertaken in the Hampstead Nurseries during the war, and had dealt with the needs and the problems of child development. Other subjects of research grew out of clinical concerns: for instance, the centre has recently become interested in the technical difficulties of working with adolescents, emotional problems arising from and linked to physical illness, to chronic disorders such as diabetes, sight or hearing impairment, problems connected with adoption, or specific to single-parent families.

During her interview with us, Anne-Marie Sandler reminded us just how much Anna Freud, who has sometimes been described as being rigid, was open to the creation of this type of work group, saying that she was always ready to give them encouragement.

194

Beyond the simple description, it would seem to us, lies the essence and the creative aspect of the whole setup: the interaction of the various services with the object of learning something new with each new case. There is an example given by Frances Marton (Chiland and Young, 1990: 237): 'Observation was undertaken by the diagnostic unit, the treatment was part of the research on simultaneous mother–child analyses, and the progress of the child was the subject of detailed observation by a research group look-ing at developmental disorders.' Mother–child interactions had been the object of careful study by Anna Freud, in her own fashion, for some con-siderable time. On this subject she wrote in 1960: 'The tool of simultaneous analysis can be profitably used to shed light on problems of development. . . . As the child progresses up the ladder of development, each stage means giving up positions, giving up previous attainments, not only on the child's part, but also on the part of the parent' (in Chiland and Young, 1990: 243). The way in which the work of the two analysts, that of the mother and that of the child, was linked is worth looking at in some detail, since it is a good illustration of the detail with which the clinical data were recorded. For sci-entific purposes, a third analyst coordinator was entrusted with the weekly reports of the first two analysts each week.

> The task was to study the way in which the phantasies of the mother and the child coexisted, overlapped and influenced each other. In addition, the co-ordinator was able to see how the interaction between the mother and the child was reflected in the analysis of the other, how events common to both were felt differently (or in a similar way) and how the disorders seemed to interact with and influence each other.
>
> (Frances Marton, in ibid., 1990: 243–4)

Her contributions to theory were all based on this unique experience of a child-guidance centre, where the direction taken was purely analytic and where child disorders were fundamentally seen as the child's having deviated from the normal road to development.

One of the procedures for collecting data had been set up very early on. The Hampstead Index was devised by Dorothy Burlingham and a group was set up to look after this very important system. The chairmanship of the group devolved to Professor Joseph Sandler in the 1960s, and in a number of significant publications he showed how important this colossal undertak-ing was. An article in the *International Journal of Psycho-Analysis* in 1962, and the book *The Hampstead Psychoanalytic Index*, written in conjunction with John Bolland and published in 1965, which related how the Hampstead Index had come into being using the case of 2-year-old Andy as a demon-stration, are but two examples. In the Preface to the book, Anna Freud expressed the hope that through the Index it would be possible to

195

construct something of a 'collective analytic memory', i.e., a storehouse of analytic material which places at the disposal of the single thinker and author an abundance of facts gathered by many, thereby transcending the narrow confines of individual experience and extending the possibilities for insightful study, for constructive comparisons between cases, for deductions, and generalizations, and finally for extrapolations of theory from clinical therapeutic work.

(A. Freud, in Bolland and Sandler, 1965: x)

For an in-depth acquaintance with the Index, we would refer the reader to this work. We would remind the reader here that this material, collected by every member of staff or trainee at the centre, is divided into two main parts, one entitled General Information on Case and the other, by far the most important, Psychoanalytical Material. Each heading carries a section and sub-sections. The material about each child is indexed on two cards, the Case Index and the Subject Index. The Case Index is used to study a given case; the Subject Index is for comparative research. These indexes are living things and can be continuously adapted to the requirements of the material. *Therapeutic Situation and Technique*, a constantly revised manual, helps the therapists to classify the material in the various sections, determine the vocabulary to be used in the writing up of the Index, and enables the researcher to find his way around the Index.

The group doing research on material, chaired by Joseph Sandler and in which Anna Freud herself took an active part, gave an account of its work in a book published in 1980 called *Techniques of Child Psychoanalysis*. 'This work does not pretend to lay out in a global and exhaustive fashion the technique of child psychoanalysis', writes Sandler, 'but it constitutes the widest commentary published on the subject to date.' It deals with a number of problems to do with the treatment programme, the therapeutic relationship, with the therapeutic alliance, resistance, fantasies, insight and transference. It also looks at the various modes of expression of the child, and at interpretation. The last part deals with the conclusion of the treatment, the goals and assessment.

Anna Freud's book *Normality and Pathology in Childhood* was published in 1965 in Britain and in 1968 in France. It is essential to the understanding of her theories and puts the colossal work of the Index into perspective. 'This book is a continuation of my book *The Ego and the Mechanisms of Defence* written 30 years ago', she writes. It reports on the work carried out during that time and the conclusions she had come to. The psychoanalytical psychology that Anna Freud was developing intended to shed light on developmental disorders as they become apparent from the study of the personality and its relationship with environment.

In this work, as she writes in the Foreword (1965), she wants to 'shed light on the complexities and inequalities of development, as they become apparent from the study of different aspects of the personality of the child and their interrelationships, as well as from the relationship between the child's personality and its external environment'.

Herein lies the originality of Anna Freud's position, which was to define the concept of developmental lines while taking into account the influence of the external world on these developmental lines.

With this concept Anna Freud embarked on research into the successive stages of these developmental lines, which would then provide the necessary basis for the assessment of emotional maturity or immaturity, of the normal or of the pathological. One such line, for example, leads from suckling and the weaning experiences in infancy to the way in which the adult feeds himself. Another line starts with the infant's first erotic games with his own and the mother's body, continues through the transitional objects described by Donald Winnicott, to play activity and finally to work.

For each child, the arrival at a given level on one of the development lines is the result of an interaction between the development of the drives, the ego/superego system and their reaction to the influence of the child's environment.

Anna Freud describes a number of developmental lines, for instance: 'From Dependency to Emotional Self-Reliance and Adult Object Relationships', or 'Some Developmental Lines toward Body Independence'. She then goes on to the correspondence between developmental lines. Her premise is that the criteria of normality for a child depend on a fairly close matching between 'growth on the individual developmental lines'. The personality is then described as harmonious. An imbalance in the evolution of these lines should lead to a closer inquiry into the circumstances which gave rise to it: is it linked to innate factors or to the influence of the child's environment? But what was essential for Anna Freud was the study of their interactions and she used metapsychology to do this. For example, she showed how, by using her development concept, she could assess whether a child had reached the level necessary to enter nursery school. She studied the level required in the developmental line which led from dependence to emotional self-reliance, the level required in the line which led towards bodily independence, or towards companionship, or which led from play to work. The assessment of the required levels in these different lines enables the relationship between the child's ego and id to be determined, in other words to show whether the child has mastered the affects and impulses or whether she is still at their mercy.

In this assessment of psychic development, Anna Freud shows how important the concept of regression is. Regression is not necessarily the sign of a disorder; on the contrary, she states that she holds regression to be a normal phenomenon, the child searching (in this return to the past which on a clinical level shows up as the loss of an attainment) for security, shelter, protection, as she had known them in the primal relationship with her mother.

From these findings Anna Freud is able to describe a large number of variations of the norm which are not all pathological, far from it. Continuing her research, she determines 'a metapsychological profile of the child', the result of all of the material collected during the diagnostic stage. This metapsychological profile is, she writes in *Normality and Pathology in Childhood* (1965: 139), 'a picture which contains dynamic, genetic, economic, structural and adaptive data'.

With these data in hand, and taking variations from the norm into account, she then goes on to look at pathology, at its assessment, and to describe a number of pathological states.

Anna Freud thus came to believe that, in serious cases, where there had been primary developmental disturbances, if a number of structuralizations had not been able to take place, the ego would be flawed; and a particular sort of interpretative work would be necessary to remedy this. An explicative interpretation would be necessary, aimed at showing that there was a deficiency and at furnishing a prosthesis, at providing something where words alone were not sufficient. The reader may find of interest a recent paper prepublished for the IPA Congress in Buenos Aires in 1991 by Peter Fonagy and George Moran on this subject. They conclude their paper, 'in thinking that the concept of structural change . . . encompasses both psychic changes achieved through modification of mental representation and the re-establishment of inhibited psychic processes' (1991: 21).

Anna Freud was a prolific writer. She produced many other papers, all published in English in a volume entitled *The Writings of Anna Freud* (1966–80), some of which were published in French in *L'enfant dans la psychanalyse* (1968). In this shaping of psychoanalytical psychology, the rigorous clinical work is easy to spot; it requires a daily effort on the part of all staff members to build a metapsychological profile for each child at a given point in her development from the data recorded in the Index. In addition, such work requires considerable theoretical consistency in a team, and this is the case at the Hampstead Clinic. It is rare in French institutions, however, where the tendency is for each individual to express his or her originality when describing childhood disorders: the result is impressionistic to say the least. We shall not debate the issue as to which of the two different concepts, English or French, is more 'psychoanalytical'; this has already been done. We shall simply confine ourselves to this one remark which is related to the fact that we have attended some working sessions on child psychoanalysis in England where we have been greatly impressed by the level of the discussions, their interest, their accuracy, all of which is of course linked by a common and very precise vocabulary, but which is also to do with an authentic study of the mind of the child.

Serious criticism could be levelled at the work of Anna Freud if one only retained the historical, linear, aspect of her concept of developmental lines. However, it is tempered by the metapsychological study, which always underlies the assessment of the developmental lines and takes the processes of change into account.

In a final contribution, which was accomplished under the direction of Joseph Sandler and a group of colleagues at the Hampstead Clinic, Anna Freud took a fresh look at her 1936 work *The Ego and the Mechanisms of Defence*. Entitled *Analysis of Defence*, this work was published in 1985 in England and in 1989 in France.

This work reveals an Anna Freud who had remained active in the psychoanalytic discussion despite her age, who did not hesitate to go back to her initial text, situating it in the context of the day. Neither did she hesitate to go forward, looking for a better definition of a concept, but always using clinical experience as a basis. She also showed she was capable of modifying her position on theory, for example, on the origin of the castration anxiety. This book is a rare document which will, it is hoped, lead French psychoanalysts to reflect on the sense of the expression 'passing on' and encourage them to rediscover a clinical psychoanalysis which is clear and precise, the only possible basis for any sort of qualitative theoretical contribution.

Anne-Marie Sandler (I. 3) believes that 'there was no question of idealizing analysis for analysis sake' in Anna Freud's scientific approach. She always tried to establish definite criteria to show that analysis was required, refusing to see a child analysed just for the sake of it. It is also true that she always believed that the most serious cases were not able to be treated by psychoanalysis. She had great reservations about the ability of analysis to change a child outside the field of neurotic disorder.

Anna Freud's work is little known in France, is not appreciated to its full extent and the very mention of her name brings immediate reticence. It is true that her work only became known in France in the 1960s, even though Serge Lebovici had been working with her concepts since 1945. It is easy to understand how the terms 'education', 'institutional', 'direct observation', and 'diagnostic interest', must have appeared heretical to a whole generation of analysts from 'leftist' backgrounds, reconverted to analysis by virtue of the ideology linked to the events of 1968, with which they are still impregnated.

Training of child psychoanalysts

Anna Freud was always actively interested in the training of child psychoanalysts. We have seen that one of her first tasks on arrival in London was to organize a private weekly training seminar.

At the end of the 'Controversies' in 1945 the training for child analysts was recognized by the British Psycho-Analytical Society. Candidates who wished to train as child analysts were, after their second, supervised, treatment of an adult, allowed to undertake treatment of children, under supervision: three types of case had to be carried out, one of a young infant, one of a child in the latency stage and one of an adolescent. This training does not come under the sole authority of Anna Freud, since the Kleinian Group may also train child analysts.

However, the compromise that had been reached did not satisfy Anna Freud, and as early as 1947 she drew up plans for a training programme for child therapists with a group of Anna Freudian analysts, Willi Hoffer and Kate Friedlander in particular. There was an agreement with the British Society that they would not be called 'analysts'. The first candidates in this training programme were some of those who had worked with her at the Hampstead Nurseries during the war. Eventually, this training programme was integrated into the activities of the Hampstead Clinic. It was Anna Freud's wish that the centre carry out a full-time, day-time training programme for a small number of carefully selected candidates from different backgrounds who were perfectly integrated into the various activities of the clinic: treatment, prevention and research. Each year the centre took in three to five new candidates for a four-year training period.

The programme consisted of a personal analysis, undertaking and supervising longitudinal observations of children, psychoanalytical treatments and psychotherapies. Clinical and technical seminars, using clinical material collected in the various departments of the Hampstead Clinic and run by psychoanalysts, completed the programme.

The training given was very quickly recognised for its quality, and the majority of the child psychoanalysts who were able to benefit from it (140 by 1990) go on to hold important positions in their respective countries, and/or chose to complete their training in an institute attached to a psychoanalytical society.

In this connection, Anna Freud expressed regret in 1960 that the International Psychoanalytical Association did not recognize the qualifications of these trainees as child analysts, whereas it did recognize those trained by the British Society. This rejection, and a number of other considerations, led her to take up the fight again for recognition of a qualification in child analysis by the IPA. The Hampstead Clinic was dependent on the donations and subsidies it received. Anna Freud had supported this lack of security less and less easily, all the more so since her old friends, who had been responsible for the first subsidies and donations, were dying off. In the United States, her friend Helen Ross was considering doing battle inside the IPA to have training for child analysts recognized, but her attempts immediately came up against the question of lay analysis, for the majority of child analysts in the United States were not trained medical practitioners. At about the same time her friend Marianne Kris founded the American Association of Child Psychoanalysis (AACP), hoping it would subsequently be recognized by the IPA. Anna Freud gave the project her backing. She was still dreaming of the ideal institute, which she had described, as we have seen, at the lecture given at the Chicago Institute in 1966 at the invitation of Heinz Kohut. Such an institute would train analysts competent in *both* adult and child analysis. About the same time her friend Jeanne Lampl de Groot from Holland had contacted her because the Dutch Psychoanalytical Society wanted to establish a child analysis training scheme which would lead to a qualification as a child analyst recognized by the IPA, but which would not include training in adult analysis. This and various other proposals were widely discussed at the International Congresses in Rome (1969), Vienna (1971) and Paris (1973).

No decision was reached in Rome, since, as Michael Balint expressed it in the name of the British Society: 'What they have done and are proposing to do is to achieve a split inside analysis . . . distinguishing the psychoanalysis of children from the psychoanalysis of adults' (in Young-Bruehl, 1988: 387). The problem was posed correctly, but political questions came to obscure the scientific ones. It is true that at a previous Congress in Amsterdam in 1965 child analysis had been prominent: Dr Samuel Ritvo had presented a paper on the analysis of an adult who, as a child, had been analysed by Berta Bornstein; Bornstein had added a comment and comparisons were made with Sigmund Freud's famous case study of obsessional neurosis, the so-called Rat-Man. The Amsterdam Congress had shown how 'the insights of adult analysis and child analysis can and should complement each other' (ibid., p. 392).

In 1970 there were many scientific meetings given over to child analysis in preparation for the discussions for the Vienna Congress in 1971. In June 1970 the European Psychoanalytical Federation organized a symposium in Geneva entitled 'The role of child psychoanalysis in psychoanalytical training' (*La Psychiatrie de l'enfant*, vol. 14, 1971). Anna Freud, Hanna Segal and René Diatkine presented the introductory reports to the discussions. In his paper entitled 'Preliminary remarks on the current state of child analysis', Diatkine asked the 'serious and fundamental question which is to know whether there can be an analytical process in children' (1971: 33). He examined the problem from three angles: the specificity of the analytical process in children, the finality of this process, and a comparison between the analytical process in children and the psychotherapeutic effects of other techniques. In this paper, full of light and shade, Diatkine intended to demonstrate that there was no radical difference between the analytical situation of the child and that of the adult. However, this did not seem to him to be sufficient to define the analytical process in the child. This process had to be examined in relation to Freudian metapsychology. The meeting between the child and the psychoanalyst, he wrote, had the effect of immediately mobilizing the ego of the patient in two different directions at the same time. One would try to master the object projected on the analyst, the other would intend to permit a better repression of unconscious desires stimulated by the libidinal gain connected with the privileged position of the child in relation to the adult analyst. Consequently,

> the productions of the child, its play activities, its drawings, should be considered as a reaction formation destined to maintain far from the child's consciousness the instinctual movements and the invested representations that the psychoanalyst perceives to be at work by recognizing the latent content around which play or drawing is organized.
>
> (p. 11)

Diatkine also questioned the 'concept of knowing' equally overdetermined in both the adult and the child. In addition, he stressed the absence of remembrance in the early analysis of the child, even if, he says, during the treatment the child relives what was already organized by a distant past. 'This is not remembrance, it is analysis in the present, which is not the same thing as analysis of present conflicts' (p. 35). Differentiating carefully between parental imagos and the real parents, Diatkine considered that only a phobia of the analytic situation itself on the part of the parents made child analysis impossible, for this would mean that they would not take the child to the sessions.

The discussions were very heated. Anna Freud returned to the question of the preparatory period from a historical point of view by referring to the work of August Aichhorn. Hanna Segal questioned the 'passage' from psychotherapy to psychoanalysis. The child analyst, perforce, takes part in the child's play activities: it is his/her participation (but to what extent?) which enables the child to change his object, but it is the interpretation of the analyst (which implies non-participation) that makes the change a mutation, in the psychoanalytical meaning of the word.

Serge Lebovici was not as optimistic as René Diatkine as to the existence of an analytical process. He questioned the quality of the transference, in particular the 'externalization of the object' as defined by Anna Freud. He also questioned the quality of interpretation by a psychoanalyst involved in a play situation with the child. Some situations, he suggests, are more to do with accompanying the child than an interpretation of content.

In the second paper of the 1970 Symposium at Geneva, Anna Freud spoke of 'Child analysis as a sub-speciality of psychoanalysis' (1970a). The titles of the various headings were evocative and directly connected with her project: 'Psychoanalysis revolutionary or conservative?', 'Child analysis: the historical angle', 'Child analysis on its own', and finally, 'Future outlooks'. It was an extraordinary paper, extremely clear and combative. She was 75, with more than fifty years of professional analytical experience. Her paper showed, yet again, her startling ability to bring separate elements of thought into a whole, which had been so useful at the Hampstead Clinic. She reminded her audience that psychoanalysis had been created in a 'revolutionary spirit'. At present, she stated, 'while there is revolution, even anarchy, the fields of theory and technique, there is rigidity, conservatism, and bureaucracy on the organizational side' (p. 209). She was inclined to believe that there was a connection between the two. The more the scientific links between the members of a society weaken, the stronger the efforts are, on both national and international levels, to keep the group together by means of rules and regulations. This sort of atmosphere went against the whole spirit of analysis, and child analysis was but one of the victims.

From a historical viewpoint, she believed that child psychoanalysis had been considered from its inception as but one of many sub-specialities of analysis. This was to do with the fact that the importance of child analysis had not been sufficiently recognized for its 'unique aspect', which was of being 'the only innovation which opened up the possibility of checking up on the correctness of reconstructions in adult analysis' (1970a: 210). She was consequently surprised that adult analysts, supposedly profoundly interested in these findings, had not bothered to experience child analysis for themselves: she noted that, on the contrary, the majority of adult analysts continued to act as if 'it were an inferior type of professional occupation' (p. 211). Over and above the superficial responses they gave to explain their attitude (school, the parents, etc.) she suspected in fact that these analysts 'vastly preferred the childhood images which emerged from their interpretations to the real children, in whom they remained uninterested' (p. 211–12). To these remarks of Anna Freud the present authors would not hesitate to add that, more often than not, adult analysts are very suspicious of the child that is in them, and that they believe that any dealings with it, libidinal in particular, are dangerous; that sometimes their unconscious desire to undergo analysis is, at least in part, connected not with a desire to learn about the child in them, but with a desire to master it.

It was after having noted this fact ('no discipline can flourish in these conditions') that Anna Freud made her plea for the recognition of child analysis as a separate branch. She based her demonstration on the experience acquired in the few areas in the world where, in her opinion, child analysis had found its place. The examples she gave were the Tavistock Clinic and the Hampstead Clinic in London, the centres in Leyden and Amsterdam in The Netherlands and, in the United States, the Association for Child Psychoanalysis and the centres in Cleveland (Anny Katan and the Furmans) and New York (Marianne Kris).

However, independence, as she had been able to gauge at the Hampstead Clinic, had both good and bad points. This is why she requested that the IPA either recognize and promote training which would include training in child analysis for everybody, or accept that child analysis was independent, like adult analysis.

The discussion surrounding her report was heated. Most of the speakers (Jeanne Lampl de Groot, James Gammill, René Diatkine, Evelyne Kestemberg) adopted a position in favour of integrated training, which would include training in child analysis, and against specialization. Joseph Sandler put forward arguments in support of this position, stressing that it was not a question of training child analysts or adult analysts, which is what specialization would lead to. He defined the practice of psychoanalysis not as a technique but as 'a method for internalizing theory'. He believed that training in child analysis had been nothing but enriching for him, but he also believed that training in adult analysis enabled the analyst to develop a new capacity, connected to what he called 'the third ear', which he defined as being 'the possibility of hearing day after day the material that one has a feeling will come out, emerge' (p. 53).

The third paper of the Geneva symposium of 1970 was one given by Hanna Segal on 'The role of child analysis in the general training of the analyst' (Segal, 1971). She centred her argument around the proposition that she thought was fundamental: psychoanalysis is made up of knowledge, theory and technique. In addition, all these facets are closely linked and of equal importance in the training of the psychoanalyst. She reminded those present that many of the major advances in analytical knowledge and theory could be attributed to child psychoanalysis, and gave as an example the considerable work done on the creation of symbols in the Kleinian school, which had originated in the analytical work done by Melanie Klein with Dick, a 6-year-old autistic child.

To teach theory, she said, was to come up against the experience on which that theory was based. Moreover, could theory be taught with clinical examples if these were not linked to technique? And, 'Can the theoretical knowledge of technique be taught without any real experience of technique?' Differentiating what was ideal from what was possible, she demanded that any institute which trained analysts should have a minimum of training in child analysis included in the programme. This minimum would include 'first of all, the complete integration into the theory of all the acquisitions arising from child analysis, secondly the observation of babies and children, and lastly lectures and clinical seminars in child analysis for all candidates'. Moreover, she would have no objection if analytical societies suffering from a lack of training analysts in child analysis called upon those from other societies.

This point also seems to have provoked much discussion. René Diatkine wanted to see acknowledged the essential difference between the observation of babies and child psychoanalysis, where 'according to the same scientific process as in adult analysis, one sees for the most part the effect of what has already been organized in an earlier phase'.

For Georges Mauco, who was one of the founders of 'Medico-Psycho-Pedagogical' (Centres (CMPP) in France along with André Berge and Juliette Favez-Boutonier, this debate was essential, because he envisaged the recognition of the status and the training of child psychotherapists in the French national education system, at least for those who might be called upon to be part of a team in an institution.

At this point Serge Lebovici intervened to explain that he was no longer in favour of the recognition of child psychotherapists. He dreamt of child psychoanalysts' being trained from among the best psychoanalysts and continuing to carry out adult analysis as well. It seemed to him that it would be better to move towards psychoanalysts who would include the practice of child psychotherapy in their field of activity. It was not a question of 'treating the child', as Mauco had put it, but of 'considering that the child's disorders were the expression not only of what the child was experiencing but also the result of its relationship with its family'. Moreover, Lebovici believed that the observation of the child, if retained, should be defined as an observation not of the baby but of the relationship between the baby and the mother, the baby and the family.

In conclusion, Hanna Segal replied to a number of those taking part in the discussion. René Diatkine and Evelyne Kestemberg had insisted on the differences between the two types of analysis, underlining the importance of the primary processes in child analysis. Hanna Segal noted the position adopted by Lebovici, who had just said in essence that only child psychotherapy existed, while child psychoanalysis did not; she herself believed in the existence of child psychoanalysis. However, if one practised this type of analysis only, one might easily deviate, one might move further and further away from psychoanalysis, in the direction of psychotherapy. 'In this [she saw] two important elements: one due to the fact that in child psychoanalysis one is more exposed to the primary processes; the other, as Joseph Sandler had emphasized, that it was a technique with unavoidable parameters.'

She summed up her position by stating that the more one worked within parameters, the more one had to spend time, as a counterbalance, with adult patients who confront us with the analytical process. In any case, she stressed, we work with psychic reality, which is the essence of analytical work. The conclusion that she drew from all this was that sound training in child psychoanalysis was needed at existing analytical institutes.

We thought it useful to present the discussions of this particular congress in detail because it was a real scientific debate, perhaps the only one within an international body in this field. In addition, the arguments that were raised struck us, twenty years on, as still being relevant.

The second congress of note in 1970 took place in London that autumn, The English Speaking Yearly Conference. The British Society was very concerned at Anna Freud's request to the IPA, as it was in danger of losing its monopoly on the training of child analysts in England. It therefore decided that the theme of its annual symposium would be infantile neurosis. The only merit of the papers given, by Elliot Jaques, 'The Kleinian concept of infantile neurosis', by Martin James, 'Evolution of concepts in infantile neurosis', and by Masud R. Khan, 'Infantile Neurosis – false organization of self', was to present the respective points of view of the various schools of thought present. We shall not dwell on these further.

At the Vienna Congress in the summer of 1971, no decision was made on the fundamental problems, in spite of the report by the committee headed by Dr Ritvo set up at the Rome Congress to give an account of the current status and future possibilities of training in child analysis. However, the Hampstead Clinic had applied to become an IPA 'study-group'. The status of study-group meant that the constitution of a second British Psycho-Analytical Society, headed by Anna Freud, was possibly in the offing. The British Society reacted immediately by proposing a compromise, which Anna Freud accepted, thus staying within the Society. She was rewarded by having the training at the Hampstead Clinic recognized as official training of the British Institute of Psycho-Analysis in child analysis. Members of the Society who so wished could now come to Hampstead and train officially in child analysis, and the child analysts trained at Hampstead would benefit from special arrangements to train in adult analysis at the Society's Institute. Anna Freud had not entirely failed. The Hampstead Clinic had been recognized by the IPA inasmuch as it would be officially taking part in the training of analysts in England. She did fail, however, and she had understood that this would be the case since the Vienna Congress, in her request to have the IPA recognize a specific training course and status for child psychoanalysts. In 1973, at the Paris Congress, the findings of the Ritvo report were rejected. To our knowledge, the question has never been discussed since.

Her final years

The final years of Anna Freud's life were also those of her final works. At the beginning of the 1970s she gradually relinquished her responsibilities at the Hampstead Clinic, entrusting more and more of the co-management to Clifford Yorke and Hansi Kennedy, who had already worked with her at the Nurseries during the war. In the 1960s she had accepted a teaching position at the Yale University Law School, where she gave a seminar on the child and the law. With Joseph Goldstein and Albert Solnit she co-authored two books: *Beyond the Best Interests of the Child and Before the Best Interests of the Child*.

Although in her eighties, Anna Freud was still in harmony with the young educator she had once been in Vienna, looking into the distress of children with the same concern, working for the recognition of their rights, especially that of children's need for continuity in their life experience. She was to propose the concept of 'psychological parents' for children who were deprived of their own family environment. If it was necessary, and if it was in the child's interest, he should be protected from the biological parents. However, in general the biological parents are the best equipped to bring up the child, and in this sense, and as far as possible, they should be protected from too much intrusion on the part of the state. *Beyond the Best Interests of the Child* had a considerable impact in the United States, for it fostered reflection on the needs and the feelings of the child; all too often judged, in her opinion, by an adult and from an adult point of view.

These works were the last of Anna Freud's great professional joys. She died at the age of 87 in 1982.

MELANIE KLEIN (1945–60): THE WORLD OF PSYCHOSIS

The final years

The last fifteen years of Melanie Klein's life were very creative ones. When the war ended in 1945 she was 63. She was now assured of a recognized position within the British Psycho-Analytical Society, and was surrounded by colleagues who had defended her well. A growing number of young analysts were becoming interested in her work and wanting to train with her group. However, she was still worried about the future of her work, in particular, whether or not it would survive her, such was the sharpness of the criticisms raised against it. She knew that although she had triumphed over her rival, Anna Freud, in London (in the sense that the latter had not been able to have her banished from the analytical world for deviation, as her father, Sigmund, had done to Adler, Jung and a few others), she was nevertheless the object of deep hostility on the part of American analytical circles. This group, which had become the most powerful after the war, never quoted her, and never missed an occasion to state their hostility to her ideas during the IPA congresses which she insisted on attending regularly. There were sessions where she was routinely interrupted for going over her allocated speaking time. In contrast to Anna Freud, who was literally venerated because she was 'the Master's daughter', Melanie Klein was given the same amount of time as everybody else, perhaps even a little less. We can remember a particular working session with Anna Freud in London in the 1970s in which the whole room, filled to capacity, and which had been patiently awaiting the arrival of Miss Freud, got to its feet as one man to applaud her when she finally entered the hall and tried to slip quietly up to the rostrum like a little grey mouse. These vexations did not seem to affect Melanie Klein. We might presume to say that the additional energy she put into her work was her way of reacting.

Gradually her faithful colleagues disappeared. We have mentioned some of them but it might be useful to remind the reader of the untimely death in 1948 of Susan Isaacs, who had been very active during the 'Controversies', the progressive remoteness of Joan Rivière, who, although never hostile, wished to put some distance between herself and Melanie Klein from the 1950s onwards because 'she felt ill at ease in the world of psychosis' in which Klein was taking more and more of an interest. In the latter years of her life she found herself in conflict with Paula Heimann, even to the extent of excluding her from her group (see above, Chapter 10). The reasons were complex and partly obscure, as we have seen. Happily, however, her new analysands rapidly took up the flame. In 1949 Hanna Segal and Herbert Rosenfeld published papers on schizophrenic patients at the IPA's Zurich Congress. They were followed by Wilfred R. Bion, Donald Meltzer, Elliot Jaques and Esther Bick, who all deepened and enriched her theoretical contributions, whether in the field of the psychoanalysis of psychoses, or of creativeness and art, or in the study of group dynamics. We shall come back to this when we discuss these authors.

The major works of this period were, first, a key article in 1946 entitled, 'Notes on some schizoid mechanisms', followed in 1948 by 'On the theory of anxiety and guilt'.

In 1952 her colleagues and students wished to mark her seventieth birthday, as had been done for Sigmund Freud. There was first the publication of *Developments in Psychoanalysis* (Klein *et al.*, 1952), followed by a special issue of the *International Journal of Psycho-Analysis* dedicated entirely to her. All these papers plus some by other authors were published in London in 1955 in a volume entitled *New Directions in Psychoanalysis* (Klein, Heimann and Money-Kyrle, 1955). The clinical section included a number of papers on child psychoanalysis, in particular that of a 3-year-old autistic child by Emilio Rodrigué, whom we shall meet again, this time in his native country, Argentina. Two of the papers were about the analysis of schizophrenic adults, one by Herbert Rosenfeld (1952), the other by Wilfred R. Bion (1953). The second part of the book gave an account of Kleinian theories as they applied to non-clinical fields. For example, there were papers by Joan Rivière from the field of literature, Hanna Segal from the field of aesthetics, and R. E. Money-Kyrle from the field of philosophy. Bion and Jaques provided two contributions from the field of sociology. In this volume Melanie Klein published her fine paper on identification (Klein, 1955), in which she analysed *If I Were you*, a novel by Julien Green. It is a nice description, and an illustration, of the dynamics of a case of massive projective identification. The whole book, *New Directions in Psychoanalysis*, was prefaced by Ernest Jones, who took the opportunity of stating his delight at the recognition of Melanie Klein's work.

The year 1952 was also marked by a paper entitled: 'The origins of transference' (1952a) given at the Amsterdam Congress. It was the first of her works to be translated into French, by Daniel Lagache. This paper, which was didactic in intent, recalled her theoretical position, but its main interest lies in the way she linked analytical technique to theory.

She could have stopped there. Her work would have been complete, having constructed her theory of the structure and development of the mind. But this was not to be. In 1955 she gave a paper about envy at the International Congress in Geneva, and then published a small volume: *Envy and Gratitude* (1957). Her new theories caused an outcry and rekindled the 'Controversies'.

In 1959, in Copenhagen, she gave a final paper entitled: 'On the sense of loneliness' (1963). It is autobiographical in a sense: at the end of her life Melanie Klein went through a period of great pessimism and depression. She once again doubted that her work would survive her. Her feeling of loneliness continued to grow and in this paper she tried to find its roots: the depressive feeling at the loss of the object, and the schizoid splits, which lead to and accentuate the feeling of being cut off from oneself. The paper was never finished.

At the same time she published the Richard case in a book entitled *Narrative of a Child Analysis* (1961). It was about the psychoanalysis of a 10-year-old boy she had conducted for a few months in Scotland during the war in 1941. The writing up of the case was linked to her desire to see her work survive her by enabling her critics to understand her work, as she had practised it, more clearly. It is a fascinating piece of work but of course gave her detractors an opportunity to renew their criticism of her, and of her interpretative technique in particular.

Her work

Let us now have a more detailed look at some of the works of this period. Trying to read her 1946 paper, 'Notes on some schizoid mechanisms' (1946) is an arduous task. In it she defines two essential elements of her analytical construction: the paranoid-schizoid position and projective identification. The reader is immediately confronted with a great feeling of anxiety because of the vertiginous nature of the world she describes. The means of defence is often rejection, i.e. to close the book, or derision. In this work Melanie Klein describes how the infant (with her rudimentary ego) has to cope with psychotic anxiety using her defence mechanisms, also psychotic, the anxieties and the defences underlain by unconscious sadistic-oral phantasies. In 1952, in the General Introduction to *Developments in Psychoanalysis* Joan Rivière was already defending Melanie Klein against the critics of the day who objected to her turning the infant into a psychotic (this criticism remains today). She stressed that, on the contrary, Melanie Klein was describing a normal stage of development in which, although anxieties and defence mechanisms are psychotic in nature, the infant itself is not. We should remember that Melanie Klein did, however, believe that the infant could become psychotic later on if there was fixation or regression at this stage. For her the paranoid-schizoid position contained the roots of later psychosis.

In this paper, starting from the Freudian distinction between the life and death instincts, Melanie Klein develops her definition of the nature of the primitive ego and primitive anxiety. In contrast to Freud, however, who talks of a (biological) organism which deflects the death instinct, Melanie Klein talks of a psychological entity, the ego, which is capable of feeling anxiety from birth, and of using defence mechanisms. 'She does not speak of an organism deflecting but of a primitive ego projecting the death instinct'. Hanna Segal stresses (1979). Inasmuch as Klein also attributes to the ego the ability of phantasizing in a primitive mode an object relationship, the projection produces a phantasy of a bad object – projection *into* the object.

Melanie Klein believed that the death instinct gave rise to a fear of annihilation in the primitive ego and that it is the defence against this fear which leads to the projection of the death instinct into the object. For her, the fear of annihilation and disintegration is the greatest fear which the death instinct can give rise to and the organization of the primitive ego arises out of this chaos through the use of the defence mechanisms of projection and introjection. The ego is constructed from the struggle between the life instinct and the death instinct, thus splitting the object into a persecutory object and an ideal object, in the same way that inside itself, and also by splitting, the ego creates a libidinal part and a destructive part. The goal of the ego is to introject the ideal object and to identify with it, so as to keep the persecutory internal and external objects at bay. It should be noted that the good object, although only a part-object at this point, is perceived as being whole and intact, whereas the bad object, hated and then becoming a persecutor, attacked by oral sadism, is fragmented and torn apart.

These ideas met with few positive opinions among the analysts working in the field of neuroses, which is understandable. However, from the outset they were of great interest to the analysts working with psychotics, for they found in it a container allowing reflection about their own experience with patients. The debate has been rekindled at a different level over the past few decades with the constructin of the atomic bomb, which caused among the public at large an immediate fear of annihilation (not of castration), sufficiently important for a number of intellectuals to see an important turning point in human civilization connected with the concrete representation in the external world of the death instinct. It is not uninteresting to note here that a movement opposed to the use of nuclear power in warfare was formed amongst psychoanalysts in which Hanna Segal, together with Moses Laufer, played a leading role. This movement still meets at each International Congress of the IPA.

In this paper, Melanie Klein also introduces a new mechanism at the service of the ego, projective identification. 'It represents the phantasy', writes Joan Rivière (in *Developments in Psychoanalysis*, 1952: 33), 'of forcing the self in part or as a whole into the inside of the object in order to obtain possession and control of it, whether in love or in hate'. It is not just parts, but the whole of the ego which can be projected into the object. In 'The Importance of Symbol Formation in the Development of the Ego' (1930a), Dick has two sorts of phantasy about his mother's body. On the one hand, his phantasies were of the mother's body as filled with the projected and terrifying parts, and on the other, his phantasy was of a mother whose inside is empty and into which he can project all of himself. He plays this out by hiding in the empty cupboard. In the paper entitled 'On identification' (in *Envy and Gratitude and Other Works 1946–1963*, vol. 3 of *The Writings of Melanie Klein*, 1975), based on the novel *If I Were You* by Julian Green, Melanie Klein shows how a personality in its totality can project itself into another, thus identifying almost totally with the other, taking its place. It is in this fashion that in a delusional construction one can become Napoleon, Jesus, and so on.

The purposes of projective identification are many, such as getting rid of a part of oneself, greedily possessing and controlling the object, emptying it, etc. Projective identification concerns not only the 'bad parts' of the ego, which will make up the persecutory object, but also the parts perceived as being good, which are thus given shelter in an object which has become idealized, or put into the object to avoid separation from it. However, the consequence is that the ego feels impoverished.

Projective identification is at the root of a narcissistic object relationship, for the object is reintrojected. Melanie Klein defines a narcissistic *state*, which is more temporary, connected to the introjection of the split/idealized object and to the identification of the ego with it, and a narcissistic *structure* with narcissistic object relations, both based on projective identification (see Klein, 1952a). The narcissistic state refers to Freud's auto-erotism.

The narcissistic structure that Klein defines was described by Freud when he talked of the narcissistic object relationship and of the narcissistic object choice, the subject in this case choosing a love object in which he can find himself again and love himself (Freud, 'On narcissism: an introduction', 1914b: 73–102). Klein described in much detail the underlying phantasies of such a choice. She thought that when we are in a narcissistic object relationship, and when projective identification is the principal mechanism, the subject can be bought to the point of being afraid of loving, or even of giving up all contact with the other for he sees himself in danger of being impoverished and of being subjugated by the other. We shall not go any further into the description of these phenomena here. We would refer the inexperienced reader to Klein's paper 'Notes on some schizoid mechanisms' (1946), for it is rich and compact, and essential reading even for the informed reader, and has opened up new fields of psychoanalytical research in the field of psychoses. First, by defining projective identification and the way it works, Klein demonstrates a means of communication, a relationship between the psychotic personality and other people, and it was thus possible to then define the nature of psychotic transference. This enabled some analysts to consider treatment of psychotic patients. In addition, her followers undertook work on defining more clearly and on recording the different forms of projective identification which can not only be excessive, as described by Melanie Klein herself, but also take less pathological forms, as we shall see with post-Kleinian authors.

From this point, and after her 1948 article entitled 'On the theory of anxiety and guilt', Klein was able to formulate a coherent theory about psychic development and its disorders. Her entire work may be said to be constructed around the paranoid-schizoid and the depressive positions, anxiety and guilt. In chapter 10 of her book *Melanie Klein* (1979) Hanna Segal takes another, gripping, look at the way in which Klein had formulated her work; we would warmly recommend it to the interested reader. We will simply give an outline here: the notion of position appears as a structural concept and not a chronological one. By defining the concept of position, Klein is able to define the organization of the ego, which includes the state of the ego, the nature of its relationships with internal objects, the nature of anxiety, and the specific defences. The concept of position also enables her to formulate a theory which encompasses both anxiety and guilt. For her, anxiety is a direct response to the internal activity of the death instinct. It can take two forms, a persecutory anxiety, belonging to the paranoid-schizoid position, and a depressive anxiety, belonging to the depressive position. Guilt appears as a resolution of the conflict between the life and death instincts, the life instincts normally prevailing gradually over the death instincts. The passage from the paranoid-schizoid position to the depressive position is the fundamental passage from a psychotic functioning to a neurotic functioning with a differentiation between internal and external reality, i.e. enabling the ego to confront its phantasies with reality. The preoccupation with the object is at the centre of the depressive position and is one of the aspects of reality-testing.

The depressive position is never totally worked through: at each stage of development a choice must be made between regression to a paranoid-schizoid functioning mode (to escape depressive pain) or working through depressive pain in order to progress. 'But the degree to which the depression has been worked through and internal good objects securely established within the ego determines the maturity and stability of the individual', writes Hanna Segal (1979).

The interest of this theory of oscillation between the depressive and paranoid-schizoid positions in an individual should be noted, for it enables the coexistence in the individual of both neurotic and psychotic parts. Taking these psychotic parts into account in the case of the healthy individual is one of the characteristics of Kleinian analytic technique. The Oedipus complex, we should remember, occurs during the depressive position and is an integral part of it. Indeed, it is when the child perceives his parents as real and whole beings and begins to perceive the relationship between them that the oedipal fears and desires manifest themselves (in the first year of life).

The formation and use of the symbol goes together with the evolution from the paranoid-schizoid position to the depressive position. In the paranoid-schizoid position, thanks to the mechanism of projective identification, a part of the ego identifies with the object in a concrete fashion. We should remember the well known example of Dick, the autistic child who cried 'Poor Mrs Klein' while watching the wood shavings that she had just made. This is the symbolic formation underlying concrete psychotic thinking. Hanna Segal would later define this stage of symbol formation with the term 'symbolic equation'. On the other hand, in the depressive position, the ego repudiates absolute power over the internal objects; it mourns for them and the symbol then becomes necessary to replace and represent the lost object. The symbol is no longer concrete and can be used in communication. Creation and sublimation thus develop in the depressive position and are intimately linked to this experience of guilt and loss, which leads to a desire for internal and external reparation of the lost internal object. Klein's research into symbol formation was to find a considerable echo in followers such as Hanna Segal and, in particular, Wilfred R. Bion.

The book *Envy and Gratitude* (1957) is worthy of special attention. Klein was 75 at the time of its publication. This last creative piece of work is moving inasmuch as in it Klein goes in search of the 'infantile roots of the adult world', which was also the title of a paper she published in 1959 ('Our adult world and its roots in infancy', Klein, 1959a). We can but think that at the approach of death Klein was re-examining the links between the infant and its parental imagos, thus continuing her work of self-analysis in the face of the growing feeling which was to be the title of her last work: 'On the sense of loneliness' (1963). In the Foreword she stresses her indebtedness to Karl Abraham, stating how close she had felt to him and to his work and how she had been able to use his work as a foundation for hers. In the first few lines of this Foreword she also intended to place her thinking in the context of the relationship uniting the infant with its mother, to denounce envy 'which undermines love and gratitude at their very foundation'. It is perhaps this self-analysis that enables Klein to state so strongly in her autobiography her love for her mother, now that the destructive elements had been eliminated. This book, which created a storm in the psychoanalytical world, reviving the 'Controversies' yet again, was perhaps the one which enabled her to find inner peace.

In this book Klein defines the concept of envy: 'I consider that envy is an oral-sadistic and anal-sadistic expression of destructives impulses, operative from beginning of life, and that it has a constitutional basis' (1957, in *Writings*, vol. 3, 1975: 176). Envy appears here to be one of the first fundamental emotions, and as such is relived in analysis, in the transference in what she calls 'memories in feeling', which can be reconstructed and verbalized with the help of the analyst. She states that envy is envy for the mother's breast, with its nourishing mental (the breast can transform a state of distress into a state of happiness) and physical properties. Envy for the breast is caused by the gratification obtained because the breast seems to be the holder of infinite wealth, but envy is also caused by frustration when the breast is experienced as enjoying for itself the wealth it distributes at other times. Klein's intention is to distinguish between envy, jealousy and greed. Jealousy is part of the oedipal triangle and is based on love and hate; envy is born in a part-object relationship and is purely destructive; greed is only destructive by accident, and is more specially connected to the mechanisms of introjection.

If excessive, envy becomes a fundamental element in disorders of the paranoid-schizoid and depressive positions. Klein renders envy responsible for a good many confusional states in psychotic patients. By attacking the good object through projection and fragmentation, envy turns it into a bad object. Klein stressed the inner constitutional aspect which was at the root of envy. This discovery somewhat modified her optimism as to therapeutic possibilities, which in turn came up against the 'biological bedrock'. If she persisted in thinking that in certain cases analysis and integration of envy could overcome the negative therapeutic reaction, thus making analysis more effective, she also believed that in other cases envy is too deeply rooted in permanent constitutional factors for integration to be possible. 'The existence of the innate factors referred to above points to the limitations of psycho-analytic therapy. While I fully realize this, my experience has taught me that *nevertheless* we are able in a number of cases to produce fundamental and positive changes' (1957: 230, emphasis added).

This 'nevertheless' of course led to discussion, which are still on-going, about the limits of psychoanalysis, limits which she must be credited with moving to include the field of psychoses.

The final point we will discuss is the connection between her theories and her technique, using the case of Richard as an illustration. Klein analysed Richard in Pitlochry, Scotland, at the beginning of the war. The analysis lasted four months, and was made up of ninety-three sessions. To a certain extent, this was not a typical analysis in that both Klein and Richard knew that it would be limited to a relatively short period of time. In addition, the analytical setting was unusual in that Klein used the premises usually used by a group of guides. She published some of the material in her paper 'The Oedipus Complex in the light of early anxieties' (1945). This work is fascinating reading and prompts a number of comments. First, we see the inner world of the child unfolding, its phantasies, its anxieties, its defences and its progressive changes. Incidentally, the work brings to light Klein's technique of this period. We can see how she goes from the interpretation of the transference to the interpretation of the relationship with the real parents, from the inner world to the outside world. She interprets the elements of reality, the impact on Richard of numerous external events (the illness of the mother, the departure and return of the father, events connected with the war) by linking them to the child's phantasies and by showing him how they colour the external events and how the external events in turn have an impact on his own inner world, increasing or diminishing his anxiety. These interpretations, contrary to some traditions (notably French) of not interpreting events in reality, were generally not well tolerated by French readers, who saw Klein literally persecuting Richard, tracking him down to the furthermost depths of his inner self. This type of analysis, which aims at interpreting the unconscious phantasy and its related anxiety, can only be carried out in a well-defined framework with four or five sessions a week. We might point out one apparent paradox: in this particular case Klein was carrying out a type of interpretation which was not confined to analysing the defences and which made her appear like a persecutor to some. In fact, by interpreting the anxiety and the underlying unconscious phantasy, she brought relief to Richard who was very grateful to her.

In addition, this paper shows clearly how she makes a point of linking interpretation of the present to that of the past, how she maintains a balance between these two interpretations, and how the nature of the relationship to internal objects, relationships which the child repeats in transference, sheds light on the child's present relationships with her environment.

The comments that Klein made in 1959 about the work she had carried out in 1941 are very interesting, for by that time she had brought to light the concept of envy as well as the mechanism of projective identification, which she had not been able to distinguish quite so readily in 1941.

As we have already noted, Klein took great pains with this book, thinking it would make her work more accessible and bring it more recognition. Hanna Segal (1979) writes that she was still working on it at the hospital shortly before her death, rereading the proofs of the index.

DONALD WOODS WINNICOTT (1896–1971): THE INDEPENDENT

Donald Woods Winnicott occupies an important and unique position within the British school of psychoanalysis. A paediatrician by training, he was interested in infants from the outset. As a young analyst he was able to profit from the particularly stimulating climate that reigned within the British Psycho-Analytical Society at a time (1925–35) when the work of Melanie Klein was having a considerable influence on the field. The main part of his voluminous work was done after World War II. He was a solitary figure and belonged to the group of Independents.

His life

Winnicott was born in 1896 in Plymouth, Devon, into a wealthy middle-class family. His father was a prosperous businessman who had twice been mayor of the town and was knighted late in life. An intelligent, calm and well-balanced man who led a busy professional life, he was perhaps somewhat absent for his son (C. Winnicott, 1977).

The family home was a vast residence consisting of many rooms surrounded by a big park. Winnicott lived there with his two older sisters and his mother until he was 12 years old. His mother was a fun-loving, vivacious musician. He was certainly very much cherished and had attention lavished on him by the many women in the household, in addition to those of his family: nannies, housekeeper, cook. 'He learnt very early on that he was loved', writes his wife Clare (1977: 30).

He therefore took for granted the security he experienced in the family home. In such a vast house all sorts of relationship were possible and there was enough room for the inevitable tensions to be isolated and resolved within its setting. With this home base in place, Donald was free to explore all the space around him at his disposal in both house and garden and to fill these spaces with bits of himself and to thus progressively build his own world. This ability of being at home was very useful throughout his life. 'Home is in my heart', says a pop song and this is what Donald must have felt. It gave him that immense liberty of feeling at home anywhere.

At the age of 13, after he had come home swearing one day, his father decided to send him to boarding school. Donald was sent to Leys School in Cambridge as a boarder. He adapted very well, played a lot of sport and made many friends, with whom he would sing or read. At 16 he broke his collarbone on the sports field and spent some time in the school sick bay. It was here that he decided he would become a doctor: he could not imagine having to depend on doctors all his life if he became sick or hurt himself again.

After school, he enrolled at Jesus College, Cambridge, where he obtained a Bachelor of Arts Degree in Biology. Then World War I broke out, and his first year of medicine was done as a nurse at Cambridge, where the colleges had been turned into hospitals. His non-medical friends went off to fight and a number of his close friends were killed; this was to mark him for the rest of his life. 'He always felt that he had a responsibility to live for those who had died, as much as for himself', wrote his wife Clare (1977). He would not rest until he too had gone out to meet the danger of war face to face, so he enlisted in the navy as a trainee surgeon even though he had not yet finished his medical studies.

After World War I he went to London to continue his studies at St Bartholomew's Hospital. He was a serious student, enthusiastic about his work but also very happy to spend his spare time with his friends, playing the piano, or going to the opera. In fact, he wanted to be a country GP (General Practitioner), but the chance discovery of one of Freud's books kept him in London so that he could undergo analysis. In 1923, at the age of 27, he became a paediatrician at the Queen's Hospital for Children and at Paddington Green Children's Hospital. He was to remain at the latter for forty years. It was here that he was to acquire his considerable clinical experience in some 60,000 mother–child consultations.

Concurrently in 1923, he began an analysis with James Strachey, which was to last for ten years. In a lecture given to the Los Angeles Psychoanalytic Society on 3 October 1962, ' A Personal View of the Kleinian Contribution', he said:

> From my point of view psycho-analysis in England was an edifice whose foundation was Ernest Jones. If any man earned my gratitude it was Ernest Jones, and it was Jones to whom I went when I found I needed help in 1923. He put me in touch with James Strachey, to whom I went for analysis for ten years, but I always knew that it was because of Jones that there was a Strachey and a British Psycho-Analytical Society for me to use.

(1965: 171–2)

One might wonder why he was so much in need of help. Perhaps he felt fettered by memories of the war and of the friends who had died in it. It is interesting to note that World War II was to have quite a different effect on him.

> Primarily interested in the child patient, and the infant, I decided that I must study psychosis in analysis. I have had about a dozen psychotic adult patients, and half of these have been rather extensively analysed. This happened in the war, and I might say that I hardly noticed the blitz, being all the time engaged in analysis of psychotic patients who are notoriously and maddeningly oblivious of bombs, earthquakes, and floods.
>
> ('Primitive emotional development', 1945 in *Through Paediatrics to Psychoanalysis*, 1958: 145)

Is it possible that his avoidance of the shock of World War II insofar as was possible was linked to what for him had been the serious psychic trauma of World War I, a time when he had just left a very protected adolescence and had been thrown into the particularly cruel reality of that War? Perhaps one should also listen to the opinion of his wife Clare when she writes: 'However, there was a time when the quality of his early years and his appreciation of them posed a serious problem that of freeing himself from his family to establish his own, separate life and his own identity while sacrificing nothing of that initial abundance. He took a long time in doing so.' (1977: 33)

It was Strachey who was to point Winnicott in the direction of Melanie Klein during his analysis. This meeting was to be one of the important moments in his life. 'This was difficult for me, because overnight I had changed from being a pioneer into being a student with a pioneer teacher' ('A Personal View of the Kleinian Contribution', 1962), in *The Maturational Processes and the Facilitating Environment*, 1965: 173). Later, towards the end of the 1930s, Winnicott was to analyse one of Melanie Klein's children (Eric) and to undergo a second analysis with Joan Rivière.

Winnicott married for the first time at the age of 28, only to divorce a few years later. In 1951, he married Clare, a social worker with whom he had worked during World War II. They did not have any children. Clare has described at length their relationship, which was a happy one:

> We played with things, our possessions, re-arranging them, taking them up or putting them aside, as the mood took us. We played with ideas, juggling with them at random, knowing that we did not need to be of the same opinion, that we were strong enough not to be hurt by one another.

In fact, the question of hurting one another did not arise because we operated in an area of play where nothing was forbidden.

(1977: 35–6)

The post-war period seems to have been a happy one for Winnicott. He had a very spacious house, which welcomed a growing number of visitors and was filled with music and various activities such as reading, painting (in particular, the Christmas cards that he and his wife liked to make) and, of course, work. This was his great creative period, as we shall see.

He took part in the setting up of the Middle Group at the British Psycho-Analytical Society with Michael Balint, the group of Independents who placed themselves between the two blocks, Kleinian on the one hand and Anna Freudian on the other. He was long considered by Anna Freud to be Kleinian, and therefore ignored. He was also rejected by the Kleinians, which caused him much grief and bitterness.

Winnicott was to continue to work with children all his life, which is rare for a psychoanalyst. He took great pleasure in meeting children and probably in giving life to the child in him. All those who saw him at work speak of their amazement at how easily he managed to make contact with children. He surprised his listeners by his ease, his unaffectedness, his simplicity and his anti-conformity; what struck one about him was the quality of his narcissistic basis. He certainly does not seem to have lived in a stage of perpetual elation, but he did appear to have the ability of self-repair. He would draw squiggles as part of his daily routine, writes his wife: 'In them he would be playing games with himself, sometimes the drawings would be terrifying, sometimes very amusing, and often they had a strong inferiority all of their own' (1977: 36). Was, as all his biographers stress, this narcissistic basis, this ability of self-repair, related to his childhood and/or to the particular quality of his two long analytical experiences?

'I have never been able to follow anyone else, not even Freud', he wrote in his 1962 Los Angeles lecture 'A personal view on the Kleinian contribution' (in *The Maturational Processes and the Facilitating Environment*, 1965: 177). It was thus that he came to belong to the group of Independents. What Freud unquestionably did provide him with was a transformation of himself, an ability to understand his emotional life, a desire to understand others and to repair them as he had done for himself. As Victor Smirnoff wrote: 'His fidelity to Freudian psychoanalysis did not consist of interpreting of texts or of idly glorifying the past but of continually challenging the everyday practice of analysis, both on the clinical and conceptual planes' (1966: 50).

He was twice elected President of the British Psycho-Analytical Society (from 1956 to 1959, and from 1965 to 1968). His later years, however, were clouded by a serious heart condition, and he died on 25 January 1971.

His work

It is difficult to give an account of Winnicott's work because not only does he not offer any system, he also puts forward a certain number of paradoxes which must be taken into account if one is to understand his theories. His whole thinking centred around the observation of the mother–child dyad in the early stages of life. Over the years his articles often came back to notions he had already described, sometimes adding a new element which enabled him to reopen and deepen his thinking.

Winnicott's entire work was devoted to temporal aspects, the study of the continual process of growth and maturation of the child; the 'already-here', potentialities, regression. His originality lies in the fact that he placed this temporal axis in the spatial domain, thus combining continuity and contiguity, highlighting for his readers the path which takes the human being from union with its mother to separation and independence, the ability to be alone, and defining areas as being inner and outer, internal reality and external reality, transitional area, and cultural area.

This constantly intertwining dual perspective makes him even more difficult to read than would appear on the surface, especially as another dimension also needs to be added. This third perspective was a permanent reflection on the use he could make of his clinical discoveries in analytical treatment. In this way he came to define a new technical approach, specific to borderline cases, through the importance he gave to the phenomena of regression and dependence, and to the entity of psychoanalyst–patient as a substitute for the mother–child dyad.

His links with the works of Sigmund Freud and Melanie Klein

'There is no such thing as an infant.' This statement was made by Winnicott at a scientific meeting of the British Psycho-Analytical Society in 1940. He came back to it in a paper in 1960 entitled 'The theory of the parent–infant relationship' and explained it thus: 'meaning of course that whenever one finds an infant one finds maternal care, and without maternal care there would be no infant' (in 1965: 39, footnote 1).

From his earliest research work he was conscious of being a creator because he was interested in a domain that Sigmund Freud had explored little: that of the very young child. This is why his meeting in 1925 with Melanie Klein, on the advice of Strachey, was to be providential for him. However, he always intended to remain in a continuum with Freud's work: 'I was probably influenced, without realizing it', he wrote in 1960, 'by one of the footnotes in Freud's 1911 work *Formulations on the Two Principles of Mental Functioning* where he wrote . . . "an organisation which was a slave to the pleasure-principle and neglected the reality of the external world could not maintain itself alive for the shortest time, so that it could not have come into existence at all. The employment of a fiction like this is, however, justified when one considers that the infant – provided one includes with it the care it receives from its mother – does almost realize a psychical system of this kind . . '" (p. 39).

However, the contribution of Melanie Klein to his work would be much greater than that of Freud, and it can be said that he followed her line faithfully for about two decades. After World War II, however, he would diverge in his theories, placing an ever increasing importance on the environment, on external reality. In the 1962 Los Angeles lecture mentioned above, in a country very much attached to the psychoanalytical values of the works of Anna Freud, he made the point of stressing Melanie Klein's contribution to psychoanalytical theory: 'The only important thing is that psychoanalysis, firmly based on Freud, shall not miss Klein's contribution' (1965: 178). After having recalled that it was due to Klein that a very rich analytical world had been opened up for him, he attempted to define what seemed to him to be the essence of her work, what he agreed with in her line of thought and what he disagreed with. He believed that Klein's principal contribution was in demonstrating the existence of the depressive position, with the ideas of restitution and reparation that she included in it: 'This is Klein's most important contribution, in my opinion', he writes, 'and I think it ranks with Freud's concept of the Oedipus complex' (p. 176). He also placed great value on her manner of devising 'a strict orthodox technique in psychoanalysis of children' (p. 178).

His greatest disagreements with her were the place given to the paranoid-schizoid position (he reproached her for having mixed up 'deep-seated' and 'primary'), his refusal of the death instinct (so essential to Kleinian theory), and the importance he placed on external reality, which he describes as being an ally of the child's ego in the maturational process. We should emphasize here, and in this agree with Masud Khan, that on this last point he moved away not only from Melanie Klein's thinking, but also from that of Freud. For Freud, external reality was not an ally, but a tyrant. 'Freud', writes Masud Khan in the Preface to the French edition of *Therapeutic Consultations in Child Psychiatry* (1971: 36), 'saw the ego doing battle with two tyrants: instinctual desires and external reality. The ego did its best to serve both in order to ensure its growth and survival.'

Winnicott also differed with Melanie Klein over the nature of destructiveness and what was for him the essential differentiation between phantasizing and internal reality. It was over the last works of Melanie Klein on envy and during the lecture she gave to the British Psycho-Analytical Society in 1956, entitled 'A study of envy and gratitude', that their split finally materialized. It is interesting to read what Winnicott wrote about it in 1956 and in 1962. In 1956, in a letter written the day after the lecture and sent to Joan Rivière, he wrote:

> After Mrs Klein's paper you and she spoke to me, and within the frame-work of friendliness you gave me to understand that both of you are absolutely certain that there is no positive contribution to be made from me to the interesting attempt Melanie is making all the time to state the psychology of the earliest stages. . . . In other words, there is a block in me. This naturally concerns me very deeply . . .
>
> (*The Spontaneous Gesture*, Winnicott, 1987: 94)

In 1962, in Los Angeles, he came back to this point again: 'I believe my views began to separate out from hers, and in any case, I found she had not included me in as a Kleinian. This did not matter to me because I have never been able to follow any one else, not even Freud' (1965: 176–7). In fact, and we will come back to his point, he had already been in the Independents for a number of years.

The paradoxes

Winnicott's work is based on a number of paradoxes which he thought essential to the understanding of his work: 'I ask that a paradox be accepted, tolerated and that it is admitted that it does not have to be resolved. The paradox can be resolved but the price to be paid is the loss of the value of the paradox' (*Playing and Reality*, 1971). For Winnicott, paradox is implied in The Maturational Process. In *Le Paradoxe de Winnicott*, Anne Clancier and Jeannine Kalmanovitch (1984), using the work of René Rousillon (1977 and 1978) as a base, distinguished two types of paradox in Winnicott's work. In the first case, the paradox is logical and is necessary in order to ensure the continuity of being of the child. They give two examples. First, his paper entitled 'The capacity to be alone' (1958, in 1965, pp. 29–36), where he states: 'The basis of the capacity to be alone is . . . paradoxical because it is the experience of being alone in the presence of someone else.' For these two authors, as for René Rousillon, the paradox here is introduced by the confusion between internal and external reality and enables communication between these two types of reality. Their second example concerns the transitional object, which, according to the Winnicott formula, they write, should be found in order to be created and created in order to be found. 'Thus an illusion is required for the object to have a basis, but at the same time, it is fundamental that the object really exist for the illusion to be of any value' (1984: 149–50).

In the second type of paradox that these authors wish to distinguish, it is a question of paradoxical defences, which come into play precisely when

continuity of being is lacking. 'These defences present themselves as a solution of continuity and their object is to preserve the real self from
annihilation or from one of the primitive agonies which threaten it' (ibid.,
p. 150). They give as a model of this type of paradox the theory put forward
by Winnicott in his paper on 'The fear of breakdown' (1974). Here, the
paradoxical reply, as Winnicott wrote, could be 'to enable the recall of
something which has not yet happened, to enable it to happen, i.e. to
reestablish a process of maturation which has not taken place' (ibid., p. 153).

Communicating and not communicating

A rereading of Winnicott's work shows that for him, as Masud R. Khan
writes in his Preface to *Therapeutic Consultations in Child Psychiatry* (1971)
'the human individual was unknowable, isolated, only able to personalize
himself by the mediation of another'. In his 1958 paper 'The capacity to be
alone', Winnicott does not question the desire to be alone but the aptitude
for being alone. For him this capacity was based, as we have seen, on a paradox, which is 'the experience of being alone, as an infant and as a young
child in the presence of mother'. This capacity can be achieved at a very
early stage, well before the interiorization of the object, 'at the moment
when the immaturity of the ego is compensated in a natural fashion by the
support to the ego offered by mother'. He calls this relationship 'ego-relat-
edness', which he is careful to differentiate from the id relationship. He
believes that at this stage it is essential that the young child be able to understand the uninterrupted existence of its mother; if this experience is
insufficient, the capacity to be alone does not develop. He sees in this ego-
relatedness one of the possible matrixes of transference.

We believe that his 1963 paper entitled 'Communicating and not communicating, leading to a study of certain opposites' (in *The Maturational
Processes and the Facilitating Environment*, 1965, pp. 179–92), is essential to the
understanding of Winnicott's work: 'Each individual is an isolated element
in a permanent state of not-communicating always unknown, never discovered in fact.' At the core of each individual is 'an element of
not-communicating which is sacred'. In fact, in favourable cases, the individual will have three modes of communication at his or her disposal: one
mode, which will always be silent, Winnicott relates to Freud's concept of
primary narcissism; an explicit mode of communication, which is a source
of indirect pleasure whose most obvious element is language; and finally, a
third, intermediate, form, which is a valuable compromise between the
two and which extends from play to cultural life. This intermediate area
does not exist for everybody. One of the best illustrations of the nature of
this area is to be found in Clare Winnicott's (1977) paper entitled 'Winnicott

in person', written after the death of her husband in which she describes their relationship, and from which we quoted earlier.

For us, it is clear that this is one of Winnicott's major contributions: the definition and emphasis he gives to this potential play area where infantile omnipotence has not been completely abandoned and where destructiveness appears happy. On this subject we should perhaps recall a passage in the autobiographical notes that Winnicott left to his wife. In it he remembers an incident from his childhood (see 1977: 31): he was 3 years old when, using a croquet mallet, he flattened the nose of a wax doll belonging to one of his sisters and with which his father was teasing him. He stressed the fact that this doll irritated him, that he had to damage it and how important it was for him to *carry out* this act. He also remembered the epilogue. Using matches to warm the wax, his father had returned the doll's face to its initial aspect. 'This first demonstration of the act of restitution and reparation undoubtedly impressed me and perhaps made me capable of accepting the fact that I myself, a dear innocent child, had indeed become violent, directly with the doll and indirectly with my father.'

His work might appear to be despairing, for not everybody has the opportunity, the good fortune, to possess this third possibility of communication. In addition, the feeling of being alive for the infant does not depend on his psyche but is totally dependent on the quality of the mother's psyche. He distinguishes between 'being alive' and 'being full of life'. Thus, ordinarily, for Winnicott, the mother of an infant has living internal objects and the infant becomes integrated into the preconception of the mother of a *living* child. However, in cases where the mother is depressed, the central internal object of the mother is dead; in this case the infant must adapt itself to the role of a *dead* object, i.e. be full of life to compensate for the preconceived idea of the mother. Winnicott sees here an anti-life factor, which is the opposite of that very lively state of the child. On reading this passage it is easier to understand why the death instinct played no part in his theories. Life is not opposed to death but becomes established out of non-existence in the same way that communication is born of silence. For him, death only begins to have meaning in one's existence with the appearance of hate, i.e. much later on. 'For myself', he wrote, 'I do not find it valid to attach the word "death" to the word "instinct" and even less valid to talk of hate and anger by using the term death instinct.' We can but stress once again the importance of his differences of opinion with Melanie Klein and with Sigmund Freud.

The process of maturation in the child

By studying the works of Donald Winnicott, one can follow the variations in his thinking about the potential capacity that the human being has of becoming a person through the mediation of a privileged partner who might be the environment–mother (in opposition to the concept of object–mother), but who might also be the analyst for his patient. With the greatest of care he studies the two partners of the dyad that, for him, was so fundamental and yet which is condemned to disintegration if the child is to develop correctly.

What happens at the child's level?

In one of his earliest papers (1941) entitled 'The Observation of Infants in a Set Situation' Winnicott, 1958, (in *Through Paediatrics to Psychoanalysis*, pp. 52–69), Winnicott recounted in detail the game of a young child with a shiny spatula. He described three stages which the child goes through. First, there is a period of reflection when the baby reaches out for the spatula; then there is a period of hesitation before she accepts the reality of her desire for the object and grabs it; finally there is the moment where she lets the spatula fall, initially by chance and then deliberately. What is important here is what he calls 'the period of hesitation'. The baby stops her movement, looks at her mother, hesitates, before deciding to grab the spatula and put it in her mouth and then uses it to bang it on the table. Winnicott sees this period of hesitation as a psychic space opening up in the child with the phantasy 'of making an angry and perhaps vindictive mother appear by its gesture if it gives in to its pleasure'. For Winnicott, the period of hesitation signifies the existence of a conflict in the child's psyche.

He was to complete his thinking on the subject in a 1945 article entitled 'Primitive emotional development' (in *Through Paediatrics to Psychoanalysis*, 1958, pp. 145–56) in which 'the period of hesitation' becomes a 'moment of illusion', owing to the acquisition by the mother and her child, over time, of a common experience. 'I think of the process as if two lines came from opposite directions, liable to come near each other. If they overlap there is a moment of *illusion* – a bit of experience which the infant can take as *either* his hallucination *or* a thing belonging to external reality' (p. 152, original emphases). It is from here that he was to conceptualize the notion of transitional object and transitional space. It is also this kind of intimacy that he would try to recreate in analytical treatment with the management that he was to bring to it. In another one of his early papers, 'The manic defence' (1935 in 1958, pp. 129–44), he insisted on differentiating between phantasizing and internal reality. Phantasizing enables access to external reality through the effort produced to escape internal reality. In addition, at this time he also saw internal reality and external reality as being separated by a membrane-frontier, which he called the psycho-soma. He took up these notions again in 1945 in his paper entitled 'Primitive emotional development'. He distinguished three processes from which internal reality originated: (1) integration, (2) personalization, and (3), following these, the appreciation of time and space and other properties of reality – in short, realization' (1958: 149). He postulates the existence of a primary state of unintegration, to which it is possible to come back by regression, using the mechanism of regressive disintegration. 'All this tends towards the establishment of a unit self', he wrote in 'Ego integration in child development' (1962: 60 in *The Maturational Processes*, 1965, pp. 56–63). He defined integration as being closely linked to the function of holding exerted by the environment and unintegration as resulting from the absence of support from the mother's ego. It is successful unintegration which gives rise to pathological dissociations.

> The term disintegration is used to describe a sophisticated *defence*, a defence that is an active production of chaos in defence against unintegration in the absence of maternal ego-support, that is, against the unthinkable or archaic anxiety that results from failure of holding in the stage of absolute dependence. The chaos of disintegration may be as 'bad' as the unreliability of the environment, but it has the advantage of being produced by the baby and therefore of being non-environmental. It is within the area of the baby's omnipotence. In terms of psychoanalysis, it is analysable, whereas the unthinkable anxieties are not.
>
> (1965: 61, original emphasis)

Here once more is a fundamental element of the theories that we will see again in the way in which he tailored treatment. The continuation of a true self is a requirement for integration. This is his definition: in the theory of the parent–infant relationship (1958: 46) 'The central self could be said to be the inherited potential which is experiencing a continuity of being, and acquiring in its own way and at its own speed personal psychic reality and a personal body-scheme.' This self must, perforce, be isolated for the sound mental health of the child and any threat of impingement troubling this isolation will give rise to a massive anxiety of psychotic level. The organization of a false self then appears to be the best possible defence, 'a defence', he writes, 'against that which is unthinkable, the exploitation of the True Self, which would lead to its annihilation' (Ego distortion in terms of true and false self', 1960: 147, in *The Maturational Processes and the Facilitating Environment*, 1965, pp. 140–52).

This new concept of false self was very popular with the public. Winnicott simply said: 'My object . . . is to point out that this modern concept of false self hiding the true self, as well as the theory of its aetiology, can have important consequences for analytical work.' We shall come back to this point.

What happens at the mother's level?

Throughout his work Winnicott returns time and again to the fundamental role of *the mother*. Three of his works are essential on this subject: 'Psychoses and child care' (1952), 'Primary maternal preoccupation' (1956), both in *Through Paediatrics to Psycho-Analysis*, 1958, pp. 219–28, and 300–5 respectively, and 'The theory of the parent–infant relationship' (1960), in *The Maturational Processes*, 1965, pp. 37–55. A number of terms are repeated constantly: primary maternal preoccupation, the good-enough mother, holding, impingement and the birth of illusion.

With the help of a few simple models, Winnicott demonstrates the importance of the environment-mother in the 1952 paper. In the first model, the environment produces a sufficiently active adaptation for the infant to survive in a state of quiet isolation. The infant can therefore make a spontaneous movement which will put it in contact with its environment without the self being affected. In the second example, it is a defective environment which, because it is not adapted, puts the child in contact with it, thus producing an impingement against which the child must react, only finding the integrity of its self by returning to isolation. It is not the impingements which are important but the reactions to impingement which the infant has to give, because they interrupt what Winnicott calls 'the going on being' of the child. An excessive reaction which is repeated leads to a fear of annihilation. With a third figure illustrating theoretical first feed, he writes that:

> The creative potential of the individual arising out of need produces readiness for an hallucination. The mother's love and her close identification with her infant make her aware of the infant's needs to the extent that she provides something *more or less*[2] at the right place and at the right time. This, much repeated, starts off the infant's ability to use *illusion*[3] without which no contact is possible between the psyche and the environment.
>
> ('Psychoses and child care, 1952: 223, in *Through Paediatrics to Psychoanalysis* 1958)

It is the holding function of the mother that he is describing here. This is natural, arising from a primary maternal preoccupation and is based on an identificatory movement, the empathy that the mother has for her child, rather than on any phenomenon of intellectual comprehension. This maternal function of holding is necessary to the child for the period of development, which takes it from absolute dependence to relative dependence and then to independence. In this last phase, the child has acquired the capacity of dispensing with care, because it has been able to introject the memory of care given in a dependable environment.

In Winnicott's concept of the good-enough mother, 'good enough' needs to be properly grasped, for it has been the subject of misrepresented meanings, notably in France, where it has often been transformed into a 'sufficiently good (i.e. adequate)' mother, suited to the needs of the child, whereas Winnicott, as we stressed in the quote above, wrote *'more or less'*. Through the repetition of situations which only she can create, the good-enough mother will enable the child's ability to use illusion to emerge. Winnicott was to represent this illusion, which facilitates the meeting of the child's psyche with external reality, in two ways: first, in the concept of transitional space, and, second, in the concreteness of the transitional object.

Winnicott was anxious to differentiate between two maternal images available to the infant. Next to the environment-mother of which we have just spoken, he placed the object-mother total or part-object, which is there to satisfy immediate needs. In his paper 'The development of the capacity for concern' (1963 in *The Maturational Processes*, 1965, pp. 73–82), he explains: 'The object-mother has to be found to survive the instinct-driven episodes. . . . Also, the environment-mother has a special function, which is to continue to be herself . . . to be there to receive the spontaneous gesture and to be pleased' (in *The Maturational Processes and the Facilitating Environment*, 1965: 76).

From the discovery of the object by the child to its use

It was after having revealed the child's 'moment of illusion', which we have already mentioned twice (the first time when he perceived it during clinical consultations at the hospital, and the second when he located it in the transitional space between the mother and the child), that Winnicott was to construct his concept of the transitional object and other transitional phenomena. He built it around a paradox which has to be accepted, i.e. 'the baby creates the object, but the object was there, waiting to be created and to become a cathected object' (*Playing and Reality*, 1971a). In his book *Playing and Reality* (1971a), Winnicott went into some depth about the specific qualities of the relationship established by the child with this transitional object. We shall not go into them here in detail, since they are well known. The reader should simply remember that the child lays claim to this much-coddled and mutilated object, which seems to have a life of its own, and to bring it warmth. This object, which for the child neither comes from inside nor is part of external reality, is located in the intermediate area, the third dimension to which Winnicott was to give a lot of his attention. He defined this space as follows: 'From the outset, the baby has the most intense experiences in the potential space between the subjective object and the object perceived objectively, between the extensions of me . . . and not-me. This potential space is situated between the domain where there is nothing but me, and the domain where there are objects and phenomena which escape omnipotent control' (1971a). This potential area of experience constitutes, from his point of view, the greatest part of the young child's experience. When the transitional object is progressively decathected because the child's cultural interests have developed, the transitional area will continue to exist, becoming, first, an area for play and then the area where interest in religion, art, music, scientific creation and imaginary life will be situated.

In the Introduction to his book *Playing and Reality*, written 20 years after his first paper on the transitional object, Winnicott felt the need to restate his thinking: 'It is now generally recognized, I believe, that what I am referring to in this part of my work is not the cloth or the teddy bear that the baby uses – not so much the object used as the use of the object' (1972a: xii). This last point would be the subject of his research in the later years of his life. In his paper entitled 'The use of an object and relating through identifications' (1969, in *Playing and Reality*, 1971a, pp. 86–94), Winnicott was to distinguish quite clearly between the relationship to an object which can be a subjective object and the use of the object, which use implies that the object is part of external reality, i.e. that thereafter it is situated outside the omnipotent area of control of the child. He describes the fundamental sequence as follows: '(1) Subject *relates* to object. (2) Object is in process of being found instead of placed by the subject in the world. (3) Subject *destroys* object. (4) Object survives destruction. (5) Subject can *use* object' (in *Playing and Reality*, 1971a: 94). It is interesting to note how the development of this theory, twenty-eight years later, is a perfect commentary of the clinical observation he had made in 1941 with the baby and the shiny spatula in his consulting room.

For Winnicott, the constancy of the object becomes established from the point of differentiation of the baby makes progressively between its phantasy where the object is still being destroyed and the reality of the object's survival in the external world. It is only at this point that the object can be used by the infant, because it is now situated outside the area of the omnipotent control of the subject. It is here that the positive value of destructiveness comes to light. As the object survives destruction, the process of 'destroying' it places it outside the area of the objects established by the mental projective mechanisms of the subject. For Winnicott 'a world of shared reality is created which the subject can use and which can feed back other-than-me substance into the subject' (1971a: 94). Winnicott was to transpose this new idea about the use of the object into treatment, where he stressed, as we shall see, the necessity for some patients of being able to use the analyst, and for that the latter must be sure that he will survive the destructiveness of the patient. In his Preface to the French edition of *Therapeutic Consultations in Child Psychiatry* (1971b), Masud Khan stresses this modification of the concept of transference, which acquires an even greater significance. 'Indeed, a new potential appears in the clinical area, and the relationship which enables the imaginary and emotional realization of self by the use of the analyst as both a transitional object and as an objective object . . . each of them will be created and found by the other.'

Regression and management of analytical treatment

Winnicott's ideas concerning regression and the development of treatment were the source of a great number of his articles. The main ones were 'Hate in the Counter-transference' (1947, in *Through Paediatrics to Psycho-Analysis*, 1958, pp. 194–203), 'Metapsychological and clinical aspects of regression', in *Through Paediatrics to Psycho-Analysis*, 1958, pp. 278–94), 'Clinical varieties of transference' (1955–6 in *Through Paediatrics to Psycho-Analysis*, 1958, pp. 295–9), 'Counter-transference' (1960, in *The Maturational Processes*, 1965, pp. 158–65), 'The aims of analytical treatment' (1962, in *The Maturational Processes*, 1965, pp. 166–70), 'Regression as therapy' (1963, in *British Journal of Medical Psychology*, vol. 36), 'Dependence in infant care, child care and in the psychoanalytic setting' (1963, in *The Maturational Processes*, 1965, pp. 249–60), and 'The fear of breakdown' (1974). Two books published after his death give an account of cases of analysis that he undertook: *The Piggle* (1978) and *Holding and Interpretation* (1986). In order to understand the progress of his thinking we need to go back to what he called 'primitive emotional development', which he placed in the first few weeks of life and which he defined as a primary narcissistic state. (In this he is closer to Anna or Sigmund Freud than to Melanie Klein.) It is at this point, if all is well, that the infant constitutes its real self through a satisfying environment. Winnicott believed that the position of the environment is fundamental to the development of the self: 'I should mention here that I am basing this on the hypothesis I have often put forward and which is not readily accepted, far from it, that the further one goes back to the theoretical beginning, the less there is personal failure and you arrive at a point where there is only lack of adaptation on the part of the environment' (1958).

In situations where the maternal environment is flawed or in general in the case of a specific inadequacy in the environment, the individual will defend its self 'by freezing the situation of inadequacy' and by building a false self. It is a defence mechanism of the ego, very well organized, a protective screen, the existence of the guardian of the self threatened by the impingements of the environment. For this author, regression is the opposite of progress, given that by progress he means the capacity that every baby has of developing towards maturation. This potential for maturation, he believes, is biological in origin, and doubtless already present during gestation. However, progress cannot simply be reversed; the individual must have at his disposal an organization which enables regression to occur and this is where Winnicott brings in management of treatment.

It is clear that, for Winnicott, regression, in psychoanalytical terms, meant that an underlying organization of the ego and chaos exists. In one of the last papers he wrote, 'The fear of breakdown' (1974), published after his death, he stated this theory more clearly. Starting from a paradoxical position, 'the fear of breakdown can be the fear of a breakdown that has already been experienced' (1974), he believed that the patient must continue to look for the detail in the past *which has not yet been experienced*. The necessity of experiencing this event seemed to him as vital for the successful unfolding of treatment as the recall described by Freud in the analysis of patients suffering from psychoneurosis.

> There are moments, according to my experience, when a patient needs to be told that breakdown, a fear of which destroys his or her life, *has already been* . . . when the patient can go to emptiness itself and endure that state through his dependence on the auxiliary ego of the analyst, to absorb can then suddenly appear to be a function which is pleasurable.
>
> (pp. 104–5 and 43)

Winnicott did not propose to apply his technique to all his patients. He believed that Freud, because of the type of patients he chose (those suffering from psychoneurosis), those 'who had been suitably provided for in early childhood' (1971a), supposed that the first process of mothering had been acquired, and this comes out in his setting of the analytical process. According to Winnicott, Freud always stated he was dealing with three people, one of whom was excluded from the analytic room. With the psychotic patients Winnicott had chosen to apply himself to, the analytical process, with the regression that it requires, revolves at best around two people (the mother and the infant) or, if regression is very advanced, from the point of view of the patient, around a single person, herself.

Because of the originality of his ideas, we thought it interesting to set out, even if it is somewhat at length, the manner in which Winnicott expounded his theories and the way he put them into practice.

> Psychotic illness is related to environmental failure at an early stage of the emotional development of the individual. The sense of futility and unreality belongs to the development of a false self which develops in protection of the true self.

231

The setting of analysis reproduces the early and earliest mothering techniques. It invites regression by reason of its reliability.

The regression of a patient is an organized return to early dependence or double dependence. The patient and the setting merge into the original success situation of primary narcissism.

Progress from primary narcissism starts anew with the true self able to meet environmental failure situations without organization of the defences that involve a false self protecting the true self.

To this extent psychotic illness can only be relieved by specialized environmental provision interlocked with the patient's regression.

Progress from the new position, with the true self surrendered to the total ego, can now be studied in terms of the complex processes of individual growth.

In practice there is a sequence of events:

1. The provision of a setting that gives confidence.
2. Regression of the patient to dependence, with due sense of the risk involved.
3. The patient feeling a new sense of self, and the self hitherto hidden becoming surrendered to the total ego. A new progression of the individual processes which had stopped.
4. An unfreezing of an environmental failure situation.
5. From the new position of ego strength, anger related to the early environmental failure, felt in the present and expressed.
6. Return from regression to dependence, in orderly progress towards independence.
7. Instinctual needs and wishes becoming realizable with genuine vitality and vigour.

All this repeated again and again.

> ('Metapsychological and clinical aspects of regression
> within the psycho-analytic set-up', 1954, in
> *Through Paediatrics to Psycho-Analysis*, 1958: 286–7)

The management of treatment was carried out on two levels: on the level of what the analyst will say, of course, as we saw in his paper on 'The fear of breakdown', but also on the level of the setting itself. Insofar as Winnicott believes that 'the couch *is* the analyst' and that the needs of the patient must be met (at this stage there is no question for him of wish, tolerance towards the patient's acting out must be extreme, as with all situations, 'if the couch gets wetted . . . that is inherent, not a complication') (p. 289).

However, the analyst cannot perfectly meet the needs of his patient, any more than the good-enough mother can. In this setback in adaptating to the patient, Winnicott sees the emergence of the possible progress of the patient.

In this repetition of a primitive setback, here and now, the patient will be able to get angry. It is this anger, new for the patient, which is a factor of progress because it puts him in touch with his self and enables him finally to live out what he feels it is to be real. Winnicott stresses the difficulties the analyst has in accompanying this regression: he needs to be highly qualified with considerable experience, and, in addition, '*A belief in human nature and in the developmental process exists in the analyst* if work is to be done at all, and this is quickly sensed by the patient' (p. 292).

We believe that two remarks should be made. First, on the technical level, it would seem that, for Winnicott, at this point in treatment, interpretation is inopportune, the patient only needing certain specific care. What is the precise nature of this care? 'Are silence and company sufficient, or should there be some type of bodily contact?' (Etchegoyen, 1991: 562). Winnicott never did fully explain this point.

In addition, on the theoretical level, many authors question so much emphasis being placed on the role of the environment in the development of the individual, doing away with personal responsibility. This particular point has given rise to many comments about Winnicott's work.

> In doing psycho-analysis I aim at:
>   Keeping alive
>   Keeping well
>   Keeping awake
>   . . . Analysis for analysis' sake has no meaning for me. I do analysis because that is what the patient needs to have done and to have done with. If the patient does not need analysis then I do something else.
> ('The aims of psychoanalytical treatment', 1962, in *The Maturational Processes and the Facilitating Environment*, 1965: 166)

The work of Donald Winnicott occupies a very special place in the psychoanalytical world. First, perhaps because, right to the very last, he was both a child and an adult analyst, and because it was from his work with children, and with psychotics, that he forged his ideas. He certainly undertook a great number of analyses of children and adults in the most orthodox fashion, but at the same time, in his consultations, he treated a great number of children in various different ways, using his experience as an analyst. *The Piggle* (1978) is a good illustration of this. Winnicott was concerned by what he considered to be the limits of psychoanalysis. He used analytical treatment each time he thought it was indicated. If the material circumstances of the patient did not permit it, or if the patient's disorder did not require it, he envisaged other forms of treatment. This position seems to us much more responsible than that of many of those today who call 'psychoanalytic treatment' many forms of intervention that have nothing to do with psychoanalysis.

Winnicott wrote a great number of papers, articles and books. He gave a great number of lectures of instructive value to varied audiences. His scientific papers, of a very high standard, provided a better understanding of the mother–child dyad and discussed the way in which psychoanalytical treatment needed to be managed for certain types of patient.

He did not escape criticism, however: what about the place of the father or the place of infantile sexuality in his work? Sexuality as such is not actually mentioned, or at most only partially, and sexual conflict was never at the centre of his work. This is perhaps explained by the fact that he did not believe that the individualized id existed at the outset of life (the area in which he was interested), since it was included in a primary ego. It was not until later on, with a differentiated ego, that an individualized id could appear.

The place of the father is not uppermost in Winnicott's thoughts, but that does not mean that it was denied. The father does appear in a number of his written texts, but only through the psychic equilibrium that he brings to the mother.

Winnicott's influence in the analytical world and on the general public was considerable. It is interesting to realize that in France his popularity was based in part on misunderstandings. We shall only mention three examples. It seems to us that it is the notion of self which is important in Winnicott's work as meaning a continuous experience of maternal care, and yet one often sees the accent put on the false self, mixed up with the 'as if' personality. One needs to remember that self and false self are metapsychological and not clinical phenomena.

In the same way, the transitional space following the transitional object has become a concrete entity; institutions that set out 'to be' a specifically intermediate space have blossomed all over France.

Finally, the term 'good-enough mother' has often been translated in French as the 'sufficiently good' mother and understood in the sense of 'perfectly good'. It is undoubtedly not just a problem of translation and we would agree with Joyce MacDougall when she writes in a joint work on Winnicott entitled *Winnicott in Practice* (1988: 52),

> As an Anglicist I can confirm that 'good enough' should indeed be translated by 'more or less adequate, nothing more'. I do not think that it is a question of a misinterpretation but indeed of an erroneous sense. . . . Why this error? Well I believe that everybody would have liked to have that good mother! Besides, a mother must be ideal in order to produce the perfect child!

Winnicott influenced the thinking of many analysts the world over even though he never founded a school, and not just amongst the group of Independents in which he placed himself, as we shall see.

Although Winnicott belonged to the Independent group in the British Psychoanalytical Society and strongly influenced them with a number of his ideas, he did not in fact 'found' this group. When he is mentioned by his colleagues he is carefully described as being one analyst among many, and in the list of well-known (now deceased) Independents that Eric Rayner mentions in his recent book on *The Independent Mind in British Psychoanalysis* (1991) one can find: 'Jones, Sharpe, Glover, Flugel, Payne, Rickman, Strachey, Brierley, Fairbairn, Winnicott, Balint, Klauber, Khan and Bowlby'.

Rayner (1991) tries to place this 'independent' mind in a dual historical perspective. A 'British' perspective, on the one hand, by stressing the moderate streak in British Protestantism which offers 'a personal, direct and moral contract with God', which 'cuts across submission to the authority of priests and Pope'. On the other hand, there is an 'internationalist' perspective, wishing to incorporate ideas coming from all horizons and all countries. The 'independent' mind also has its roots in the philosophies of empiricism and pragmatism with their traditional concern for an open mind. The attitude of this group was to 'evaluate and respect ideas for their use and true value, no matter whence they came'.

This group of Independents was initially called the Middle Group and was born out of the 'Controversial Discussions' which took place in the 1940s, after which a majority of members (see Rayner, 1991: 9) did not want to belong exclusively to either the Melanie Klein or the Anna Freud group. For the purposes of training, it was decided initially that a candidate's second supervisor could be chosen neither from Group A (Melanie Klein) nor from Group B (Anna Freud), but from a middle group, whence the name 'Middle Group'. Later, in the 1950s, candidates were allowed to choose both supervisors from one group if they wished. On a social level, Rayner points out that today the members of these different groups get on well in spite of their differences of opinion on theory, even if these differences can still sometimes lead to bitter arguments.

On a theoretical level, this Independent group is opposed to any extremist or totalitarian thinking, qualities which are suspected in the other two British groups. For instance, although one might acknowledge the existence of the paranoid–schizoid position, one is not obliged to see it as Melanie Klein did. One can, like Fairbairn, consider it as a reactional development to do with the interactions between the baby and its environment and trauma. In the same fashion, envy is acknowledged as a sort of complex emotion, but its innate and instinctual nature is denied. Other diverging views are related to the role of the environment at the beginning of existence, and to that of the death instinct, which leads to differences in treatment techniques. In the same way, for the Independents, countertransference 'arises' more from the relationship between the patient and the analyst than from projective identification alone.

As to how treatment is conducted, Christopher Bollas has proposed the term of 'shared potential space' between the patient and the analyst. He also calls it an 'intermediate space', which term was also used by Winnicott (1971a). Bollas stresses the difference between this and transitional space which is an 'area of experience that is felt as both self and not-self. An intermediate space is an interpersonal phenomenon: one where two or more people experience that there is a *commonality between them but that they are separate*' (in Rayner, 1991: 247).

Above all, however, the Independents wanted to be open-minded so as to be able to use, if they so desired, the work of Sigmund Freud, Melanie Klein, Anna Freud, or of others without being obliged to feel that they had to conform to any one of them in particular; they rejected conformity. As Eric Rayner has remarked, that made their position weaker in the battle over ideas, because of a certain eclecticism which is not always convincing, and a liberalism which, by definition, does not try to convince. The presence of Winnicott in this group, however, strongly marked its ideology, and contributed to its developing child analysis. Eric Rayner concluded his book with the following paragraph:

To their tradition of open-minded empiricism and humanism the Independents have added their theory in terms of transitions and creativity. They have brought, perhaps, a mood of paradox, of mutuality yet examination, of spontaneity yet discipline, into the dialogue of emotions which is clinical psychoanalysis. They have fun exploring, yet keep to the rules imposed by reality. The Independent contribution is only a part of the whole fabric that is psychoanalytic knowledge, but it is a valuable one.

(p. 298)

CONCLUSION

Moving on from this study of the various tendencies, we now take a look at four points which seem to us to characterize the present climate in the psychoanalytical field in Britain:

- the compromise reached on the training of child analysts;
- the attention given by Esther Bick to the specific difficulties of child analysis;
- the fruitful rivalry between the three schools of thought which led to the appearance of a large number of theorists in the field of psychoanalysis;
- the current renewal, connected with the dialogue, which now seems to be taking place between the various tendencies.

Training in child analysis

The compromise reached between the various groups at the end of the 'Controversies' brought about recognition within the British Society of the need to make candidates sensitive to child analysis, and this was to be included in the training of every analyst, with specific training in child analysis for those analysts wishing to do so.

This acknowledgment, which exists in no other society affiliated to the IPA, had a considerable effect. On the one hand, discussions concerning child analysis are commonplace in the British Society; it is included in the various scientific events. For instance, at a week-end conference in October 1990, entitled 'The Treatment Alliance and the Transference', we were able to listen to Betty Joseph and Anne-Marie Sandler, among others, present a report on child analysis.

Moreover, this recognition and the training which ensued was certainly the beginning of a real differentiation between child analysis, on the one hand, and the domain of psychoanalytical psychotherapy of the child, on the other – both being taught differently, to different students, and carried out within well-defined and different structures. Child psychoanalysts are currently trained at the British Society's Institute and at the Anna Freud Centre (formerly the Hampstead Clinic). They also receive training in adult analysis: the framework is well-defined with its five, weekly, 50 minute sessions. Only child analysis, as opposed to psychoanalytical psychotherapy, enables research in psychoanalysis to be carried out, says Hanna Segal: 'There can be no discovery in psychotherapy because the processes cannot be observed in enough detail.' (I. 1) Psychoanalytical psychotherapy is one of the many forms of child psychotherapy practised in Britain, and is practised in the form of one, two or three weekly sessions at consulting centres which usually refuse to undertake psychoanalysis. Psychotherapists are trained in psychoanalytical psychotherapy centres. The two most well known of these are the Anna Freud Centre and the Tavistock Clinic. For Hanna Segal,

> psychoanalytical psychotherapy does not offer a sufficient container to enable the child to be given a distressing interpretation, if one does not see it the following day. Moreover, it appears [to me] that the psychotherapist should avoid the psychotic core; finally, the psychotherapist can help improve the child's state, but his work cannot produce any basic modifications.
>
> (I. 1)

The difficulties specific to child analysis

In a paper given to the IPA Congress in Edinburgh in 1961 Esther Bick spoke on the subject of 'Child analysis today'. She first underlined the historic nature of the meeting, inasmuch as it was the first symposium on child analysis to have taken place at an international psychoanalytical congress. She recalled the British Society's 1927 symposium, at which Melanie Klein had spoken, examining even at that early date the reasons for the lack of success in the development of child analysis.

Bick first stressed the progress that had been made in the field of child analysis, both in the range of cases treated and in its techniques, which had come into their own. However, she noted the very small place it occupied in relation to the whole field of psychoanalysis whether 'in terms of practice of child analysis, of training, of scientific discussions and publications'. She presumed that there were specific difficulties which impeded the development of child analysis and which did not apply to adult analysis to the same degree. She then went on to examine the differences existing between child and adult analysis from the point of view of the trainee analyst, and from that of the practising analyst. She proposed to look at 'stresses and gratifications, both external and internal'.

The external stresses are to do with the financial difficulties and the timetable problems with which the parents are faced. The timetable that the analyst proposes does not necessarily fit in with that of the child or its parents. Keeping in contact with the parents, caring for the play room, all this takes time and this time is not rewarded financially. These are real difficulties which should not be underestimated as they are often used as a rational cover for the emotional problems of studying and practising child analysis, she writes. She singles out two categories of emotional problems. First, there is the internal stress linked to pre-established anxieties, concerning the treatment of children as such and there is the specific question of counter-transference. In this first stress category she includes the 'general' anxieties of the young psychoanalyst as to whether she feels competent enough to communicate with the young child, to take on the dual responsibility involved (towards the child on the one hand, and towards the parents on the other), with the feeling that the less the maturity of the patient's ego, the greater the analyst's responsibility for its development. The young analyst must be able to assess clearly her responsibility when she analyses the child, even if it clashes with what she feels the parents expect of her. The analyst must also independently determine the objectives of her analysis, such objectives often being distinct from curing the symptoms, the original motive for the treatment. The young analyst might also be afraid of becoming excessively attached to the young child, or of being hurtful. All this can be heard in supervision, but sometimes a more detailed analysis is required if the young analyst is to overcome the unconscious conflicts that are inhibiting her. Anxieties of this type are close to those of the second category, having to do with the phenomenon of countertransference.

Bick believed that the countertransference stresses are greater for the child analyst than for the adult analyst, with perhaps the exception of psychotic patients, and are linked to two specific factors. First, the unconscious conflicts which arise with regard to the child's parents. Second, the nature of the material provided by the child. In the first case, she stresses, the child analyst has to deal with the constant problem of his own unconscious identifications. He can identify with the child against the parents, or with the parents against the child, or even take a protective parental attitude towards the child. 'These conflicts often lead to a persecutory and guilty attitude towards the parents, making the analyst over-critical of them and over-dependant on their approval' ('Child analysis today', in *Collected Papers of Martha Harris and Esther Bick*, pp. 104–13, 1987: 107). In addition, she underlined the difficulty the young analyst had in understanding the twofold nature of the relationship between the child and its parents: 'His normal and healthy dependence on them, relative to his age, and the infantile elements in the relationship, due to his internal difficulties' (p. 107).

The second specific factor related to the nature of the material is to be found at the level of

> the strain imposed on the mental apparatus of the analyst, both by the content of the child's material and its mode of expression. The intensity of the child's dependence, of his positive and negative transference, the primitive nature of his phantasies, tend to arouse the analyst's own unconscious anxieties. The violent and concrete projections of the child into the analyst may be difficult to contain. Also the child's suffering tends to evoke the analyst's parental feelings which have to be controlled so that the proper analytic role can be maintained. All these problems tend to obscure the analyst's understanding and to increase in turn his anxiety and guilt about his work.
>
> (pp. 107–8)

Another interesting detail is that Esther Bick also underlines the great difficulty that the analyst can be faced with concerning the child's play material or its non-verbal communication. She concluded from this that the child analyst was someone who had to depend to a greater extent on her own unconscious, which at the appropriate time would enlighten her as to the significance of the 'primitive' communication.

Bick ends her paper on the necessity for training in child analysis with a plea for the quality of such training, which should, by overcoming her anxieties, enable the analyst to see the existing, inherent gratification in this sort of work.

We have given a perhaps somewhat detailed account of Bick's paper because it seemed to us to epitomize the conceptual and clinical rigour of the thinking of a number of English analysts. Also it echoed our own work in child analysis; and finally, because this type of work needs to be encouraged and continued.

The great fruitfulness of the different schools of thought

The different 'rival' English schools were outstandingly fruitful. Both Anna Freud and Melanie Klein attracted to them a large number of fascinating figures who often had considerable influence not just on child psychoanalysis but on psychoanalysis in general. The 'pupils' often took the concepts of these two great child psychoanalysts and used them to develop theories in relation to psychoanalysis in general or to particular fields of application in psychoanalysis.

In Anna Freud's camp, we have already mentioned her 'Viennese' or 'Berlin' friends and followers, and a number of them either preceded or followed her to London: for example, Kate Friedlander, Dorothy Burlingham, Hedwig and Willi Hoffer; Kate Friedlander was involved in the Nurseries and it was she who came up with the original idea for the Hampstead Clinic. She was also one of the first to open a pilot psychoanalytical consultation in 1945, at the East End Hospital in London. She died prematurely in 1949.

As we shall see further on (Chapter 12), others were to develop Anna Freud's teachings in the United States. Heinz Hartmann was one of those, and he based his ego psychology on Anna Freud's theories; it is one of the most widespread theories in the psychoanalytical world today. Even if French and Argentinian psychoanalysts, for example, have not come round to it, and even if Anna Freud herself did not entirely hold with it, in particular criticizing the too 'adaptive' position of this construction, it is nevertheless an interesting example of the impact that discoveries in child analysis have had on psychoanalytical theory in general.

Yet others were trained in London. This was the case of Ilse Hellman, who we have mentioned several times. Her path was an interesting one: also Viennese, she was initially a social worker, and worked with Charlotte Bühler on infant psychology where she met a variety of interesting people, such as Jean Piaget, René Spitz and Esther Bick. In 1930, she went to France to study psychology at the Sorbonne. For three or four years she worked at a centre for delinquent children near Paris. In 1937–8 Bühler sent her as her representative to London with a view to opening an Institute of Psychology. Bühler's 'first assistant' did not wish to leave her country on the grounds that 'glorious events' were brewing (the annexation of Austria by

Hitler). Ilse Hellman was later to thank her for her 'patriotism', which had enabled her, Ilse, to go to London, where she remained in 1939 when war was declared, since she did not wish to return to her homeland. It was thus that she was able to meet the Viennese girl, Anna Freud, in London. Consequently, she worked at the Nurseries with Anna and underwent analysis with Dorothy Burlingham, and was to practise the psychoanalysis of children and adolescents for the rest of her life. As we have already mentioned, some of her theoretical work can be found in her book *From War Babies to Grandmothers* (1990).

She also played a role in administrative bodies and, in particular, was part of the IPA committee which inquired into the Lacan group in France, 'because I spoke French', she says modestly.

When we interviewed her (I. 4) she was 82 years old and still practising; in particular, the analysis of adolescents, with whom, she stressed, she had better contact than some of the younger analysts, 'probably because there are not the same erotic temptations, and also because they prefer grandmothers. . . . When they come to see me, they are checking to see if I am still alive.'

Among some of the better known of Anna Freud's followers Joseph Sandler should be mentioned. He took over the management of the Index research project at the Hampstead Clinic from Dorothy Burlingham and worked on getting it into shape. He directed the work and the discussions about the Index and this led to the publication of *The Hampstead Psychoanalytic Index*, co-edited with John Bolland (1965), and *The Technique of Child Psychoanalysis* with Hansi Kennedy (who continued her work on the Index) and Robert L. Tyson (Sandler, Kennedy and Tyson, 1980). Sandler's book *The Analysis of Defence* (1985) enabled Anna Freud to take another look at her earlier work *The Ego and the Mechanisms of Defence* (1936) in the light of forty years' experience at the Hampstead Clinic. Sandler was the first holder of the Chair in Psychoanalysis founded in Jerusalem and was, until his recent retirement, the Professor of the Freud Memorial Chair in London, and a past president of the IPA. He has recently published a work on projective identification (1988).

Anne-Marie Sandler, his wife, has been quoted frequently in this book. Swiss by birth, she was one of the first to undergo training in psychoanalysis at the Hampstead Clinic before becoming a member of the British Society. She is the spokesperson for the child psychoanalysts of the Contemporary Freudian group (formerly Anna Freud's group) with the most authority. She has also contributed to the conceptualization of child psychoanalysis with her numerous articles.

Alex Holder, who ran the Hampstead Clinic's 'Bulletin', Clifford Yorke, former director of the Hampstead Clinic, George Moran, who followed him as director and who died recently, Peter Fonagy, the present head of scientific research at the Anna Freud Centre, and many others, should also be mentioned.

So should Thomas Freeman, who also worked on the Index at the Hampstead Clinic and who developed Anna's Freud's work on Psychoses. His works study the relationships between the psychopathology of the 'deviant' (or psychotic) child and adult schizophrenia using Anna Freud's concepts, which he did not hesitate to compare with those of Melanie Klein. Freeman worked in Scotland and Ireland.

As to Melanie Klein's followers, we have already looked closely at Paula Heimann, Susan Isaacs and Joan Rivière. Klein's followers developed her theories, not only by deepening the understanding of child analysis, but often also the understanding of more general phenomena, such as psychoses or the psychoanalytical study of groups, or indeed society at large.

Hanna Segal (née Poznanska) was born in Poland in 1918. Her father was a lawyer in Warsaw who emigrated to Geneva at the beginning of the 1930s to run an international newspaper. She was 12 when the family left Poland, but always remained attached to her Polish roots. At 16 she persuaded her parents to let her return to Warsaw, where she finished her secondary schooling and began her medical studies. When war broke out she was in Paris with her parents. When Paris was occupied by the Nazis she emigrated to Britain and finished her medical studies in Edinburgh, where the university ran a special course for Poles. Through Fairbairn she came into contact with the works of Melanie Klein and began analysis with David Matthew (who had himself been analysed by Melanie). She continued her analysis with Klein herself in London: this was the period of the 'Controversies'. Her supervisors were Paula Heimann and Joan Rivière, and then Melanie Klein for a child psychoanalysis. Admitted to the British Society in 1947, she became its President for a time, and was vice president of the IPA until recently.

In France Hanna Segal is best known for her presentation of Melanie Klein's works in two books which revealed Klein to the French public: *Introduction to the Work of Melanie Klein* (1964) and *Melanie Klein* (1979). These are solid works, well documented, well written and very informative. Notably, child psychoanalysis was only one chapter among many others defining Klein's work. It is a body of general psychoanalytical theory which, of course, uses child psychoanalysis as the starting point and from which child psychoanalysis itself can benefit, in both its practical and its theoretical applications, but which, moreover, is related to psychoanalysis as a whole. Her papers covering the period 1947–81 were printed in a book entitled *The Work of Hanna Segal: A Kleinian Approach to Clinical Practice* (1981), in which her numerous interests can be seen, including child analysis and the analysis of psychotics, aesthetics and freedom of thought, the function of dreams and the fear of death. Among others, she created the concept of 'symbolic equation'. She used this term to describe non–differentiation between the thing symbolized and the symbol itself, which is part of the disturbed relationship between the ego and the object, on which the concrete thought of the schizophrenic is based. Her latest work, *Dream, Phantasy and Art* (1991), has just been translated into French and contains a number of other extremely creative studies on the 'royal road', 'mental space' and 'art and the depressive position'. Segal's theories about the death instinct led her to chair and be very active in an international association of psychoanalysts against nuclear warfare.

Segal still does a lot of teaching and knows how to put her human warmth and humour, her in–depth knowledge of her subject and a great simplicity of expression to good use. In this context, we are particularly grateful for her considerable contribution to our own training in psychoanalysis of child psychoses.

Wilfred Ruprecht Bion (1897–1979) was born in an India still under British rule, of a father who was a civil engineer sent to the 'colonies', and of a mother 'not as well-educated but who possessed a great intuitive understanding' (Anzieu, 1980). Separated from his family at the age of 8 and sent to boarding school in England, Bion left school in 1916 and went into the army, where he was attached to a tank regiment. This was a traumatic but essential experience for him. The memory of his friends being burned alive in their tanks and the fact that he had survived played a role comparable with that of the concentration camps for Bettelheim. His only tangible reward was the Distinguished Service Order and the Legion d'Honneur. He studied history at Oxford and then medicine in London, and then appears to have spent a year in France (Green, 1991). In 1934, he started work at the Tavistock Clinic, and had his private consulting rooms in the famous Harley Street. Here he met Rickman, with whom he underwent a first phase of analysis in 1938, interrupted in 1939 by the war. Mobilized once again, as a psychiatrist, he was asked to deal with the 'skivers' in the British Army at the Northfield Military Hospital. He then ran the officer-selection board. It was while he was in the army that he undertook his initial work on groups. The war over, he went back to his consultations and underwent analysis with Melanie Klein for a number of years.

The change in Bion's personality caused by this analysis was astonishing: all his theoretical work was written during or after this experience. The terms of this change have been well documented by Donald Meltzer (1978). In 1968, at the age of 70, he emigrated to the United States, settling in Los Angeles, where there was a growing interest in the work of Melanie Klein. His later works date from this American period and from symposiums he attended in São Paulo and Rio de Janeiro, Brazil.

Bion's work, which will remain fundamental to the history of psychoanalysis, is only just beginning to be understood. Some of the concepts he put forward are often used drained of their essence, and sometimes even quite erroneously. We are thinking of his 'maternal reverie' or his notion of container–contained. In fact, it was a reworking of much of Melanie Klein's work, starting from the analysis of psychotics, which he was one of the first to practise using the analyst's couch. It has been said that his work was 'general Kleinism' (P. Geissmann *et al.*, 1991) (in reference to the general theory of relativity) in which all the Kleinian concepts (notably the paranoid-schizoid and depressive positions, projective identification, the early object relation and the early superego) were reformulated (and often hard to understand), and applied not only to the early development of the child, to adult psychoses and to groups, but also to psychopathology in general. His conceptualization, which had used child psychoanalysis as its starting point, came back to child analysis, where it is starting to be used both in the understanding of treatment and in group work in institutions caring for children.

Betty Joseph underwent analysis with Michael Balint in Manchester and then did a second phase with Paula Heimann in London. A member of the British Psycho-Analytical Society in 1949, one of her postgraduate supervisors was Hanna Segal. She was soon to develop a style of her own in her work, which Segal describes as being characterized by listening carefully to her patients and noting the minute-by-minute psychic changes in relation to the constant interaction between the analyst and the patient and their effect on transference and countertransference. She became a training analyst somewhere in the mid-1950s and her postgraduate seminar evolved to become a creative workshop.

In her workshop, too, it was the technical details of each moment of the treatment that were examined in detail. This way of doing things, says Hanna Segal, tends to eliminate any 'theory of technique' which would evolve in the direction of fixed and monolithic applications, and what has characterized her students is the way they have acquired different styles in relation to their different personalities. During the long interview she was kind enough to give us, we were indeed struck by the minute detail of her descriptions and the masterly manner in which she could weave the details into a coherent whole. Psychoanalysts of the Kleinian school, although they always interpret 'in the transference', i.e. in the here and now, vary in the importance they give to relating these interpretations to the patient's childhood history. Betty Joseph uses the 'acting in' of the patient to make the situation more characteristic and establishes the relationship between the transference and the childhood history less frequently than others. Segal describes her work as being characterized by the rare combination of a very finely honed intuition and a great intellectual and technical rigour. In the 1989 publication of her collected works (1959–89), the topics covered include repetition compulsion, the psychic change that takes place during the analytical process, the analysis of perversion, the 'total situation' in transference, projective identification and envy in every day life.

Betty Joseph was a child analyst for some considerable time, and in fact still practises as a child analyst. Nowadays, she told us (I. 8), cases have become rarer, perhaps for social and economic reasons. In addition, thanks to child analysis, there has been considerable progress in adult analysis over the last twenty-five years so that, paradoxically, the most experienced child analysts put their experience at the disposal of adult analysts and the children are analysed by younger specialists.

Donald Meltzer, an American living in Oxford who practised child analysis for a long time, was one of the last to undergo analysis with Melanie Klein. He tried to see Kleinian theories gain ground by fostering the growth of ideas in Bion's sense of the word, Bion being one of his reference points. Meltzer's inventive genius led him to propose new formulations within Melanie Klein's world. His 1967 book entitled *The Psychoanalytical Process* was an attempt at a systematic description of the process of analytical treatment in general, using child analysis as a paradigm. In 1973 *Sexual States of Mind* was a collection of papers where the accent was on the central role that sexuality plays in psychoanalysis. His work was in general centred on the analytical treatment of children but he also examined some of the applications, as in the chapter entitled 'Pedagogic implications of the structural psychosexual theory'. As with other Kleinian authors, Meltzer also outlined political and social applications, such as when he described tyranny as being 'a social perversion in defence against depressive anxieties . . . a social process for commerce in seemingly hopelessly mutilated internal objects' (Meltzer, 'Tyranny', in 1973: 144–5).

In 1975 he published *Explorations in Autism* (see Meltzer *et al.*, 1975) in which he demonstrated how cases of child autism, supervised by him in his team, had been treated using authentic analytical methods consisting of five 50-minute sessions a week, systematic investigation and no compromise in the transference: 'The method of treatment did not differ from that . . . described by Melanie Klein.' This demonstration by Meltzer of the possibility of psychoanalytical treatment for autistic patients was in itself an invaluable contribution. In addition, it enabled him to describe new views on autistic states proper, about dismantling, about post-autistic obsessional states and about dimensionality as a parameter of mental functioning. His three 1978 studies published as *The Kleinian Development* are of prime importance and very instructive for anyone wanting to understand the connection between the work of Sigmund Freud and that of Melanie Klein, and between the work of Melanie Klein and that of Wilfred R. Bion.

His later works were more speculative and concerned subjects such as the aesthetic object, a concept which he placed short of the paranoid-schizoid position, as a return to the utopian idea of the golden age. He was getting some way away from Kleinian theories here. Probably because of this distance, but also because his colleagues took exception to his lack of rigour in technique in his later years, he is no longer considered representative by the Kleinian school, and is no longer a member of the British Society.

Meltzer nevertheless continues his teaching activities, both in England and in France, in the form of seminars, very 'collective' supervisions (1–200 people!) and conferences. We ourselves are indebted to him for this form of teaching and, in addition to his theoretical abilities, we have been able to appreciate his clinical sense in appreciating a situation, his ability to detect unconscious phantasies and the rapidity of his interpretations.

Herbert A. Rosenfeld, who died in 1986, was born in Germany and studied medicine in Munich. Fleeing the Nazi persecutions, he emigrated to Britain in 1935, finished off his studies in Edinburgh and then settled in London, where he became a psychotherapist at the Tavistock Clinic. He underwent analysis with Melanie Klein during the war, became a member of the British Society in 1947 and was one of its training analysts for a long time.

He did not practise child psychoanalysis, but centred much of his work in line with Melanie Klein's thinking on the psychoanalysis of psychoses. He was one of those who put patients with severe mental disorders on the couch, an attitude considered bold at that time, and which fits in with the fact that Kleinian child psychoanalysts were anxious to carry out treatment in as similar a fashion as possible to that of adult neurotics. He developed a considerable number of new concepts about psychoses, the massive denial of affects, early Oedipus complex in psychotics, transference psychosis, collusion. Unlike Meltzer, he gave more attention to the role of the analyst as container than to the self-observation of the countertransference, which seems to be closer to Melanie Klein's thinking. His theories on feedback have enriched the conceptualization of child psychoanalysis and of psychoanalysis in general. To date, two of his books have been translated into French: *Psychotic States: A Psychoanalytical Approach* (1965) and *Impasse and Interpretation* (1987).

Esther Bick was born in Poland. She studied psychology at Vienna University, working with Charlotte and Karl Bühler, and chose the subject of child development for her PhD thesis. She did statistical research, studying a considerable number of the children who were submitted to the range of tests developed by the Bühlers.

On her arrival in Britain, just before the war, Bick joined Michael Balint in Manchester. After the war she moved to London and underwent analysis with Melanie Klein. Very quickly, she became interested in the observation of the young infant, but with the eye of the psychoanalyst. At the request of John Bowlby she began to teach a course on infant observation at the Tavistock Clinic, and gave papers on the subject to the British

Society in 1963. Indeed, her paper entitled 'Notes on Infant Observation in Psychoanalytic Training' (1964) is still considered the main reference on the subject. The observation of the baby was part of the course at the London Institute of Psycho-Analysis from 1960 onwards. At the same time she continued her activities as a child analyst, and presented a report on the specific difficulties of child analysis at the 1961 IPA Congress. We have already mentioned this remarkable report in detail (see pp. 238–40).

In 1968, Bick's paper "The experience of the skin in early object-relations' marked an epoch in Britain. She wanted to demonstrate the need that a child has for a containing object experienced like a skin.

> The need for a containing object would seem, in the infantile unintegrated state, to produce a frantic search for an object – a light, a voice, a smell, or other sensual object – which can hold the attention and thereby be experienced, momentarily at least, as holding the parts of the personality together. The optimal object is the nipple in the mouth, together with the holding and talking and familiar smelling mother'
> (in *Collected Papers of Martha Harris and Esther Bick*, 1987: 115).

For Bick, 'disturbance of the primal skin function can lead to the development of a second-skin formation' (ibid.), and she goes on to develop the characteristics and the consequences of this on the infant's mind.

Towards the end of her life, Bick travelled to Israel frequently, and helped to train a number of psychoanalysts there (I. 11).

The work of Frances Tustin was original and very creative, centred on the study of the analysis of children with psychogenetic autism, on which subject she wrote four books: *Autism and Childhood Psychosis* (1972), *Autistic States in Children* (1981), *Autistic Barriers in Neurotic Patients* (1986) and *The Protective Shell in Children and Adults* (1990).

She began to take an interest in autistic children at the beginning of the 1950s. She underwent analysis with Wilfred Bion for many years and then briefly with Stanley Leigh. 'My Kleinian training', she wrote (1986: 58). She worked at the Tavistock Clinic, where she supervised child psychotherapy. She was not, however, a member of the British Society. Although she acknowledged having received advice from a number of her contemporaries (Herbert Rosenfeld and Donald Meltzer) and that for her theoretical bases she had used the theoretical work of Klein, Winnicott, Margaret Mahler, Bick and Segal, she exercised her art in a solitary fashion for fifteen years, alone, at home with the autistic children that she was treating. In her interview (I. 9) she told us in picturesque fashion how her husband, a physicist, was at that time a very necessary representative of reality: he had manifested astonishment when, following one particular child, she had gone out into the street after the child and sat down on the pavement outside her house with the child and a basin of water.

In the second part of her life, she travelled a lot, taking part in numerous work groups in France, Italy and Spain, where she supervised a considerable number of cases of autism.

Tustin's work on the personality of the autistic child is most enlightening. Her theories were outlined gradually, as she acquired experience in the analytical treatment of these children. She developed a number of concepts from her clinical observations such as the autistic barriers, autistic shapes, autistic objects and the black hole. 'Patients who are prone to autistic ways of behaving have had this early state of communion traumatically disturbed [the model is early suckling experiences]. This means that, instead of a psychic core which hold them together, they have an unmourned sense of loss – "black hole with a nasty prick," as John . . . so graphically described it' (1986: 30).

In this work (*Autistic Barriers in Neurotic Patients*) she tackles the problem of autistic encapsulations within the personality of the neurotic patient. They are expressed clinically in a number of ways: a major phobia, of course, and fits of panic, but also in addictive or psychopathic behaviour, or they may be at the bottom of psychosomatic disorders. Tustin discusses the repercussions of these autistic encapsulations on psychoanalytical treatment. for her, the fact that they had not been considered might account for a number of never-ending analyses, characterized by a transference whose nature she questioned. Here she provides us with an excellent example of what child psychoanalysis has brought to psychoanalytical theories in general. Frances Tustin died in 1994.

A number of Melanie Klein's other pupils took an interest in extra-clinical subjects. This was the case of Roger E. Money-Kyrle, who wrote the introduction to *New Directions in Psychoanalysis* and edited the complete works of Melanie Klein in Britain. His own papers (1927–77) were collected and published for his fiftieth jubilee in the form of the *Collected Papers* (1978). He became interested, from an ethical viewpoint, in the general aspects of a personality able to free itself from its blind spots and tackle the depressive position. Such a person, he said, would be able to experience a feeling of unprojected guilt and would seek to work in a humanistic and democratic system. His six months' experience in 1946 with the 'Research Section on German Staff', a British committee set up to select a sufficiently democratic German administrative staff, resulted in the publication in 1951 of *Psychoanalysis and Political Horizons*, in which he developed this idea. However, he also wrote numerous articles on his clinical work such as one on the death instinct (1955, in *Collected Papers*, 1978, pp. 285–96), or the 1956 one on countertransference (in Money-Kyrle, *Collected Papers*, 1978, pp. 330–42).

Elliot Jaques, who as well as being a psychoanalyst was a doctor and professor of sociology, also used Kleinian concepts to study conflicts inside businesses. His 1955 article on 'Social Systems as Defence against

Persecutory and Depressive Anxiety' is an impressive example of this view-point. One of his conclusions is that this type of study throws light on the reasons why it is so difficult to bring about social change, and why so many social problems are apparently insolvable. Jaques also published papers on his clinical work, such as his work on 'Death and the mid-life crisis' (1963).

Isabel Menzies Lyth practised psychoanalysis on a part-time basis in private practice and carried out research and social consultancy for businesses the remainder of the time. Her studies on food for pleasure (chocolate, ice-cream, etc.), on the use of Bion's theories about groups in social institutions (factories, hospitals), road safety or the recruiting of London firemen, to mention but a few, show the diversity of possible applications of psycho-analysis. The title of one of her books *Containing Anxiety in Institutions* (1988), speaks volumes about the sort of work she did.

Several other famous psychoanalysts trained by Melanie Klein returned home to their native Argentina (for example, José Bleger, Enrique Racker and Emilio Rodrigué). We shall mention them in Chapter 13.

A renewed dialogue

It would seem that as the years go by antagonism is abating. Amicable relationships with and esteem for people belonging to other groups is now possible. 'We can now listen to each other, from one group to the other, says Anne-Marie Sandler (I. 3). As the publication about the 'Controversies' in 1991 (see King and Steiner, 1991) proves, it would appear that there is a common desire for understanding and to discuss the somewhat tumultuous past.

Hanna Segal and Betty Joseph, expressing themselves as Kleinians, both stress the evolution in Kleinian thinking. In her report at the Week-end Conference for English-Speaking Members of European Societies held in the autumn of 1990 on the subject of 'The Treatment Alliance and the Transference', Betty Joseph (1990) mentions the case of Jane, for whom the interpretation of the unconscious phantasy was not enough. 'Interpretations about her projecting her own feelings of smallness and stupidity into me, clearly could not reach her; interpretations about how she saw me as stupid, unable to understand, seemed nearer, so long as the feelings were left in me' (p. 22). She stressed that it may be necessary to assess the state of the ego and to interpret certain phantasies as a means of defence for the ego against the anxiety which assails it. As in the case of Jane, it was the interpretation which enabled her to listen to the analyst and to remain calm because she needed 'to keep me and whatever I said, out of her mind, her ears, and close the drawbridge between us' (p. 22). For her part, expressing herself as a Contemporary Freudian at the same week-end conference on the same subject, Anne-Marie Sandler stated at the end of her paper that 'the analyst needs to take into account the nature of the child's ego, the form of his resistances and their source. An understanding of the unconscious phantasy, while essential, is not in itself enough' (1990: 26).

In a more general fashion, and without drawing up an exhaustive catalogue, we can mention some of these changes. Anna Freud was hesitant as to whether analysis could really change the young child in very difficult cases. At the Anna Freud Centre, at present, the analysis of very young children has been taken on board and research is being done into very difficult cases and into autism. The report presented at the IPA Congress in Buenos Aires in 1991 by Peter Fonagy and George S. Moran is a good reflection of these new concerns (Fonagy and Moran, 1991).

According to Anne-Marie Sandler (I. 3), one can now mention the internal object and projective identification at the Anna Freud Centre, and to envisage early forms of the superego is no longer taboo.

For their part, the Kleinians now speak of and interpret the defence mechanisms of the ego, it being understood of course that unconscious phantasies underlie these defensive mechanisms.

However, the child's history still plays an essential role for Contemporary Freudians, and aggressiveness is still secondary to frustration in the sequence attachment–frustration–aggressive discharge. This remains a fundamental difference from the Kleinians' view, because the way they observe and listen to the child is quite different and the interpretation made to the child is based on other factors.

Finally, the interpretation of a negative transference has become commonplace for Contemporary Freudians, but here the sense of the interpretation is different, for, unlike the Kleinians, it is not based on the recognition of the existence of the death instinct.

It is true that few members of the British Society who are analysts train in child analysis, but it seems essential that this training exists, for, due to it, the identity of child psychoanalysis had been preserved.

Notes

1 We would like to take this opportunity of thanking Dr Riccardo Steiner, member of the British Psychoanalytical Society, for sending us the text of a report that he gave at a particularly interesting meeting of the International Association for the History of Psychoanalysis, which took place in London in July 1990.

2 Our emphasis.

3 Winnicott's emphasis.

12

The United States of America

Child psychoanalysis developed in the United States in several stages. Initially, after the celebrated voyage of Sigmund Freud and Carl Jung in 1909, psychoanalytical ideas spread very quickly and met with both an immediate success and indignant reaction.

Abraham A. Brill, who had worked at the Burghölzli in Zurich and then in Vienna, founded the New York Psychoanalytic Society in 1911. In that same year the American Psychoanalytic Society was formed to bring together all the societies that might be founded in the various states. In 1914 a society was founded in Boston with James Putnam as its first President. Other cities were soon to follow suit: Los Angeles, Washington, Chicago, Philadelphia. The Americans brought dynamism, pragmatism, efficiency and advertising sense to bear on the development of psychoanalysis. They also brought some shortcomings: they forbade the practice of lay analysis, in order to guarantee therapeutic content; and they let a climate of *laissez-faire* take hold in training and perhaps even in conceptualization, which led Freud to remark in 1926 in *The Question of Lay Analysis*: 'I venture to assert that – not only in European countries – doctors form a preponderating contingent of quacks in analysis. They very frequently practise analytic treatment without having learnt it and without understanding it' (1926a: 230). And Samuel Goldwyn's offer to Freud (which, of course, he refused) in 1925 of $100,000 to collaborate on the film *Anthony and Cleopatra* would have done nothing to make him change his mind.

One of the consequences of the rapid spread of psychoanalysis throughout the United States was the excessive application of the ideas of the pioneers of psychoanalysis to the up-bringing of children (in proportion to the size of the new continent and its possibilities of absorption – the 'melting-pot' phenomenon). Physical or emotional shock to children from

251

upper- and middle-class backgrounds in American society had to be avoided at all costs, since such trauma was supposed to lead to neuroses. Not only should children not be physically punished (which would cause masochistic phantasies), they should not be frustrated either. The child should only be given its bottle when he wanted it and all whims should be catered to. The child should be given a sexual education. It was common for American parents to consult their psychoanalyst in order to assess their own guilt in their children's up-bringing. Analysts had no hesitation in giving parents the 'recipes' they demanded, which increased yet again the size of their clientele. We wonder whether the incredible number of cases of obesity in young Americans is totally unrelated to this type of education. Such a gigantic departure from the original concept of psychoanalytical up-bringing could perhaps not be avoided, but it also contributed to the disrepute into which psychoanalysis itself then fell. 'America', Freud joked one day, 'is a mistake, a huge mistake it is true, but nevertheless a mistake' (Jaccard, 1982a: 279). The difficulties that psychoanalysis met with are generally attributed to the fact that from 1927 onwards it could only be practised by doctors. In our opinion, this is only one of the factors, because psychologists, like doctors, are quite capable of talking rubbish.

However, American psychoanalytical societies did try to adhere to doctrine at certain levels, in particular by maintaining relations with Vienna. Horace W. Frink went to train with Sigmund Freud. Ruth Mack Brunswick was a member of both the Vienna and New York societies, and underwent analysis with Sigmund Freud from 1922 onwards, becoming one of Anna Freud's friends. She became interested in the psychoanalysis of psychoses and in this context devised a theory about the pre-oedipal phases, but was not interested in child analysis. Otto Rank, who went to New York episodically from 1924 and then finally moved there, had considerable influence on the newly formed psychoanalysts. Sandor Rado, who was one of Sándor Ferenczi's friends, underwent analysis with Karl Abraham in Berlin. His analysands included Otto Fenichel, Heinz Hartmann and Wilhelm Reich. Roazen (1976) mentions that, when the Americans needed a stimulating and experienced professor to head the training of analysts at the New York Institute they would offer the position to Rado. Sigmund Freud apparently gave his blessing to Rado's departure for the United States n 1931. Gradually, he was to take a different position from that of Freud by envisaging the personality as a whole, by insisting on the analysis of feelings and by reviving Freud's early theory of psychical trauma. Franz Alexander, another Hungarian, also came from Berlin at this time and became interested in psychosomatics in Chicago. Alexander, like Rado, had been among those in Berlin who had best demonstrated their lack of understanding of child psychoanalysis, of Melanie Klein's type of child analysis in particular. In a letter to her husband dated 14 December 1924, Alix Strachey recounts the episode where 'Die Klein' [Melanie] had offered her ideas and her experience on *Kinderanalyse* [child analysis] at the meeting of the Berlin Society:

> at last the opposition showed its hoary head – & it really was *too* hoary. The *words* used were, of course, psycho-analytical: danger of weakening the Ichideal, etc. But the *sense*, was, I thought, purely anti-analysis: We mustn't tell children the terrible truth about their repressed tendencies, etc. And this, altho' die Klein demonstrated absolutely clearly that these children (from 2¾ upwards) were already wrecked by the repression of their desires & the most appalling *Schuld bewusstsein* [= too great, or incorrect oppression by the Ueberich]. The opposition consisted of Drs Alexander & Rado, & was purely affective & 'theoretical,' since apparently noone knows anything about the subject outside die Melanie and Frl Schott, who is too retiring to speak, but who agrees with her. Abraham spoke sharply to Alexander, and Dr Boehm (a faded, but possibly a very clever analyst, youngish & birdlike in manner) rushed in too to defend die Klein. In fact, everyone rallied to her and attacked the 2 swarthy Hungarians.
>
> (Strachey and Strachey, 1985: 145)

Karen Horney was also present at this meeting. She emigrated to New York in 1932.

In the *Psychoanalytical Quarterly* (1933: 143), Alexander renewed his criticism of Melanie Klein for having incorrectly interpreted Freud's death instinct, and for her 'exaggerated stress on the ideational content'. He called her an 'artiste'.

Peter Blos was one of the educators at the school founded by Anna Freud for the children of Dorothy Burlingham and a few others. There he practised the 'project method', which endeavoured to implement a modern approach to education, but which was not specifically psychoanalytical. After emigrating to the United States, Blos became a psychoanalyst specializing in adolescents and is well known for his work in this field. In 1986 he was chosen to give the Sigmund Freud Lecture at Vienna University on the subject of 'Freud and the Father Complex', in the presence of the President of Austria.

Erik Homburger Erikson, a painter, made contact with the world of Freud in 1927 while hitch-hiking around Europe. His friend Peter Blos suggested that he paint portraits of the Burlingham children. Since he seemed to get on well with children, it was suggested that he become a child analyst. Roazen (1976) believes that Anna Freud and Dorothy Burlingham wanted to attract men to child analysis, which would have been an innovation at that time. As we saw when we looked at the pioneers of psychoanalysis, many of them undertook analyses of children, but not for long. It was Anna Freud who undertook Erikson's analysis and he soon became one of the inner circle. August Aichhorn also contributed to his training. He became a member of the Vienna Psychoanalytical Society in 1933, and then came in for criticism by Anna Freud because his papers about the play activities of children smacked too much of Melanie Klein for her liking. Anna Freud recommended him to American psychoanalysts as a training analyst and he moved to Cambridge, Massachusetts. He remained a child analyst, perhaps because that was his only training, and he gained a considerable reputation in the United States.

Erikson published numerous works on children's play activities, on anthropology, on the development of the ego. He developed the concept of identity (including the notion of a social identity) and that of the strength of the ego. Influenced by Anna Freud and Heinz Hartmann, he also worked with anthropologists (Gregory Bateson and Margaret Mead to name but two) and studied in such diverse, and famous, universities as Yale, Harvard and Berkeley. He believed that society had an important role to play in human development and was strongly in favour of psychotherapeutic applications, even though he recognized the founding role of psychoanalysis.

Although he does not seem to have been a psychoanalyst himself, Ernst Kris nevertheless devoted much of his work to the psychoanalytical psychology of children. He is the author of an important Yale psychoanalytical research study into the longitudinal observation of children. This was a behavioural study of children from 0–5 years old undertaken by a multidisciplinary team of people familiar with psychoanalysis. The mothers of the families, selected in obstetrical clinics, had to have a good record of mental health and give an assurance of remaining in the New Haven area for at lest five years. They were offered complete paediatric assistance and a place in the kindergarten at the study centre. (Comments on this study can be found in *La connaissance de l'enfant par la psychanalyse*, Lebovici and Soulé, 1970: 200–6.)

In this same work, the authors analyse an article (1958) by Kris on the recall of childhood memories in psychoanalysis which shows that he was interested in children, but through adult analysis. How the memories of a traumatic experience are distorted, telescoped or diluted with time comes out in the treatment of adult. There was also a very fine observation of a little girl called Dorothy, who was being followed by the Yale research group, in whom the traumatic events could be observed at the time they occurred, as could the initial distortion of these events by her memory.

Most of the Viennese and Berliners who emigrated to the United States did so a little later on, before or during World War II. Heinz Hartmann came to occupy an eminent position. We saw in Chapter 5 how his ideas closely followed those of Anna Freud and led him to develop his ego psychology, his theory of the autonomous ego, integrating the data pertaining to direct observation of the child into psychoanalysis. This trend rapidly became dominant in the United States, and still is. However, he did not contribute to the development of child analysis at all. Neither did any of the other *émigrés*: Kurt Loewenstein, Herman Nunberg, Theodor Reik, Erich Fromm, Wilhelm Reich or Hanns Sachs. The latter had already been invited to the United States in 1932, where he was to teach at the Harvard Medical School.

These second-generation psychoanalysts neither practised child analysis nor contributed new theories to it, but their influence on it quickly became preponderant.

THE POST-WAR PERIOD

René A. Spitz (1887–1974) lived long enough both to have undergone a training analysis with Sigmund Freud himself in 1910 (the first to have done so, according to Jaccard, 1982a) and to have been one of the most modern 'American' authors. Spitz is a perfect example of the 'genetic' trend in psychoanalysis, for whom the object relationship is the result of an evolving relationship between the child and its mother. This point of view complements what the Americans call the 'structuralist' trend, which is based on Freud's second theory of the psychical apparatus in which he described the structuring agencies of the personality as being made up of the id, the ego and the superego. Genetic psychoanalysis is based on studies of genetic psychology or developmental psychology.

Spitz was one of the 'younger' generation who gathered around Anna Freud even before the founding of the Vienna Institute. There, at the *Kinderseminar* he came into contact with Heinz Hartmann, Wilhelm Reich, Jeanne Lampl de Groot, Willi Hoffer, Robert and Jenny Waelder, and Richard Sterba. At the same time he began his research work in Charlotte Bühler's department of experimental psychology, where he met Ilse Hellman (who was not yet interested in psychoanalysis) and Jean Piaget. He would have had to assert himself, for Frau Bühler would not have Sigmund Freud mentioned in her presence, nor have any Freudians around her (I. 4). However, he remained faithful to the Bühlers' ideal of research, since the test he used in his own research (*The First Year of Life*, 1954) was the Bühler–Hetzer baby-test. The Vienna University's Department of Psychology had used this test between 1928 and 1938 on all the children taken in by the Vienna *Kinderübernahmestelle* (Child Welfare Department), about 5,000 babies in all. Spitz chose as the title of his book (published first in a short version in 1954 and then full-length in 1965), *The First Year of Life: A Psychoanalytic Study of Normal and Deviant Development of Object Relations*, almost the same title as Charlotte Bühler's 1930 work *The First Year of Life*.

He would use this test in the United States in a crèche and with abandoned children. He was probably one of the first to use film in the observation of babies and in 1933 invented a method of fast-motion shooting to obtain good slow-motion replays for effective observation. His first writings date from 1935 in Vienna. As he himself says in the Foreword: 'In 1935 . . . I worked alone.' Since then, however, a number of authors have worked in the same field. It is clear that he is the forerunner of the research done and the films made by Brazelton, an American paediatrician, who has recently (1979) given a boost to work on the interactivity between mother and child.

Spitz's research work enabled him to present a number of important discoveries in genetic psychology and provided a good foundation to his psychoanalytical conceptualization. A number of these discoveries are well known, in particular what he called the 'crucial points', in a lecture given at the Sorbonne in 1934, later to be named 'psychic organizers', which mark certain critical levels in the integration of the personality, represented on a symptomatic level by the smile on the mother's face, anxiety in the eighth month and the gesture 'no'.

We should also mention the discovery of the effects of hospitalization and the notion of anaclitic depression. However, an attentive study of his work shows such a large number of intuitions and discoveries concerning the detailed observation of babies that it is not possible to go into them here. The interested reader will find these notions developed in his book *The First Year of Life* (1954). We can nevertheless mention his work on the genesis of verbal and non-verbal communication (which he had also been working on in Vienna, following in the footsteps this time of Karl Bühler, Charlotte's husband), and a study of the role of nuzzling as a preliminary step to communication (Spitz, 1957).

His psychoanalytical conceptualization was very much Anna Freudian, close to the ego psychology of Heinz Hartmann. He backed them up, somewhat excessively we feel, by saying that he had *seen* the phenomena in his experiments, and made a number of bald assertions. In the first edition of *The First Year of Life*, presenting his research, he declared:

> This organism [the neonate] still lacks consciousness, perception, sensation, and all other psychological functions, be they conscious or unconscious.
>
> It also follows from this proposition concerning the neonate's state of nondifferentiation that at birth there exists no ego, at least not in the usual sense of the term . . . Obviously, one can speak even less of the existence of an Oedipus complex or that of a superego at birth. Similarly, symbolism and thinking in symbols are nonexistent, and symbolic interpretations are inapplicable. Symbols are more or less contingent on the

acquisition of language. Language, however, is non-existent during the whole of the first year of life.

(1965: 4–5)

René Spitz, on the other hand, acknowledged the 'theorems' of psychoanalysis, and in addition states that his viewpoint is genetic. He believed that 'all psychological phenomena are based on the reciprocal interaction of a congenital factor with a factor emanating from the family environment' (ibid.). Congenital factors can be chromosomal, infectious, or due to neonatal anoxia. Spitz did not believe in birth trauma, as described by Otto Rank, or, even less, in the 'naivety' of authors who maintain that the foetus expresses its unpleasure in the uterus. The cry of the child at birth is more to do with the silver nitrate put in its eyes or the slaps on the bottom 'administered with gusto' by the midwife (*The First Year of Life*, 1965). *The First Year of Life* (1965) is an updated and considerably enlarged version of the first edition published in 1954. The way Spitz formulated his ideas was now less abrupt: 'I have refrained from using any hypothesis positing the operation of intrapsychic processes in the infant at birth', or 'at birth, there exists no ego, at least not in the general sense of the word' (p. 5).

Georges Mauco, who wrote Spitz's obituary in *Revue française de psychanalyse* (1975), mentioned that he spent some time in Paris before emigrating to the United States in 1937, giving lectures at the Paris Institute of Psychoanalysis from 1934 onwards. We have found eight papers in French which were published in that magazine between 1934 and 1966. In 1966 the paper was the introductory report he gave to the 26th Conference on Romance Languages in Paris and entitled: 'Implications métapsychologiques de mes recherches sur les données du développement infantile' ['The metapsychological implications of my research into data on infantile development']. Here he is even less categoric: 'In early childhood the ego is still non-existent, or in the process of being formed' or, further on, 'My observations confirm Edward Glover's supposition that some discrete *nuclei* of the ego first of all show an organizing tendency. These are crystallization nuclei', and finally, 'I would go as far as accepting the notion that the baby does experience things and that these would be the *forerunners* of a consciousness of *self*'. Then aged 78, Spitz still clung to the idea he had upheld all his life, but was able to perceive the trend in ideas.

Spitz exerted considerable influence on psychoanalysis both in France and in the United States, and he was elected President of the Colorado Psychoanalytical Society in 1957. Was he able to practise as a psychoanalyst over this long period, between emigration and his travels? It is highly likely that he was, since a number of his works concern notions of clinical psychoanalysis. For example, 'Countertransference: comments on its varying roles in the analytic situation', was the title of an article published in the

Journal of the American Psychoanalytical Association in 1956. But this great researcher into child psychoanalysis does not seem to have carried out child analysis himself; it was probably not his vocation and, in any case, his theories would not have permitted him to do so.

In her preface to the 1954 book, Anna Freud obviously appreciated Spitz's opposition to Kleinian theories, which were described without being named as such. She uses a phrase which, although purporting to be Freudian orthodoxy, leaves us somewhat perplexed: 'To trace the happenings in the first year of life, he advocates the use of direct observation and of the methods of experimental psychology, in contrast to those analytic authors who prefer to rely only on the reconstruction of developmental processes from the analysis of later stages' (Anna Freud, Preface to *The First Year of Life*, 1954: vii).

Phyllis Greenacre (1894–1989) was an American from Chicago, a contemporary of the second-generation Viennese analysts. Her first vocation, influenced by Adolf Meyer, was to be a psychobiologist and she worked at the Phipps Clinic, Johns Hopkins Hospital, from 1916–27. After moving to New York she ran a public health organization for children until 1932 and then became Professor of Clinical Psychiatry at Cornell University Medical College. She underwent analysis at this time and became a member of the New York Psychoanalytic Institute in 1937. At one point she was President of the Institute, and in 1961 she became Vice-President of the IPA. She published ninety-nine papers in her long life and two books.

Greenacre worked with Ernst Kris, who prefaced her book *Trauma, Growth and Personality*, published in 1953, which is a compilation of the papers she wrote between 1941 and 1951. We should also mention her work on the parent–infant relationship which was the subject of a report to the 22nd International Psycho-Analytical Congress in Edinburgh (1960).

Although her work falls more in the domain of genetic psychoanalysis and her centres of interest were firstly directed towards the biological approach to the birth of personality and direct observation. Greenacre disregarded the work of René Spitz, though it is true that some of his work was later than hers. Her conclusions are also different: she attributes an important role to birth; although she does not give the trauma of birth a role as important as Otto Rank does, she demonstrates that its role is not insignificant. She insists on the fact that birth is 'certainly' the prototype of human anxiety. In her first paper on psychoanalysis, 'The predisposition to Anxiety' (1941), she indicates, contrary to Spitz, that the foetus possesses a certain reactivity. It reacts to a *feeling* of discomfort, even if it is only a question of reflexes. She offers some reflections on the erection at birth and the sucking of the thumb. She reminds us that Sigmund Freud had spoken of the 'narcissistic libido' of the foetus. 'Although the prenatal period', she writes, 'is, as Ferenczi pointed out and Freud emphasized, practically a continuum with postnatal life, the cæsura of birth has not only the organizing effect of a single momentous event, but it also marks the threshold at which "danger" (first probably in the sense of lack of familiarity) begins to be vaguely apprehended and it is therefore the first dawn of psychic content' (pp. 86–7). Her opinions were very much criticized in the United States before it was recognized that, in fact, she was somewhat in advance of her contemporaries.

Although connected to the Anna Freud school of thought, and to Harmannian psychoanalysis, Greenacre did not hesitate to quote Melanie Klein (which was rare in the context of that period of conflict) or to adopt some of her viewpoints. 'I think, as does Melanie Klein, that this high degree of aggressiveness in early childhood, with the reflected severity of the threatening primitive figures, plays a very important role in the development of schizophrenia'. It seems that she is using the word 'aggressiveness' to describe the death instinct, without naming it. However, she defines aggressiveness as being the manifestation of a *positive* developmental force, like the violence of development in expansion, a force which is not hostile, similar to Jean Bergeret in France (Bergeret, 1984). In general, moreover, she relates the psychobiological or developmental notions that she uses to possible uses in treatment. The same applies for the predisposition to anxiety, whose consequences Greenacre examines in the treatment of severe neuroses, and the handling of transference. The method recommended for severely disturbed patients 'is necessarily situated somewhere between psychoanalytical technique and methods used with children'.

We thought it interesting to indicate the variety of psychoanalytical conceptualizations one could arrive at from the same basic theories, depending perhaps on the personal history and the flexibility of the authors' egos, and also on whether they were primarily experimentalists and theorists (Spitz) or whether they had considerable clinical experience in psychoanalysis (Greenacre).

The contributions that Margaret Mahler has made to our understanding of the pre-oedipal stage, said James Anthony in 1986,

> have certainly had an impact on the dynamic approach to child development in the United States. . . . Based on the direct observation of children just starting to walk, but *not* on their analysis, the primary focus, as with Klein, was on the mother–child relationship and the intrapsychic struggles of the child within this dyad. It is of special interest that the two child analysts, Klein and Mahler, both emphasized the significance of depression (a normative depressive 'position' and a 'basic depressive mood' during the crucial rapprochement crisis) that needed to be resolved before an orderly classical psychosexual development could ensue. As a result, the general psychoanalyst has become more accepting of the concept of

depression as a primary affect that makes its presence felt from the earliest years and contributes to later psychopathology.

('The contributions of child psychoanalysis to psychoanalysis',
1986: 80–1)

Margaret Mahler also went to the United States from Vienna (see Mahler, 1978). Her particular vocation dated back, she said, to an episode that stood out in her mind (as a screen-memory) from when she was 5 years old and had tried to open up the eyes of some newborn kittens so that they could see the world into which they had just arrived. In Hungary one of her childhood friend's was Alice Balint. Through this friendship she briefly met Sándor Ferenczi; her father was a doctor, and her meeting with Ferenczi reinforced her paternal identification. After studying medicine, she specialized in paediatrics and worked in this field in Vienna, while at the same time frequenting the hospital's child psychiatry unit. At this time she published seven articles, showing her interest in research and writing even at this early stage. One of Anna Freud's lectures led to her decision to enrol at the Vienna Psychoanalytical Institute. She was one of August Aichhorn's more assiduous pupils, and at his instigation founded Austria's first psychoanalytically oriented child guidance centre. She was an enthusiastic student at Anna Freud's seminar on child analysis, and no doubt underwent psychoanalysis herself at that time.

While still in Vienna, Margaret Mahler had become interested in 'atypical' children, and this would be her main centre of interest in New York, where she probably arrived in 1938. Her first psychoanalytical paper seems to date from 1940. It was a paper given to the New York Psychoanalytical Society on 'Pseudo-imbecility' and published in 1942 under the name of Mahler (Schoenberger). She was then working as a consultant in the children's section of the New York State (University of Columbia) Psychiatric Institute. Next, she worked at the Municipal Hospital in the Bronx, and after that at the Masters Children's Centre in New York City. Her work was much appreciated by the authorities, and this meant that it benefited from numerous subsidies, in particular from the National Institute of Mental Health, USPHS. She was also Professor of Psychiatry at the Albert Einstein Medical School.

She relates (Mahler, 1968) how difficult it was to get recognition for children with 'schizophrenia-like' syndromes who were neither mentally retarded nor severely neurotic. 'There has been a great resistance, emotionally tinged, against acknowledgement of the existence of schizophrenia-like derangement in little children . . . the only concession that adult psychiatry would make was to acknowledge the existence of an "early infantile autism", described by Kanner a few years earlier.' (1968: 1–2). Up to the mid-1950s she worked on establishing the differences between the autistic syndrome and the syndrome of symbiotic psychosis, which she went on to describe. She then worked on developing a form of treatment using a 'corrective symbiotic experience' with 'infusions of auxiliary forces of the ego'. She was less interested in treatment for autistic children, who she said must be lured out of [their] autistic shell with all sorts of devices, such as music, rhythmic activities, and pleasurable stimulation of [their] sense organs' (ibid., p. 168). She proposed a classification of infantile psychosis in terms of the predominance of one or other of the primitive psychotic organizations of defence, i.e. depending on whether autistic or symbiotic defences were dominant.

As with other theorists of child psychoanalysis, she was not able to escape from the necessity of defining the origin of the object relationship. The second volume of her work (Mahler *et al.*, *The Psychological Birth of the Human Infant: Symbiosis and Individuation*, 1975), with Pine and Bergman, starts with the incisive sentence: 'The biological birth of the human infant and the psychological birth of the individual are not coincident in time' (p. 3). She instituted the theory of separation–individuation, a process which takes place between the fourth and thirty-sixth months. Separation is the 'child's emergence from a symbiotic fusion with the mother', and individuation consists of those achievements marking 'the child's assumption of his own individual characteristics'.

Margaret Mahler's support of the ideas of Anna Freud, Heinz Hartmann and René Spitz, her honesty with regard to the results of her observation, and her desire to conform to that singular form of denial of Melanie Klein's work observed among American psychoanalysts at the time, meant that she never mentioned Klein. But she could not say that the ego *did not exist at all* at birth, and so she wrote (1968): 'Only a rudimentary ego exists at birth', and further on mentions an 'undifferentiated ego'. But the newborn baby arriving at term 'evidently possesses an inborn talent which leads it to make a sensorimotor distinction between a living part object and inanimate matter.' The mother is the catalyst in these reactions and only interaction (in symbiosis) with her enables the resulting development of personality.

One way of getting round this dilemma was to note 'the shifting in normal intrapsychic development, between the permanence of the object (in Piaget's sense) and the acquisition of the permanence of the libidinal object, in Hartmann's sense'. However, the problem is thereby only put off, for this slow acquisition of the libidinal object leaves intact 'the realization of the permanence of the object', which is almost contemporaneous with birth. The difference consists in saying that this perceived object is not libidinal, not invested. It is the need which gives place to desire. In the permanence of the object, the maternal image has become intrapsychically available to the child.

However, without ever citing Melanie Klein, Mahler indicates that the phase of permanence of the (libidinal) object is reached when the ego no longer has to use the splitting of the object as a defence. What sort of splitting?: 'so as to preserve the image of the good object, the child separates (during mother's absence) the desired image and the hated image from the love object. Expectation was fixed on the "good" mother' (ibid.).

Mahler tried to summarize as follows the contradictions that one necessarily comes across on the subject of the transformation of a 'biological' embryo into a child who develops an ego in relation to objects, and this was the only time she ever mentioned Klein's name:

> Analysts have taken positions that vary along a broad spectrum regarding efforts to understand the preverbal period. At one extreme stand those who believe in innate complex oedipal fantasies – those who, like Melanie Klein and her followers, impute to earliest extra-uterine human mental life a quasi-phylogenetic memory, an inborn symbolic process . . . At the other end of the spectrum stand those Freudian analysts who look with favour on stringent verbal and reconstructive evidence . . . yet who seem to accord preverbal material little right to serve as the basis for even the most cautious and tentative extension of our main body of hypotheses. . . . We believe that there is a broad middle ground among analysts who, with caution, are ready to explore the contributions to theory that can come from inferences regarding the preverbal period.
>
> (Mahler *et al.*, 1975: 14)

This is the place to recall the deep emotional resonance that the work of Melanie Klein had with her contemporaries, and still does today. American psychoanalysts seem to be struck with terror at the idea of notions such as the existence of an object relationship at the beginning of life and, in particular, the unfolding consequences of the acceptance of the death instinct concept. Refuge in extreme, negative positions (Spitz), or the search for a compromise position which might attenuate the anxieties of the theorist (Margaret Mahler), should not be seen just as reflecting a struggle between trends or a battle for power, but as the deep-seated rejection of an unacceptable idea.

The work and ideas of the 'Viennese' in the United States, when compared with their earlier, mostly less creative work, has given rise to some speculation. James Anthony put the question to Margaret Mahler somewhat abruptly: 'If you had stayed in Europe, do you think you would have created or produced as much work?', giving her a line of possible response: 'For many people with creative potential, stress can stimulate creativity' (Mahler, 1978). In a remarkable reply, Mahler wrote:

> Some people, when they go into new territory, react with a regressive drive and become dependent, lost and miserable. Yet others bend their new

environment to make it fit their purposes and paranoid psychosis follows. I believe that, in positive cases, emigration is followed by a second individuation, a new psychological birth and perhaps a new vision of the world.

And further on:

[in Vienna] I was surrounded by the titans of my profession. I lived in the shadow of their ideas and received their teachings. It was a significant and uniquely enriching experience. But, and this 'but' is crucial, my ideas, my orientation and my own approach to development seem not to have been able to take shape as long as I had not succeeded in (or rather, as long as I was not forced) separating myself from these primary sources and therefore live my own particular individuation as a contributor. This then is what emigration was for me: it tore me and my sleepy ideas away from that psychological capsule which was Vienna in those days, and exposed me to a foreign environment whose newness aggravated the vulnerabilities of transition. But once the initial anxieties and insecurity had been mastered, it led me to become productive again and to the emergence of my theory of development.

(Mahler, 1978)

This is indeed a remarkable synthesis, in which one sees the author explaining the circumstances of her creativity in terms of the theories she herself had developed. In doing this she also shows the theoretical potential of her theories, underlining the possibility they hold for new concepts and discoveries in and for child psychoanalysis, to be of value for phenomena touching on the whole of psychoanalytical thought and its application in other fields, psychological and social in particular.

In *The Empty Fortress* (1967: 408), Bruno Bettelheim wrote:

It is unfortunate that Mahler, who was among the first to study infantile autism from a psychoanalytic viewpoint, was kept from recognizing infantile autism as an autonomous response on the part of the child by her belief that the young child is 'only half an individual.'

For Bettelheim, the golden age is a myth, from which the theories of primary narcissism and of the passivity of the child follow on. 'I believe that in his nursing, for example, the infant is eminently active in what to him is a central event in his life. At such times he may not feel he is moving mountains, but as if he were sucking them dry.' (ibid., p. 15).

Well before the study of fantasized interactions, of which Serge Lebovici is the recognized specialist in France, Bruno Bettelheim had described the process of mutuality: 'For breast feeding to be fully satisfying, the child must be hungry for food and the mother must want relief from the pressure of the milk in her breast' (ibid., p. 19).

263

Although he occupies a special position in American child analysis, Bruno Bettelheim (1903–90) nevertheless followed a path similar to other second generation Viennese. In his memoirs (Bettelheim, 1986), he describes his initial contact with psychoanalysis: it was purely by chance. In 1917, at the age of 13, he was a member of the Jung Wandervogel Youth, a pacifist, socialist movement. Here he met the young Otto Fenichel, who was a few years older and on leave from the army. Fenichel was already strongly promoting the ideas of Sigmund Freud and the adolescents found him a very charming and attractive person. His charm seemed to succeed in particular with a girl on whom the young Bruno had also set his heart. Things did not go any further, and Bettelheim rapidly got his girlfriend back, but he concluded that to be found attractive one needed to know about psychoanalysis. He therefore began to read the works of Sigmund Freud. However, until 1927, he sought his way in philosophy and art history; the business circles in which his father moved did not interest him and a university career was closed to Jews.

Bettelheim's depressive nature, his feeling of inferiority and, finally, a crisis in his married life led him to Richard Sterba, with whom he underwent analysis. He greatly appreciated the way in which his analyst proceeded, his neutrality, which was not at all in contradiction with the very personal touch he had given to the decoration of his waiting room and his treatment room. Bettelheim uses this detail to draw attention to the unfortunate trend of modern American analysts, who prefer to offer their patients 'impersonal and rather sterile settings'. He also believes that in the same fashion, American psychoanalysts make their patients feel just how superior they (the analysts) are, which has led to the general public calling them 'headshrinkers', or 'shrinks' for short.

It was in Sterba's waiting room that Bettelheim met his first psychotic child. Edith Sterba, who shared a waiting room with her husband, was at the time (1925–35) one of the earliest second-generation child psychoanalysts and was undertaking the analysis of a little boy called Johnny. Bettelheim met Johnny in the waiting room. In general, he did not respond to Bettelheim's attempts at conversation with more than a few monosyllabic and unintelligible utterances. He was also in the habit of chewing the leaves he had picked from a prickly cactus growing in a pot in the waiting room. One day Bettelheim said to him: 'Johnny, I don't know how long you have been seeing Dr Sterba, but it must be at least two years, since I have known you for that long, and here you are still chewing these awful leaves!' The child stood upright, 'looking down' on him, and said disdainfully: 'What are two years compared with eternity?' (Bettelheim, 1986: 32). This was the first time Bettelheim had heard him say a complete sentence. It was a considerable event for him, for it enabled him to understand *his own* problem all of a sudden (concern for others often conceals a need for concern about oneself), the value of time ('Trying to hurry up the process has more to do with one's own anxieties than with anything else') (ibid., p. 34), and the problems of child psychosis (a backward, mute, child was not only capable of speaking to him as an equal but also of informing him about things which he had not understood). He had just been given a lesson on oral sadism, masochism, self-mutilation and transference – what the child was eating were the mutilating leaves of Dr Sterba.

Bettelheim had another early experience with autistic children. From 1932–8 he provided lodgings for two of them in his own home. He tried to form a therapeutic environment for them and did not hesitate to make many changes in his home to adapt it to their needs. 'This was my initial experience with trying to create a very special environment that might undo emotional isolation in a child and build up personality' (1967: 8).

> Because of our fascination with child psychoanalysis, which had just then begun to develop, my wife and I brought in a child who suffered from infantile autism (a 'hopeless case') in order to find out whether the new discipline could help her . . .
> . . . the girl improved over the years she lived with us and grew into a charming and most talented adolescent.
>
> (*A Home for the Heart*, 1974: 12)

In 1936, after his own analysis was complete, Bettelheim envisaged becoming a member of the Vienna Psychoanalytical Society. He already had a number of friends who were members: to Otto Fenichel, who has already been mentioned, we should add Wilhelm Reich, Edith Buxbaum and Annie Reich.

However, 1938 opened a wound that was never to heal: it was the year Austria was annexed by the Third Reich and the year the Nazis marched into Vienna. As a Jew who had undertaken political activities against them (Bettelheim, 1943), the Nazis sent Bettelheim to Dachau concentration camp in the spring of 1938. At the end of the summer he was transfered to Buchenwald. While being transferred to Dachau he had received a bayonet wound and had been hit violently on the head. He lost his glasses, which left him virtually blind. He evidently tried valiantly to resist these aggressive attacks and he did finally manage to get a new pair of glasses sent to him. He fought against his nature by trying to remain lucid. He studied his traumatic dreams, observing that they were different from the nightmares he had had once before following a traffic accident. He even found some colleagues with whom he undertook a psychosocial study of the camp inmates. Ernst Federn, son of Paul Federn, a Viennese psychoanalyst mentioned earlier (Chapter 1), was interned with him and remembered how they tried to help their unfortunate comrades to overcome their difficulties using (brief) sessions of psychotherapy (Federn, 1988).

The fact that he had been one of the first to be interned explains how he was able to get out of the camps by being 'bought out'. At that time the camps were for punishment and not yet for extermination.

However, what Bettelheim had experienced there marked him for the rest of his life. His means of defence had been to use the observations he had made in the camps to develop his psychoanalytical thought, his creativity. The feeling of guilt at having survived is a theme which runs through all his work; it is a theme common to all surviving former inmates of the concentration camps, and a number of psychoanalytic works are still studying this particular form of guilt and shame. Papers on the subject were given as recently as 1991 at the IPA conference in Buenos Aires.

It was in this dramatic context that Bruno Bettelheim emigrated to the United States. He was welcomed by his colleagues and Franz Alexander, who was then the director of the Chicago Institute, admitted him to the Psychoanalytical Society, even though he was not a medical practitioner.

Bettelheim continued to search for the motives for the work he was doing. 'Why and how had the concentration camp experience . . . led me to work with psychotic children? Why had I selected this particular field to quiet the question: "Why was I spared?" (1974: 12). The authors of the present work, who as children experienced the Nazi persecutions in France during the war, wholeheartedly understand that question.

As soon as he arrived in the United States Bettelheim began by exposing the concentration camps and tried to alert public opinion to their existence and object. His paper entitled 'Individual and mass behaviour in extreme situations', written in 1942, was refused by a number of psychiatric and psychoanalytical publications for more than a year. The reasons for their refusal are interesting: he had not made any 'notes' while he was in the concentration camp; the facts were not verifiable; the findings could not be reproduced experimentally; the conclusions were exaggerated; or else the readers would not accept them. It was finally published in 1943 and read. However, the failure to recognize the nature of the camps was such that at the end of the war General Eisenhower made it obligatory reading for all the staff officers of the US Army stationed in Germany. 'Rather late', Bettelheim was to remark.

In 1944, Bettelheim was named Principal of the University of Chicago's Sonia Shankman Orthogenic School. We do not know where the term 'orthogenic' comes from but it would appear to date back to the time when the school took in backward and encephalopathic children. When Bettelheim announced his intention of running the school on psychoanalytical lines, the staff left fairly rapidly. They were replaced by some of his students from the University of Chicago and the school began to function properly in 1947.

The description of this school and the work done there has been the subject of a number of books: *Love is not Enough* and *Truants from Life* were published in 1950 and 1955 respectively. A number of papers preceding these works appeared in psychoanalytical journals: the *Menninger Clinic Bulletin* (1948), the *Psychoanalytic Review* (1949) and the *Psychoanalytical Study of the Child* (1950). Then came *The Empty Fortress* (1967) and *A Home for the Heart* (1974). As we shall see, further works by this author deal with other subjects. Bettelheim ran the school until 1973 when he resigned, at the age of 70, and the position went to his assistant, Jacqui Sanders. It would seem that she was not able to continue the work he had begun and the orthogenic school changed its outlook. By this time Bettelheim was no doubt so identified with his school that it was bound to disappear with him, but he knew that others would take up the torch of what can only be called the 'fight' against child psychosis, among other things.

Bettelheim's ideas for the treatment of psychotic children were founded on the triptych of:

1 The psychoanalytical theory, with Anna Freud's contributions concerning children.
2 His work on life in the concentration camps and in 'extreme situations'.
3 His social preoccupations, focused in particular on the fight against the traditional psychiatric institutions.

1. *From the psychoanalytical point of view*, his position, as we have seen, was clearly in favour of an active newly born baby interacting, functioning in 'mutuality', with its mother. He was therefore critical of the positions of René Spitz, Margaret Mahler, Erik Erikson and even of Donald Winnicott (1967).

On the other hand, he did assimilate Bowlby's notions on early clutching. He distinguished three critical phases in child development: between birth and 6 months the child 'must have experienced that the world is essentially a good place'; from the sixth to the ninth month people are recognized as individuals; from 18 months to 2 years the child can either approach the world or avoid contact.

Bettelheim also only mentions Melanie Klein once (ibid., p. 59), to say that he does not believe in the depressive and paranoid–schizoid positions, but he does in fact adopt the views of Klein and of Bion about autism, where mentally painful reality leads the child to turn 'destructively on his capacity for verbal thought'.

The autistic child cannot develop through the normal phases because of an autistic *Anlage*: a state which is perhaps partly constitutional and partly due to very early traumatic events, the extreme situation. The mother is not responsible for the autistic process; on this point he paraphrases Anna Freud: 'Fortunately, psychoanalysts are beginning to deny the haunting image of the rejecting mother' (ibid., p. 69). Anna Freud's quote dates from 1954, so Bettelheim was indeed the first to expose this myth. The authors of the present work strongly share these views, which even today have still not gained enough ground to have become overriding, even in the psychoanalytical world. 'The figure of the destructive mother (the devouring witch) is the creation of the child's imagination, though an imagining that has its source in reality, namely the [unconscious] destructive intents of the mothering person' (ibid., p. 71). Elsewhere, he adds that *all* mothers, and not just mothers of autistic children, have destructive intentions which run parallel to their loving intentions, as do all fathers. 'It is not the maternal attitude that produces autism, but the child's spontaneous reaction to it' (ibid., p. 69).

In *The Empty Fortress* (1967), an enormous work of almost 500 pages, more than 100 pages towards the end of the book are given over to a discussion of the literature.

2. *Bettelheim's experience of life in the concentration camps* 'permitted' him actually to experience what he was then to develop as an 'extreme situation'. The prisoners presented symptoms of marasmus, catatonia or melancholia, and even paranoid, criminal or regressive states. 'These [reactions] deteriorated to near autistic behaviour when the feeling of doom penetrated so deep that it brought the added conviction of imminent death. Such men were called "moslems" in the camps . . .' (ibid., p. 65).

An extreme situation occurs when what is experienced appears to be irrevocable: it is impossible to circumvent, the duration is uncertain but leads inescapably to death, and no human fight or rage is conceivable; one is totally at the mercy of a destructive outside world in the face of which the only alternative is total submission. All emotion must disappear, including pain, even physical pain. A human being's natural aggressiveness is suppressed. Bettelheim observed that, in modern times, atomic war had taken over from the SS. 'The image of the atomic explosion suddenly seems to have abolished any freedom or partial freedom of choice we may have of the way in which we confront the danger of war'.

Bearing this in mind, he thus arrives at a definition of child autism as being 'a mental state that develops in reaction to feeling oneself in an extreme situation, entirely without hope' (ibid., p. 68).

3. Hope was precisely what Bettelheim was proposing to give back to autistic children. *He therefore invented a system of institutional psychoanalytical treatment* in which the children would live in maximum comfort and extreme tolerance. For that a team of sufficiently devoted and motivated specialists was required who knew how things stood concerning their countertransference reactions. The psychiatric institution thus created would therefore have almost exactly the opposite characteristics of the traditional psychiatric hospital. *A Home for the Heart* (1974) describes at length and in detail the necessary requirements to succeed in these challenging circumstances. Respect for the child first, then respect for all the other members of

the team, including those doing the cooking and cleaning, is one of the characteristic features.

It can therefore be said that Bettelheim proved that psychoanalytical theory is useless unless it is enclosed within a framework within which it can be applied.

Bettelheim's work goes beyond what he did with autistic children. His study of kibbutz children (*Children of the Dream*, 1969) and his *The Uses of Enchantment* (1952b) should be mentioned in particular, as well as the many shorter papers which can be found in *Surviving and Other Essays* (1979), *Recollections and Reflections* (1986) and other works.

Although for a long time he managed to remain aloof from disputes and quarrels, Bettelheim's work was the object of both fascination and rejection at least equal to that given, as we have seen, to Melanie Klein and her work, in spite of the fact that Bettelheim absolutely did not hold with Kleinian theories. For instance, in the Translator's Foreword to the French edition of *The Empty Fortress* it is stated that Bettelheim was 'almost unknown in France', whereas on the cover of *A Home for the Heart* it is stated: 'Bruno Bettelheim, who is known throughout France today thanks to television'. His work was indeed the subject of a number of television programmes in France made by Tony Lainé and Daniel Karlin, and these increased its attraction, but at the same time they triggered a press campaign in the most serious French daily newspapers, with crass arguments such as 'He is not a doctor', or 'The children he treats are not really autistic', or 'He makes parents feel guilty', all the while heavily stressing the harmful role of psychoanalysis. At the time of his death at the age of 87, a similar campaign appeared in the United States, where he was accused of using violence on children and of having locked them away. Echoes of this campaign were picked up and propagated in France with the addition of the particularly sinister insinuation that there was a connection between the 'orthogenic' school and eugenics. That accusations of totalitarianism could, in such a fashion, be brought against a person who had spent his whole life and his work trying to repair the effects of the Holocaust, leaves us somewhat bewildered. Because he had had such a courageous attitude towards the Nazis, because he was a psychoanalyst concerned with anxieties about death, because he had dealt with autistic children, all this aroused a similarly deep anxiety in the public, which perhaps goes some way to explaining these extraordinary releases of aggressiveness.

It is obviously not possible to retrace the *entire* history of child analysis in the United States within the framework of this work. American society is structured in such a fashion that schools are founded and develop, and sometimes even disappear, without there necessarily being a link between them and it is not possible to talk about the pre-eminence of one or other even if, on the whole they all followed the personal or written teachings of

Anna Freud and the psychoanalytical ideology of Heinz Hartmann's ego psychology. We could have mentioned Edith Sterba in Detroit, Edith Buxbaum in Seattle, Berta Bornstein in New York, Marianne Kris at the Yale Child Study Center in New Haven, and many others. We could also have mentioned the work of the students and successors of Carl Jung, Alfred Adler or Wilhelm Reich.

These child analysts, in addition to their treatment of neurotic or 'atypical' children, developed child centres all over the United States, and trained psychiatrists and social workers. They concerned themselves with the problems of children in hospital, whether it be for medical or surgical treatment. We have seen that a number of them did scientific research based on direct observation (Spitz, Mahler, Ernst Kris, to be followed later by Marianne Kris and Selma Fraiberg).

CHILD PSYCHOANALYSIS TODAY

After 1945 the need was felt for specific training in child psychoanalysis. The psychoanalytic institutes of the APA (American Psychoanalytical Association) did not entirely fill the need, inasmuch as the theoretical status of child analysis was not (and is still not) clear, and the situation was not helped by the ban on training lay analysts, since most of the specialists wanting to go into child analysis were not medical practitioners.

But, as Erna Furman pointed out in an article in the *Journal de la psychanalyse de l'enfant* (Furman, 1986), the idea of a specific curriculum for training in child analysis did not arise until after World War II with the Hampstead Child Therapy Course in London, founded by Anna Freud. In 1948 Erik Homburger Erikson chaired a committee on child analysis which raised the question of specific training and that of lay analysts, but to no avail. Those Americans who wanted to train in child analysis either went to private seminars run by the 'immigrants' or went to the Hampstead Clinic in London.

In 1958 Anny Katan (see Chapter 9) 'dared to take a decisive step' (Furman, 1986) and organized the Cleveland Analytic Child Therapy Course, modelled on that of Hampstead. In order to conform to American Psychoanalytical Association rules neither Katan herself nor Dr Robert Furman were teachers or supervisors in these classes, the teaching remaining, paradoxically, in the hands of non-medical practitioners.

With a greater number of child analysts available, child analysis and specific consultations for children were made available in psychiatric institutions. Such analysts were even 'occasionally invited to attend the APA's scientific meetings'. But with the continuing impossibility of non-medical practitioners becoming full members of their various psychoanalytical societies, Marianne Kris founded the American Child Psychoanalysis Association in 1965. The scientific activities of the association are important. Its members are those with diplomas from the recognized training programmes and individually proposed candidates who can prove that they do hold a qualification in child analysis. Erna Furman reports that in 1986 there were 435 American members, 58 per cent of whom were doctors. However, Furman says that there is no room for complacency. Since the 1960s the succession of economic crises has hit child analysis broadside on and it has been the victim of budgetary restrictions. Public bodies are opting for 'short' treatments, and health insurance programmes, whether private or public, severely limit admission, preferring medical (drug) or behavioural treatment (child fixing). In view of their declining incomes, a number of former child analysts now prefer to treat adolescents or adults. However, in other countries, as we shall see with Argentina (Chapter 13) the situation is somewhat different.

With Cleveland, Erna Furman (trained at the Hampstead Clinic), provides us an example of how child analysis is currently practised in the United States. At the Hanna Perkins Therapeutic School (HPTS) and the Cleveland Center for Research in Child Development (both run by Anny Katan), Erna Furman works with a group of child analysts which holds meetings every Monday and Friday. The Monday evening meetings take place at the HPTS and between twenty-five and thirty child analysts, experienced or in training, are present. With a view to remedying the crisis in child analysis, this group founded a Child Analytic Clinic in 1964 with the assistance of the Cleveland Psychoanalytical Society. Children at this Clinic can benefit from psychoanalytical treatment whether the parents are rich or poor (Furman says that this is the only such instance in the whole of the United States). In 1986, thirty-eight children were being treated. The structure was completed in 1966 by the creation of a non-profit association looking after overall management and able to collect funds. The non-medical analysts were to be supervised by a medical director. In order to survive, this group of analysts decided that they would have to keep their expenses to a minimum. The members are therefore not paid when they participate in study forums, do research, or write reports or papers. They accept being paid at a rate which is about one-third of average private fees for the treatment of the clinic's patients, less for those treated at the HPTS. These details might appear trivial, but they illustrate clearly the various parameters of the situation.

The scientific work of Erna Furman and the Cleveland group encompasses the problems of mourning, learning disabilities at nursery school, emotional trauma, adoption, the effects of somatic disorders on psychic development, foster care, cruelty to children, as well as working on more theoretical subjects such as phantasy and reality, the latency phase or seduction.

As is the case with most American authors, Erna Furman refers to the work of Anna Freud and Heinz Hartmann. She also mentions that of Margaret Mahler and Donald Winnicott. In another article in the *Journal de la pychanalyse de l'enfant* (Furman, 1987) she describes an original approach to the problem of psychotic children. First of all she calls them 'atypical children,' and says that psychosis does not enter into it because (a) there is no regression in these cases: development simply stops or departs from the norm; (b) there are no hallucinations; and, (c) catamnesis shows that they are not developing towards psychosis. However, the treatment she adopts is not very different from that of Margaret Mahler. On the other hand, unlike Bruno Bettelheim, she does not separate the children from their parents. On the contrary, she includes them in the treatment, particularly at the start. For instance, she proposes a preparatory phase, which may take several months, or even a year or two. Then, when it is possible, the child undergoes analytical treatment at the rate of five 55-minute sessions a week. Erna Furman's metapsychological description of the disorders of the 'atypical' child does not differ greatly from that of authors who have described psychotic children except perhaps in that the processes are looked at in another perspective, in terms of whether the independent functions of the ego develop or not, in particular, the organizing function, and the integrating function. What we mean by this is that, whatever the theorization envisaged, it remains psychoanalytical as long as it keeps a firm footing in clinical practice.

TRAINING IN THE UNITED STATES

In 1976, another institute was founded in Los Angeles, along the lines of the Cleveland Clinic. In a paper paying tribute to Anna Freud, Leo Rangell (1982) indicated that the Hampstead model had also been followed at Boston, Yale, New York, Detroit, Ann Arbor (Michigan), Chicago and La Jolla (California).

The American example shows to what extent the problem of lay analysis (by non-medical practitioners) interferes with child analysis, to the point that the difficulties met in the recognition of child analysis have been attributed to the question of the possession, or not, of a medical diploma. In reality, the doctors have met (and continue to meet today) just as much difficulty as the others in having child analysis recognized by their adult analysis colleagues and by psychoanalytical institutions. The numerous examples we have just given, especially that of Anny Katan and Robert Furman, demonstrate this.

In fact, with time, the APA softened its position, largely due to the efforts of the child analysts themselves and of Anna Freud. In 1968 Helen Ross and

Bertram Lewis wrote a report on the teaching of psychoanalysis in the United States, part of which included child analysis. In 1958 also, the APA recommended that each institute organize 'a course in child analysis', a recommendation that was not followed up to any great extent. In 1964 it organized a round table on child analysis. In 1978 it published its 'Training Standards in Child and Adolescent Psychoanalysis'. More recently (1991) it has admitted lay analysts as members, forced to do so by a court case, but this has not solved the problem of child analysis, as we have seen.

In a paper published in *The Psychoanalytical Study of the Child* (1987), Jules Glenn, professor at the New York Medical Center and teaching analyst at the Psychoanalytic Institute (a member of the APA), investigated the supervision of child analysts. Supervision occurs, of course, after the candidate has undergone personal analysis and after extensive preparation (including lectures on psychoanalytical theory and practice, and the study of child development). The candidate's experience with children continues throughout his training period and includes direct observation. Lectures on psychoanalytical technique specific to children and to adolescents are also available as are case-study seminars and clinical lectures. The APA requires, however, that this curriculum be preceded by some experience in adult analysis, so that the candidate has acquired solid notions about technique 'with a minimum of parameters'. In addition, in this way the candidate will be better trained to handle interpretations. Glenn then goes on to look at supervision of the first consultations, analysis of the child proper, the styles of the analyst and of the supervisor, modes of communication with the child, the non-psychoanalytical tendencies of the candidate who has previously exercised in the field of child psychotherapy (as is often the case), and the problem of the parents.

Numerous Freudian child analysts meet the parents, Glenn says, in order to maintain a therapeutic alliance with them, to help them with the difficulties they experience in having a child undergoing analysis, and in order to obtain information about the child's past and present, and eventually to try to modify or stabilize the family environment. This entails a specific task for the supervisor. Next, after having looked into the relationship between the supervisor and the candidate being supervised, especially from the point of view of transference and countertransference. Glenn looks into the problem of the development of a 'child analyst identity', quoting the work of Joseph and Widlöcher (*The Identity of the Psychoanalyst*, 1983). Does the child psychoanalyst identify automatically with his own analyst or with his supervisor? Does he, for example, risk becoming automatically Kleinian or Anna Freudian? He concludes by saying that the child analyst must feel independent and choose his own path.

It can therefore be seen that the idea that child psychoanalysis should be integrated into the field of psychoanalysis as a whole is progressing in the

United States. It is taught both in private institutes by the Association for Child Psychoanalysis and officially by the APA. Although the Anna Freudian tendency (in its Hartmannian version) remains predominant in this training, Kleinian theories are timidly beginning to break through. Perhaps this means that one day we will be able to see child analysis in the United States get a harmonious development. The annual publication since 1945 of a large volume (500–700 pages) of the *Psychoanalytic Study of the Child* (initially sponsored by Anna Freud and the Kris and Eissler couples) should help considerably.

— 13 —

Argentina

Arminda Aberastury was the founder of child psychoanalysis in Argentina. She was born in Buenos Aires, into an aristocratic family of Basque origin. Her father was a lawyer and land-owner. When, after her secondary-school studies, the young Arminda wanted to study medicine, her family forbade her: it was not done in their circles. In those days the age of majority was 25, so she studied educational science and eventually gained a PhD in that subject. She became engaged to Enrique Pichon-Rivière[1] when she was very young, and while he was studying medicine. She attended lectures with him and thus underwent the same training, although she could not obtain the corresponding diplomas. Sidonia Mehler, one of her friends, to whom we owe this information, says she was a beautiful, fascinating and intelligent woman, astute and cultivated (I. 7). She was nicknamed 'La Negra' (the dark one) (Ferrer and Garma, 1973).

Her husband, Enrique Pichon-Rivière, was a brilliant man, with a very original personality. He became one of the masters of psychiatry and then of psychoanalysis in Argentina. In a report to the First Agentinian Congress on Child and Adolescent Psychopathology in 1969, Arminda Aberastury stated: 'My technique was first of all based on what Anna Freud and Sophie Morgenstern had created in child analysis. From 1940 onwards I was influenced by the theories and techniques of Melanie Klein onto which, year after year, I grafted my own ways of doing things, my own discoveries and those of my colleagues who worked and are still working with me' (Aberastury, 1972: 13).

From 1952 onwards she often visited Melanie Klein in London. Klein had asked her to stay in Britain but she preferred to return to Argentina. In her later years she reproached Melanie Klein with a certain lack of culture and was no longer 'an out and out Kleinian' (I. 7). She worked hard to disseminate Klein's ideas, however, and she herself described a primary genital phase, which appears in the first year of life of the baby, and consists in a growth in the genital instinct, with a definite predominance in the corresponding erogenous zone (Ferrer and Garma, 1973: 619–25).

Between 1960 and 1971, the date of her death, she also became interested in group psychotherapy ('orientation groups' made up of child psychoanalysts, groups of paediatricians and children's dentists, and groups of parents) and the techniques of family therapy. In the 1950s she developed one of Erik Erikson's ideas and created a 'house' construction test ('El constructor infantil') with little wooden cubes in order to determine structures such as the child's inner space, for example. This test was used by Susanna Ferrer and Edoardo Salas (1951).

Arminda Aberastury also founded research groups in child psychoanalysis, and one of the departments of child psychoanalysis within the Argentinian Psychoanalytical Association (APA) was given her name when it was created by Susanna Ferrer two or three years after her death. She travelled a lot in South America, to Brazil in particular, advocating that training in child analysis should be incorporated into training courses in psychoanalysis. Sidonia Mehler remembers having seen her successfully treat a 7-month old child who had had uncontrollable rhinitis from the age of 8 days. With Angel Garma she presented this case to the Aula Magna of the Faculty of Medicine in Buenos Aires in the presence of 2,000 people. (I. 7) Her training activities were recognized and much appreciated and in 1956 she became the head of the APA's training institute. Her first contact with Melanie Klein was through the latter's works. In 1951 the supervision of the case of one particular child was undertaken by Klein, by correspondence. They then remained in touch by correspondence (Francois Caille, 1989) and, as we have seen, she often went to see Klein. Aberastury practised five sessions per week, which enabled her to analyse the deep-rooted anxieties of children, and of analysts. 'We do five sessions because we "can" do them', says David Rosenfeld (I. 5). It was Aberastury who translated Klein's book *The Psychoanalysis of Children* into Spanish, although Klein and her theories were already known and accepted in Argentina. Among other authors who had influenced her Aberastury cites (1973a) Hermine Hug-Hellmuth, Gerald Pearson (whose contribution concerning relationships with parents she appreciated), Sigmund Freud and his 'Juanito' (little Hans).

Enrique Pichon-Rivière dealt with psychotics using Kleinian theories. His pupils, such as José Bleger, David Liberman, Joël Zak and Léon Grinberg, continued along the same lines. The next generation of Argentinian analysts, trained from 1955 onwards, also took an interest in serious disorders *and* in children. Emilio Rodrigué was a doctor and did his psychoanalytical training in London. Upon his return to Argentina he turned his teaching towards the study of groups (the theories of Bion and Jaques) and of children. However, like many other child analysts (and not only those in Argentina) he finally abandoned child analysis to become a training analyst.

David Rosenfeld (I. 5) remembered having worked with Rodrigué in a seminar on child analysis that he was running at that time with Rebecca Grinberg. Emilio Rodrigué wrote to us to report that he had left the Argentinian Psychoanalytical Association in 1972, following the 'Plataforma' movement with Marie Langer, Diego and Gilberte Garcia Reynoso and many others. Since 1974 he has been working as a training analyst in Salvador de Bahia (Brazil), where he cooperates with the Lacanian School of Psychoanalysis.

Beyond her role as leader, Arminda Aberastury developed a number of personal ideas and new applications. She applied herself to the task of differentiating between child psychoanalysis and psychotherapy: going back to the definitions of Laplanche and Pontalis (1967), on the one hand, and of Wolberg, on the other, she pointed out an omission made by Laplanche and Pontalis: 'Wolberg insisted on the necessity of specialized training for the application of *any type of psychotherapy.*' Whether it is a question of psychotherapy or of psychoanalysis, a long period of training over a number of years is required in order to be able to understand the non-verbal language of the child (Play activities, drawings, bodily expressions, certain verbal expressions). For the understanding of play activities she drew inspiration from Sigmund Freud (understanding the underlying traumatic situation and compulsion of repetition), from Melanie Klein (the phantasies of masturbation underlying all play activity, projective identification and early object relationships), from Erik Erikson (play activity as an expression of an ego function) and from Waelder (play as a constructive process, comparable in its repetitive nature with the digestion of ruminants). Play acquires significance when the child is 4 months old. Drawing is also an essential component of the child's non-verbal language and is used from the age of 3 years to early adolescence. In addition to the well-known functions of drawings, Arminda Aberastury believed they had important correlations with the development of body image and spatial relationships. In child psychoanalysis proper play activities and drawings must be interpreted for their content, and for the defences they signify, in the transference relationship. She had a legendary ability for analysing them right down to the last detail.

She distinguished two currents amongst psychoanalysts: those who used non-verbal interpretation (play activity) and those who spoke to children. For her part, she believed that 'only words can render the unconscious conscious, and this is the goal that we are trying to attain in interpretation' (Aberastury, 1972: 18). Child therapists have difficulty in accepting that children can *understand* our words, and yet interpretations in child analysis have the same characteristics as for adult analysis; it is simply a question of adapting the formulation to the age of the patient, in particular when the children are very young, say between 12 and 18 months.

> One assumption consistent with this technique is that, when the treatment is over, even a very young child will be equipped with a minimum amount of verbal language enabling it to express its ideas without having recourse to non-verbal language. This use of verbal language was an indispensable prerequisite for Melanie Klein for considering that the child's analysis was completed.
>
> (ibid., p. 18)

In addition, she chose to treat the positive and negative aspects of transference equally, to use regression, but without recourse to any 'historical' work, to use anxiety to facilitate transference (and, consequently, anxiety should not be reduced artificially), and she fixed a structural and dynamic change as the goal of analysis, not the disappearance of symptoms, as is the case with psychotherapy.

In her book *Child Psychoanalysis and its Applications* (1972), Aberastury studied in minute detail the technical approach to analytical work with children. It is not our intention to go into these here. Examples of the ways in which she thought child psychoanalysis could be usefully applied can be seen in the kinds of group she created (orientation groups for parents, groups of paediatricians, groups of children's dentists ['odontopediatras'], and child analysts), and in her recommendations concerning psychotherapy for children who are to undergo surgery. Much work has been done in the wake of her ideas, in particular concerning psychoanalysis and psychotherapy prior to surgery. It might be of interest to those in France or in other countries who have ever tried to carry out this sort of psychoanalytical work individually in an odontological clinic or public hospital. The work she herself did in Argentina with children's dentists was facilitated by the fact that the director of the odontological clinic, Marie Ines Egozcue, had undergone analysis with Angel Garma.

In another of her books (1967) she looked at the history of the psychoanalytical movement in Argentina, and at the legislation concerning the practice of psychoanalysis there.

Aberastury's unfinished work (1973b) on how children perceive death should also be mentioned.

Among her abundant contributions, Aberastury's reflections on some of the practical and theoretical difficulties in child psychoanalysis should be mentioned, in particular her paper entitled 'Transference and countertransference', given in Paris in 1951. In it she notes that a child undergoing analysis finds itself in a difficult position in relation to its family environment 'so that some child analysts, fearing reactions on the part of the child, tend to modify the treatment and in doing so depart from psychoanalysis proper' (Aberastury de Pichon-Rivière, 1989 [1952]: 249).

Why are there more adult analysts than child analysts? 'To say that this is explained by the fact that the technique is more difficult, is to give a conscious explanation of a much more complicated unconscious fact. . . . The work that is done with the child and the way the child experiences and manifests transference awaken deep rooted anxieties in the analyst which go back to his own early childhood, which nobody really ever successfully overcomes' (ibid., p. 250) (these are the paranoid and depressive anxieties described by Melanie Klein). When this anxiety acts in an unconscious manner, it distances the analyst from his work with the child. When the child's transference is intense, this anxiety is (unconsciously) fixed on the child's mother. The analyst 'is under the impression that he has stolen the child from its mother, an impression which is a repetition of what he, as a child, felt with regard to his own mother' (ibid., p. 251). When the child openly says that it would like to exchange her analyst for her mother, an old anxiety is awakened in the analyst, the anxiety born of the phantasy of stealing the contents of his own mother and of not being able to restore them. 'This anxiety on the part of the analyst has led some to deny that the child is able to effect transference, or to believe that it is not a question of true transference neurosis' (ibid., p. 251). Sometimes, on the rebound, the analyst feels an aversion towards the mother. Thus by tactless questions or statements, determined by his own unconscious, the analyst can arouse feelings of guilt in the mother concerning her child's neurosis, which in turn leads to an abrupt interruption in treatment or to termination.

Why are there so few men analysts among child psychoanalysts? We have seen in previous chapters that following Jung, Sigmund Freud and others, there has been a general trend in the psychoanalytical movement to entrust the task of child analysis to women because they are generally considered more 'gifted' in these matters. Arminda Aberastury believed that the fact of 'taking up the maternal role' (being the object of a maternal transference), which is much more evident when a child is being analysed, 'is what keeps men away from the sort of work which arouses in them anxieties connected with their passive-feminine position, their rivalry with their mothers, and their phantasies of taking her place and stealing her children', as mentioned earlier (ibid., pp. 253–4).

Although we agree with Aberastury's analysis, and although there are indeed few men child psychoanalysts, one might well ask the same question concerning paternal transference in women analysts.

In addition, Aberastury writes, some men might feel the following anxiety: 'If someone opened the door and saw me playing with a child, is there not a chance that he might find me effeminate, in other words a homosexual?' Yet others might fear that 'their attitude might lead to people thinking that they were unbalanced, mad, i.e. castrated' (ibid., 254).

In fact, there are more men child analysts in Argentina than in other countries. This is certainly not due to the 'Latin' culture of Argentinians, but is perhaps the result of some of Aberastury's discerning reflections.

The fact that she was able to highlight such matters in her seminars and supervisions of trainees was largely due to her detailed study of counter-transference in candidate analysts. She also used this information when looking for fresh forms of *training* for child analysts. Although the essential point for Aberastury was still the candidate's own personal analysis, meaning a complete and 'finished' analysis, including the paranoid and depressive positions, some procedures appeared to make things easier: for the children with whom there was hesitation in carrying out an analysis, Aberastury had created a section made up of a paediatrician with analytical training and candidates undergoing training.

> Depending on the case, the child goes through three or four play sessions in which no interpretation is done. The candidates have to observe the play activity and general conduct of the child. Once the child has left, they have to make a written summary of the session with all the details, i.e. symbolic content of play and a description of the child's general behaviour. The supervising analyst then discusses with the candidate the significance of the session and possible interpretations, with their verbal formulation. We have found it very useful for candidates, before they begin child analysis proper, to have sufficient practice in this sort of work before they have finished undergoing their own training analysis. Contact with the child is then less tense because, since they do not have to interpret or take responsibility for the treatment, the candidates are free to observe all the details of play activity, so important when they do finally begin to practise analysis themselves.
>
> (ibid., pp. 252–3)

In the same way, candidates are taught to question the children's parents without hurting their feelings or arousing unnecessary feelings of guilt.

As part of the next stage of their training at the Psychoanalytical Institute, candidates who have treated two children under supervision (one under 5 and one in the latency period) must then try out their skills in analysing adults. Conversely, adult analysts practise doing child analysis, which is very useful for their training. However, although this curriculum is recommended, it is not obligatory.

As to the position in Argentina forty years after Arminda Aberastury's work, Estela and David Rosenfeld have told us that although child analysis sections exists in both the Psychoanalytical Association of Argentina and in the Psychoanalytical Association of Buenos Aires, it does not follow that the training institutes train child analysts. Teaching and training (supervision, seminars) are dispensed to those who are already experienced psychoanalysts. While some seminars on child analysis are recommended for all, including those who only treat adults, and while one of the two control cases may be a child (if the candidate so requests and if the request is accepted), one can nevertheless become an adult psychoanalyst in Argentina without ever having analysed a child. This is a state of affairs which our Argentinian colleagues seem to deplore. On the other hand, once one has become a psychoanalyst, one can do additional training in the specialist study groups (psychoses, children, families, etc.) of the Psychoanalytical Association of Buenos Aires, for example, or in 'private' research groups. Many analysts set up private seminars where an admission fee is charged and which may have an attendance of several hundred people. This sort of system does enable the spread of child psychoanalysis, but can also lead to 'uncontrolled' and even deviant practice. These seminars are open to doctors and psychologists as well as to psychoanalysts who want to study a particular field. No certificates are given out; people attend simply because of their 'pleasure in knowing'. In addition, since 1974, the date of the creation of the Freudian School of Buenos Aires under the impetus of the philosopher Masotta, study groups made up of followers of Lacan's theories are on the increase and, as in France, they are split in many different leanings.

Although no statistics are available, it would appear that Argentina is one of the countries, if not *the* country in the world where child psychoanalysis is most widespread. If only for this reason it is worth examining.

Psychoanalysis made its appearance in Argentina towards 1940, although the complete works of Sigmund Freud in twenty-four volumes had been translated (and supervised by Freud himself) as early as 1923 and had been widely disseminated. The movement was started by Angel Garma, who had come back from Berlin, having undergone analysis with Theodor Reik. After having practised psychoanalysis in Spain (his birthplace) from 1931–6, he moved to France, and then emigrated to Argentina in 1938. He was to be joined by Celes Carcano, analysed in Paris by Paul Schiff, and Marie Langer, analysed in Vienna by Richard Sterba. Langer in turn analysed Enrique Racker, who then did two supervisions with Melanie Klein. Enrique Pichon-Rivière, who ran the adult psychiatry unit, Arminda Aberastury and Arnaldo Raskovsky all underwent analysis with Garma in 1942. It was they who founded the Argentinian Psychoanalytical Association in 1943, with Garma and Hardoy rapidly recognized by the IPA. Their journal, *Revista de psicoanálisis*, reached a circulation of 5,000 with its first edition. As we have already seen, the works of Melanie Klein were also translated into Spanish early on, so that her ideas were much more widespread than one might expect from the perceived proximity of Argentina to the USA.

It was in this atmosphere that Arminda Aberastury founded child psychoanalysis, with the energy we have seen. To these favourable factors must be added the nomination of heads of departments in a number of large hospitals which were open to psychoanalytical ideas. As early as the 1950s there was quite a change in care at the Children's Hospital: thanks to the new Dean, mothers could stay with their children who were being hospitalized. A psychotherapy department was created and run by some of the child psychoanalysts trained by Arminda Aberastury, such as Maria L. Pelento, Susana Lustig de Ferrer and Edoardo Salas. A Swiss-trained psychoanalyst became head of a psychopathology unit. The instituting of outpatient consultations led to the setting up of psychopathology units in other hospitals, where residents, child psychologists and child psychotherapists could be trained.

After 1970 a number of Argentinian psychoanalysts who wanted to work differently, among whom a significant percentage were child psychoanalysts, founded the Psychoanalytical Association of Buenos Aires, also recognized by the IPA. The association's magazine *Psicoanálisis*, published since 1978, is very lively, and several issues have been given over entirely to child and adolescent psychoanalysis. The editor is Dr Alfredo Kargieman and Dr Narciso Notrica is the secretary. Recently, it has decided to exchange articles with the *Journal de la psychanalyse de l'enfant* published in Paris. Another literary venture was launched in Buenos Aires in 1991 in the form of the magazine *N/A Psicoanálisis con niños y adolescentes*, edited by Rodolfo Urribarri. It also intends to have the same kind of exchange of articles, in particular with the French magazine *Adolescence*.

International recognition for the outstanding position of psychoanalysis in Argentina was made concrete by the holding of the international IPA conference in Buenos Aires in 1991, at which Horacio Etchegoyen, a member of the Psychoanalytical Association of Buenos Aires, was elected as the new IPA president. As we were able to experience for ourselves, this conference took place in a very vibrant atmosphere, quite different from that of European conferences. It was attended by more than 3,000 delegates, the majority of whom were from South American countries.

We were also struck by how open our Argentinian colleagues were to psychoanalytical research from other countries, quite a contrast to what one finds in France or the United States. This country, which is in a chronic social and economic crisis, has recently emerged from a severe political crisis. The military dictatorship posed many serious problems to psychoanalysts confronted with the ordinary difficulties of their fellow citizens which were made worse by specific moral dilemmas: refusal to take part in interrogations, the problem of kidnapped children, and so forth. A number of them finally emigrated, to Spain in particular; Léon and Rebecca Grinberg were among the latter.

The economic situation has made it increasingly difficult for child psychoanalysts to continue with the usual four sessions a week, unless the child is seriously ill and/or the parents can afford to pay. Otherwise it is frequent to give only two or three sessions a week, which amounts to psychoanalytical psychotherapy.

The spread of population and urban distribution in Argentina means that it is easier to practise several sessions a week then, say, in Britain, where distances are so great between the large urban centres and even, during peak-time traffic, in London itself. In Argentina 30 per cent of the population and 60 per cent of the intelligentsia live in Buenos Aires, a city where it is possible to move about easily, in spite of its population of six million.

No doubt, the combined effects of the teachings of Arminda Aberastury and the economic crisis have paradoxically lead to the fact that in Argentina many analysts prefer to do child analysis. Although, as elsewhere, very young children are less often treated, Argentinian analysts seem to find sufficient pleasure in analysing children, all the more so since it is easier to find child patients as clients than adults. Parents are more prepared to pay for treatment for their children than they are for themselves. This is true in Buenos Aires and in other cities, such as Rosario and Mendoza.

Unless they have taken out a special type of health insurance, parents must pay the full cost of treatment for their children. However, psychoanalytical psychotherapy (two sessions a week for a year) at hospitals is free of charge. There are facilities for supervising the analysts who carry out the treatment, which is done in children's hospitals or in children's wards in general hospitals.

We tried to find out how the analysts who carried out treatment in hospitals were paid. The reaction to our questions was one of great hilarity. Estela and David Rosenfeld replied: 'In Argentina you work in hospitals for nothing! You literally have to pay to work there, and to learn your craft. But you can get meals there!' As to those who teach, Professor Urribarri told us that he was paid $US100 a month for the teaching he did at the university.

In one of the hospitals (the Italian Hospital) the chief psychiatrist of the child psychiatric unit trained in the United States, and has organized an observation unit for babies and a team of consultants who can be moved around as required to the other units and are available in emergencies.

The practice of child psychoanalysis in Argentina has been complicated by the fact that in 1954 a law was passed under the Peronist regime whereby only medical practitioners could practise psychoanalysis. This law was only changed in 1983. Until then candidates had to study medicine.

At present, although less noticeably than elsewhere, child psychoanalysis is practised mostly by women, and the majority of them are non-medical psychologists. However, it does not seem to have decreased the status of child psychoanalysis, at least if one can judge by the number of those training. Although psychoanalytical institutes have retained the paradigm of the adult neurotic, they are not opposed, as we have seen, to additional training in child psychoanalysis, and they organize the curriculum. However, those who choose this path are not taking the easiest of routes:

> Child psychoanalysis is more difficult, and more distressing than the psychoanalysis of adults: play activities and non-verbal language are much more difficult to grasp than verbal language. Relationships with the parents are difficult. You have to put up with their psychoses, their negative reactions to the treatment, their difficulties in paying the analyst, their difficulties in bringing the child along, those who are in the process of divorcing, or who take long holidays. It is strange to note that the families of psychotics are less exhausting than those who have children undergoing analysis.
>
> (Estela and David Rosenfeld, I. 5)

Our investigations in Argentina have shown that child psychoanalysis there benefits from an exceptionally favourable climate and throws light on a number of phenomena which are more or less concealed in other, more economically wealthy, countries, which are, however, poorer from this point of view.

Note

1 Enrique Pichon-Rivière does not seem to have been related in any way to the French psychoanalyst Edouard Pichon, one of the founders of the SPP (Paris Psychoanalytical Society).

— 14 —

France

The development of psychoanalysis in France has suffered from one specific difficulty since its inception, that of wanting to 'translate' it into French. The present authors suppose, as do others, that the difficulties contained in the (literal) translation of Sigmund Freud's works were connected with the (ideological) problem of translating Freud's thought. It is known that after Morichau-Beauchant in Poitiers in 1910, it was Regis and Hesnard of Bordeaux who, in 1914, published the first account in French of psychoanalytical theory (ed. Alcan). Freud did not really appreciate the criticisms of these authors, who appeared to him to have distorted his ideas. In 1915 Sándor Ferenczi took it upon himself to attack them in an article entitled 'Psychoanalysis as seen by the Bordeaux Psychiatric School'. Regis and Hesnard insisted that if a theory (ed. Alcan) was to be accepted in France it should be 'synthetical and clearly expressed'. The two authors omitted, however, to mention the unconscious in their definition of psychoanalysis, and supposed that psychoanalysis was 'inspired by a vast system of interpretation'. For them, the notion of 'pansexualism' replaced that of infantile sexuality. They thus tried to differentiate the origin of a disorder from its cause, which is, perforce, organic and cerebral. They suggested that words such as 'libido', 'sexuality', etc., should be replaced by the word 'affect'. In addition, the method was too 'subjective', and would it not be better to 'reduce the complex to silence by an even greater intensification of repression, rather than uncovering it?'

This critical attitude undoubtedly influenced the following decades. We have seen how Eugenie Sokolnicka had found credit mainly with the writers of the Gallimard publishing house. 'Did this craze really serve the cause of analysis?' questioned Victor Smirnoff (1979) in an article about the origins of 'psychoanalysis *à la française.*' During the winter of 1921–2 it was

fashionable to talk about psychoanalysis in Parisian *salons*,' mostly with blissful admiration or else in tones of mockery, equally superficial and equally
tiresome', wrote Edouard Pichon (1934).

In 1924, in An Autobiographical Study Freud wrote:

> I now watch from a distance the symptomatic reactions that are accom-
> panying the introduction of psycho-analysis into the France which was
> for so long refractory. . . . Objections of incredible simplicity are raised,
> such as that French sensitiveness is offended by the pedantry and crudity
> of psycho-analytic terminology . . . the whole mode of thought of
> psycho-analysis, so he declared, is inconsistent with the *génie latin*. Here
> the Anglo-Saxon allies of France, who count as supporters of analysis, are
> explicity thrown over.
>
> (1925a: 62)

The first translation into French of this paper was done in 1928 by Marie
Bonaparte. She inserted a footnote that did not appear in later translations.
She wrote: 'The understanding of psychoanalysis on the part of the Anglo-
Saxon was facilitated by his spirit of realism and his courage when faced
with the facts – qualities which incidentally contributed to his conquering
the world'. A number of traits of the French national character make such
understanding more difficult for them: a love of logical clarity, the cult of
'common sense' and of 'good taste'. However, the phenomena of nature are
unfortunately not always in 'good taste' and common sense would have you
believe that the sun goes round the earth and does not permit you to 'see'
microbes. Lastly, 'in France, the mention of things sexual is often mistaken
for licentiousness; it is a subject that should be made light of, mentioned by
insinuation so as to be understood between witty people; out of this attitude
to things sexual has come our facile literature of the *theâtre du boulevard*
which foreigners find so amusing, but which does not necessarily mean that
we are held in great esteem by them' (ibid.). According to Marie Bonaparte,
the sexual is thus devalued.

In 1925 Freud wrote an article in French which appeared in *La revue juive*
entitled 'Resistances to psychoanalysis' (1925b). Guy Rosolato (1979)
believes that this article is about the resistance met by psychoanalysis specifically in French scientific and philosophical circles. After having noted the
conscious resistance, Freud says that he believes that its depth can only be
explained by (unconscious) 'emotional forces'. Above all, it is a question of
resistance to the problems of the sexual instinct in general. Freud reminds
the reader that

> Psycho-analysis disposed once and for all of the fairy tale of an asexual
> childhood. . . . To adults their prehistory seems so inglorious that they
> refuse to allow themselves to be reminded of it; they were infuriated

when psycho-analysis tried to lift the veil of amnesia from their years of childhood. There was only one way out: what psycho-analysis asserted must be false and what posed as a new science must be a tissue of fancies and distortions.

(1925b: 220–1)

MARIE BONAPARTE AND THE *IMMIGRÉS* OF THE PARIS PSYCHOANALYTICAL SOCIETY

Her Royal Highness Princess George of Greece, *née* Marie Bonaparte (1882–1962) was the daughter of Roland Bonaparte (a grandson of Lucien, one of the brothers of Napoleon I) and of Marie-Felix Blanc (born of a German mother) (source: Elisabeth Roudinesco, 1986). She had lived in France all her life. At the age of 25 she married the son of the King of Greece, George I. It seems to have been a marriage of convenience which enabled her to become a free and emancipated woman. She befriended such well-known people as Aristide Briand and Gustave Le Bon. Towards 1923 she became interested in female sexuality in Parisian hospitals. Her father died in 1924 and in 1925 she consulted René Lafforgue, who sent her to Sigmund Freud for analysis. Freud was at first reluctant, but a solid transference was established and the analysis was in fact to last until 1938, with many interruptions. 'The Princess' as she was called in Paris, quickly became an ardent supporter and propagator of Freudian ideas, the truth of which she had been able to experience personally.

She was one of a small group of people which, on 4 November 1926, was, at last, to found the first French psychoanalytical society, the Paris Psychoanalytical Society (SPP). The others were Eugenie Sokolnicka, Angelo Hesnard, René Allendy, Adrien Borel, René Lafforgue, Rudolf Loewenstein, Georges Parcheminey and Edouard Pichon. She was given the 'non-medical section' of the *Revue française de psychanalyse,* founded the same day. Until her death in 1962 she was thus the most authentic of Freud's representatives at the SPP. With great generosity, she also financed the psychoanalytical movement.

This first 'French' group was therefore in fact made up of a large number of 'immigrés' who thought it their duty to instil an authentically Freudian and international spirit in a debate which has been commented on in detail by Elisabeth Roudinesco (1986). It is therefore not our intention to go into these discussions. However, it should be remarked that the attempt to create from the outset a form of psychoanalysis *à la française* ran parallel to a collective feeling of permanent rebellion against the IPA. This feeling, the consequences of which can still be felt today, was justified rationally and consciously, but differently, according to the period. In the 1930s the IPA was criticized for wanting to impose a 'Viennese' view of things and, in addition, for claiming the right to oblige the psychoanalysts of the time to accept the principle of lay analysts. Later on, when the majority of the IPA was made up of North Americans, it was criticized for the opposite, for not letting lay analysts practise. Over the years, in addition to its bureaucratic ways, the IPA was criticized for being in favour of ego psychology, for intervening in the affairs of its constituent societies, and, more recently, for insisting that treatment consisting of fewer than four, 45-minute sessions weekly should not be considered as psychoanalysis. Its 'recommendations' were often considered to be arbitrary decrees. However, it was not reproached for its 'recommendations' concerning the setting up of training courses in child psychoanalysis; they were simply ignored.

As we have seen, the small group of immigrants within this first French psychoanalytical group included Eugenie Sokolnicka and Sophie Morgenstern, supported by Marie Bonaparte, who played the commercial traveller between Paris and Vienna. It also included Rudolf Loewenstein. The Swiss analysts Raymond de Saussure, Henri Floumoy and Charles Odier were soon to join them.

Born in Lodz in 1898, Rudolf Loewenstein studied medicine in Poland and then in Zurich, where he studied psychiatry. He underwent analysis with Hans Sachs and moved to Berlin, where he took up his medical studies again. After this cosmopolitan period of training began a 'French' period which was to last from 1925 to World War II. He was a defender of Freudian theories in France and his couch received a great number of psychoanalysts, including Jacques Lacan, for whom he had no esteem whatsoever. Loewenstein called Lacan a 'cheat' and said that 'what he did later on had nothing whatsoever to do with psychoanalysis'. When war broke out he emigrated once again. He moved permanently to the United States, where, as we know, he was one of the eminent proponents of ego-psychology, with Heinz Hartmann and Ernst Kris.

1930–40: CHILD PSYCHOANALYSIS FIRST APPEARS

The specific situation of child psychoanalysis in France was somewhat complex. We shall try to determine a number of parameters.

We saw in Chapters 7 and 8 how Eugenie Sokolnicka and more especially Sophie Morgenstern were the first in France to introduce this form of analysis. They gave an Anna Freudian stamp to child psychoanalysis, which it still bears today.

However, in 1950, Serge Lebovici, having in turn worked in Professor Heuyer's unit, showed that Sophie Morgenstern did not actually practise psychoanalysis: her treatment was in fact psychoanalytically inspired psychotherapy. It was too short, and by examining what sorts of adult some of the children she had treated had become, he noted that the disorders they had presented as children had persisted, relapsed or got worse. A careful reading of Jean Losserand's paper (1991) will confirm this.

Marie Bonaparte was very conscious of the difficulties of introducing psychoanalysis in general, and child psychoanalysis in particular, into the French psychiatric and psychoanalytical world. In 1930 she gave a report to the 5th Conference of French Language Psychoanalysts on 'Prevention in Children of Neuroses' the full-length version of which was published in the *Revue française de psychanalyse*. Even at that time she stressed the difference between psychoanalysis and psychotherapy. Quoting Freud, Bonaparte compared this difference to that of two ways of repairing a leak under a paving stone in the street:

> The ordinary psychotherapist resembles a workman who accumulates materials on the pavement, at the point where the water is welling up, in order to stop the flow of water, with varying degrees of success. On the contrary, the psychoanalyst resembles the workman who pulls up the paving stones, digs down, removing the earth until he has found the source of the underground leak in the pipe and repaired it, replacing the earth and paving stones once he has done so. Psychoanalysis is a causal treatment and any possible educational measures it might offer for the preventive treatment of neuroses are also [causal].
>
> (Bonaparte, 1930: 112)

She mentions those who represent the old order in society as those who 'fear the removal of the familiar paving stones in the traditional street', and this is what 'repressive psychotherapists' are. As part of the anti-psychoanalytical movement, she mentions the encyclical 'On Christian education for young people' dated 31 December 1929 in which Pope Pius XI stigmatizes sexual education, saying that one must not 'imprudently light and fan the fire of evil in the simple, delicate heart of the child' (ibid., p. 114).

By contrast, the Archbishop of Canterbury, Dr Lang, found 'great progress in the full and free discussion of sexual matters'. 'We want to liberate the sexual instinct – which is part of the heritage of humanity – from the impression that it should always be surrounded by warnings and negative restrictions, and put it in its place among the great creative things offered to each healthy young woman and young man' (ibid., p. 115).

'It is not surprising', said Marie Bonaparte,

> that this priestly voice should have precisely been raised in England, in that race which prides itself, rightly so, on knowing how to face facts and which these past few years has been able to move away from the cant of

the past with which it was so burdened towards greater sincerity. Psychoanalysis is more in tune with the mores of Anglo-Saxon countries than in Latin countries.

(ibid., p. 114)

At the end of this long, fifty-page article, she recalls what Freud had to say on the subject:

Child analysis constitutes, for at least two thirds of children, not a luxury but a necessity. The most favourable age is the onset of the latency period, around five or six years old, the period of the first repressions. In order to carry out these analyses, thousands of analysts, mainly women, need to be trained, and this point alone shows to what extent the training of analysts goes beyond the mere question of medical training.

(ibid., p. 134)

It has to be said that an article by Edouard Pichon and Georges Parcheminey, entitled 'On Freudian Inspired Short Psychotherapeutic Treatment for Children', did appear in the *Revue française de psychanalyse* in 1928. However, after the report by the 'Princess' and that of Sophie Morgenstern which followed, the Paris Psychoanalytical Society was obliged to make an effort and, in numbers 3 and 4 of 1930–1 and number 1 of 1932, the *Revue française de psychanalyse* published articles by both Anna Freud ('Introduction to child psychoanalysis') and Melanie Klein ('The psychological principles of child analysis', and 'The early stages of the Oedipus complex'). But it was doubtless to no avail: very few French analysts seemed to be *truly* interested in children in the period prior to 1940.

This point is also raised by Robert Barande (1975) and Didier-Jacques Duche (1990). They note, for example, that Dr Odette Codet reported on the short analytical treatment of three cases of mental anorexia at the Paris Psychoanalytical Society meeting on 18 June 1935. In the discussion that followed, Dr Odier remarked: 'Why are we always so acutely interested in the analysis of children?' and Dr Lacan asked 'How far should the psychoanalysis of a child go?' Georges Mauco wrote a long article for the *Revue française de psychanalyse* entitled 'Child psychology and its relationship with the psychology of the unconscious' (Mauco, 1936). In that same year René Lafforgue wrote the first report on 'Family Neurosis' for the 9th Conference of French Language Psychoanalysts, and John Leuba a second report on 'The neurotic family and family neuroses', with the following remark in the introduction: 'Children have no greater enemy than their own parents.' So, says Leuba, 'what can we do to prevent family neuroses? It is simple: mankind itself needs to be reformed.' In other words, something which will take several centuries. In the meantime, analyses must be carried out and only a small number of patients can be treated. 'We tend to treat adults first and foremost, but with varying success.' 'Our greatest efforts should be brought to bear on the younger generations.' How? Educate the educators, instruct those who are in charge of instruction; but, above all, he says, 'we must train the greatest possible number of psychoanalysts specializing in the treatment of children, the only really rational treatment, all things considered'. Unfortunately, this suggestion was not taken up again in the very long discussions that followed.

In 1936, too, Edouard Pichon published *Le developpement psychique de l'enfant et de l'adolescent*, a psychological study viewed in the light of psychoanalysis. It is only at the end of the book that the author reflects on the problems of education and then on 'orthopsychopedia'. He talks about psychotherapy and mentions Anna Freud; as for psychoanalysis as practised in adults, he says it can be applied from the age of 17 onwards. Before this, it is premature, since the only results obtained are unreliable, unless the special technique of 'pedopsychoanalysis' is used. On this subject, Raymond de Saussure observes that the book makes no mention of anxiety, castration complex or of superego; however, linguistic questions (Pichon's speciality) were well developed.

In 1938, an article by Madeleine L. Rambert, of Lausanne, was published in the *Revue française de psychanalyse* presenting, in line with the theories of Anna Freud, 'puppet play' as a new technique which could be used in child analysis. The author describes herself as a child psychoanalyst and presents the technique as being one which could be used alongside drawings and plasticine. We found no response to this paper from Switzerland, apart from a comment by Serge Lebovici in 1950, and perhaps the use of puppets in psychotherapy ten or twenty years later, but here we are getting away from child psychoanalysis.

FRANÇOISE DOLTO

Françoise Dolto, *née* Marette (1908–88), holds an intermediate position in the development of child psychoanalysis in France. Her biography has been related so often by herself and by others that we will not go into it here. A short, simple and warm presentation of her was made by Colette Destombes in the *Journal de la psychanalyse de l'enfant* (1989). The interested reader should also read the well-documented book by Yannick François (1990). From a bourgeois, Catholic Parisian family, Françoise Marette discovered psychoanalysis early on in her life through René Lafforgue, who was treating her brother for depression. It was Lafforgue himself who suggested she undergo analysis with him. This is understandable in the atmosphere of that period (1934). She quickly became a member of the small circle of psychoanalysts belonging to the Paris Psychoanalytical Society, probably in 1936, and took part in its discussions. In June 1938 she became an associate member, and in 1939 a full member. She was encouraged by Lafforgue to undertake analyses of adults under supervision, which was undertaken by Heinz Hartmann, Angel Garma, Rudolf Loewenstein and René Spitz (according to herself and to Colette Destombes) or by Nacht and Daniel Lagache (according to Roudinesco, 1986).

At the same time she finished her medical studies. She was a non-resident medical student in 1934, and in 1936 was taken on as such in Professor Heuyer's unit. This was the unit in which Sophie Morgenstern worked, and it was therefore she who introduced Dolto to child psychoanalysis and taught her how to use drawings as a replacement for free association. Morgenstern supervised her first cases.

In 1938, Françoise Marette became Odette Codet's assistant in Edouard Pichon's outpatient department at Bretonneau Hospital. There she prepared her thesis, which she defended in July 1939, on the subject of 'Psychoanalysis and Paediatrics'. The thesis consists of a fairly lengthy account of conventional psychoanalytical theory as it was taught at the time, simplified so as to make it accessible to the medical profession, putting the accent on traumas and the castration complex. This part of the thesis was then followed by an account of sixteen cases seen in Pichon's outpatient department. There were also therapeutic consultations (in the sense that Winnicott was to give to this expression later on). One can clearly see that Françoise Marette's technique and inspiration were not very different from those of Sophie Morgenstern: interventionist, but combined with undoubted clinical intuition.

When the Germans entered Paris in 1940 Morgenstern committed suicide, the immigrants went into exile and a number of French analysts joined the Resistance. Pichon, who also died that year, was not to see the triumph of his nationalistic ideas. Others continued to work in Paris and met, albeit infrequently. This was the case of a number of those analysed by René Lafforgue: André Berge, Georges Mauco, Juliette Boutonier and Françoise Marette. Jacques Lacan was also working in Paris. It is also known that although Lafforgue sheltered a number of Jews and had at one time been a member of the LICA (League Against Anti-semitism), he also collaborated with the Nazis and tried, without success, to set up a psychotherapy society under the benevolent aegis of one of Goering's cousins (the Paris Psychoanalytical Society having suspended its activities).

Françoise Marette moved into this institutional void, treating adults and children, and consulting at the Trousseau Hospital. She married Boris Dolto in 1942.

In 1945, at the end of the war, she thus appeared as an experienced child analyst. Although she had only been practising since 1938, she was the only one to be practising this particular speciality in Paris, since all the

others had gone. This also perhaps explains why she worked in relative isolation all her life outside the two main currents (Anna Freudian and
Kleinian), without reference to any master in particular, but with a number
of friends and pupils who grew rapidly in number and who built her a reputation far beyond her real historical importance. We believe that she was
not wary enough of her friends, for behind the role of guru that she was
ultimately forced to play, was the silhouette of a competent child psychotherapist, with considerable intuition and great goodwill towards others.

Her style was very personal and quite inimitable. As an example we
would like to try to translate the following passage from a paper entitled
'Personology and body image': 'This place which houses the affects [the
heart] bears the name of the pulsating viscera that nestles behind the tits
between these arms which convey to us the sense of that very first embrace;
these viscera are connected with the earliest exchanges current, it is living
before the breath and only dies after it' (1961: 63).

Dolto's solitary approach and her training cut short by the war doubtless
help explain the fact that she discovered the notion of body image without
any reference whatsoever to Paul Schilder, a Viennese psychoanalyst who
had emigrated to the United States in 1928, where he married Lauretta
Bender, and died in 1940. However, Schilder wrote a 350-page volume on
the subject in 1935. He was not the only one, as Jean-Louis Lang reminds
us (1983): we also owe the notion to Melanie Klein (1921).

Her personal theories about the beginnings of mental life led Dolto to
solve the problem by imagining a pre-ego, a pre-ego ideal and a pre-super-
ego, but the difference between this and Melanie Klein's primitive superego
is not made explicit.

It is, of course, not possible to go into the different aspects of her clinical
work and her theories here. Her friendship with Lacan led her to share his
vicissitudes with psychoanalytical institutions, but she never really adhered
to his theories. However, she was excluded from the IPA at the same time
as Lacan, but for different reasons. It was Winnicott himself, whom she had
nevertheless held in high esteem, who decided that she was not to be permitted to be a training analyst. He said that her patients and students had a
'wild [and therefore harmful] transference' on to her. She had too much
intuition and not enough method to be a training analyst. The IPA criticized her for the way in which she transmitted psychoanalytical knowledge
as if it were mystical or initiatory in nature, which contrasts considerably
with the prudence necessary to the problems of analysts' training.

In 1978, Dolto gave up her psychoanalytical practice to become a popu-
larizer of psychoanalysis, and thereafter was to be heard on the radio, where
she gave advice on the air ('SOS psychanalyst' – a psychological helpline),
and be seen on television. She actually did contribute to the spreading of a
number of psychoanalytical notions about children to the general public,

even if she also claimed exclusive paternity of these ideas for herself and systematically forgot to mention the work of any of Freud's other successors. A large section of the public also appreciated the fact that she believed in God, and her book *L'Evangile au risque de la psychanalyse* (1977) ('Gospel at the risk of psychoanalysis') reassured many. She certainly helped to give new moral standards to a society which had lost its bearings.

She also supported the founding of institutions such as the 'Maison Verte', where she took up Anna Freud's early ideas – without ever referring to her, however.

Towards the end of her life, the media effect was such that for the French public the name Françoise Dolto was synonymous with child psychoanalysis, not without ambivalence, for the epithet of 'witch' was also used. She did not found a school and did not have any pupils as such, since her practices and style were said to be inimitable.

At the same time, as we shall see, another image of child psychoanalysis was beginning to take form in France.

SERGE LEBOVICI AND HIS SCHOOL

Serge Lebovici was born in Paris in 1915. His father, a doctor, had emigrated from Romania and been deported to Auschwitz during the war. Lebovici himself had to work clandestinely for some time. He became a member of the Paris Psychoanalytical Society in 1946 after having undergone analysis with Sacha Nacht. His role in the development of child psychoanalysis in France was considerable and his influence extended to the international level. Not only are his theories known by psychoanalysts the world over, and we have heard them quoted in all the countries we have visited, but this celebrity was to lead to his election as Vice President of the IPA from 1967–73 and President from 1973–7. He was the only French IPA President and the fact that this international tribute was paid to a child psychoanalyst is particularly significant for us. Very early on he organized an annual forum (quickly baptized by his friends as the 'Lebovici Forum'), which was also attended by foreign colleagues.

We will go rapidly into the theories of Serge Lebovici. The particular circumstances of professional life in Paris mean that, to our knowledge, no one has yet done so, a fact which is not without its significance.

His first paper in the *Revue française de psychanalyse* (1950a) on psychotherapy with puppets was, even at that early date, an 'Introduction to an exhaustive study of analytical transference in children'. A second paper that same year (1950b) studied the 'Diagnosis of Infantile Neurosis'. It discusses the analytical psychotherapies of Sophie Morgenstern, little Hans, and the spontaneous curability of infantile neurosis, and the contrasting opinions of

Anna Freud and Melanie Klein. Lebovici states that he stops analytical treatment 'when children reach oedipal relations'. He criticizes the notion of maladjustment as a criterion for treating children, and shows that the criteria to be taken into consideration for the analysis of a child should be the child's biography, the personality of the parents, and the pathological defences of the ego, among which is the 'permanent fantasizing of its life'. As with the adult, he says, 'analysis for the child does not exist without an analysis of the transference in the light of past experience'. He concludes by saying that psychotherapy for children must be 'treatment pursued by very experienced analysts so as to justify the hopes that we all believe we should bring to it'. The author has never contradicted this assertion.

In the *Revue française de psychanalyse* alone we have counted more than seventy-five articles written by Lebovici between 1950 and 1991, some of them reviews of books, but all of which touch on child psychoanalysis. Among those which we believe are the most important, we would like to mention the studies of child obsessions, also with Diatkine (1957), indications and contraindications for psychoanalysis, with Nacht (1955), and also his report to the Paris Congress (Lebovici, 1979) on models of infantile neurosis and transference neurosis.

This report was very important for the development of psychoanalytical thought and provoked a very valuable discussion. In it Lebovici demonstrates that transference does exist for children (p. 794) and that the child can organize a transference neurosis: the only problem is its interpretation. It is also important that the transference neurosis be clearly distinguished from infantile neurosis, which is characterized either by semiology nor by symptoms: 'Structurally it is the working through of archaic psychotic positions. Ontogenetically it is the fruit of the interactional particularities of development' (p. 818). Infantile neurosis does not simply interlock with the transference neurosis: 'What is repeated is only valid in the situation relating to the transference neurosis which makes a past occur in order to give it a sense' (p. 832). This 'infantile neurosis' is therefore a development concept which should be carefully distinguished from 'a neurosis of the child', which is a clinical reality with serious and often permanent symptoms, resulting from a failure of the defence systems, with manifestations which are sometimes hysterical, phobic or obsessional, and which is an indication for psychoanalytical treatment, contrary to the fluctuating and passing symptoms, often less evident to the observer, which are only signs of a 'normal' infantile neurosis.

Unfortunately, it is not possible to go into such a discussion here, which has numerous, complex implications, precisely, we believe, because it concerns the central problem of the theory of child psychoanalysis.

In 1958, with Julian de Ajuriaguerra and René Diatkine, Lebovici founded a journal called *La psychiatrie de l'enfant*, which was to play a considerable role, both in France and elsewhere, in having psychoanalytical ideas taken into consideration in child psychiatry, a new field which was just opening up and in which he himself played a considerable part. In the first issue of the new journal Lebovici published a 100-page article he had written with Diatkine and Evelyne Kestemberg (1958), an assessment of ten years' practising psychodrama with children and adolescents. He also published there several other important papers and a number of reviews of books.

His own books contributed to the training of many child psychoanalysts and had a great influence on psychiatrists: *Les tics chez l'enfant* (1955), *Les centres de guidance infantile*, with Buckle (1958), *Un cas de psychose infantile, étude psychanalytique*, with Joyce MacDougall (1960), *La connaissance de l'enfant par la psychanalyse*, with Michel Soulé (1970). We should also mention one of his most recent books: *Le nourisson, la mère et le psychanalyste, les interactions précoces* (1983).

This list is not exhaustive, we have mentioned only the works which have had a particular influence on us. But we thought it necessary to mention them, since for us Lebovici is above all a theorist.

Lebovici's position on the theory of child psychoanalysis is very personal, both firm and subtly balanced. He adopted a number of Anna Freud's positions: her prudence concerning treatment, the necessity of sound preparation and the restrictive indications. But at the same time he included in his theories the Kleinian concepts of position and projective identification, in particular, for the treatment of psychotic children, while rejecting Klein's interpretative system and the concept of early object relationship. He found in the work of Spitz and Bowlby the basis for his ideas about the early fantasized interaction between mother and baby that he is currently working on.

His on-going clinical and experimental research has already contributed much to the theory of treatment itself and has foreseeable implications on preventive social work. Is this child psychoanalysis? To this question Lebovici responds: 'I don't know. I am a psychoanalyst and I work with babies. It is enriching for the child psychoanalyst.' (I. 2)

Being a psychoanalyst in France does not easily combine with a career in hospital or university. Lebovici had been a non-resident medical student, a house physician, and then an assistant working in Professor Heuyer's department. When Professor Michaux became head of department, he refused to appoint Lebovici as a professor and invited him to leave the department with the words which have remained engraved in his memory: 'You may stay for two more weeks . . .'. Lebovici had to wait until the age of 55 to be appointed a full professor, and became tenured at an age when others were taking retirement.

On leaving Professor Heuyer's department, Lebovici did consultation work at the Institute of Psychoanalysis. It was at this time that, with Philippe

Paumelle, he founded the Child Mental Health Centre in the 13th arrondissement of Paris. (There will be a rapid presentation of the Child Guidance Centres and the Mental Health Centre below.) However, we should stress one point here: Lebovici was no longer alone in promoting this type of body, than he was in his way of thinking. While in Heuyer's department he seems to have already shared his scientific interests with others. In his theoretical work it is often difficult to disassociate him from René Diatkine, who himself was a figure of considerable importance in France. We can give many other examples: Evelyne Kestemberg, Michel Soulé, Myriam David, Colette Chiland, Simone Decobert, Roger Misès, and we are sure that we will be guilty of important omissions in doing so. All these authors have independent approaches to both theory and practice, sometimes diverging very distinctly, and yet this has not engendered any institutional conflict or schisms. We see in this fact one remarkable aspect of Lebovici's teaching: he is able to accept the independence of his colleagues and friends, which is not something much in evidence in a country such as France, where the notion of hierarchy carries considerable weight. One only need think for a moment of the power of the Professor holding the Chair in France (in Paris in particular). It is truly paradoxical that Serge Lebovici should be identified with this professorial image, and be criticized for it by those same people who were followers of, and who identified themselves with, Jacques Lacan, who, although he was not a professor, nevertheless acted as if he were one.

CHILD GUIDANCE CENTRES AND OTHER MENTAL HEALTH CARE INSTITUTIONS

According to Victor Smirnoff (1966), the term 'guidance centre' can be traced back to the Juvenile Psychopathic Institute founded by William Healy and Augusta Bronner in Chicago in 1909, followed by the Judge Baker Foundation in Boston in 1915. Initially, they were for juvenile delinquents, but the consultation clinics rapidly came to include other types of psychological disorder. We saw in Chapter 5 how the efforts of Anna Freud and her colleagues in Vienna led to the creation of guidance centres, amongst other things. Another example would be the Tavistock Clinic in London. Was it the same notion as that which had lead to the outpatient consultations given, for example, by Sophie Morgenstern in Professor Heuyer's department? It is not evident, since in this sort of set-up the psychoanalyst is alone, stuck in like an additional examination between X-rays and blood tests. Pierre Male (1964), who did much for psychoanalytical psychotherapy for adolescents, had also had a consultation clinic in child psychiatry with Gilbert Robin as early as 1927. In fact, although the Child Guidance Centres (Buckle and Lebovici, 1958) retained the name, they rapidly developed, both in France and elsewhere, into outpatient consulting clinics where parents could be advised and each child 'examined from a medical, psychological and social point of view', which required the intervention of a number of different specialists and where it would seem that psychoanalysis entered by the back door, in places where the psychiatrist or psychologist on the team happened to be a child psychoanalyst. However, Lebovici considered that although it was rare that true psychoanalytical treatment be 'prescribed' for a child, 'the action of the guidance centres first of all in Anglo-Saxon and then in Latin countries is . . . one application of child psychoanalysis'. However, many other types of intervention are also advocated with an eye to re-educating or modifying the parental environment. It was also here that the first notions of prevention and general activities out in the community were developed. Towards 1950, under the impetus of psychiatrists such as Daumezon or Lucien Bonnafé, there was a movement by French psychiatric hospitals to set up medico-psychological centres, which tried to function somewhat like guidance centres.

We shall mention two ventures in particular which were psychoanalytical in origin and which tried to give structure to these guidance centres: 'medico-psycho-pedagogical' centres (CMPP) and the Child Mental Health Centres (CSMI). The idea can be roughly described as follows: to set up an administrative framework able, in turn, to create structures where all children could be seen, with their parents, and where the diagnosis and treatment could be psychoanalytical or psychoanalytically inspired, by taking advantage of the particular social and political climate of the time: after the defeat of the Nazis, the country had to be rebuilt and some kind of real social policy could be envisaged. It was then possible (just as it had been in Vienna after the 1914–18 war) to ask the state to help children in difficulty.

THE CMPP ('MEDICO-PSYCHO-PEDAGOGICAL' CENTRES)

The first 'psycho-pedagogical' centre, given the name Claude Bernard because it was located in the secondary school of the same name, was opened on 15 April 1946. The project had been discussed by three of the four members of the 'St Genevieve Four' (the name given to the four psychoanalysts who had continued to meet regularly in Paris during the Occupation: André Berge, Juliette Boutonier, Françoise Dolto and Marc Schlumberger). Schlumberger does not seem to have treated children and Dolto did not pursue the project. It was therefore Berge and Boutonier, with Georges Mauco, who went ahead with it.

Like Berge and Boutonier, Georges Mauco had undergone analysis with René Lafforgue. He was a specialist in human geography and had written a book in 1932 entitled *Les étrangers en France et leur adaptation* 'Foreigners

Adapting to Life in France'. He became interested in teaching very early on, and this was probably one of the reasons he underwent analysis. After having been a member of General de Gaulle's cabinet in 1945, he was appointed General Secretary of the Committee on Family and Population in 1946. After having studied how the Vaud Educational Medicine Office (run by Dr Lucien Bovet in Lausanne) worked, Mauco's position enabled him to persuade the French authorities to create the first CMPP. The idea was that centres should have a 'psychoanalytic activity', otherwise 'it is difficult to see what purpose they serve' (Mauco, 1967).

Another of those analysed by Lafforgue, Juliette Boutonier (later Favez-Boutonier), professor of psychology and a doctor, also played an important part in the development of psychoanalytical psychology in France. A tolerant, generous woman with a very open mind and keen and subtle intelligence, Boutonier had agreed to be a patron of the Claude Bernard Centre and, while she was teaching in Strasbourg, was the originator of a similar centre there in 1947. She died in 1994.

Born in 1902, André Berge, grandson of the French President Félix Faure, initially obtained a Bachelor of Arts degree in Philosophy. He became interested in psychology and literature very early on. He became a writer and was one of those who frequented the publishers Gallimard, and the surrealists. In 1930 he took part in the founding of *L'école des parents* ('The school for parents'). In 1936, he wrote *L'éducation familiale* ('Education in the Family'), which was the first of his works to do with up-bringing. He told Michel Mathieu (1988) how he had come to psychoanalysis. He had begun to undergo analysis with Lafforgue in 1939 and had begun his medical studies shortly afterwards. His thesis, given in 1945 at the age of 43, entitled 'The Psychic Factor in Enuresis', enabled him to become a psychiatrist. During the war he too had been a non-resident medical student to Professor Heuyer's department and it was no doubt here that he had been given his first case of psychotherapy, which would have gone to Sophie Morgenstern before her death. He is one of the rare French psychoanalysts to have kept out of the 'scrum' during the divisions which occurred in the psychoanalytical societies, telling Mathieu (1988): 'You have to understand, we began in child analysis. Neither Nacht nor Lacan had this experience. For me this is the essential dichotomy of the situation: some started in child analysis and worked up to adults, some started with adults and worked a little back to children.' Berge liked to think of himself as a humanist.

When the Psycho-pedagogical Centre opened the medical director was Juliette Boutonier and the administrative and educational director Georges Mauco. André Berge headed the organization from 1947–74.

It is likely that Berge influenced the French CMPPs with his particular brand of ideology. They were set up along the lines of the child guidance centres (see above) following Anna Freud's ideas on psychoanalytical up-bringing, management being split half and half between doctors and psychologists representing child psychoanalysis, on the one hand, and Ministry of Education staff (seconded by the department), on the other, with the overall assistance of specialists in psychomotor re-education, speech therapists, social workers and secretaries in the consulting rooms. This institution, said Berge, was a melting pot where 'all sorts of different disciplines could meet and collaborate in an atmosphere of trust and friendship'. However, this would appear to have been wishful thinking. 'At first', wrote Georges Mauco (1967), 'the analytical action of the psycho-pedagogical centres had to be discreet so as to avoid triggering off anxious or aggressive opposition to psychoanalysis'. Yet all the child psychotherapy was conducted by psychoanalysts – in addition to André Berge, Juliette Boutonier and Georges Mauco, Mireille Monod, Françoise Dolto and Serge Lebovici were to be found there in the early months.

The conflict between the desire to create a psychoanalytical consulting centre and the resistance of the authorities is evidenced in a remark made by Mauco (1967):

> This psychoanalytical information appears to us to be very necessary at precisely the time when public services are tending to go down the wrong path. They are multiplying consultation centres and projects for children in difficulty without the vital psychoanalytical understanding of the reasons for disturbed behaviour.

The same could also be said today.

The psycho-pedagogical centre therefore developed into a 'medico-psycho-pedagogical' centre in order to satisfy the desires of the authorities. But the 'medico' was not necessarily a psychoanalyst nor even a psychiatrist. In 1964, legislation was introduced to set up the CMPP, and they spread throughout France from that date onwards. One of the present authors (Claudine Geissmann) was thus able to set up a CMPP in Bordeaux in 1965, presided by Roland Doron and Jacques Wittwer. She was the medical director. Psychoanalytical work was possible and enabled children to be treated, but it was also possible to set a trend, make young psychiatrists more aware of psychoanalysis, train psychotherapists and produce scientific studies.

However, the constant battle required to maintain a psychoanalytical approach at that time was exhausting, and we stopped trying in 1971. We were not alone; this happened in the hundreds of CMPPs which were eventually to be opened throughout France. New teams are continually trying to win acceptance for the sort of collaboration that would enable child psychoanalysis to be carried out, and these sincere and devoted efforts are continually being reduced almost to nothing by a natural resistance to problems that seem to arise whenever the unconscious is mentioned.

At present, although there are some centres where psychoanalysis is accepted, in many cases the opposite is true, and the proportion of different types of re-education and psychotherapies which are not psychoanalytical in approach is constantly increasing. All too often, so-called 'psychoanalytical psychotherapies' (at the rate of one 30-minute session a week) are undertaken by psychotherapists with inadequate training in psychoanalysis. These 'de-psychoanalysed' CMPPs have become centres for the treatment of learning disabilities, where serious neuroses and psychoses are not accepted and where the Ministry of Education rules.

THE EDOUARD CLAPARÈDE INSTITUTE

In 1949, just after the Claude Bernard Centre was founded, the Edouard Claparède Institute (named after the famous Swiss psychoanalyst and educationalist) opened in Paris, in premises offered by a Swiss charitable trust, on rue du Ranelagh. Later the Institute moved to Neuilly (Decobert, 1989a).

Based on the principles of child guidance, the Claparède Institute was distinguished from the outset by an entirely medical management board, initially run by its founder, the psychoanalyst Henri Sauguet. According to Simone Decobert (I. 10), this medical psychiatric board, which is always headed by a psychoanalyst, had the support at the time of Professor Heuyer and of Sacha Nacht. Henri Sauguet worked with Georges Mauco in the drafting of the legislation for the CMPPs, but does not seem to have succeeded in getting his own institution included.

The idea was that the Claparède Institute should be run somewhat on the lines of the Hampstead Clinic founded in London by Anna Freud. One can imagine a relationship between this psychoanalytical management board and the destiny of the Institute, in comparison with that of the CMPPs as mentioned above. At present, there are thirty-five cases of child psychoanalysis being carried out at the Institute by psychoanalysts trained at the Paris Psychoanalytical Society, at the rate of at least three sessions a week. Training seminars are conducted there, attended either by candidates at the Paris Institute of Psychoanalysis or by psychotherapists (I. 10).

Initially, Henri Sauguet entrusted Pierre Luquet with the job of running the section dealing with child psychoanalysis, supervision and organization of treatment (Luquet, 1989). The Claparède Institute, says Luquet 'was a big slice of my life which has been dedicated to the development of child psychoanalysis'. In the picture he painted of the way this sort of work has evolved since 1949, he shows that we are moving towards an approach which is to treat increasingly early on, first, in order to fight the ill at its roots and, second 'so as to extend such possibilities to the more serious cases of arrested development or elementary disorders which are hindering

301

normal development'. The growth of the Institute cannot be separated from the progress made in psychoanalytical theory. Interpretation, for example, he says, 'is often the representation given to the silent phantasy or the unformulated desire. It constitutes a partial release of them in the pleasure of thought.' He also says: 'We should try to understand the way a child thinks from the outset and where the blockages occur. Re-establishing the possibility of a displacement, permitting condensations to occur, helping to organize symbolism through the relationship, these are our real tasks.'

Simone Decobert, the present director of the Claparède Institute, shows clearly the connection between psychoanalytical work and psychoanalytical theory (1989a). She centres her thinking, among other things, on the development of work with the family. The family must be helped to help its child. It is a solution of a different kind which she offers to the theoretical conflict between Anna Freud and Melanie Klein over their approach to parents. The problem needs to be looked at 'in terms other than those highlighting the resistance to the application of psychoanalysis to the interrelations between people, rather than to the psyche of the individual taken in isolation in treatment'. The real obstacle is not that of dependence on parents, but is related to the fact that 'the foundation of the family is in fact the sexual link', whose expression is repressed or denied in the family group, in spite of the 'conscious' advance of sexuality in society in general. She thus places great hopes in 'psychoanalytical family therapy' which is based on the theories and experience of Didier Anzieu and René Kaes of the group psychic apparatus, on those of Serge Lebovici and his team in psychoanalytical psychodrama and group transference, as well as the work of Ruffiot, Caillot and Decherf (1989c).

We will quote in full the conclusion to the introduction to the Proceedings of the psychoanalytical Forum held at Claparède in 1989:

> These considerations and discoveries seem to have improved the framework of child psychoanalysis proper and to have made it more secure. Instituting the analysis of a child, which means attendance at therapy sessions four times a week, is certainly an important event for the child, but it is also an event for the family, which is anyway questioned, involved and may even be altered. The use of group dynamics means that rejection, resistance, or even suffering, which might otherwise hinder both family therapy and relationships within the family, can be avoided. The practical formula generally associated with the child's analysis is therefore the therapeutic consultation which enables parents to adapt to the evolving situation and to get the most out of it.
>
> (1989b)

There are, of course, other psychoanalytical guidance and assessment centres in France, among which the Psychotherapeutic Rehabilitation

Centre (CEREP) in Paris should be mentioned, founded in the 1950s by Denise Weill and Raymond Cahn. Initially, the object of the guidance centres was to treat children in their natural environment by, as we have seen, using applications of child analysis, wherever possible. This sort of treatment is in total opposition to the solution which has been used by traditional psychiatry for a long time, i.e. to place children in 'specialized' institutions for children when they show 'characterological or behavioural disorders', or when their intellect is judged to be deficient by intelligence tests. These kinds of establishment go by various names: reform school, borstal, asylum, children's home, medico-educational boarding school or observation centres. They were started up by the consulting clinics of large hospitals, or by the health authorities, and more often than not by associations for the 'rehabilitation' or 'protection' of children. These associations are mostly non-profit-making organizations where the devotion of those running them does not always make up for the lack of technical training of those in charge of the children. This sort of placement is still extremely common and in general such institutions do not allow for psychoanalytical intervention, or even simple psychiatric treatment. Even today, when the usefulness of psychoanalytical intervention is virtually no longer questioned, economic factors mean that it cannot be put into practice.

However, there are occasions when child psychoanalysts are called in and things do change. One example is the Vallée Foundation, where Roger Misès has demonstrated this in masterly fashion. The history of the foundation has been documented by Misès himself (1980). He starts with a description of the lunatic asylum for children founded at the end of last century. This institution made remarkable strides under the direction of Bourneville, who tried to set up an educational structure (Gateaux-Mennecier, 1989). On Bourneville's death it returned to the state of asylum and even disappeared as an institution for children in 1920. The Vallée Foundation became 'just a place offering assistance for children considered to be uneducable and promised a life of being shut up in a psychiatric institution' (Misès, 1980). Although classes were introduced by the Ministry of Education in 1950s, it was not until Misès was appointed chief physician in 1957 that the institution underwent a complete metamorphosis.

A member of the Paris Psychoanalytical Society, Roger Misès had also benefited from the teaching of Serge Lebovici. His influence on the Vallée Foundation shows just what short of impact a child psychoanalyst can have on psychiatry without losing his identity as a psychoanalyst. Children were treated, instead of the 'backward' being 'placed'. Factors which might influence the development process favourably or unfavourably at various levels were sought out. The approach was psychoanalytical, but nevertheless multidimensional. Misès (1980) demonstrated the evolving nature of the various diagnoses and how 'the mechanisms of reintegration underpinned by treatment often lead to successful transformations, if one acts early and brings sufficient means to bear'. The Foundation was attached to the psychiatric sector (see below) and from that point the percentage of admissions decreased and facilities outside the hospital were diversified (a guidance centre and a day hospital in particular). It also 'meant that admission to residential care was rarely indicated, as the decision was based on therapeutic criteria and no longer on any criteria of assistance' (Misès, 1980: 12).

This is a clear example of the influence a child psychoanalyst can have on a 'classic' type of institution. In turn, the work he did at the Foundation enabled Misès to produce a number of scientific works showing, in particular, other nosological contexts better adapted to the psychoanalytical understanding of children: severe disharmonic states (Misès and Barande, 1963), psychoses expressing themselves by deficiency (1975) and, very recently, borderline disorders in children (1990). As to the difficult problem of the status of treatment in an institution, we have already seen that Hermine Hug-Hellmuth and Anna Freud had already addressed this subject. Misès mentions three possibilities:

1 Systematic treatment carried out solely by psychoanalysts, the educational element only being a support.
2 All members of the team (doctors, nurses, educators, etc.) undertake psychoanalysis and interpret. In this case, 'the educational function is dissolved in by the blanketing hypertrophia of the identification of meaning and its reiterated manipulation'.
3 A third solution, and the one advocated by Misès: treatment should consist of both educational (educators) and psychotherapeutic (psychoanalysts) elements. 'What is at stake is that there should be a dialectical link between the two, with no break or mix-up between them' (Misès, 1980).

Among a number of possible other examples we would also mention Raymond Cahn, if only because of the part he played in our own psychiatric training. We mentioned above the psychoanalytical nature he was able to give to the CEREP. He also transformed the Vitry-sur-Seine Observation Centre, run at that time by Georges Amado, and published a study about the development of psychopathological structures for maladjusted children which has become a classic on the subject (1962). His psychoanalytical works (on both children and adults) have been much appreciated, and in 1981 and 1982 he was elected President of the Paris Psychoanalytical Society. His latest work is also very much connected with our subject: *Adolescence et folie* 'Adolescence and Madness' (1991). This book deals with this particular subject with great subtlety and contains a study of the fate of the psychopathological modes of organization in adolescence.

CHILD MENTAL HEALTH CENTRE, 13TH *ARRONDISSEMENT*, PARIS: THE
PSYCHIATRIC SECTOR

A turning point was reached in relation to these experiments with child analysis inside existing psychiatric institutions when Philippe Paumelle and Serge Lebovici founded an original structure centred around the consulting clinic in 1954. The objective was continuity in care, limiting the work to a population which was in geographical proximity, forming teams by sector or sub-sector headed by psychoanalysts, the creation of psychiatric institutions of a new type, based on needs, a structure which was sufficiently flexible and which could be modified if the needs of the children required, and, above all, work in the community. It was defined thus by Lebovici (1984a):

> Community psychiatry aims to remedy the inertia of the type of consultation structures that currently exist in both public and private hospitals. It aims to ensure unity and continuity of care wherever the help and treatment is given to the children and their families. It stresses preventive action and is therefore based on child care programmes where teams made up of people from various disciplines work together, each with their own 'key person'. It tries to step in when there is a crisis, in situations where risks may exist and to help vulnerable families. The ambition of the child psychiatry teams is to work in the community, for the community and with the community.

> (1984a [1980]: 359)

Lebovici surrounded himself with colleagues with whom he had worked in Professor Heuyer's department.

> the essence of community psychiatry was to put psychoanalysts out to work into the community. The work might be in the domain of psychiatry or psychoanalysis but it would be done out in the community because they are used to putting a certain distance between themselves and their work. There was no question of founding a psycho-analytical clinic, rather what we wanted was a modern psychoanalytically oriented psychiatric team. (I. 2)

In 1958 three sub-sectors were created in the 13th *arrondissement* of Paris. In 1959 Paumelle and Lebovici pushed for the creation of a non-profit-making association to give a legal framework the whole set up. In 1961 the 13th *arrondissement* Mental Health Association (as it was called) signed an agreement with various state and social security departments so as to be entitled to practise officially. In 1963 the Alfred Binet Centre had six sub-sector teams dealing with children. At the same time, a day hospital able to take twenty-five psychotic children had also been opened. The fact that a similar structure for adult psychiatry existed meant that the teams worked well together (Paumelle, 1966).

This new way of organizing the work was also to lead to the development of an intense amount of research work and the creation of new facilities. René Diatkine became interested in the problems of language, in the disharmonies of development, of what happens, for example, when the non-organization of the child neurosis deprives the child of the mental functions he requires to go through the Latency period. Diatkine was also interested in the way analysis worked with children and in its interpretation. Since 1982 this research has been published under the title *Les textes du Centre Alfred Binet*. In the first issue, Diatkine says that

> the child's unconscious is only reached through its preconscious . . . by making the preconscious elements more coherent, one enables the child to tell its own story in a different way. For many of those we treat, it is also means they discover that they have a past, that they don't just live in the present, that the projections are not the only way of seeing things and that their desires can be developed in the direction of the future and of the discovery of the pleasure of desiring.
>
> (1982: 7)

It is in this context that Myriam David published her work (1960, 1962) on family placement and the problems of prevention, that Professor Colette Chiland published her now famous work *L'enfant de 6 ans et son avenir (The Six-year Old and its Future)* (1971), and that Evelyne Kestemberg (1972) published her work on adolescents, psychodrama and mental anorexia. The total sum of research, innovation and new psychoanalytical theories, closely allied to clinical work undertaken from a psychoanalytical approach is such that is impossible to draw up a complete list here.

As Lebovici demonstrates, this type of community work means that psychoanalysts have to learn to identify with other members of the team, without giving up anything of their understanding of child disorders. They also need to be able to use their capacity to identify without having their feelings of omnipotence reinforced, feelings with which their reactivated infantile desires might interfere. They must be at ease with their identity as psychoanalysts so as to have an effective influence on the other members of the team and on community representatives (Lebovici, 1984a).

This must have been the case, since, in the debate within the administration between 1960 and 1975 on the subject of child psychiatry in France, it was the organizational structure of the 13th *arrondissement* of Paris which was used as a model by French authorities. This brings us to the notion of the model. The legislative text setting up 'Sectors of child and adolescent psychiatry' per population group of 100,000–200,000 inhabitants centred around the consultation clinic, having offshoots in the form of day hospitals, outpatient units and even hospital services, presupposed that for every 100,00–200,00 inhabitants in France it was possible to provide a Lebovici, Diatkine, Kestemberg, Chiland or David, not to mention all the others. Society had laid a trap for psychoanalysis: since your theories about the unconscious enable children to live happier lives, put them into practice all over the country. But just copying the organizational structure set up in the 13th *arrondissement* to give a psychoanalytical direction to psychiatry is, of course, not sufficient. Just as with the CMPPs, although not quite as markedly, wild psychoanalysis was rife. Much of the psychotherapy carried out was done unquestionably with great devotion, but often without the necessary training. This dilemma is that of the practical problems of child psychoanalysis in essence.

One of the present authors (Pierre Geissmann) set up a child mental health centre working on the sector system, and based on the experience acquired in the 13th *arrondissement* in Paris, in Bordeaux in 1972. The fact that Bordeaux is considerably different from Paris solved most of the problems related to population stability and made the possibility of epidemiological studies much easier. This in turn meant that one of the authors (Claudine Geissmann) was able to set up a day hospital for psychotic children in 1973, where we tried to apply psychoanalytical theories in the form of child analysis and a psychoanalytical approach to problems encountered in institutions. This enabled us to come up with some new theories, in particular using the works of Wilfred Bion and the teachings of Hanna Segal (see C. and P. Geissmann, 1984). The community care approach brings requirements to light more readily and we were thus able to set up a unit specializing in family placement, a system of hospitalization in the home for very young children in great difficulty (Geissmann, et al., 1991, 1993), a special class at nursery-school level, and a day hospital for adolescents who had undergone treatment for psychosis as children but who had not shown sufficient improvement.

The example of the 13th *arrondissement* is therefore quite exciting. It gave birth to numerous initiatives, our own among them, but it is also very demanding and, with the training of child psychoanalysts in its present state, very difficult to keep up.

Among other psychoanalysts who have worked on the theory of child psychoanalysis in France we need to mention Michel Soulé who also set up the Paediatric Nursing Institute (Institut de Puériculture) in Paris along psychoanalytical lines. This was yet another study and training centre for psychoanalysts, but more directed towards very young children because of its paediatric nature.

Some psychoanalysts (such as André Green or Didier Anzieu, who developed the skin-ego theory) although not practising child psychoanalysis themselves, have nevertheless taken an interest in advanced theories of the metapsychology of the beginnings of psychic life.

CHILD PSYCHIATRY AND PSYCHOANALYSIS AND THEIR RELATIONSHIP WITH INSTITUTIONS

We are perfectly aware of the somewhat fragmentary nature of this presentation of the way in which the child psychoanalysts of the Paris Psychoanalytical Society operate as regards theory and institutions. The reader will perhaps be wondering: is the application of psychoanalysis to psychiatry legitimate, and by doing so is there not a risk of distorting the practice and perhaps even the theory of psychoanalysis? We believe that we have partially answered these two questions throughout this book.

1. Child psychoanalysis has had an extraordinarily fertile impact on child psychiatry, whether at the level of diagnostic procedures, nosology, institutional and psychiatric treatment (apart from psychoanalysis proper), or prevention, and most child psychiatrists recognize this. Of course, there are still those who are opposed to any psychoanalytical approach whatsoever, but they are in the minority, if only because all French child psychoanalysts aim to take a multidimensional approach. For example, they will collaborate willingly with specialists of non-psychoanalytical theory (even in their work on the theory of psychiatry) and take biological or systemic theories into consideration. The option of psychoanalytical work within psychiatric institutions has been championed in a book (which is still very valid today) entitled *Le psychanalyste sans divan* (1970) ('The Psychoanalyst without His Couch') edited by Paul-Claude Racamier, which includes chapters by Serge Lebovici, René Diatkine and Philippe Paumelle. Continuing along these lines, one might reflect upon the continued resistance on the part of society to such action by psychoanalysis.

> Psychoanalysis will provide the light for a better, if still incomplete understanding of the forces which irresistibly push some individuals, some groups, and to a certain extent, our society, to fiercely resist an undertaking which consists in 'de-alienating' the mentally-ill patient and psychiatric care. It would appear that people prefer to see the psychoanalyst stick to the confines of his consulting rooms rather than to emerge from it and become involved in the running of care systems themselves.
> (Racamier, 1970: 62)

2. Is there any danger of a loss of 'psychoanalytical purity' if the psychoanalyst works in institutions? We have seen that, to function correctly in an institution, psychoanalysts must possess and be able to maintain their own strong identity and that, in return, this type of work provides a considerable

quantity of material enabling advances to be made in theory proper. We should perhaps reiterate that institutions run on 'psychoanalytical' lines do, of course, permit proper analytical treatment of children. We should also add that, in the prevailing difficult economic conditions (although Hermine Hug-Hellmuth and Anna Freud have both already suggested this possibility), the analytical treatment of children in an institution is slowly becoming the only way of seeing a child four or five times a week. Few parents have the time to take the child to the analyst so often, not to mention the money.

THE ANTIPSYCHIATRY MOVEMENT AND ITS INFLUENCE ON VARIOUS GROUPS

To understand the criticism about 'psychoanalytical purity' we must have a quick look at some specifically French phenomena. The splits in the French psychoanalytical movement do not seem to have had any lasting effect on child psychoanalysis itself. We shall therefore not go into any of the details of the numerous episodes involved in these splits; they have been described often enough elsewhere over the past few years and are mostly anecdotal anyway. In any case, conflicts within psychoanalytical groups have existed in all countries and have either led to splits or to some sort of 'gentleman's agreement' (as in Britain). France is no different.

However, there is something specifically French in the 'Back to the Freud' position of Jacques Lacan, which led him to consider that the only thing that had the right to be called psychoanalysis was the model type of treatment (i.e. using classic techniques, 'pure psychoanalysis', with neurotic adults) and even then not always. He believed that the only real form of treatment was the training analysis. Under these circumstances, child psychoanalysis could only be one application of psychoanalysis, in other words, a by-product. The child here was therefore not acknowledged as a subject because it could not talk (the infant), and the mother had an awful reputation (the witch).

Also specifically French was the fortuitous arrival of the Lacanian phenomenon at the same time as the French version of the English antipsychiatry movement, when in fact Lacanism and antipsychiatry are two quite separate and different ideologies. This version of the movement exploded in the midst of the French psychiatric establishment after 1968 and had a great influence, not only on many young psychiatrists (and some not so young), but on a preconscious level it also influenced the formulations and practices of many others.

According to antipsychiatry concepts, patients did not have to be treated, since they were only sick because society had decreed they were sick. For example, the expression 'patients said to be psychotic' was used. In addition, this generous ideology recommended widespread egalitarianism; patients and doctors no longer existed, rather there were those undergoing treatment and those undertaking treatment. There were no longer masters and pupils, but teachers and taught. As to the patients they were called analysands. In some institutions psychotic children took part in institutional meetings and in the decision-making processes concerning the running of their unit and these decisions were taken by the majority. It is not difficult to see how such a system could lead to manipulation on the part of psychiatrists skilled at such games, leading to power play 'coups' far more oppressive than the traditional system had been. But this would seem to be true of all revolutions. The altruistic nature of this system of thought appealed to many French psychiatrists and psychoanalysts, to the point that, even today, it is difficult to challenge such utopian ideas without bringing down wrath on one's own head.

Arguments of this sort can be found under the pen of Michel Gribinski in a journal called *La Nef* (1971). According to this author, psychiatry should be separate from medicine, for a number of reasons: the mad may not in fact be sick, the people who look after them may not need to be doctors. As to diagnosis, he states, 'a quality relationship with the insane can only be founded on the refusal of a diagnosis. . . . A medical ideology which works in two directions at the same time: clericalism on the one hand, and the separation of the body from the mind, on the other', should be rejected.

Likewise, in a journal called *Partisans* (1969), one can read the following written by Gantheret and Brohm: 'What does to be cured signify? . . . It implies coercion, that willy nilly, the patient has "got back into line."'

In an article by Robert Lefort entitled 'La parole et la mort' ('Word and Death') (1971) there is a particularly good demonstration of the link between antipsychiatry, Lacanian thinking and political ideology. Quoting the work of Rosine Lefort on *L'enfant au loup* (1956) he mentions (1971) the mothers of psychotic children, in what appears to us to be one of the constants of the system:

> They tune in to their child even before it is born, in a symbolic refusal and it is from this refusal that the child's real gains dimension; it is only in front of the mirror that the full extent of the situation is brought to light. The child is confronted with his double, like an image of mortal horror (Schreber's leprous dead body), where he appears to be what the other is really lacking.

For this author

> with its experience with adults (mainly in England) and with children (mainly in France – e.g. the experimental school in Bonneuil[1] only antipsychiatry raises the question of speech and of the discourse of madness as a challenge to society and its defences, even if madness misses its

objective. This in turn raises the question of the politicizing of the psychoanalytic and psychiatric movements.

Then comes a quote from Maud Mannoni: this politicizing 'makes sense inasmuch as it enables questions to be opened up that bourgeois ideology tried to debar' (1970: 176).

The influence of Robert and Rosine Lefort and of Maud Mannoni should not be underestimated. Their ideas permeated several generations of young psychiatrists and psychoanalysts, to the extent that today, over twenty years on, they can still be found, quite unchanged for some, and in a latent state for others who can no longer recall, or do not wish to recall, their rebellious past, from which their theories nevertheless directly stem.

The influence of the Lacanian school of thought, and of the antipsychiatry movement as far as child psychoanalysis is concerned, is all the more important as the question of training in this school is governed by one of Lacan's maxims: 'The analyst is his own sole authority', which led to an excessive increase in the number of 'child psychoanalysts', some of whom manage, outside any control on the part of the IPA institutes, to 'come across' acceptable training, while the greater number do not have that training. The situation is all the more complex in that, according to Jacques Lacan, child psychoanalysis as such cannot exist, and this is well understood in a number of Lacanian schools. However, some of these groups do quite a lot of 'psychoanalysis with children'.

The same goes for the Psychoanalytical Association of France (APF), which is nevertheless affiliated to the IPA, but which, as a group, does not recognize child psychoanalysis. However, at its beginnings the APF had used 'The analysis of a phobic child' by Berta Bornstein (1949), and 'The observation of Frankie' by Samuel Ritvo which followed on, as the theme of its two-day forum in 1965. Jean-Louis Lang, director of an institution in Jouy-en-Josas and author of numerous papers and books on child psychoanalysis, wrote reports on the subject, as did Daniel Widlöcher, author of a book about children's drawing and a long-time director of a seminar on child psychotherapy. Victor Smirnoff, who wrote a didactic work on *La Psychanalyse de l'enfant* in 1966, and who ran a psychotherapy clinic for children for thirty years, took part in the discussion, as did Cécile Dinard, who tried to promote child psychoanalysis in Marseille. But, with the exception of a stand by the APF in 1966 and a report by Jean-Louis Lang in 1970, the attempt was short-lived. However, Anne Anzieu does run a group which *supervises* child psychotherapy.

Some Lacanians came up with formulations, the humour of which we can appreciate, even though we do not agree with them. Anne Porge, for instance, said: 'Once again stifled in the name of rigid analytical knowledge, the child-king has become the child-object.' Eric Porge came up with: 'If it is School [the education system] which forges the child, one can easily see that, as far as child psychoanalysis goes, there is really no need to add anything. This would only reinforce the child in its ghetto. The child cannot be the object of psychoanalysis simply because *parlêtres* [speaking-beings] called children undergo psychoanalysis.' Gérard Pommier stated: 'The only child in psychoanalysis is that which every *parlêtre* [speaking-being] represents from birth to death and this particular parlêtre [speaking-being] wants nothing to do with the conceptual rattle that is "child psychoanalysis," which is about as useful to him as gaiters are to a rabbit' (Pommier, 1978: 127–8).

We have therefore seen that in the period since 1945 child psychoanalysis in France has developed a number of special features:

1 The creation of institutions in which psychoanalysts themselves get involved, and which in turn enables psychoanalysis to develop.
2 Psychoanalysis *à la française* (in the style of Gallimard) as established before the war, was to make a comeback in the schismatic movements. Jacques Lacan was nevertheless influenced, among others, by Edouard Pichon and René Lafforgue.
3 The explosion on the scene of the antipsychiatry movement in 1968 gave an original flavour to the development of psychoanalysis in France, but its effect was mainly felt in the Lacanian school of thought.

The Kleinian school

Contrary to the successors and followers of Anna Freud, the Kleinian school did not care much for institutions. Kleinian psychoanalysts were quite happy to undertake supervision or treatment in such structures but do not seem to have wanted to get involved in the politics of institutions.

It was an American, James Gammill, who introduced the Kleinian school of psychoanalysis to France at the beginning of the 1960s. A member of the British Psychoanalytical Society and of the Paris Psychoanalytical Society, Gammill was born in Nashville (Tennessee). After studying psychiatry in the United States, notably with Karl Menninger in Topeka, he decided to undergo analytical training with the Kleinian group in London, against Menninger's advice. From 1952 onwards he underwent analysis with Paula Heimann and later, between 1957 and 1959, submitted to a weekly supervision of a case of child analysis (a young child) with Melanie Klein herself. Gammill was to remain under the spell of her genius. He seems to have personally accepted the main criteria Klein used for judging a colleague: 'Truly and deeply devoted to psychoanalysis.'

With the assistance of Jean Bégoin and Florence Bégoin-Guignard from Geneva, Gammill was to introduce Kleinian theories of child analysis in

France. From the outset they saw themselves as teachers, and were not interested in founding institutions. They would offer to undertake supervision of any analyst or psychotherapist interested, and would run seminars on texts. To start with they were little known, but their audience soon grew, particularly among young child psychotherapists confronted with difficult cases in the institutions in which they were working. As Florence Bégoin-Guignard (1985) puts it in one of her papers, 'The development of technique in child analysis', they made a case for a strict framework, five long sessions a week, and proper training: 'Through what shortsightedness and in the name of what taboos are we depriving ourselves of the conceptual and technical means developed by Melanie Klein to explore, describe and better understand the way in which the neurotic mind is organized?'

The arrival in this group of Donald Meltzer, an old friend of Gammill, and the opening up of the supervision sessions to a larger public, in principle to all 'analysts undergoing training', was to give them an audience even in the distant provinces. People were going to Paris for 'Meltzer week-ends' three or four times a year. This type of operation was the subject of much criticism. Some saw it as information rather than training. Others were shocked by the use young psychotherapists made of their newly found knowledge when they returned to their institutions: they did not always seem to have really understood all what they had heard. In general, they were criticized for wanting to create a Kleinian group in France based on the London model and they were accused of being 'cliquish'.

From 1970–75 Gammill took part in many working groups in the provinces. For a number of years he went regularly to Brest (with Didier Houzel), to Bordeaux, Toulouse and Montpellier. We believe that this work carried out in small groups was important and very beneficial. It enabled Klein's work to be understood, not just as an intellectual and bookish exercise, but based on the understanding of the clinical material provided by the analysis of severely disturbed young children.

Lastly, he was able to persuade his students to take an interest in analytical observation, following Esther Bick's methods, or the work of Frances Tustin. Some members of the group underwent supervision with Bick and/or Tustin.

As the years went by, Meltzer's influence, and his psychoanalytical research, was to prevail, especially during the Parisian week-ends, and today we think it would be more correct to speak of a Meltzerian group. Divergence over theory and practice led the Kleinian group in London and the British Psycho-Analytical Society to separate from Donald Meltzer in the early 1980s.

Training

Training for child psychoanalysis was treated differently in all the main groups.

The Lacanians do not envisage any additional training for child analysts, first, because the very existence of child analysis is very much disputed, and, second, because they believe that the only person who is fit to decide on the use of the qualification is the analyst himself.

The Psychoanalytical Association of France does not think it necessary to give any additional training in child analysis to the psychoanalysts it trains. In recent years there has been discussion on the subject but proposals to do so have been rejected. In the 1989 report to the International Association for the History of Psychoanalysis (AIHP) entitled 'Training in the French Psychoanalytical Society and in the Psychoanalytical Association of France', Jean-Claude Arfouilloux (1989: 364) wrote:

> There is another problem which is subject to differences of opinion within the APF and that is the problem of child analysis. Its status is still uncertain, although that is not peculiar to the Association, and training in this field is not even envisaged. Some believe that 'child analysis' is not in fact analysis at all, but at the best psychotherapy, and that it is bespattered with educational objectives. Others insist that it should exist in its own right.

The present authors should add that they were among those who 'insist that it should exist in its own right', and confirm the accuracy of Arfouilloux's remarks.

In 1986 a small group of child analysts from the Association decided to found a specialized journal, called the *Journal de la psychanalyse de l'enfant*, so as to be able to express themselves freely without being restricted by the rules governing the APF. Currently, it has a wide distribution.

The Paris Psychoanalytical Society organizes seminars and lectures on the subject of child analysis. It allows discussion of the subject in the congresses it organizes and does not seem to consider psychoanalysts who practise child analysis as second-rate analysts. However, no special training for child analysis is organized by the Society. Those who wish to specialize in this field frequent the institutions mentioned above and take part in seminars, lectures, supervisory sessions and working groups, and this gives them a fairly solid background.

Outside of the analytical associations, some groups organize working week-ends once or twice a year. This cannot be described as training, but we do believe that the information dispensed could be useful because it can give people a taste for the subject and a desire to train. In recent years Pierre Ferrari has been regularly organizing an International Forum on child analysis in Monaco, which usually attracts about a thousand people.

314

Training for psychoanalytical psychotherapy has many angles. Some child psychotherapists are psychoanalysts who have trained in institutes. This is the solution advocated by Serge Lebovici (I. 2): 'Child psychotherapy is what a psychoanalyst does when he works with children, when he is not carrying out an analysis in the strict sense of the word.' We would remember that Lebovici does not see any clear cut difference between psychoanalysis and psychotherapy, since a fixed, tangible spatio-temporal framework is so difficult to establish both in theory and in practice. In addition, he believes that child analysis could only be difficult and distressing for the analyst. The analyst must therefore be well trained and must practise adult analysis at the same time. Often those who practise child analysis abandon it after a few years, he says.

Some institutions, often run by psychoanalysts themselves, do care about the training of their psychotherapists and will either try to set up some kind of in-house training, or point their psychotherapists in the direction of other places or people where they can get proper training.

More often than not, however, psychiatrists and psychologists call themselves 'psychotherapists'. The more serious among them will have undergone analysis themselves and been supervised. Others have no previous practical training. To show just how complex the situation is, we need to remember that in France a psychiatrist can set up practice as a child psychotherapist without having specialized in child psychiatry, and even child psychiatry courses do not necessarily include a child psychotherapy component. A psychologist can set up as a child psychotherapist if she so wishes without ever having met a child before. It also has to be remembered that child psychotherapy carries considerable economic weight for many young psychiatrists and psychologists who set up in practice and are trying to build up a clientele.

Some question the need for proper training for child psychotherapists. But in that case, as Lebovici puts it, is there not a risk of launching people who are 'not sufficiently hardened into a difficult field, where they risk committing themselves without sufficient thought and with the feeling that as far as counter-transference is concerned they would not become deeply involved'? (I. 2).

The problem is not an easy one to solve, and yet countries such as Britain have managed to do so. At the Anna Freud Centre students, in addition to their training in child analysis (which among other things includes the monitoring of treatments undertaken on the basis of five sessions a week), are trained in psychotherapy with the supervision of treatments undertaken on the basis of two sessions a week. This is explained by the fact that they believe that the goals and the techniques of child psychoanalysis and child psychotherapy are different. Should psychoanalysts in France also be trained in both child psychoanalysis and child psychotherapy? Should the many psychotherapists needed by children also be trained in child psychoanalysis, or should anybody be allowed to do anything they like? And, in any case, can they be prevented from doing so?

Note

1 Founded in 1969 by Maud Mannoni, with the assistance of Jean Ayme, Pierre Fedida and Françoise Dolto (Fages, 1991).

PART IV

And tomorrow?

15

The basis of child psychoanalysis: psychoanalytical treatment

Child psychoanalysis does exist and today has reached an advanced age.

The field of child psychoanalysis might appear to be heterogeneous. It is true that it had two founders and that this contributed to the difficulties it has had in developing. There is also no doubt that this helped to contribute to its image. Although the position of Melanie Klein is quite clear, centred as it is on analytical treatment, having read this book and the various sections it contains on Anna Freud, the reader might well have got the impression that the field of psychoanalysis is heterogeneous because of the many different terms employed: psychoanalytical observation, psychoanalytical up-bringing, psychoanalytical psychology, to mention but a few. In fact, and this is the essential point, although Melanie Klein and Anna Freud were interested in different fields and differed in the definition of those fields, they both firmly believed that child analysis could only be based on the psycho-analytical treatment of the child. The treatment of the child is the place of research, the laboratory in which the psychoanalyst can carry out his investigations and which enables him to formulate theories.

We should remember that at the Anna Freud Centre all research on theory was, and is, based on treatment of children, whether for the Index or to draw up the metapsychological profile, even if in some cases data from direct observation were, and are, also used. Contrary to what has often been said, Anna Freud did not fail to distinguish between treatment and observation or up-bringing. It is the theoretical knowledge and the experience acquired during treatment that enables problems of up-bringing to be broached or psychoanalytical psychology to be created, she wrote in 1970.

The driving force behind the work of both Klein and Freud was their curiosity of mind. Melanie Klein had an intense need to know, and it was partly an absence of her son's thirst for knowledge and partly an inhibition of his epistemophilic instinct that led her to undertake the treatment of Erich–Fritz. It was this curiosity about how human beings functioned, linked to the recognition of the existence of the unconscious, that led her to talk about an epistemophilic instinct in her early work. It was this same desire to lift the inhibitions to the thirst for knowledge as far as possible that, for more than fifty years, drove Kleinian analysts in England to have preventive analysis carried out on their own children, at about the age of 3 years, by one of their colleagues. Contrary to accepted opinion, and one which is rife in some anti-analytical circles, none of these children suffered from this early analysis. They turned out none the worse for it, rather the contrary. Erich–Fritz insisted on saying so himself in Paris in 1981 at the scientific forum on the work of his mother, Melanie Klein. As we saw in Chapter 1, little Hans became a famous opera producer, and Hilda Abraham became a famous London analyst.

This curiosity about how human beings operate, what motivates human beings, may appear to some to be less evident in Anna Freud's work. However, it *was* an essential element in her work and she insisted on saying so a number of times. Towards the end of her life, in 1976, at the IPA symposium on 'The identity of the analyst', she said: 'We decide to become analysts for one particular reason, our curiosity about what makes human beings tick . . . and I believe that it is this eternal curiosity which accompanies the analyst throughout his professional life and which creates his identity (if you wish to call it such), or rather his identification with psychoanalysis' (p. 271).

What does the future hold for child psychoanalysis?

This question merits reflection if one considers how rarely child psychoanalysis is in fact practised in the strict sense of the term, the almost total absence of proper training for child analysts in most countries, how fragile the identity of the child analyst is, and, finally, the proliferation of its applications whether in the field of observation, up-bringing or treatment.

The rarity of the practice of the analytic treatment of children

We should, first, remember that for both Anna Freud and Melanie Klein, as well as for Donald Winnicott, the term child psychoanalysis can only be applied to treatment consisting of five (sometimes four) sessions of analysis lasting 50 minutes each per week. Today both the Anna Freud Centre and the Kleinian school recognize this necessity, in spite of the practical difficulties it implies. 'Psychoanalytical research is not possible outside this framework', states Hanna Segal (I. 1). We do not question this requirement, which we ourselves apply after having undertaken this type of treatment in psychotic children. However, it does explain, from an economic viewpoint, why it is done so rarely. But that is not the only explanation. Without going back to Esther Bick's report to the IPA congress in Edinburgh in 1961 (see Chapter 3), we should, however, remember the considerable importance of the great resistance to child analysis on the part of psychoanalysts themselves, related to its specific difficulties. Bick distinguished 'two categories of emotional problem: the internal stress related to preestablished anxieties to do with the treatment of children as such, and the specific questions related to counter-transference'. Today the question is whether this resistance can be overcome. After all, why shouldn't it, thanks to good training?

The almost total absence of proper training for child psychoanalysis in most countries

This problem has already been discussed at length. Britain is the only country in the world (with the possible exception of Argentina) which has incorporated into its institutions the necessity for making analysts aware of child analysis, along with specialist training in child analysis for those who so wish, over and above that for adult analysis. And it is precisely in these two countries that over the past forty years the most important theoretical developments in psychoanalysis in general have occurred. One could also add that this remarkable creativity has a lot to do with the positive emulation caused by the rivalry between the three schools of thought.

Child analysis is a difficult art. The identity of the child analyst is undoubtedly more difficult to sustain than that of the analyst who limits herself to the treatment of neuroses. During the Geneva conference in 1970, Hanna Segal expressed this idea clearly: 'In using parameters when working in close contact with the primary processes, there is a risk of being led away from the current of psychoanalytical thinking' (p. 75). We believe that the identity of the analyst is based on his recognition and taking into account of the change that occurred within himself, related to the discovery of his own unconscious, when he underwent his own analysis. This identity is shaped by the experience we gain in daily practice, from the way we are able to develop it and to confront it with the work of those who have gone before or of those who are doing the same work today. History shows just how fragile this identity is, and that training is absolutely essential.

The proliferation of the applications of child psychoanalysis

Whether it be psychoanalytical up-bringing, the observation of babies or the practice of psychotherapy, the proliferation of the applications of child psychoanalysis is considerable. Is this a case for rejoicing? Or for complaining? We believe that it is a case for rejoicing but that vigilance is required. We cannot forget the pessimistic words of Anna Freud (1968) after forty years' experience of 'psychoanalytical up-bringing'. 'On the whole, there is no way of preventing neurosis. By definition, the various psychical agencies, id, ego and super-ego have opposite purposes, whence the disagreements and clashes which become conscious in the form of psychical conflict.' We probably need to reflect carefully before responding to the demands which society often places upon us.

In all the countries to which we have travelled, the demands of society are also considerable concerning requests for the *psychotherapeutic treatment of children* on the basis of one or two sessions a week. In his paper entitled 'Child psychotherapy' (in *Psychiatrie de l'enfant*, 1982: 458) René Diatkine states that: 'The history of child psychotherapy is full of examples where good concepts have covered bad habits.' Before going any further, one should perhaps think about what is specific to the psychotherapeutic process, and how it differs from the psychoanalytical process. The absence of training for psychotherapists remains a worry; and yet even in the 1960s Anna Freud was regretting that the training of psychotherapists was being left to non-analysts, more often than not.

Psychoanalytical observations of babies are also being multiplied, in various contexts and with teams which are often mixed. The transition is often rapid, the distortion evident when it is the behaviour of the child which is observed and not the phantasized interaction between mother and child. What is analytical about some of the observations of babies we are asked to peruse? We should perhaps remember what André Green had to say on the subject of the discoveries made by Donald Winnicott:

> What I mean is that if Winnicott saw children as he saw them, if he heard them as he heard them, if he was so intuitively penetrating and profound about them it is not just simply because he was a pediatrician, but because he had experienced analysis as an adult: it was therefore his passage through psychoanalysis which enable him to see the child with the eyes of the adult who, having undergone analysis, has found the child within himself in all its vulnerability and creativity.
>
> (1984: 190)

There can be no question of confining the study of mother–child inter-relationships to the field of psychoanalysis, even if these investigations appear to be especially fruitful when they are carried out by a psychoanalyst. However, we believe that is essential to know from what point of view one is speaking. For, as Kestemberg and Lebovici remark in their paper entitled 'Reflexions sur le devenir de la psychanalyse' (1975), the application of the discoveries of psychoanalysis as to the importance of the mother–child unit and the work on 'attachment,' with the ethological references which are included, lead to something quite different from psychoanalysis, in particular to the behaviourist positions and to studies about conditioning favourable to the programming of improvements in behaviour. This is one particular illustrative example of the use of psychoanalysis for purposes which are totally foreign to it.

(p. 48)

To conclude, we would stress the considerable contribution that child psychoanalysis has made to the body of psychoanalytical theory in general. Decidedly, the fate of psychoanalysis in general is closely linked to that of child psychoanalysis. Psychoanalysts will not be able to continue to ignore the problem of training in child analysis for much longer. Two pitfalls must be avoided: one consists in thinking of the psychoanalytical function as being similar to the ecclesiastical function, which means that once 'ordered' the psychoanalyst can or knows how to do everything. The other consists in denying the disinterest of the analyst for child analysis, which is often expressed in the following way: 'I [the analyst] am interested in the child because I am interested in the child that is in the adult, as brought to light in the treatment of the latter.'

The child brought to light in the treatment of the adult should not be confused with the child whose treatment a child analyst decides to undertake. It is true that the identity of the child analyst is built around the identity of the analyst who undertakes adult treatment, but the former should not be confused with the latter. Perhaps precisely because there is a child inside each adult, whether that adult be a psychoanalyst or a patient, all psychoanalysts should have *experience* of the analytical treatment of children, after having undergone psychoanalysis themselves. This is the lesson we have gleaned from the experience of all the child analysts we have met all over the world and throughout history. Beyond their own personal career, what stands out is that they are all passionately curious about what makes human beings tick, they are interested in their psychic life, and they are certain that it can be changed (why not for the better?) if the child is permitted to understand itself and to acquire a greater freedom of thought. In a very exacting manner, they have carried out this research on themselves. It is an adventure which they have offered to other human beings since the beginning of this century, a humanistic adventure.

Bibliography

Collected works

The First Psychoanalysts. *Minutes of the Vienna Psychoanalytic Society*, ed. H. Numberg and E. Federn.
  I. 1906–1908, 1962. New York: International Universities Press.
  II. 1908–1910, 1967. New York: International Universities Press.
  III. 1910–1911, 1974. New York: International Universities Press.
  IV. 1912–1918, 1975. New York: International Universities Press.
1970. Symposium de Genève sur la Psychanalyse de l'Enfant. In *Psychanalyse de l'Enfant*, 1(14), 1971. Paris: PUF.
1970. Colloque des Psychanalystes de Langue Anglaise. London, 1970. In *Psychanalyse de l'Enfant*, 1(15), 1972. Paris: PUF.
1985. *Mélanie Klein aujourd'hui*. Ouvrage Collectif. Lyon: Cesura.
1991. *The Freud–Klein Controversies 1941–1945*, ed. Pearl King and Riccardo Steiner. London: Tavistock/Routledge, 1991.

Individual works

Aberastury, (Pichon-Rivière) A. (1952) 'Quelques considérations sur le transfert et le contre-transfert dans la psychanalyse d'enfants', *Revue française de psychanalyse*, 16(2): 230–53. Repris in *Journal de la psychanalyse de l'enfant*, 1989, 6: 228–55.
Aberastury, A. (1951 and 1966) *El juego de contruir casas*. Buenos Aires: Païdos.
Aberastury, A. (1962) *Teoría y técnica del psicoanálisis de niños*. Buenos Aires: Païdos.
Aberastury, A. (1967) *Historia, enseñandza y ejercicio legal del psicoanálisis*. Buenos Aires: Bibl. Omeba.
Aberastury, A. (1968) *El niño y sus juegos*. Buenos Aires: Païdos.
Aberastury, A. (1971) *Aportaciones al psicoanálisis de niños*. Buenos Aires: Païdos.
Aberastury, A. (1972) *Compiladora: El Psicoanálisis de niños y sus aplicaciones*. Buenos Aires: Païdos, SAICF.

324

Bibliography

Aberastury, A. (1973a) 'Psicoanálisis de niños', *Revista de psicoanálisis,* 30(3–4): 631–87.

Aberastury, A. (1973b) 'La percepción de la muerte en los niños', *Revista de Psicoanálisis,* 30(3–4): 689–702.

Abraham, H. C. (1974) 'Karl Abraham: An unfinished biography with a comment by Anna Freud and Introductory note by Dinora Pines', *International Review of Psycho-Analysis,* 1: 15–72.

Abraham, K. (1913) 'Mental after-effects produced in a nine-year-old child by the observation of sexual intercourse between its parents', in *Selected Papers of Karl Abraham.* London: Hogarth, 1927.

Abraham, K. (1917) 'Some illustrations on the emotional relationship of little girls toward their parents', in *Clinical Papers and Essays on Psychoanalysis.* London: Hogarth, 1955.

Abraham, K. (1974) 'Little Hilda: Daydreams and a symptom in a seven-year-old girl', *International Review of Psycho-Analysis,* 1: 5–14.

Adler, A. (1925) 'Enfant inéducable ou théorie incorrigible? Remarques sur le cas Hug', *Wiener Arbeiterzeitung,* 63(5).

Aichhorn, A. (1925) *Wayward Youth.* New York: Viking Press, 1935.

Alexander, F. (1933) Review of *Die Psychoanalyse des Kindes* by M. Klein, *Psychoanalytic Quarterly,* 2: 141–52.

Anderson, R. (ed.) 1992) *Clinical Lectures on Klein and Bion.* London: Routledge.

Anthony, J. (1986) 'The contributions of child psychoanalysis to psychoanalysis', *Psychoanalytic Study of the Child,* 41: 61–89.

Anzieu, D. (1980) 'W. R. Bion 1897–1979', *Documents et débats,* 17.

Anzieu, D. (1982) 'Comment devient-on Mélanie Klein? *Nouvelle Revue de Psychanalyse,* 26: 235–51.

Anzieu, D. (1985) 'Jeunesse de Mélanie Klein', in *'Melanie Klein Aujourd'hui'.* Lyon: Cesura, pp. 11–35.

Anzieu, D. (1986) *Freud's Self-Analysis.* London: Hogarth and the Institute of Psycho-Analysis.

Arfouilloux, J. C. (1989) 'La formation dans la Société Française de Psychanalyse et dans l'Association Psychanalytique de France: Histoire d'un malaise dans la culture analytique', *Rev. Int. histoire de la psychanalyse,* 2: 343–68.

Barande, R. (1975) *L'histoire de la psychanalyse en France.* Toulouse: Privat.

Berge, A. (1936) *L'éducation familiale.* Paris: Editions Montaigne.

Berge, A. (1968) *Les psychothérapies.* Paris: PUF.

Berge, A. (1988) *De l'écriture à la psychanalyse. Entretiens avec Michel Mathieu.* Paris: Clancier-Guenaud.

Bergeret, J. (1984) *La violence fondamentale.* Paris: Dunod.

Bergeret, J. (1987) *Le Petit Hans et la Réalité.* Paris: Payot.

Bettelheim, B. (1943) 'Individual and mass behavior in extreme situations', in *Surviving and Other Essays* (1952b).

Bettelheim, B. (1950) *Love is not Enough,* Glencoe, Illinois, Free Press.

Bettelheim, B. (1952a) *The Uses of Enchantment.* London: Thames & Hudson.

Bettelheim, B. (1952b) *Surviving and Other Essays.* London: Thames & Hudson, 1979.

Bettelheim, B. (1955) *Truants from Life.* Glencoe, Free Press.

Bettelheim, B. (1967) *The Empty Fortress: Infantile Autism and the Birth of the Self.* New York: Free Press.

Bettelheim, B. (1969) *The Children of the Dream.* New York & London: Macmillan-Collier.

Bettelheim, B. (1974) *A Home for the Heart.* London: Thames & Hudson.

Bettelheim, B. (1986) *Recollections and Reflections.* London: Thames & Hudson, 1990.

Bettelheim, B. and Sylvester, E. (1950) 'Delinquency and morality', *Psychoanalytic Study of the Child,* 5: 329–42.

Bible, *Genesis* 11, vv. 1–9, King James version.

Bick, E. (1961) 'Child analysis today', in *Collected Papers of Martha Harris and Esther Bick,* pp. 104–13.

Bick, E. (1964) 'Notes on infant observation in psychoanalytic training', *International Journal of Psycho-Analysis,* 45: 558–66.

Bick, E. (1968) 'The experience of the skin in early object relations', *International Journal of Psycho-Analysis,* 49: 484–6.

Bick, E. (1987) *Collected Papers of Martha Harris and Esther Bick,* ed. M. G. Williams. Perthshire: The Clunie Press.

Bion, W. R. (1955) 'Language and the schizophrenic', in Klein *et al. New Directions in Psycho-Analysis,* pp. 220–39.

Bion, W. R. (1961) *Experiences in Groups.* London: Tavistock.

Bion, W. R. (1963) *Elements of Psycho-Analysis.* London: Heinemann.

Bleandonu, G. (1985) *L'école de Mélanie Klein.* Paris: Centurion.

Blos, P. (1986) 'Freud and the father complex', *Psychoanalytic Study of the Child,* 42 (1987): 425–41.

Boix, M. (1990) *La vie et l'œuvre de Hermine Hug-Hellmuth.* T. 1. Mémoire CES de Psychiatrie, Université de Bordeaux-II.

Bolland, J. and Sandler, J. (1965) *The Hampstead Psychoanalytic Index.* New York: International Universities Press.

Bonaparte, M. (1930) 'De la prophylaxie infantile des névroses', *Revue française de psychanalyse,* 4(1): 85–135.

Bornstein, B. (1949) 'The analysis of a phobic child: Some problems of theory and technique in child analysis', *Psychoanalytic Study of the Child,* 3–4: 181–226.

Brazelton, T. B. (1979) 'Comportement et compétence du nouveau-né'. *Psychiatrie de l'enfant,* 24(2) (1981): 275–96.

Britton, R., Feldman, M. and O'Shaughnessy, E. (1989) *The Oedipus Complex Today,* ed. J. Steiner. London, Karnac Books.

Buckle, D. and Lebovici, S. (1958) *Les centres de guidance infantile.* Geneva: OMS.

Bühler, Ch. (1922) *Das Seelenleben des Jugendlichen. Versuch einer Analyse und Theorie der psychischen Pubertät.* Jena: Fischer.

Bühler, Ch. (1930) *The First Years of Life,* trans. Pearl Greenberg and Rowena Ripen. New York: John Doyle.

Burlingham, M. J. (1989) *The Last Tiffany, a Biography of D. Tiffany-Burlingham.* New York: Atheneum.

Cahn, R. (1962) 'Les structures psychopathologiques des enfants inadaptés', *Psychiatrie de l'enfant.* 1: 255–316.

Cahn, R. (1991) *Adolescence et folie.* Paris: PUF.

Caille, F. (1989) 'Editorial', *Journal de la psychanalyse de l'enfant,* 6: 7–18.

Chiland, C. (1971) *L'enfant de 6 ans et son avenir.* Paris: PUF.

Chiland, C. (1975) 'La psychanalyse des enfants en 1920 et en 1974', *Psychiatrie de l'enfant,* 18(1): 211–18.

Chiland, C. (1980) *Homo psychanalyticus.* Paris: PUF.

Chiland, C. and Young, J. C. (1990) *L'enfant dans sa famille. Nouvelles approches de la santé mentale.* Paris: PUF.

Clancier, A. and Kalmanovitch, J. (1984) *Le paradoxe de Winnicott.* Paris: Payot.

Codet, O. (1935) 'A propos de 3 cas d'anorexie mentale', *Revue française de psychanalyse,* 11(2) (1939): 253–72.

Cucurullo, A., Fainberg, H. and Werder, L. (1982) 'La psychanalyse en Argentine', in R. Jaccard, *Histoire de la psychanalyse.* Paris: Hachette, T2, pp. 453–511.

David, M. (1960) *L'enfant de 2 à 6 ans.* Toulouse: Privat.

David, M. (1962) *L'aide psycho-sociale.* Paris: PUF.

Decobert, S. (1989a) *Historique de l'Institut Edouard Claparède. Sauv. Enf.* 3 (1989): 161–5.

Decobert, S. (1989b) 'Introduction', in *Avancées métapsychologiques: L'enfant et la famille.* Paris: Apsygée, 1991, pp. 7–10.

Decobert, S. (1989c) 'Métapsychologie et thérapie familiale psychanalytique', in *Avancées métapsychologiques: L'enfant et la famille.* Paris: Apsygée, 1991, pp. 135–46.

Delay, J. (1956) *La jeunesse d'André Gide.* 2 vols. Paris: Gallimard.

Destombes, C. (1989) 'Françoise Dolto', *Journal de la psychanalyse de l'enfant,* 6: 291–6.

Deutsch, H. (1944) *The Psychology of Women,* 2 vols. New York: Grune & Stratton.

Deutsch, H. (1973) *Autobiography.* New York: Norton.

Diatkine, R. (1971) 'Preliminary remarks on the current state of child analysis', Symposium de Genève sur la Psychanalyse de l'enfant, *Psychiatrie de l'enfant,* 14(1) (1971), Paris: PUF.

Diatkine, R. (1982a) 'Les références au passé au cours des traitements psychanalytiques d'enfants', *Les textes du Centre Alfred Binet,* ed. ASM XIIIè, 1: 1–8.

Diatkine, R. (1982b) 'Propos d'un psychanalyste sur les psychothérapies d'enfants', *La Psychiatrie de l'enfant,* 25(1).

Dolto, F. (1939) *Psychanalyse et pédiatrie.* Thèse de Médecine, Paris, Amédée Legrand.

Dolto, F. (1961) 'Personnologie et image du corps', *La Psychanalyse*, 6: 59–92.

Dolto, F. (1977) *L'Évangile au risque de la psychanalyse*. Paris: J. P. Delarge.

Duche, D. J. (1990) *Histoire de la psychiatrie de l'enfant*. Paris: PUF.

Duhamel, P. (1988) *Eugénie Sokolnicka, 1884–1934. Entre l'oubli et le tragique*. Mémoire CES de Psychiatrie, Université de Bordeaux-II.

Dujols, D. (1990) *La vie et l'oeuvre de Hermine Hug-Hellmuth*, T. 2. Mémoire CES de Psychiatrie, Université de Bordeaux-II.

Erikson, E. (1966) *Childhood and Society*, London: Imago.

Etchegoyen, R. H. (1991) *The Fundamentals of Psychoanalytic Technique*. London: Karnac Books.

Fages, J. B. (1991) *Histoire de la psychanalyse après Freud*. Toulouse: Privat.

Federn, E. (1988) 'La psychanalyse à Buchenwald. Conversations entre Bruno Bettelheim, le Dr Brief et Ernst Federn', *Revue International d'histoire de la psychanalyse*, 1: 109–15.

Fendrick, S. I. (1989) *Fiction des origines*. Paris: Denoël.

Ferenczi, S. (1908) 'Psychoanalysis and education', in Sándor Ferenczi, *Final Contributions to the Problems and Methods of Psychoanalysis*, ed. Michael Balint, trans. Eric Masbacher *et al.* New York: Basic Books, 1955, pp. 280–90.

Ferenczi, S. (1913) 'A little chanticleer', in Sándor Ferenczi, *First Contributions to Psychoanalysis*, trans. Ernest Jones. London: Hogarth Press, 1952, pp. 240–52.

Ferenczi, S. (1915) 'Die psychiatrische schule von Bordeaux über die psychanalyse', *Internationale Zeitschrift für ärtzliche Psychanalyse*, 3: 352–69.

Ferenczi, S. (1920) 'The further development of an active therapy', in Sándor Ferenczi, *Further Contributions to the Theory and Technique of Psycho-Analysis*, compiled by John Rickman, trans. Jane Isabel Suttie *et al.* London: Hogarth Press and Institute of Psycho-Analysis, 1926.

Ferenczi, S. (1933) Thalassa: A theory of genitality', *Psychoanalytic Quarterly*, 2: 361–403.

Ferenczi, S. and Rank, O. (1924) 'Perspectives de la psychanalyse', in *Oeuvres complètes de Ferenczi*. Paris: Payot T. III, pp. 220–36.

Ferrer, S. Lustig de, Garma, A. (1973) 'Arminda Aberastury, aproximación a su vida e obra', *Revista de psicoanálisis* 30 (3–4): 619–25.

Fleury, M. (1988) *Sophie Morgenstern, Eléments de sa vie et de son oeuvre*. Mémoire CES de Psychiatrie, Université de Bordeaux-II.

Fonagy, P. and Moran, G. S. (1991) 'Understanding psychic change in child psychoanalysis', *International Journal of Psycho-Analysis*, 72: 15–22.

François, Y. (1990) *Françoise Dolto*. Paris: Centurion.

Freeman, T. (1976) *Childhood Psychopathology and Adult Psychoses*. New York: International Universities Press.

Freeman, T., Cameron, J. L. and McGhie, A. (1965) *Studies on Psychosis*. London: Tavistock.

Freud, A. Major writings can be found in *The Writings of Anna Freud*, 8 vols. New York: International Universities Press, 1966–80.

Freud, A. (1922) 'Beating fantasies and daydreams', in *Introduction to Psycho-Analysis*, vol. 1 of *The Writings of Anna Freud*. London: Hogarth Press and Institute of Psycho-Analysis, 1974.

Freud, A. (1926) 'Phase préparatoire à l'analyse des enfants', in *Le traitement psychanalytique des enfants*. Paris: PUF, 1981.

Freud, A. (1927) *Einführung in die Technik der Kinder analyse*. Vienna: Internationales psychoanalitischer Verlag. Published in English in 1928 in the USA, in Britain in 1946, as *The Psycho-Analytic Treatment of Children*, this version in *Writings*, vol. V *Introduction to Child Analysis*. London: Hogarth and Institute of Psycho-Analysis, 1974, pp. 13–69.

Freud, A. (1930) *Four lectures on Psychoanalysis for Teachers and Parents*, in *Introduction to Psycho-Analysis, Writings*, vol. 1. London: Hogarth Press, 1974, pp. 71–133.

Freud, A. (1936) English translation 1937, as *The Ego and the Mechanisms of Defence*. London: Hogarth Press and the Institute of Psycho-Analysis. *Writings* vol. 2.

Freud, A. (1946) *Wartime: The Psycho-analytical Treatment of Children*. London: George Allen & Unwin.

Freud, A. (1951) [1950] 'Observations on child development', in *Indications for Child Analysis and Other Papers 1945–1956*, Vol. 4 of *The Writings of Anna Freud*. London: Hogarth Press and Institute of Psycho-Analysis, 1969, pp. 143–62.

Freud, A. (1965) [1964] 'Heinz Hartmann: A tribute', in *Research at the Hampstead Child-Therapy Clinic and Other Papers 1956–1965*. Vol. 5 of *The Writings of Anna Freud*. London: Hogarth Press and Institute of Psycho-Analysis, 1970, pp. 499–501.

Freud, A. (1965) *Normality and Pathology in Childhood*. Vol. 6 of *The Writings of Anna Freud*. London: Hogarth Press and the Institute of Psycho-Analysis, 1966.

Freud, A. (1966a) 'A short history of child analysis', in *Problems of Psychoanalytic Technique and Therapy 1966–1970*. Vol. 7 of *The Writings of Anna Freud*. London: Hogarth Press and Institute of Psycho-Analysis, 1972, pp. 48–58.

Freud, A. (1966b) 'The ideal psychoanalytic institute: A utopia', in *Problems of Psychoanalytic Technique and Therapy 1966–1970*. Vol. 7 of *The Writings of Anna Freud*. London: Hogarth Press and Institute of Psycho-Analysis, 1972, pp. 73–93.

Freud, A. (1967) 'About losing and being lost', in *Indications for Child Analysis and Other Papers 1945–1956*. Vol. 4 of *Writings*. London: Hogarth Press and Institute of Psycho-Analysis, 1968, pp. 302–16.

Freud, A. (1970a) 'Child analysis as a sub-speciality of psychoanalysis', in *Problems of Psychoanalytic Technique and Therapy 1966–1970*. Vol. 7. of *Writings*. London: Hogarth Press and Institute of Psycho-Analysis, 1972, pp. 204–19.

Freud, A. (1970b) 'The infantile neurosis: Genetic and dynamic considerations', in *Problems of Psychoanalytic Technique and Therapy 1966–1970*. London: Hogarth Press and Institute of Psycho-Analysis, 1972, pp. 189–203.

Freud, A. (1976) 'L'identité du psychanalyste', *Monographie de l'API*. Paris: PUF, 1979, pp. 267–72.

Freud, A. and Bergmann Th. (1965) *Les enfants malades*.

Freud, A. and Burlingham, D. (1942) *Young Children in Wartime*. London: George Allen & Unwin.

Freud, A. and Burlingham, D. (1944) *Infants Without Families*. New York: International Universities Press.

Freud, S. Major writings can be found in *The Standard Edition of the Complete Psychological Works of Sigmund Freud*, ed. J. Strachey, 24 vols. London: Hogarth Press, 1953–66. (All references to this work are in the form '*S.E.*' 17, etc.)

Freud, S. (1893) 'Zur Kenntnis der cerebralen Diplegien des Kinderalters', *Beiträge zur Kinderheilkunde*, 3.

Freud, S. (1900) *The Interpretation of Dreams*, *S.E.* 4–5.

Freud, S. (1905) *Three Essays on The Theory of Sexuality*, *S.E.* 7, pp. 125–245.

Freud, S. (1907) 'The sexual enlightenment of children', *S.E.* 9, pp. 129–39.

Freud, S. (1909) *Analysis of a Phobia in a Five-Year-Old Boy*. (Little Hans!) *S.E.* 10, pp. 3–149.

Freud, S. (1910) [1909] *Five Lectures on Psycho-Analysis*, *S.E.* 11, pp. 3–56.

Freud, S. (1912) *Totem and Taboo*, *S.E.* 13, pp. ix–162.

Freud, S. (1913a) 'On beginning the treatment (further recommendations on the technique of psycho-analysis)' *S.E.* 12, pp. 121–44.

Freud, S. (1913b) 'The theme of the three caskets', *S.E.* 12, pp. 289–301.

Freud, S. (1914a) *On the History of the Psycho-Analytic Movement*, *S.E.* 14, pp. 3–66.

Freud, S. (1914b) 'On narcissism: An introduction', *S.E.* 14, pp. 67–102.

Freud, S. (1915) 'Instincts and their vicissitudes', *S.E.* 14, pp. 109–40.

Freud, S. (1918) [1914] *From The History of an Infantile Neurosis* ('The Wolf Man'), *S.E.* 17, pp. 3–123.

Freud, S. (1919a) [1918] 'Lines of advance in psycho-analytic therapy, *S.E.* 17, pp. 157–68.

Freud, S. (1919b) 'A child is being beaten: A contribution to the study of the origin of sexual perversions', *S.E.* 17, pp. 175–204.

Freud, S. (1919c) [1915] 'Letter to Dr Hermine von Hug-Hellmuth, *S.E.* 14, p. 341.

Freud, S. (1919d) 'The uncanny', *S.E.* 17, pp. 217–56.

Freud, S. (1920) *Beyond the Pleasure Principle*, *S.E.* 18, pp. 3–64.

Freud, S. (1921) *Group Psychology and the Analysis of the Ego*, *S.E.* 18, pp. 67–143.

Freud, S. (1923) *The Ego and the Id*, *S.E.* 19, pp. 3–66.

Freud, S. (1924) 'The economic problem of masochism, *S.E.* 19, pp. 157–70.

Freud, S. (1925a) [1924] *An Autobiographical Study*, *S.E.* 20, pp. 3–74.

Freud, S. (1925b) [1924] 'The resistances to psycho-analysis', *S.E.* 19, pp. 213–24.

Freud, S. (1925c) 'Negation', *S.E.* 19, pp. 235–9.

Freud, S. (1925d) 'Preface to Aichhorn's *Wayward Youth*', *S.E.* 19, pp. 271–5.

Freud, S. (1926a) *The Question of Lay Analysis*, *S.E.* 20, pp. 179–258.

Freud, S. (1926b) *Inhibitions, Symptoms and Anxiety*, *S.E.* 20, pp. 77–175.

Freud, S. (1930) [1929] *Civilization and its Discontents*, *S.E.* 21, pp. 59–145.

Freud, S. (1933) [1932] *New Introductory Lectures on Psycho-Analysis*, *S.E.* 22, pp. 3–182.

Freud, S. (1937) 'Analysis terminable and interminable', *S.E.* 23, pp. 209–25.

Freud, S. (1960) *Correspondence 1873–1939.* Paris: Gallimard, 1966 and 1979.

Freud, S. and Abraham, K. (1965) *A Psycho-Analytic Dialogue: The Letters of Sigmund Freud and Karl Abraham, 1907–1926,* ed. Hilda Abraham and Ernst L. Freud. London: Hogarth Press and The Institute of Psycho-Analysis.

Freud, S. and Andreas-Salome, Lou (1972) *Letters,* ed. Ernst Pfeiffer. New York: Harcourt Brace Jovanovich.

Freud, S. and Ferenczi, S. (1993) *The Correspondence of Sigmund Freud and Sándor Ferenczi,* ed. E. Brabant *et al.,* trans. P. T. Haffer. Cambridge, MA: Harvard University Press.

Freud, S. and Jones, E. (1993) *The Complete Correspondence of Sigmund Freud and Ernest Jones 1908–1939,* ed. R. A. Paskauskas. Cambridge, MA: Harvard University Press.

Freud, S. and Jung, C. G. (1974) *The Freud/Jung Letters,* ed. W. McGuire, trans. R. Manheim and R. F. C. Hull. London: Hogarth Press and Routledge & Kegan Paul.

Freud, S. and Rie, O. (1891) 'Klinische Studie über die halbseitige Cerebrallähmung der Kinder', *Beiträge zur Kinderheilkunde,* 3.

Furman, E. (1986) 'Pratique de la psychanalyse des enfants aux Etats-Unis', *Journal de la psychanalyse de l'enfant,* 3: 66–85.

Furman, E. (1988) 'L'expérience du travail avec les enfants atypiques', *Journal de la psychanalyse de l'enfant,* 5: 14–32.

Furman, R. E. (1993) 'Obituary: Anny Katan', *International Journal of Psychoanalysis,* 74: 834.

Gammill, J. (1985) 'Quelques souvenirs personnels sur Melanie Klein', in '*Mélanie Klein Aujourd'hui*'. Lyon: Cesura, pp. 37–54.

Gateaux-Mennecier, J. (1989) *Bourneville et l'Enfance Aliénée.* Paris: Centurion.

Geissmann, C. (1987) 'Transfert ou névrose de transfert. La controverse Anna Freud/Mélanie Klein', *Journal de la psychanalyse de l'enfant,* 4.

Geissmann, C. and Geissmann, P. (1984) *L'enfant et sa psychose.* Paris: Dunod.

Geissmann, P., Geissmann, C. and Stourm, C. (1991) 'Situation des parents dans l'hospitalisation à domicile des enfants', *Neuropsychologie. de l'enfance,* 39 (11–12): 563–66.

Geissmann, C. *et al.* (1993) 'A propos d'une forme de traitement précoce de l'autisme et des psychoses infantiles: l'hospitalisation à domicile', in *Hommage à Frances Tustin.* St-Andre de Cruzières: Audit Editions.

Gero-Brabant, E. (1986) 'Introduction à l'ouvrage du Dr Istvan Hollos: "*Mes adieux à la maison jaune*"', in *Coq-Héron,* 100.

Gide, A. (1925) *Les faux monnayeurs.* Paris: Gallimard.

Glenn, J. (1987) 'Supervision of child psychoanalyses', *The Psychoanalytic Study of the Child,* 42: 575–96.

Goldstein, J., Freud, A. and Solnit, T. (1973) *Beyond the Best Interests of the Child.* New York: Free Press.

Goldstein, J., Freud, A., and Solnit, T. (1979) *Before the Best Interests of the Child*. New York: Free Press.

Graf, H. (1972) *Memoirs of an Invisible Man*. Opera News: New York.

Graf-Nold, A. (1980) *Hermine Von Hug-Hellmuth. Werte und Leben der ersten Kinderpsychoanalytikerin*. Zurich: Unveröffenlichte lizentiatsarbeit.

Graf-Nold, A. (1988) 'Der Fall Hermine Hug-Hellmuth München-Wien', *Verlag International Psychoanalyse.*

Green, A. (1977) 'La royauté appartient à l'enfant', *Revue L'Arc*, 69.

Green, A. (1984) 'Winnicott et le modèle du cadre', in *Le Paradoxe de Winnicott*. Paris: Payot.

Green, A. (1991) 'Lettre ouverte à W. R. Bion', in *W. R. Bion une théorie pour l'avenir*, pp. 15–21. Paris: Metailié.

Greenacre, P. (1941) 'The predisposition to anxiety, Part 1, *Psychoanalytic Quarterly*, 10: 66–94.

Greenacre, P. (1952) *Trauma, Growth and Personality*. New York: International Universities Press.

Greenacre, P. (1960) 'Considerations regarding the parent–infant relationship', *International Journal of Psycho-Analysis*, 41: 571–84.

Gribinski, M. (1971) 'La médecine et la psychiatrie', *La Nef* 42: 117–32.

Grosskurth, P. (1986) *Melanie Klein: Her World and Her Work*. New York: Alfred A. Knopf.

Guignard, F. (1985) 'L'évolution de la technique en analyse d'enfants', *Melanie Klein aujourd'hui* (sous la direction de J. Gammill), Lyon, C.L.E., pp. 55–6.

Hall, S. (1914) 'A synthetic genetic study of fear', *American Journal of Psychology*, 25: 321–92.

Harris, M. and Bick, E. (1987) *Collected Papers of Martha Harris and Esther Bick*, ed. Meg Harris Williams. Perthshire: Clunie Press.

Heimann, P. (1942) 'A contribution to the problem of sublimation and its relation to processes of internalization', *International Journal of Psycho-Analysis*, 23: 8–17.

Heimann, P. (1950) 'On countertransference', *International Journal of Psycho-Analysis*, 31: 81–94.

Heller, P. (1990) *A Child Analysis with Anna Freud*. Madison, WI: International Universities Press.

Hellman, I. (1990) *From War Babies to Grandmothers*. London: Karnac Books.

Heuyer, G. (1952) *Introduction à la psychiatrie infantile*. Paris: PUF.

Houzel, D. and Catoire, G. (1986) 'La psychanalyse des enfants', *Psychiatric*, 37812 A 10, pp. 1–12, Paris, Enc. Med. Chir.

Huber, W. (1980) 'La première psychanalyse d'enfants', in *Psychoanalyse als Herausforderung* Festschrift Caruso. Ed. Ass. des Soc. Scientifiques d'Autriche; and in Boix, M. (1990), *La vie et l'oeuvre de Hermine von Hug-Hellmuth*, pp. 69–85.

Hug-Hellmuth, H. (1912a) 'Analyse eines Traumes eines Fünfeinhalbjährigen', *Zentralblatt für Psychoanalyse und Psychotherapie*, 2(3): 122–7 (transl. George MacLean); and in *Psychiatric Journal, University of Ottawa*, 11/1 (1986): 1–5.

Hug-Hellmuth, H. (1912b) 'Beiträge zum Kapital "Verschreiben" und "Verlesen"', *Zentralblatt für Psychoanalyse und Psychotherapie*, 2(2): 227–80.

Hug-Hellmuth, H. (1912c) '"Verprechen" eines kleinen Schuljungen', *Zentralblatt für Psychoanalyse und Psychotherapie*, 2(10–11): 603–4.

Hug-Hellmuth, H. (1912d) 'Das Kind und seine Vorstellung vom Tode', *Imago*, 1(3): 286–98 (transl. Anton Kris in *Psychoanalytic Quarterly*, 34 (1965): 499–516).

Hug-Hellmuth, H. (1912e) 'Über Farbenhören: Ein Versuch das Phänomen auf Grund der psycho-analytischen Methode zu erklären', *Imago*, 1(3): 228–64.

Hug-Hellmuth, H. (1913a) 'Vom Wesen der Kinderseele', *Sexual-probleme*, 9: 433–43.

Hug-Hellmuth, H. (1913b) *Aus dem Seeleneben des Kindes. Eine psychoanalytische Studie*, ed. S. Freud. Leipzig and Vienna. (English trans. J. Putnam and M. Stevens, 1913.)

Hug-Hellmuth, H. (1914a) 'Kinderbriefe', *Imago*, 3(5): 462–76.

Hug-Hellmuth, H. (1914b) 'Kinderpsychologie, Pädadogik', *Jahrbuch für Psycho-analytische und psychopathologische Forschungen*, 6: 393–404.

Hug-Hellmuth, H. (1919) *Journal d'une petite fille*. Fr. transl., 1928, Paris: Gallimard; 1975 et 1988, Paris: Denoël.

Hug-Hellmuth, H. (1921) 'A propos de la technique de l'analyse des enfants. *Int. Zeitschrift für Psychoanal*, 7: 179–97. Fr. transl. in *Psychiatrie de l'enfant*, 1975, 18(1): 191–210.

Hug-Hellmuth, H. (1924) *Neue Wege zum Verständnis der Jugend*. Leipzig and Vienna: Franz Deuticke.

Hug-Hellmuth, H. (1991) *Essais Psychanalytiques*. Paris: Payot.

Isaacs, S. (1943) 'The nature and function of phantasy', in King and Steiner, eds. 1991, pp. 264–321. Also in Melanie Klein *et al.* (1952) *Developments in Psycho-Analysis*. London: Hogarth Press and The Institute of Psycho-Analysis, pp. 67–121.

Jaccard, R. (1982a) 'La psychanalyse aux Etats-Unis', in *Histoire de la psychanalyse*, R. Jaccard. Paris: Hachette, pp. 271–95.

Jaccard, R. (1982b) *Histoire de la psychanalyse*. Paris: Hachette (2 vols.).

Jaques, E. (1955) Social systems as a defence against persecutory and depressive anxiety, in M. Klein, P. Heimann and R. E. Money-Kyrle (eds.) *New Directions in Psycho-Analysis*. London: Tavistock, pp. 478–98, 1955.

Jaques, E. (1963) 'Death and the mid-life crisis', *International Journal of Psycho-Analysis*, 46: 502–14.

Jones, E. (1935) 'Early female sexuality', *International Journal of Psycho-Analysis*, 16: 263–73.

Jones, E. (1953, 1955, 1957) *Sigmund Freud: Life and Work*, vol. 1 1953, vol. 2 1955, vol. 3 1957. London: Hogarth Press.

Joseph, B. (1989) *Psychic Equilibrium and Psychic Change*, edited by M. Feldman and E. Bott Spilius. London: Routledge.

Joseph, B. (1990) (Unpublished Report:) 'The treatment alliance and the transference', weekend Conference for English-Speaking Members of European Societies, 12–14 October 1990.

Jung, C. G. (1910) 'Conflicts of the infantile mind', *Jahrbuch*, II: 1.

Jung, C. G. (1912) 'Uber Psychoanalyse beim Kinde', *G. W.* 4, pp. 231ff.

Kestemberg, E. and Lebovici, S. (1975) 'Réflexions sur le devenir de la psychanalyse', *Revue français de psychanalyse*, 39(1–2).

Kestemberg, E., Kestemberg, J. and Decobert, S. (1972) *La faim et le corps*. Paris: PUF.

King, P. and Steiner, R. (eds.) (1991) *The Freud-Klein Controversies, 1941–1945*. London: Tavistock/Routledge.

Klein, M. Major writings can be found in *The Writings of Melanie Klein*, 4 vols.: vol. 1, *Love, Guilt and Reparation and other Works, 1921–1945*; vol. 2, *The Psycho-Analysis of Children*; vol. 3, *Envy and Gratitude and Other Works, 1946–1963*; vol. 4, *Narrative of a Child Analysis*. London: Hogarth Press and the Institute of Psycho-Analysis, 1975; and New York: Free Press, 1984.

Klein, M. (1921) 'The development of a child', in *Writings*, vol. 1, pp. 1–53.

Klein, M. (1926) 'The psychological principles of early analysis', in *Writings*, vol. 1, pp. 128–38.

Klein, M. (1927) 'Symposium on child analysis', in *Writings*, vol. 1, pp. 139–69.

Klein, M. (1928) 'Early stages of the Oedipus conflict', in *Writings*, vol. 1, pp. 186–98.

Klein, M. (1930a) 'The importance of symbol-formation in the development of the ego', in *Writings*, vol. 1, pp. 219–32.

Klein, M. (1930b) 'The psychotherapy of the psychoses', in *Writings*, vol. 1, pp. 233–5.

Klein, M. (1931) 'A contribution to the theory of intellectual inhibition', in *Writings*, vol. 1, pp. 236–47.

Klein, M. (1932) *The Psycho-Analysis of Children*, *Writings*, vol. 2.

Klein, M. (1933) 'The early development of conscience in the child', in *Writings*, vol. 1, pp. 248–57.

Klein, M. (1935) 'A contribution to the psychogenesis of manic–depressive states', in *Writings*, vol. 1, pp. 262–89.

Klein, M. (1940) 'Mourning and its relation to manic–depressive states', in *Writings*, vol. 1, pp. 344–69.

Klein, M. (1945) 'The Oedipus complex in the light of early anxieties', in *Writings*, vol. 1, pp. 370–419.

Klein, M. (1946) 'Notes on some schizoid mechanisms', in *Writings*, vol. 3, pp. 1–24.

Klein, M. (1948a) *Contributions to Psycho-Analysis 1921–1945*. London: Hogarth Press and the Institute of Psycho-Analysis.

Klein, M. (1948b) 'On the theory of anxiety and guilt', in *Writings*, vol. 3, pp. 25–42.

Klein, M. (1952a) 'The origins of transference', in *Writings*, vol. 3, pp. 48–56.

Klein, M. (1952b) 'Some theoretical conclusions regarding the emotional life of the infant', in *Writings*, vol. 3, pp. 61–93.

Klein, M. (1952c) 'On observing the behaviour of young infants', in *Writings*, vol. 3, pp. 94–121.

Klein, M. (1952d) 'The mutual influences in the development of ego and id', in *Writings*, vol. 3, pp. 55–60.

Klein, M. (1955a) 'The psycho-analytic play technique: Its history and significance', in *Writings,* vol. 3, pp. 122–40.

Klein, M. (1955b) 'On identification', in *Writings*, vol. 3, pp. 141–75. Also in Klein *et al.* (1952) *New Directions in Psycho-Analysis*, pp. 309–45.

Klein, M. (1957) 'Envy and gratitude', in *Writings*, vol. 3, pp. 176–235.

Klein, M. (1958) 'On the development of mental functioning', in *Writings*, vol. 3, pp. 236–46.

Klein, M. (1959a) 'Our adult world and its roots in infancy', in *Writings*, vol. 3, pp. 247–63.

Klein, M. (1959b) Unpublished autobiography, cited by D. Anzieu in 'Jeunesse de Melanie Klein' (1985).

Klein, M. (1960) 'A note on depression in the schizophrenic', in *Writings*, vol. 3, pp. 264–7.

Klein, M. (1961) *Narrative of a Child Analysis*, in *Writings*, vol. 4.

Klein, M. (1963) 'On the sense of loneliness', in *Writings*, vol. 3, pp. 300–13.

Klein, M. and Rivière, J. (1937) *Love, Hate and Reparation*. London: Hogarth Press.

Klein, M., Heimann, P., Isaacs, S. and Rivière, J. (1952) *Developments in Psycho-Analysis*. London: Hogarth Press and the Institute of Psycho-Analysis.

Klein, M., Heimann, P. and Money-Kyrle, R. E. (eds.) (1955) *New Directions in Psycho-Analysis*. London: Tavistock.

Kris, E. (1958) 'The recovery of childhood memories in psychoanalysis', *Psycho-Analytic Study of the Child*, 11: 54–88.

Laforgue, R. (1926) 'Schizophrenie, Schizomanie und Schizonoïa', *Zeitschrift fün die gesamonte Neurologie und Psychiatrie.*

Lang, J. L. (1965) *Commentaires techniques sur 'Analyse d'un enfant phobique'* de Berta Bornstein. Document de travail de l'APF.

Lang, J. L. (1970) 'La psychanalyse des Enfants', report to the APF, *Documents et Débats*, 1: 87–111.

Lang, J. L. (1983) 'Le modèle kleinien en psychopathologie infantile: aujourd'hui en France', *Psychanalyse à l'université* 8(32): 511–57.

Laplanche, J. (1981) 'Faut-il brûler Mélanie Klein?' *Psychanalyse à l'université*, 8(32), September, 83.

Laplanche, J. and Pontalis, J. B. (1973) *The Language of Psycho-Analysis*. London: Hogarth Press and the Institute of Psycho-Analysis.

Laurent, E., Pommier, G., Porge, E. (1978) 'Les psychanalystes chez les enfants', *Ornicar*, 16: 120–8.

Lebovici, S. (1950a) 'Une introduction à l'étude exhaustive du transfert analytique chez l'enfant', *Revue français de psychanalyse*, 16(1): 116–18.

Lebovici, S. (1950b) 'A propos du diagnostic de la névrose infantile', *Revue française de psychanalyse*, 14(4): 581–95.

Lebovici, S. (1961) *Les tics chez l'enfant*. Paris: PUF.

Lebovici, S. (1971) *Les sentiments de culpabilité chez l'enfant et chez l'adulte*. Paris: Hachette.

Lebovici, S. (1979) 'L'expérience de psychanalyste chez l'enfant et chez l'adulte devant le modèle de la névrose infantile et de la névrose de transfert', *Revue français de psychanalyse*, 44, 1980: 5–6.

Lebovici, S. (1983) *Le nourrisson, la mère et le psychanalyste. Les interventions précoces*. Paris: Centurion.

Lebovici, S. (1984a) 'La psychiatrie de l'enfant et la communauté in Anthony et Chiland', in *Prévention en Psychiatrie de l'enfant en un temps de transition*. Paris: PUF, pp. 359–76.

Lebovici, S. (1984b) 'L'oeuvre d'Anna Freud', *Psychiatrie de l'enfant*, 27(1): 5–34.

Lebovici, S. and Diatkine, R. (1957) 'Les obsessions chez l'enfant', *Revue français de psychanalyse*, 21(5): 647–83.

Lebovici, S. and Diatkine, R. (1962) 'Fonction et signification du jeu chez l'enfant', *Psychiatrie de l'enfant*, 5(1): 207–53.

Lebovici, S. and MacDougall, J. (1960) *Un cas de psychose infantile*. Paris: PUF.

Lebovici, S. and Nacht, S. (1955) 'Indications et contre-indications de la psychanalyse', *Revue français de psychanalyse*, 19(1–2): 135–88.

Lebovici, S. and Soulè, M. (1970) *La connaissance de l'enfant par la psychanalyse*. Paris: PUF.

Lebovici, S., Diatkine, R. and Kestemberg, E. (1958) 'Bilan de 10 ans de pratique psychodramatique chez l'enfant et l'adolescent', *Psychiatrie de l'enfant*, 1(1): 63–79.

Lefort, R. (1971) 'La parole et la mort', *La Nef* 42(1): 3–116.

Lieberman, E. J. (1985) *Acts of Will: The Life and Work of Otto Rank*. New York: The Free Press.

Losserand, J. (1991) 'La psychanalyse d'enfant: Le début en France, S. Morgenstern', *Le Coq Héron*, 119.

Luquet, P. (1989) 'De la représentation à l'élaboration des fantasmes', in *Avancées Métapsychologiques: L'enfant et la famille*. Paris: Apsygée, 1991, pp. 13–23.

MacLean, G. and Rappen, U. (1991) *Hermine Hug-Hellmuth: Her Life and Work*. New York/London: Routledge.

Mahler (Schoenberger), M. (1940) 'Pseudo-imbecility', *Psychoanalytic Quarterly*, 11, 1942: 149–64.

Mahler, M. (1968) *On Human Symbiosis and the Vicissitudes of Individuation*. New York: International Universities Press.

Mahler, M. (1978) 'Epilogue', in *Yearbook of the International Association for Child Psychiatry*, ed. E. J. Anthony, C. Chiland and C. Koupernik. New York: J. Wiley.

Mahler, M., Pine, F. and Bergman, A. (1975) *The Psychological Birth of the Human Infant. Symbiosis and Individuation.* New York: Basic Books.

Male, P. (1964) *Psychothérapie de l'adolescent.* Paris: PUF.

Mannoni, M. (1970) *Le psychiatre, son fou, et la psychanalyse.* Paris: Le Seuil.

Marton, F. (1990) 'Le travail actuel au Centre Anna Freud', in C. Chiland and J. G. Young (eds.) *Nouvelles approches de la santé mentale.* Paris: PUF, pp. 236–51.

Mauco, G. (1932) *Les étrangers en France et leur adaptation.* Paris: Colin.

Mauco, G. (1936) 'La Psychologie de l'enfant dans ses rapports avec l'inconscient', *Revue française de psychanalyse,* 9(3): 430–517, end 9(4): 658–710.

Mauco, G. (1967) *Psychanalyse et éducation.* Paris: Aubier-Monaigne.

Mauco, G. (1975) 'René Spitz', *Revue Française de Psychanalyse,* 39(3): 548–9.

Meltzer, D. (1967) *The Psycho-Analytical Process.* London: Heinemann.

Meltzer, D. (1973) *Sexual States of Mind.* Perthshire: Clunie Press.

Meltzer, D. (1978) *The Kleinian Development.* Perthshire: Clunie Press.

Meltzer, D. *et al.* (1975) *Explorations in Autism.* Perthshire: Clunie Press.

Menzies-Lyth, I. (1988) *Containing Anxieties in Institutions.* London: Free Association Books.

Menzies-Lyth, I. (1989) *The Dynamic of the Social.* London: Free Association Books.

de Mijolla, A. (1982) 'La Psychanalyse en France (1935–1965)' in *Histoire de la psychanalyse,* sous la direction de R. Jaccard. Paris: Hachette.

Mises, R. (1975) *L'enfant déficient mental.* Paris: PUF.

Mises, R. (1980) *La cure en institution.* Paris: ESF.

Mises, R. (1990) *Les pathologies limites de l'enfance.* Paris: PUF.

Mises, R. and Barande, I. (1963) 'Les états dysharmoniques graves', *Psychiatrie de l'enfant,* 6(1): 1–78.

Money-Kyrle, R. E. (1951) *Psychoanalysis and Politics.* London: Duckworth.

Money-Kyrle, R. (1956) 'Normal countertransference and some of its deviations', in *Collected Papers.*

Money-Kyrle, R. E. (1978) *Collected Papers of Roger Money-Kyrle,* ed. D. Meltzer with the assistance of E. O'Shaughnessy. Perthshire: Clunie Press.

Moreau-Ricaud, M. (1990) 'La création de l'Ecole de Budapest', *Revue International d'histoire de la psychanalyse,* 3: 419–37.

Morgenstern, S. (1927) 'Un cas de mutisme psychogène', *Revue français psychanalyse,* 1(3): 492–504, +18 planches. (Repr. in *Journal de la Psychanalyse de l'Enfant* 1990, 8: 211–43.)

Morgenstern, S. (1928) 'La psychanalyse infantile', *L'hygiène mentale,* 6: 158–69.

Morgenstern, S. (1930) 'La Psychanalyse infantile et son rôle dans l'hygiène mentale', *Revue française de psychanalyse,* 4(1): 136–62.

Morgenstern, S. (1931) 'Conception psychanalytique de la dépersonnalisation', *L'Evolution psychiatrique,* 2è Série, 2: 83–102.

Morgenstern, S. (1932) 'Psychanalyse et éducation', *L'Évolution psychiatrique,* tome III, fasc. III, pp. 45–64. (Conférence faite au 'Groupe d'Etudes Philosophiques et Scientifiques', Sorbonne, 18 June 1932).

Morgenstern, S. (1933) 'Quelques aperçus sur l'expression du sentiment de culpabilité dans les rêves des enfants', *Revue française de psychanalyse*, 4(2): 155–74.

Morgenstern, S. (1934a) 'Les bourreaux domestiques,' *L'Évolution psychiatrique,* fasc. III, pp. 39–58.

Morgenstern, S. (1934b) 'La pensée magique chez l'enfant', *Revue française de Psychanalyse*, 7(1): 98–115.

Morgenstern, S. (1937a) *Psychanalyse infantile (Symbolisme et valeur clinique des créations imaginatives chez l'enfant)*. Paris: Denoël.

Morgenstern, S. (1937b) 'Contribution au problème de l'hystérie chez l'enfant', *L'Evolution psychiatrique*, fasc. II, pp. 3–33.

Morgenstern, S. (1938) 'La structure de la personnalité et ses déviations', *Revue française de psychanalyse*, 19(4): 591–667.

Morgenstern, S. (1939) 'Le symbolisme et la valeur psychanalytique des dessins infantiles', *Revue française de psychanalyse*, 10(1): 39–48.

Neyraut, M. (1974) 'Préface' to *Journal d'une petite fille*. Paris: Denoël, 1988.

Nin, A. (1967) *Journal 1934–1939*. New York.

Parcheminey, G. (1947) 'Sophie Morgenstern', *L'Evolution psychiatrique,* 1: 12–13.

Paumelle, P. (1966) *L'organisation du travail d'équipe dans le XIIIè Arrondissement de Paris*. Fascicule édité par l'ASM XIIIè.

Peters U. H. (1979) *Anna Freud*. London: Weidenfeld and Nicolson.

Petot, J. M. (1979 and 1982) *Mélanie Klein*, 2 vols., trans, Christine Trollope. Madison CT: International Universities Press, 1990 and 1991.

Pfeiffer, S. (1919) 'Ausserungen der infantil–erotischer Triebe in Spiele', *Imago*, 5: 243–82.

Pfister, O. (1913) *Die Psycho-analystische Methode,* Leipzig et Berlin Klinkhardt.

Pfister, O. (1914) 'Zur Ehrenrettung des Psychoanalyse', *Zeitschrift für Jugenderziehung und Jugendfürsorge*, 5(11): 305–12.

Pichon, E. (1934) 'Eugénie Sokolnicka', *Revue française de psychanalyse*, 7(4): 590–603.

Pichon, E. (1936) *Le développement psychique de l'enfant et de l'adolescent*. Paris: Masson.

Pichon, E. and Parcheminey, G. (1928) 'Sur les traitements psychothérapiques courts d'inspiration freudienne chez les enfants', *Revue française de psychanalyse,* 2(4): 711–20.

Pommier, G. (1978) *Les psychanalystes chez les enfants*. Paris: Ornicar.

Pontalis, J. B. (1977) *Entre le rêve et la douleur*. NRF, Paris: Gallimard.

Racamier, P. C. (1970) *Le psychanalyste sans divan*. Paris: Payot.

Rambert, M. L. (1938) 'Une nouvelle technique en psychanalyse infantile: le jeu de guignols', *Revue française de psychanalyse*, 14(4): 581–95.

Rangell, L. (1983) 'The Anna Freud Experience', in *Psychoanalytic Study of the Child*, 39, 1984: 29–43.

Rank, O. (1922) *The Don Juan Legend*, trans. and ed.. David G. Winter. Princeton NJ: Princeton University Press.

Rank, O. (1924a) *The Trauma of Birth*. London, 1929.

Rank, O. (1924b) 'Zur Rolle der Frau in der Entwicklung der menschlichen', *Imago*, 10.

Rayner, E. (1991) *The Independent Mind in British Psychoanalysis*. London: Free Association Books.

Regis, E. and Hesnard, A. (1914) *La psychanalyse des névroses et des psychoses: ses applications médicales et extramédicales*. Paris: Ed. Alcan, 1929.

Rimband, A. (1872) *Voyelles*, in *Oeuvres Complètes*. Paris: Gallimard, p.53.

Rivière, J. (1936) 'The genesis of psychical conflict in earliest infancy', *International Journal of Psychoanalysis*, 17: 395–422. Also in *The Inner World and Joan Rivière*.

Rivière, J. (1991) *The Inner World and Joan Rivière: Collected Papers 1920–1958*, ed. A. Hughes. London: Karnac Books.

Roazen, P. (1975) *Freud and his Followers*. New York: Knopf.

Roazen, P. (1990) 'Tola Rank', *Revue internationale d'histoire de la psychanalyse*, 3: 439–55.

Rodrigué, E. (1955) 'The analysis of a three-year old mute schizophrenic', in Klein *et al. New Directions in Psycho-Analysis*, pp. 140–79.

Ronvaux, M. (1986) 'André Gide et Sokolnicka', *Ornicar*, 37.

Rosolato, G. (1979) 'L'analyse des résistances', *Nouvelle revue de psychanalyse*, 20: 183–215.

Rosenfeld, H. A. (1955) 'Notes on the psycho-analysis of the super-ego conflict in an acute schizophrenic patient', in Klein *et al.*, *New Directions in Psycho-Analysis*, pp. 180–219.

Rosenfeld, H. A. (1965) *Psychotic States*. London: Hogarth Press and the Institute of Psycho-Analysis.

Rosenfeld, H. A. (1987) *Impasse and Interpretation*. London: Tavistock.

Rossolato, G. (1979) 'L'analyse des résistances', *Nouvelle Revue de Psychanalyse*, 20: 183–215.

Roudinesco, E. (1986) *Histoire de la psychanalyse en France*. T. I et II. Paris: Le Seuil.

Rousillon, R. (1977) 'Paradoxe et continuité chez Winnicott: la défense paradoxale', *Bulletin de Psychologie*, 34(350): 503–9.

Rousillon, R. (1978) *Du paradoxe incontestable au paradoxe contenu*. Thèse de 3è Cycle, University of Lyon II.

Sandler, A. M. (1990) Report on 'The treatment alliance and the transference', Weekend Conference for English-speaking Members of European Societies, 12–14 October 1990.

Sandler, J. (1962) 'The Hampstead Index as an instrument of psychoanalytic research', *International Journal of Psychoanalysis*, 43: 287–91.

Sandler, J. (1988) *Projection, Identification, Projective Identification*. London: Karnac Books.

Sandler, J. and Bolland, J. (1965) *The Hampstead Psychoanalytical Index: A Study of the Psychoanalytic Case Material of a Two-Year-Old Child*. New York: International Universities Press.

Sandler, J. with Freud, A. (1985) *The Analysis of defence: The Ego and the Mechanisms of Defence Revisited.* Madison, WI: International Universities Press.

Sandler, J. Kennedy, H. and Tyson, R. L. (1980) *The Technique of Child Psychoanalysis: Discussions with Anna Freud.* Cambridge, MA: Harvard University Press.

Schilder, P. (1935) *L'image du corps.* Paris: Gallimard 1968.

Segal, H. (1964) *Introduction to the Work of Melanie Klein.* London: W. Heinemann.

Segal, H. (1971) 'The role of child analysis in the general training of the analyst, Symposium de Genève sur la Psychanalyse de l'enfant', in *Psychiatrie de l'enfant,* 14(1) 1971, Paris: PUF.

Segal, H. (1979) *Klein.* New York: The Viking Press.

Segal, H. (1981) *The Work of Hanna Segal.* New York/London: Jason Aronson.

Segal, H. (1991) *Dream, Phantasy and Art.* London: Routledge.

Smirnoff, V. (1966) *La psychanalyse de l'enfant.* Paris: PUF.

Smirnoff, V. (1971) 'D. W. Winnicott', in *Nouvelle Revue de Psychanalyse,* 3, *Lieux du corps.* Paris: Gallimard, pp. 49–51.

Smirnoff, V. (1979) 'De Vienne à Paris', *Nouvelle Revue de Psychanalyse,* 20: 13–58.

Sokolnicka, E. (1916) *Kurz Elementary – Zoologi – Botaniki – Mineralogji.* Warsaw.

Sokolnicka, E. (1920) L'analyse d'un cas de névrose obsessionnelle. *International Zeitschrift für Psychoanalyse,* 6, Fr. transl. in *Revue de Neuro-Psychiatrie et d'hygiène mentale de l'enfance,* 16: 477–87.

Sokolnicka, E. (1932) 'Un cas de guérison rapide', *Revue française de psychanalyse.*

Soubrénie, D. (1991) *Hermine von Hug-Hellmuth: Essais psychanalytiques.* Paris: Payot.

Spillius, E. Bott (1988) *Melanie Klein Today,* vols. I and II. London: Routledge.

Spitz, R. A. (1956) 'Countertransference: Comments on its varying roles in the analytic situation', *Journal of the American Psychoanalytic Association,* 4: 256–65.

Spitz, R. A. (1957) *No and Yes: On the Genesis of Human Communication.* New York: International Universities Press.

Spitz, R. A. (1965a) *The First Year of Life: A Psychoanalytic Study of Normal and Deviant Development of Object Relations.* New York: International Universities Press.

Spitz, R. A. (1965b) *De la naissance à la parole.* Fr. transl. Paris: PUF, 1968.

Spitz, R. A. (1966) 'Implications métapsychologiques de mes rechechers sur le données du développement infantile', *Revue française de psychanalyse.*

Steiner, R. (1990) Rapport au Congrès, 'Histoire de la Psychanalyse', London.

Stern, W. (1913–14) 'Die Anwendung der Psychoanalyse auf. Kindheit und Jugend. Ein Protest mit einem Anhang v. W. v. C. Stern: Kritik einer Freudschen Kinder-Psychoanalyse', *Zeitschrift für angewandte Psychologie,* 8 (1913–14): 71–101.

Strachey, J. and Strachey, A. (1985) *Bloomsbury/Freud: The Letters of James and Alix Strachey 1924–1925,* ed. by Perry Meisel and Walter Kendrick. London: Chatto & Windus.

Thurnauer-Barbey, L. (1989) 'Propos sur le destin dramatique d'Hermine Hug-Hellmuth, premiére psychanalyste d'enfants', *Journal de la psychanalyse de l'enfant*, 7: 286–306.

Tustin, F. (1972) *Autism and Childhood Psychosis*. London: The Hogarth Press.

Tustin, F. (1981) *Autistic States in Children*. London: Routledge & Kegan Paul.

Tustin, F. (1986) *Autistic Barriers in Neurotic Patients*. London: Karnac Books.

Tustin, F. (1990) *The Protective Shell in Children and Adults*. London: Karnac Books.

Waelder, R. (1937) 'The problem of the genesis of psychical conflict in earliest infancy', *International Journal of Psycho-Analysis*, 18: 456–73.

Widlöcher, D. (1965a) Structure et changement. Document de travail de l'APF.

Widlöcher, D. (1965b) *L'interprétation des dessins d'enfants*. Brussels: Dessart.

Widlöcher, D. (1968) 'Commentaires de l'analyse d'un cas de névrose obsessionnelle infantile (Sokolnicka)', *Revue neuropsychiatrie et hygiène mental de l'enfant*, 16: 5–6.

Winnicott, C. (1977) 'Winnicott en personne', *Revue l'Arc*, 69, Aix en Provence.

Winnicott, D. W. (1958) *Through Paediatrics to Psycho-Analysés*. London: Tavistock.

Winnicott, D. W. (1965) *The Maturational Processes and the Facilitating Environment*. London: Hogarth Press and the Institute of Psycho-Analysis.

Winnicott, D. W. (1971a) *Playing and Reality*. London: Tavistock.

Winnicott, D. W. (1971b) *Therapeutic Consultations in Child Psychiatry*. London: Hogarth Press and the Institute of Psycho-Analysis..

Winnicott, D. W. (1974) 'Fear of breakdown', *International Review of Psycho-Analysis*, 1: 103–10.

Winnicott, D. W. (1978) *The Piggle*. London: Hogarth Press and the Institute of Psycho-Analysis.

Winnicott, D. W. (1986) *Holding and Interpretation*. London: Hogarth Press and the Institute of Psycho-Analysis.

Winnicott, D. W. (1987) *The Spontaneous Gesture: Selected Letters of D. W. Winnicott*, ed. F. R. Rodman. Cambridge MA: Harvard University Press.

Winnicott, D. W. (1989) *Psycho-Analytic Explorations*. London: Karnac Books.

Wolberg, L. R. (1954) *The Technique of Psychotherapy*. New York: Grune and Statton.

Young-Bruehl, E. (1988) *Anna Freud*. New York: Summit.

Interviews

Name Index

Aberastury, Arminda 187, 275–84
Abraham, Hilda 34–6, 174
Abraham, Karl 9, 24, 34–9, 45, 113, 118, 119, 126, 127, 161, 166, 181, 214, 252
Adler, Alfred 44, 47, 54
Aichhorn, August 66, 84, 86, 88, 89, 91–4, 106, 158, 260
Ajuriaguerra, Julian de 295
Alexander, Franz 252, 253, 266
Alfred Binet Centre 305–6
Amado, Georges 304
American Association of Child Psychoanalysis 201, 271
American Psychoanalytical Society 251, 270
Andreas-Salomé, Lou 45, 80, 83, 84, 85, 161
Anna Freud Clinic 250
Anthony, James 259–60, 262–3
Anzieu, Annie 311
Anzieu, Didier 12, 110, 114, 115, 118, 243, 302, 307
Arfouilloux, Jean-Claude 314

Baginski, Adolf 11
Balint, Alice 121, 260
Balint, Michael 174, 201, 219, 244, 246
Barande, Robert 290, 304
Barbey-Thurnauer, Loïse 40
Bauer, Otto 159
Baumgarten Institute 83–4, 90
Bégoin-Guignard, Florence 313
Bennett, Ivy 98

Berge, André 205, 292, 298, 299, 300
Bergeret, Jean 17, 21, 259
Berlin Psychoanalytical Society 125, 166
Bernard, Claude 298
Bernfeld, Siegfried 46, 48, 49, 66, 83, 84, 86, 88, 90, 106, 158
Bettelheim, Bruno 3, 263–9
Bick, Esther 27, 189, 208, 236, 238–40, 246–7, 313, 321
Bion, Wilfred Ruprecht 4, 65, 71n, 128, 146, 169, 179, 187, 208, 213, 243–4, 245, 247, 249, 307
Blander, Eugene 49
Bleuler, Eugen 24, 25, 30, 148
Bleuler, Manfred 30, 148–9
Bloomsbury Group 166
Blos, Peter 89, 165, 253
Boix, Marcel 40
Bolland, John 195, 196, 241
Bollas, Christopher 235–6
Bonaparte, Marie 140, 141, 171, 188, 193, 286, 287–8, 289–90
Bornstein, Berta 107, 201, 311
Boston Psychoanalytical Society 164
Bourget, Paul 138
Boutonier, Juliette 292, 298, 299, 300
Bowlby, John 246, 296
Breuer, Josef 12
Brill, Abraham A. 251
British Psycho-Analytical Society 75–6, 119, 127, 165–6, 167, 168, 169, 170, 173, 174, 175, 182, 189, 190, 200, 206, 207, 216, 219, 220, 221, 237, 312

343

Subject Index

abreaction 12, 23n
aggressiveness 155, 259; as defence 127;
  domestic tyrants 156; fixation of libido
  and 129; projection and 121, 129;
  towards analyst 127, *see also* destructive
  impulses
anal stage: phantasies at 128
annihilation: fear of 210, 211, 227
antipsychiatry movement 309–12
anxiety 124, 129, 131, 151, 210; birth
  and 258–9; conscious and unconscious
  127; death instinct and 212; depressive
  212; fixation of libido and 129;
  interrelationship between genital and
  pregenital stage 181; manifested in
  drawings 154; persecutory 129, 212;
  primitive 210; psychotic 129, 173,
  210; transference and 279, *see also*
  defence mechanisms
Argentina: child psychoanalysis in
  275–84
asexual libido 56
'atypical children' *see* psychosis
autism 126, 131, 247, 260–1; mothers
  and 131, 267–8; treatment of 245,
  248, 265, 268–9, *see also* psychosis
auto-eroticism 172, 178, 180, 211–12

birth: anxiety and 258–9; trauma of 161,
  257, 258
body: fear of destruction of 130, 210; of
  mother 128, 130–1
boys: attachment to mother 130;
  castration complex 130; Oedipus

complex and 130; pregenital stage
  130; preoedipal stage 130, *see also* girls
breakdown: fear of 231
breast: destructive impulse towards 121;
  envy and 121, 214; good and bad 127,
  129; introjection of 179–80;
  relationship of child to 121, 127, 128;
  trauma of weaning 128, *see also*
  mother
breast feeding 178, 263
Britain: Barker Report 189; Child
  Guidance Clinics 189, 297; child
  psychoanalysis in 172–83, 189–250;
  development of psychoanalytical
  psychology 190–207; difficulties of
  child analysis 238–40; Independents in
  219, 235–6; psychiatric treatment in
  189; schools of thought 240–9;
  training of psychoanalysts 182, 190,
  193, 199–206, 235, 237, 250; in wartime 190–2

castration complex 130, 143; domestic
  tyrants and 156
catharsis 12
child analysis 100–8, 151–3; centres for
  65–6; difficulties of 122–3, 238–40;
  environment and 265; first session
  63–4; free association 153; goal of
  60–1; initial contact 63, 152;
  interpretation 70, 215, 277–8;
  management of analytical treatment
  232–6; men and 279–80; by parents
  27–9, 36, 65, 117–18;

348